The Rigveda Samhita

A Scientific, Spiritual and Socio-political Commentay with
Exegetical, Grammatical and Accentual notes

Vol. 1

By

Dr. Ravi Prakash Arya

Amazon Books, USA
in association with
Indian Foundation for Vedic Science
1051, Sector-1, Rohtak, Haryana, India Pin124001
Ph. No. 09313033917; 09650183260
Email : vedicscience@gmail.com; vedicscience@rediffmail.com
Web: www.vedicscience.net

First Edition

Kali era : 5119 (2019 CE)
Kalpa era: 1,97,29,49,119
Brahma era: 15,55,21,97,29,49,119

ISBN 10 Digits: 8187710268

ISBN 13 Digits: 9788187710264

Preface

I would not like to delve deep into the Introduction of the Vedas, especially the Ṛgveda, their recensions and principles of Vedic interpretation etc., as this work has already been carried out in detail by the author of present lines in his most popular and famous work '*Introduction to the Vedas*'. This work is easily available on various the websites of Amazon Books, USA. So, the scholars or researchers who are interested to acquaint themselves with the Vedas, their components, their recensions and principles of Vedic interpretations should first of all go through the above Introduction of this translation, so as to understand the *Ṛgveda* and its present translation in right earnest. Herein it has been attempted to render a scientific, metaphysical and socio-political Commentay of the *Ṛgveda* with exegetical, lexicon, grammatical and accentuation notes. If this style of translation is followed, it is going to be a very bulky work. So, first of all, a specimen copy is produced for the perusal and comments of the scholars. Accordingly, we may proceed further.

This commentary is going to be the first ever systematic exhaustive and extensive attempt in the history of Vedic interpretation. The present work deals with the first five Sūktas comparising of 50 mantras. The saṁhitā pāṭha of the *Ṛgveda*, is supplied with padapāṭha; each vocable has been rendered with grammatical, accentutation, lexicon and exegetical notes, so as to present full exposition of each and every vocable. In the present work a humble attempt has been made to render ādhidaivika, adhyātamika and ādhibhautika translation of Vedic lores following Padapāṭhakāras, Brāhmaṇas, Nairuktas, Aitihāsikas, Naidānas, ancient commentators like Skandhswami and Sāyaṇa and modern interpretators of the Veda like Swami Dayananda Saraswati and Sri Aurobindo.

This specimen copy of the translation of the *Ṛgveda* will be a torch bearer to fathom the depth and range of the Vedic wisdom. Hope the readers and researchers will be benefitted by this humble effort.

Here it may also be pointed out that Vedas consists of the most advance knowledge system which may not have been discovered until now. We don't have the scientific, cultural and philosophical background behind which this knowledge was revealed to the seers of yore. This is the direct knowledge gained by high profile seers in their samādhi, so a high profile yogi who has visualised the phenomenon at the same level as that of the Vedic seers can perfectly interpret the Vedic lores. Swami Dayanand Saraswati and Yogi Aurobindo, who were great yogis, were been successful to show the right direction of the interpretation of the Vedas. Though, the present interpretor is not a yogi, but given the present background of scientific development and indepth study of other Śāstras, including Brāhmaṇas, Āraṇyakas, Upaniṣads, Darśanas, Astronomical texts have helped a lot in decoding the background of the Vedic lores. So, hereunder an attempt is made to read the intended sense into the Ṛgvedic lores. This volumes contains first 50 Vedic Mantras from 4 Sūktas. Hope the readers and other scholars will appreciate this effort and get a new direction to proceed on the path of interpretation of the Vedas.

Dr. Ravi Prakash Arya

The Ṛgveda Saṁhitā

First Maṇḍala

ANUVĀKA I

सूक्त-1

ऋषि– मधुच्छन्दा वैश्वामित्र। **देवता–** अग्नि। **छन्द–** गायत्री।

Seer : Madhucchandā son of Viśvāmitra

Devatā : Agni **Chanda :** Gāyatrī

Devata (subject matter) of the above *Mantra* is *Agni. Agni* signifies different things in different contexts. In spiritual context, *Agni* signifies Almighty God. In scientific context, *Agni* denotes energy of observer space and geothermal energy of our earth. In scientific context, it means starry world. In conventional sense, *Agni* denotes fire. In Socio-political context *Agni* represents a scholar surcharged with knowledge, and also a ruler who has fire like qualities. As per Yaska's *Nirukta*, *Brāhmaṇa* texts, and other Vedic texts, the *Ṛgveda* owes its origin to *Agni* which is located in the observer space and geothermal energy of our earth. Thus the Ṛgvedic *Agni* refers to energy of observer space.

१. ॐ अग्निमीळे पुरोहितं यज्ञस्य देवमृत्विजम्।
होतारं रत्नधातमम्॥१॥

अग्निम्। ईळे। पुरःऽहितम्। यज्ञस्य। देवम्। ऋत्विजम्। होतारम्।
रत्नऽधातमम्॥

Saṁhitāpāṭha

Auṁ agním iḍé puróhitáṁ yajñásya devám ṛtvíjam.
hótaráṁ rátnadhā´tamám.

Padapāṭha

agnim. īḍe. puraḥ+hitam. yajñasya. devam. ṛtvijam.

hotāraṁ. ratna+dhātamam.

Grammatical Notes

ॐ (Aum)—Bhvādigaṇa root √ ava 'to protect', 'to go', 'to shine', 'to love'+man (Uṇādi suffix)[1].

अ॒ग्निम् (Agnim)—Accusative sing. of Agni. Bhvādigaṇa root √aga 'to go'+ni (Uṇādi suffix)[2]. Here both root and suffix are accented as per rule of accentuation. For example as per rule of accentuation[3], 'a' of root 'aga' will be accented. On the other hand 'i' of suffix 'ni' will also be accented[4]. But the main rule[5] says that, there can be only one acute accent in one word (formed of root and suffix). As such, in case of two acute accents in a word, one is destined to go. Consequently, one acute accent has to be dropped from Agni. According to the further rules of accentuation, the acute accent which comes first in the process of word formation will have to go first[6]. As such suffix accent will prevail over the root accent. Consequently, Agni is accented on the root.

There are two concepts about the formation of words. First concept, enjoyed by Etymologists like Yāska and Śākaṭāyana, is that every word is formed of roots[7]. As per this concept, Agni gets acute accent on the suffix as cited above. According to another view, held by Gārgya

1. See *Uṇādi sūtra* (1.142)—अवतेष्टिलोपश्च। *avateṣṭilopaśca*
2. See *Uṇādi sūtra* (4.50) —अङ्गेर्नलोपश्च *aṅgernalopaśca.*
3. Cf. Pāṇini—धातोः - 6.1.162
4. Cf. Pāṇini—आद्युदात्तश्च- 3.1.3.
5 Cf. Pāṇini—अनुदात्तं पदमेकवर्जम्-6.1.158
6. Cf. *Vārttika*—सति शिष्टस्वरो बलीयान्- Pāṇini 6.1.158
7. नामानि आख्यातजानीति शाकटायनो नैरुक्तसमयश्च न सर्वाणि इति गार्ग्यो वैयाकरणानाम् चैके - Nir. 1.12

and others, it is not necessary that all the words are formed from roots. In case of second view also when Agni is one single word unbreakable into the root and suffix, it gets acute accent on its final syllable following the rule of Phiṭ sūtra (1)[1].

ई॒ळे (īḍe)—Adādigaṇa root √iḍ 'to appreciate', 'extol'+laṭ lakāra (present tense) first person singular. It remains unaccented being followed by non-verbal form[2] in a hemistich.

पु॒रोहि॑तम् (Purohitam)—Accusative sing. of Purohita. Attributive of Agnim. Puras (prefix)+Juhotyādigaṇa root √dhā 'to possess', 'to bring up'+kta (primary suffix). Here 'dha' is replaced by 'ha'[3]. Attributive of Agni. In 'purohita', 'purs' is a particle named 'gati' by Pāṇini [4], and 'hitam' is word ending in -kta suffix. As per rule of accentuation[5], when a particle called 'gati' is is followed by a word ending in -kta suffix, it receives its natural accent. 'Puras' is formed from 'pūrva+as' and gets accented naturally on the root i.e. 'o'. As such, in purohitam, the first member 'puras' will retain its natural accent as per above rule of accentuation.

य॒ज्ञस्य॑ (Yajñsya)— Gen. sing. of Yajña. Bhvādigaṇa √ yaja 'to worship gods', 'to unite', 'to donate'+naṅ[6] suffix. It is accented in the final syllable.

दे॒वम् (Devam)—Acc. sing.of deva. Divādigaṇa root √ div 'to play', 'desire to win', 'to deal with', 'to illuminate',

---

1. फिषोऽन्त उदात्तः।
2. Cf. Pāṇini—तिङ्ङतिङः - 8.1.28
3. See Paṇini— *dadhāterhi*—
4. पुरोऽव्ययम् - 1.4.67.
5. See Pāṇini—गतिरनन्तरः - 6.2.49.
6. Cf. Pāṇini, 3.3.90—यज-याच-यत-विच्छ-प्रच्छ-रक्षो नङ् (*yaja-yāca-yata-viccha-praccha-rakṣo naṅ).*

'to glorify', 'to be happy', 'to be intoxicated', 'to sleep', to shine' and 'to go' or Curādigaṇa root √div 'to crush', 'to chirp'+ac suffix[1]. Being formed of cit (of which ending 'c' is elided) suffix, it is accented on the final syllable.[1] Devam is Attributive of Agni.

ऋत्विजम् (Ṛtvijam)—Acc. sing. of ṛtvik. Ṛtu+Bhvādigaṇa

√yaja 'to worship gods', 'to unite', 'to donate'.+kvin suffix in vocative, instrumental and accusative meaning[1]. (Bhvādigaṇa root ṛ 'to move,' to make it to reach'+tu (Uṇādi suffix)[1]. It is accented on the second member, being preceded by a word ending with a primary suffix (kṛdanta)[1]. Attributive of Agni.

होतारम् (Hotāram)—Acc. sing. of Hotṛ. Juhotyādigaṇa root

√hu 'to give and to take'+tṛn suffix in nominative sense[1]. Being formed of 'nit' suffix (of which final 'n' is elided), it is accented on the first syllabl[2]. Attributive of Agni.

रत्नधातमम् (Ratnadhātmam)—Acc. sing. of Ratnadhātama.

[Bhavādigaṇa root √ramu 'to play', 'to enjoy'+n (Uṇādi suffix)[3]+[Juhotyādigaṇa root √dhā 'to sustain', 'to possess', 'to bring up'+kvip suffix in nominative meaning+tamap (superlative degree suffix[4]].

Word meanings:

ॐ (Aum)—Name of God

Agnim—To Agni[5]

---

1. Cf. Pāṇini—तृन् - 3.2.135
2. Cf. Pāṇini—ञ्नित्यादिर्नित्यम् - 6.1.197
3. Cf. *Uṇādi sūtra*—रमेस्त च 3.14.
4. Cf. Pāṇini—अतिशायने तमबिष्ठनौ-5.3.55
5. अग्निः कस्मादग्रणीर्भवति। अक्नोपनो भवतीति स्थौलाष्ठीविर्न क्नोपयति न स्नेहयति। त्रिभ्य आख्यातेभ्यो जायत इति शाकपूणिः। इतादक्ताद्दग्धाद्वानीतात्। स खल्वेतेरकारमादत्ते

(Agni God[1] in spiritual sense; energy[2]-geothermal, field and solar energy and others-in scientific sense; star[3] in scientific sense; intellectuals (scholar, teacher etc.)[4],

---

गकारमनक्तेर्वा दहतेर्वा नी: पर: नि० 7.14. विराडग्नि: श० 6.2.2.34. यो वै रुद्र: सोऽग्नि: श० 5.2.4.13. अग्निरेष यत्पशव: श० 6.3.2.6. अग्निर्हि देवानां पशु: ऐ० 1.15. अग्निर्वै देवानां वसिष्ठ: ऐ० 1.28. शिर एवाग्नि: श० 10.1.2.4. अग्नि: सर्वा देवता: ऐ० 2.3. अग्निर्वैसवेषां देवानामात्मा श० 14.3.2.5. आत्मैवाग्नि: श० .7.1.20. अग्निर्वै देवतानां मुखं प्रजनयिता स प्रजापति: श० 3.9.1.6. अन्नादोऽग्नि: श० 2.1.4.28. अग्निर्देवानां जठरम् तै० 2 .7.12.3. अयं वै लोकोऽग्नि: श० 14.9.1.14. संवत्सर एषोऽग्नि: श० 3.7.1.18. वागेवाग्नि: श० 3.2.2.13. तेजो वाऽअग्नि: श० 2.5.4.8. अग्निर्वै रक्षसामपहन्ता कौ० 8.4.10.3. तपो वाऽअग्नि: श० 3.4.3.2. अग्निर्वै देवानां व्रतपति: श० 1.1.1.2. अग्निर्वै मृत्यु: श०14.6.2.10. पुरुषोऽग्नि: श० 10.4.1.6. मन एवाग्नि: श० 10.1.2.3. प्राणो वा अग्नि: श० 9.5.1.68. वीर्यंवा अग्नि: तै० 1.7.2.2. गायत्री अग्नि: श० 3.4.1.9. अग्निरेव ब्रह्म अग्निर्वै श० 10.4.1. 5. पर्जन्यो वा अग्नि: श० 14.9.1.13. आयुर्वाऽग्नि: श० 6.7.3.7. अग्निमतिथिं जनानाम् तै० 2.4.3.6. अमृतो ह्यग्नि: श० 1.9.2.20. असौ वा आदित्य एषोऽग्नि: श० 3.4.1.1. अग्निर्वैश्वानर: ता० 13.11.23. अनूचानमाहुरग्निकल्प इति मुखं ह्येतदग्नेर्यद् ब्रह्म श० 6.1.1.10. अग्निर्वै धर्म: श० 11.6.2.2. अग्निर्वैद्रष्टा गो० उ० 2.19. प्रजापतिरग्नि: श० 6.2.1.23. अग्निर्वाव पुरोहित: ऐ० 8.27. प्राणा अग्नि: श० 6.3.1.21. अग्निर् ऋषि: मै० 1.6.1. अग्नि: पशुरासीत्तमालभन्त तेनायजन्त इति च ब्राह्मणम् नि० 12.41.।

1. *agnireva Brahma* (Agni denotes Brahma)—Ś.Br. (10.4.1.5). *brahma vā agni* (Brahma is verily called as Agni)—K. Br. 9.1.5; T.Br. 3.9.16.3.

2. *sa yadasya sarvamasyāgram asṛjyat tasmadgnir agnir ha vai tamagnir ityācakṣate prokṣam.* Since the energy was created as the prototype of the entire creation, so it was called as agni indirectly—Ś.Br. 6.1.1.11). *agniḥ sarvāḥ devatāḥ* (All natural powers are formed from energy)—A.Br. 2.3; T.Br. 1.4.4.10.

3. *ayaṁ vā agnir arkaḥ* (This agni denotes sun)—Ś.Br. 2.5.1.4. *yadveva āha svarṇagharmaḥ svāhā, svarṇārkaḥ svāhā, ityesyevetāni agner nāmāni.* (When we say oblations to golden light, oblations to golden sun—all these names are denoted by agni itsef).—Ś.Br. 9.4.2.25.

4. *brahma vā agniḥ kṣatraṁ soma.* (Agni denotes Intellectual power and soma denotes physical power). K.Br. 9.5. Agnir ṛṣiḥ (Agni also denotes a seer, a researcher). MS. 1.6.1. agnir vai draṣṭā

Saṁnyāsī (Peripetitic monk)[1], king[2], commander in figurative sense). In Nighaṇu (5.4), Agni is read in the list of *padanāmas* (technical terms denoting various constituents of universal creation).

Iḍe—I extol

Purohitam—leader, forerunner, prototype[3], controller, Agni (geothermal energy), Vāyu (field energy) and Āditya (solar energy) have been called as purohita (foreunner)[4].

Yajñasya[5]— of the process of cosmic creation in the form

(Agni denotes a seer)—Go. Br. (Second part) 2.19.

1. *agniṁ atithiṁ janānām* (Peripetetic monks wh do visits people without any fixed date or time are called as Agni)—T.Bs. 2.4.3.6
2. *agne pṛthivīpate*—(Agni is the king upon earth). T.Br. 3.11.4.1
3. *pura enaṁ dadhati*—Nir. 2.12
4. *ādityo vāva purohitaḥ, vāyurvā purohitaḥ, agnirvāva purohitaḥ*—Ait. Br.8.27
5. यज्ञः-यज्ञ नाम निघं० 3.17. यज्ञः कस्मात? प्रख्यातं यजतिकर्मेति नैरुक्ताः। याच्ञ्यो भवतीति वा यजुरुन्नो भवतीति वा बहुकृष्णाजिन इत्यौपमन्यवो यजूंष्येनं नयन्तीति वा नि० 3.19. स (सोमः) तायमानो जायते स यन् जायते स यन् जायते तस्माद् यञ्जो यञ्जो ह वै नामैतद् यद् यज्ञ इति श० 3.9.4.23. प्राणः (यज्ञस्य) सोमः कौ० 9.6. अध्वरो वै यज्ञः श० 1.2.4.5. यज्ञोवै मखः श० 6.5.2.1. तै० 3.2.8.3. तां० 7.5.6. मख इत्येतद् यज्ञनामधेयम् गो० उ० 2.5. यज्ञो वै नमः श० 7.4.1.30, 2.4.2.24, 2.6.1.42. यज्ञो वै स्वाहाकारः श० 3.1.3.27. यज्ञो वैभुज्युः (यजु० 18.42.) यज्ञो हि सर्वाणि भूतानि भुनक्ति श० 9.4.1.11. यज्ञो भगः (यजु० 11.7.) श० 6.3.1.19. गातुं वित्त्वेति यज्ञं वित्वेत्येवैतदाह। श० 1.9.2.28, 4.4.4.13. यज्ञो वै देवानां महः श० 1.9.1.11. एष ह वै महान् देवो यद् यज्ञः गो० पू० 2.19. यज्ञो वै बृहन्विपश्चित् श० 3.5.3.12. यज्ञो वा अर्यमा तै० 2.3.5.4. यज्ञो वै ताप्र्यम् तै० 1.3.7.1, 3.9.20.1. यज्ञो वै वसुः (यजु० 1.2.) यज्ञो वै श्रेष्ठतमं कर्म (यजु० 1.1.) श० 2.7.1.5. यज्ञो हि श्रेष्ठतमं कर्म तै० 3.2.1.4. ब्रह्म यज्ञः श० 3.1.4.15. ब्रह्म हि यज्ञः श० 5.3.2.4. ब्रह्म वैज्ञः ऐ० 7.22. एष वै प्रत्यक्षं यज्ञो यत् प्रजापतिः श० 4.3.4.3. यज्ञः प्रजापतिः श०11.6.3.8. यज्ञ उ वै प्रजापतिः कौ० 10.1.13.1. तै० 3.3.7.3. एष वै यज्ञ एव प्रजापतिः श० 1.7.4.4. प्रजापतिर्यज्ञः ऐ० 2.17, 4.26. इन्द्रो वै यज्ञस्य देवता श०1.

of creation of mass energy)[1], social order, education

Devam [2]—illuminating[1], originating in day time[2].

4.1.33, 1.4.5.4. विष्णुर्यज्ञः गो०उ० 1.12. तै० 3.3.7.6. यज्ञो वै विष्णुः स यज्ञः श०5.2.3. 6. स यः स विष्णुर्यज्ञः सः, स यः स यज्ञोऽसौ आदित्यः श० 14.1.1.6. विष्णुर्वै यज्ञः ऐ० 1.15. यज्ञो विष्णुः तां० 13.3.2. गो० उ० 6.7.

1. *tāyamāno jāyate sa yan jāyate tasmād yañjo yañjo ha vai nāmaitad yad yajña iti* (Since this creation is a continuous process of expansion, so it is called as *yañja* and this *yañja* came to be known as *Yajña*)—Ś.Br. 3.9.4.23. *yajñe hi sarvaṇi bhūtāni viṣṭāni* (In this creation are included all the living and non—living entities of universe). *Ś.Br.* 8.7.3.11. *eṣa vai pratyakṣaṁ yajño yat prajāpati* (the creation of universe is a perceptible *yajña*)—*Ś.Br.* 4.3.4.3.

2. देवो दानाद्वा, दीपनाद्वा, द्योतनाद्वा, द्युस्थानो भवतीति वा। यो देवः स देवता निघं० 7.15. दिवा वै नोऽभूदिति। तद् देवानां देवत्वम् तै० 2.2.9.9. दिवा देवानसृजत नक्तमसुरान् यद्दिवा देवानसृजत तद् देवानां देवत्वम् ष० 4.1. तद् देवानां देवत्वं यद् दिवसमभिपद्यासृज्यन्त श० 11.1.6.7. प्राचीनप्रजनना वै देवाः प्रतीचीनप्रजनना मनुष्याः श० 7.4.2.40. प्राची हि देवानां दिक् श० 1.2.5.17. देवानां वा एषा दिग्यत्प्राची ष० 3.1. यद्वै मनुष्याणां प्रत्यक्षन्तद् देवानां परोक्षमथ यन्मनुष्याणां परोक्षन्तद् देवानां प्रत्यक्षम् तां० 22.10.3. द्राघीयो हि देवायुषं ह्रसीयो मनुष्यायुषम् श० 7.3.1.10. देवानां वै विधामनु मनुष्याः श० 6.7.4.9.। त्रयो वै देवाः। वसवो रुद्रा आदित्याःश० 4.3.5.1. एते वै त्रयो देवा यद् वसवो रुद्रा आदित्याः श०1.3.4.12., 1.5.1.17.,1.8.3.8. त्रयस्त्रिंशद् देवताः तां० 4.4.11. त्रयस्त्रिंशद्वै देवताः तै० 1.2.2.5., 1.8.7. 1., 2.7.1.3-4. त्रयस्त्रिंशद्वै सर्वा देवताः कौ० 8.6. त्रयस्त्रिंशद्वै देवाः प्रजापतिश्चतुस्त्रिंशः श० 12.6.1.37. अग्निर्वायुरादित्य एतानि ह तानि देवानां हृदयानि श० 9.1.1.23. अग्निर्वै देवानामवमो विष्णुः परमस्तदन्तरेण सर्वा अन्या देवताः ऐ० 1.1. तद्यदेतस्मिन्नाके स्वर्गे लोके देवा असीदंस्तस्माद्देवा नाकसदः श० 8.6.1.1. द्यौर्वै सर्वेष, देवानामायतनम् श० 14.3.2.4. देवगृहा वै नक्षत्राणि तै० 15.2.6. नरो वै देवानां ग्रामः तां० 6.9.2.। यो वै देवानामात्मा श०9. 3.2.7. सर्वेषां वाऽएष भूतानां सर्वेषां देवानामात्मा यद् यज्ञः श० 14.3.2.1. विद्वांसो हि देवाः श० 3.7.3.10. तस्मात् प्राणा देवाः, श० 7.5.1.21. प्राणा देवाः श० 6.3.1.15. चक्षुर्देवः गो० पू० 2.11.मनो देवः गो० पू० 2.10. मनो वै देववाहनं मनो हीदं मनस्विनं भूयिष्ठं वनीवाह्यते श०1.4.3.6.वाक् च वै मनश्च देवानां मिथुनम् ऐ० 5.23. वागेव देवाः श० 14.4.3.13. वाग्देवः गो० पू० 2.10. वाग्वै देवानां पुरान्नमासीत् तै० 1.3.5.1. वागिति सर्वे देवाः जै० उ० 1.9.2. वायुर्वै देवःजै० उ० 3.4.8.। यशो देवाः श० 2.1.4.9. तस्माद् (देवाः) यशः श० 3.4.

Ṛtvijam [3] —performing/creating/controlling in different times, or as per time or bound with time[4].

Hotāram[5]—presenter, provider

2.8. देवा वै यशस्कामा: सत्रमासत तां० 7.5.6. परोक्षकामा हि देवा: श० 6.1.1.2.,7.4.1.10., परोक्षप्रिया इव हि देवा भवन्ति प्रत्यक्षद्विष: गो० पू० 2.21. यदु ह किं च देवा: कुर्वते स्तोमेनैव तत्कुर्वते यज्ञो वै स्तोमो यज्ञेनैव तत्कुर्वते श० 8.4.3.2. मनो ह वै देवा मनुष्यस्याजानन्ति श० 2.1.4.1., 2.4.1.11. मनो देवा मनुष्यस्याजानन्ति श० 3.4.2.6. सत्यमेव देवा अनृतं मनुष्या: श० 1.1.1.4.यज्ञेन वै तद्देवा यज्ञमयजन्त यदग्निनाऽग्निमयजन्त ते स्वर्गं लोकमायन् ऐ० 1.16. अग्निर्वै देवानां होता ऐ० 1.28, 3.14. अग्निरेव देवानां दूत आस श० 3.5.1.21. वरुणो वै देवानां राजाश० 12.8.3.10. तस्मादाहुर्विष्णुर्देवानां श्रेष्ठ इति श० 14.1.1.5. रुद्रो वै ज्येष्ठश्च श्रेष्ठश्च देवानाम् कौ० 25.13. अन्नमु देवानां सोम: जै० 3. 174. दिवा वै मनुष्या यज्ञेन चरन्ति नक्तं देवा: मै० 4.5.1.

1. *devo dānādvā, dīpanādvā, dyotanādvā, dyusthāno bhavatīti vā. yo devaḥ sa devatā* (Deva is that which donates, illuminate, or that which is located in the celestial sphere)—*Nir.* 7.15.

2. *divā vai no'bhūditi, tad devānāṁ devatvaṁ*—T.S. 2.2.9.9. *divā devān asṛjat naktam asurān, yad divā devān asṛjat tad devānāṁ devatvam—Ṣaḍviṁśa Br.* 4.1.

3. ऋत्विक् ईरण:, ऋग्यष्टा भवतीति शाकपूणि:। ऋतुयाजी भवतीति वा नि० 3.19. ऋतव: ऋत्विज: श० 11.2.7.2. ऋत्विजो हैव देवयजनम् श० 3.43.41. आत्मा वै यज्ञस्य यजमानोऽङ्गान्यृत्विज: श० 9.5.2.16.

4. *ṛgyaṣṭā bhavatīti Śākapuṇi. ṛtuyājī bhavatīti vā* (According to Ācārya Śākapuṇi Rtvik is a person who creates thing from time to time (seasonally) or say who performs yajña seasonally)—Nir. 3.19. *ṛtvijo ha vai devayajñanam* (cosmic *yajña*/creation is called *ṛtvija*)—Ś.Br. 3.1.1.5.

5. होतु:-ह्वातव्यस्य नि० 4.26. होतारम् ह्वातारम् निघं० 7.15. होता-यद्वा स तत्र यथाभाजनं देवता अनुमावहामुमावहेत्यावहति तदेव होतुर्होतृत्वम् ऐ० 1.2. मध्यं वा एतद् यज्ञस्य यद्धोता तै०3.3.8.10. आत्मा वै यज्ञस्य होता कौ० 9.6. (ऋ० 6.16.10., यजु० 11.35.) अग्निर्वै होता श० 1.4.1.24. अग्निर्वै देवानां होता ऐ० 1.28. अग्निर्वै होताऽधिदैवं वागध्यात्मम् श० 12.1.1.4. वाग्वै होता (यजु० 13.7.) कौ० 13.9.17.7. वाग्वै यज्ञस्य होता श० 12.8.2.23. वाग्घोता षड्ढोतृणाम् तै० 3.12.5.2. मनो होता तै० 2.1.5.9. प्राणो वै होता ऐ० 6.8. असौ वैहोता योऽसौ (सूर्य:) तपति गो० उ० 6.6. पुरुषो वाव होता गो० उ० 6.6. क्षत्रं वै होता ऐ०

Ratnadhātmam[1]—possessor of precious stones, precious knowledge. The word is ratnadhātama, lit. holder of gems is very much precise in the context of geothermal energy of earth. The geothermal energy which exists in the centre of earth as a biggest natural nuclear reactor. It gives birth to volcanoes, hot water springs, movement of lithosphere plates, mid plate earth quakes, hotspots, tsunamis, Mountain building, precious gems and global heat flow value on the surface of the earth. This source of energy figures in 12th hymn of the 'Bhūmi Sūkta' of Atharvaveda which reads as follows:—

yat te madhyam prithivi yaccha nābhyāṁ yāsta urjaḥ tanvaḥ saṁbhuvuḥ
tāsu no dhehyabhi naḥ pavasva mātā bhūmiḥ putro ahaṁ prithvyāḥ

O Earth In the midst of your body there is a source of energy, situated exactly at the center, in your navel. This is your most thematic feature, energizing your entire body. We ought to focus our full attention here only. This is your sanctum sanctorum. The energy transmitted from center sterilizes the entire global surface there by enabling us to inhabit it. You are vitalizing and sheltering the entire civilization as the mother feeds and looks after her children.

Anvaya (Sequencial placement of words)

yajñasya purohitaṁ, devam, ṛtvijaṁ, hotāraṁ, ratnadhātamam, agnim, īḍe

Meaning of Mantra in different contexts :

Spiritual: (ईळे) I extol (अग्निम्) Almighty Brahman,

6.21. संवत्सरो वै होता कौ० 29.8. हेमन्तो होता तस्माद्धेमन्तवषट्कृताः पशवः सीदन्ति श०11.2.7.32. होतैव भर्गः गो० पू० 5.15. होता हि साहस्त्रः श० 4.5.8.12. प्राची दिग् होतुः श० 13.5.4.24. उत्तरत आयतनो वै होता तै० 3.9.5.2.

1. रत्नं धननाम निघं० 2.10.। रत्नधातमम्-रमणीयानां धनानां दातृतमम् नि० 7.15.

(पुरोहितम्) Who is the forerunner of (यज्ञस्य) entire process of creation, (देवम्) Who is highly effulgent, (ऋत्विजम्) creator of different things according to their need and time, (होतारम्) presenter or provider of several facilities and Who (रत्नधातमम्) possesses precious traits.

Scientific 1: (ईळे) I extol (अग्निम्) geothermal energy of the earth/planets, (पुरोहितम्) that which is the forerunner of (यज्ञस्य) creation on the earth (Note : if a planet is devoid of her geothermal energy she would become a desert planet), (देवम्) that which is highly effulgent, (ऋत्विजम्) that which create things according to their need and time, (होतारम्) that which provides several facilities worth living on the earth and that which (रत्नधातमम्) possesses precious gems available on the earth.

Scientific 2: (ईळे) I extol (अग्निम्) energy of the universe, (पुरोहितम्) that which is the prototype of (यज्ञस्य) matter particles n the observer space, (देवम्) that which is highly effulgent, (ऋत्विजम्) that which converts into matter particles according to the time and need, (होतारम्) that which provides infrastructure for creation of heavenly bodies in the observer space and that which (रत्नधातमम्) possesses starry matter in the observer space (universe).

Scientific 3: (ईळे) I extol (अग्निम्) stars/sun of our solar system, (पुरोहितम्) that which is leads (यज्ञस्य) creation on our earth/ planets, (देवम्) that which is highly luminous body, (ऋत्विजम्) that which create various climates, (होतारम्) that which provides life energy and that which (रत्नधातमम्) possesses precious light.

Socio-political 1: (ईळे) I extol (अग्निम्) ruler of state or nationa, (पुरोहितम्) who is the leader of (यज्ञस्य) nation, (देवम्) who is endowed with effulgence of physical prowess, (ऋत्विजम्) who takes actions for the welfare of his people, (होतारम्) who provides different facilities to the people at different times and need and who (रत्नधातमम्) possesses all qualifications required and expected of a good ruler.

Note : Here the mantra advises to the rulers to take care of the people and provide them with all sort of facilities worth living. The ruler should have qualifications required to rule a nation. The rulers should be strong enough to take decisions at the time of emergency.

Socio-political 2: (ईळे) I extol (अग्निम्) a seer/ intellectual/ teacher, (पुरोहितम्) who is the leader of (यज्ञस्य) Jñāna yajña, (देवम्) who is endowed with effulgence of knowledge, (ऋत्विजम्) who provides education according to time and need of a nation, (होतारम्) who inculcates values among his students and who (रत्नधातमम्) possesses all qualifications required and expected of a good teacher.

२. अ॒ग्निः पूर्वे॑भि॒रृषि॑भि॒रीड्यो॒ नूत॑नैरु॒त। स दे॒वाँ एह व॑क्षति॥२॥

अ॒ग्निः। पूर्वे॑भिः। ऋषि॑भिः। ईड्य॑ः। नूत॑नैः। उ॒त। सः। दे॒वान्। आ। इ॒ह।
व॒क्षति॑॥

Samhitāpāṭha

agniḥ pūrvebhir ṛṣibhir īḍyo nutanair uta. sa devān eha
vakṣati.

Padapāṭha

agniḥ. pūrvebhiḥ. ṛṣibhiḥ. iḍyaḥ. nutanaiḥ. uta. saḥ.
devān. ā. iha. vakṣati .

Grammatical Notes:

अ॒ग्निः (**Agniḥ**)—Nom. sing.of Agni. Bhvādigaṇa root √aga
'to go'+ni (Uṇādi suffix)[1]. Here both root and suffix
are accented as per rule of accentuation. For example as
per rule of accentuation[2], 'a' of root aga will be
accented. On the other hand 'i' of suffix 'ni' will also
be accented[3]. But the main rule[4] says that, there can be
only one acute accent in one word (formed of root and
suffix). As such, in case of two acute accents in a
word, one is destined to go. Consequently, one acute
accent has to be dropped from Agni. According to the
further rules of accentuation the acute accent which
comes first in the process of word formation will have
to go first[5]. As such suffix accent will prevail over the
root accent. Consequently, Agni is accented finally on
the root.

---

1. See *Uṇādi sūtra* (4.50) —अङ्गेर्नलोपश्च *aṅgernalopaśca.*

2. Cf. Pāṇini—धातोः - 6.1.162

3. Cf. Pāṇini—आद्युदात्तश्च- 3.1.3.

4. Cf. Pāṇini—अनुदात्तं पदमेकवर्जम्-6.1.158

5. Cf. *Vārttika*—सति शिष्टस्वरो बलायान्- Pāṇini 6.1.158

There are two concepts about the formation of words. First concept, enjoyed by Etymologists like Yāska and Śākaṭāyana, is that every word is formed of roots[1]. As per this concept, Agni gets acute accent on the suffix as cited above. According to another view, held by Gargya and others, it is not necessary that all the words are fromed from roots. In case of second view also when Agni is one single word unbreakable into the root and suffix, it gets acute accent on its final syllable following the rule of Phiṭ sūtra[2].

पूर्वेभिः (Pūrvebhiḥ)—Bhvādigaṇa root √pūrva pūrṇe+an suffix. Inst. pl. of pūrva. Here it may be informed that some scholars try to derive 'purva' with the '-ac' suffix. But the accent on the first syllable of the 'pūrva' does not allow us to form this word with the suffix '-ac'. Keeping in veiw of its accent, Sāyaṇa derives it with the (Uṇādi suffix) 'an', so that it can have its first syllable accented. But Uṇādi koṣa available to us does not mention this word formed with suffix '-an'. It seems that the word 'pūrva' is not governed by Pāṇinian system of grammar. As such, initially accented word 'pūrva' can be regularised by adding a new supplementary formula—पूर्वतश्चोपसंख्यातव्यम् - after Uṇādi—5.33—क्लिशेरन् लो लोपश्च। Being formed of 'nit' (of which final 'n' is elided) suffix, it is accented on the first syllable. It is a pronominal attributive of Ṛṣi.

ऋषिभिः (Ṛṣibhiḥ)—Inst. pl. of ṛṣi. Tudādigaṇa root √ṛṣi 'to go'+in (Uṇādi suffix)[3]. Being formed of nit suffix, it is

---

1. नामानि आख्यातजानीति शाकटायनो नैरुक्तसमयश्च न सर्वाणि इति गार्ग्यो वैयाकरणानाम् चैके - Nir. 1.12
2. फिषोऽन्त उदात्तः -1
3. Cf. *Uṇādikoṣa—igupadhāt kit*—4.120.

also accented on the first syllable[1].

ईड्यः (Iḍya)—Adādigaṇa root √iḍ 'to appreciate', 'to extol'+ṇyat suffix. Due to—ṇyat suffix, it carries accent on the first syllable[2].

नूतनैः (Nūtanaiḥ)—A pronoun attributing ṛṣi. Inst. pl. of nūtana. nava+tanan suffix. Nava is replaced by nu[3]. Being formed of 'nit' (of which the ending sound 'n' is elided) suffix, it carries acute accent on its first syllable. Here it may be informed that the available editions of Kāśikā mentions -tnan and -tanap suffixes, as such the grammarians forms nūtana word with -tanap suffix. But the accent on the first syllable shows that 'nūtana' word is formed from -tanan suffix and not from -tanap suffix. Perhaps that is why Sāyaṇa also derives this word with -tnan suffix instead of -tanap. According to the information of Sāyaṇa -tanan suffix has been mentioned in Mahāvārtika i.e. a Vārttika in Mahābhāṣya. In fact, Mahābhāṣyakāra mentions suffix -tnan under Pāṇini 5.4.30. Lohitan maṇau. Under the circumstances, with extant Pāṇinian system of grammar, it appears that present form of 'nūtana' is not governed by any rule of Pāṇini and his followers,Vārttikakāras and Iṭikāras. Regularisation of this form can be done by supplementing Pāṇini's rule—पादार्घाभ्यां च-5.4.25 with one more supplementary formula as—तनन् इत्यस्यापि छन्दसि उपसंख्यानं कर्त्तव्यम्।

उत (Uta)—A particle. According to the rule of accentuation, it should have been accented on the first syllable[4]. But it is not so. Pāṇini reads several particles in the group of svara particles (svrādigaṇa) as accented

---

1. Cf. Pāṇini—ञ्नित्यादिर्नित्यम्- 6.1.197.
2. Cf. Pāṇini—ईड-वन्द-वृ-शंस-दुहां ण्यत्- 6.1.197.
3. Cf. *Vārttika*—नवस्य नू आदेशस्-त्नन्-तनप्-खाश्च- Pāṇ. 5.4.25.
4. Cf. *Phiṭ sūtra*—निपाताः आद्युदात्ताः - 80.

on final syllable under his aphorism—स्वरादीनिपातमव्ययम् - 1.1.37. But he makes no mention of 'uta' among such particles. As such 'uta' may also be added to the list of particles mentioned in svarādigaṇa as—उत छन्दसि। Its accent on final syllable is also governed by Phiṭ sūtra [1].

सः (Saḥ)—Nom. sing. masc. of demonstrative pronoun 'Tad'. It is accented following the norms set by Phiṭ sūtra.[2]

देवान् (Devān)—Acc. sing.of deva. Divādigaṇa root √ div 'to play', 'desire to win', 'to deal with', 'to illuminate', 'to glorify', 'to be happy', 'to be intoxicated', 'to sleep', to shine' and 'to go' or Curādigaṇa root √div 'to crush', 'to chirp'+ac suffix[3]. Being formed of cit (of which ending 'c' is elided) suffix, it is accented on the final syllable.[4] Devam is Attributive of Agni.

आ (ā)—A prefix meaning proximity, conjunction and simli. Being a prefix, it is accented on the first syllable[5].

इह (iha)—Demonstrative Pronoun idam (loc.case)+ha suffix[6]. It carries accent on suffix 'ha'[7].

वक्षति (Vakṣati)—Bhvādigaṇa root √vaha 'to send'+leṭ (subjunctive) first person sing. It remains unaccented being followed by non—verbal form [8]in a hemistich.

---

1. एवादीनामन्तः (evādinām—antaḥ)—(82).
2 Cf. Sāyaṇa on *RV.* 1.2.1.
3. Cf. Pāṇ. नन्दिग्रहिपचादिभ्यो ल्यु-णिनि-अचः - 3.1.134
4. चित् स्वर, see Pāṇini—चितः - 6.1.163.
5. Cf. *Phiṭ sūtra*—उपसर्गाश्चाभिवर्जम् -81.
6. Cf. Pāṇini— इदमो ह-5.3.11.
7. See Pāṇini—आद्युदात्तश्च-3.1.3
8. Cf. Pāṇini—तिङ्ङतिङः - 8.1.28

Word meanings:

Agniḥ[1]—God in spiritual sense; geothermal, field and solar energy in scientific sense; star in scientific sense; king, teacher, commander in figurative sense.

Pūrvebhiḥ—previous, ancient

Ṛṣibhiḥ[2]—Researchers

Iḍya—worth extolled

Nutanaiḥ—modern

Uta—and, or—उत अपि नि० 1.6. च नि० 10.27

Saḥ—that

---

1. अग्निः कस्मादग्रणीर्भवति। अक्नोपनो भवतीति स्थौलाष्ठीविर्न क्नोपयति न स्नेहयति। त्रिभ्य आख्यातेभ्यो जायत इति शाकपूणिः। इतादक्ताद्दग्धाद्वानीतात्। स खल्वेतेरकारमादत्ते गकारमनक्तेर्वा दहतेर्वा नीः परः नि० 7.14. विराडग्निः श० 6.2.2.34. यो वै रुद्रः सो ऽग्निः श० 5.2.4.13. अग्निरेष यत्पशवः श० 6.3.2.6. अग्निर्हि देवानां पशुः ऐ० 1.15. अग्निर्वै देवानां वसिष्ठः ऐ० 1.28. शिर एवाग्निः श० 10.1.2.4. अग्निः सर्वा देवताः ऐ० 2.3. अग्निर्वैसर्वेषां देवानामात्मा श० 14.3.2.5. आत्मैवाग्निः श० .7.1.20. अग्निर्वै देवतानां मुखं प्रजनयितास प्रजापतिः श० 3.9.1.6. अन्नादोऽग्निः श० 2.1.4.28. अग्निर्देवानां जठरम् तै० 2.7.12.3. अयं वै लोकोऽग्निः श० 14.9.1.14. संवत्सर एषोऽग्निः श० 3.7.1.18. वागेवाग्निः श० 3.2.2.13. तेजो वाऽअग्निः श० 2.5.4.8. अग्निर्वै रक्षसामपहन्ता कौ० 8.4.10. 3. तपो वाऽअग्निः श० 3.4.3.2. अग्निर्वै देवानां व्रतपतिः श० 1.1.1.2. अग्निर्वै मृत्युः श० 14.6.2.10. पुरुषोऽग्निः श० 10.4.1.6. मन एवाग्निः श० 10.1.2.3. प्राणो वा अग्निः श० 9.5.1.68. वीर्यं वा अग्निः तै० 1.7.2.2. गायत्री अग्निः श० 3.4.1.9. अग्निरेव ब्रह्म श० 10.4.1.5. पर्जन्यो वा अग्निः श० 14.9.1.13. आयुर्वाऽग्निः श० 6.7.3.7. अग्निमतिथिं जनानाम् तै० 2.4.3.6. अमृतो ह्यग्निःश० 1.9.2.20. असौ वा आदित्य एषोऽग्निः श० 3.4.1.1. अग्निर्वैश्वानरः ता० 13.11.23. अनूचानमाहुरग्निकल्प इति मुखं ह्येतदग्नेर्यद् ब्रह्म श० 6.1.1.10. अग्निर्वै धर्मः श० 11.6.2.2. अग्निर्वैद्रष्टा गो० उ० 2.19. प्रजापतिरग्निः श० 6.2.1.23. अग्निर्वैयमः श० 7.2.1.10. अग्निर्वाव पुरोहितः ऐ० 8.27. प्राणा अग्निः श० 6.3.1.21. अग्निर् ऋषिः मै० 1.6.1. अग्निः पशुरासीत्तमालभन्त तेनायजन्त इति च ब्राह्मणम् नि० 12.41.

2. ऋषयः पदनाम निघं० 5.6. ऋषीन्-सप्त ऋषीणानि ज्योतींषि नि० 3.26. ऋषिः दर्शनात् स्तोमान्ददर्शेत्यौपमन्यवः। इन्द्रियाणि नि० 12.36. प्राणा वा ऋषयः ऐ० 2.27. प्राणा ऋषयः श० 7.2.3.5. एते वै विप्रा यदृषयः श० 1.4.2.7. श० 1.7.2.3.

Devān[1]—illuminating forces of creation, divine forces, divine personalities (high spirited yogis and high profile scholars), radiation, rain.

1. देवो दानाद्वा, दीपनाद्वा, द्योतनाद्वा, द्युस्थानो भवतीति वा। यो देवः स देवता निघं० 7.15. दिवा वै नोऽभूदिति। तद् देवानां देवत्वम् तै० 2.2.9.9. दिवा देवानसृजत नक्तमसुरान् यद्दिवा देवानसृजत तद् देवानां देवत्वम् ष० 4.1. तद् देवानां देवत्वं यद् दिवसमभिपद्यासृज्यन्त श० 11.1.6.7. प्राचीनप्रजनना वै देवाः प्रतीचीनप्रजनना मनुष्याः श० 7.4.2.40. प्राची हि देवा नां दिक् श० 1.2.5.17. देवानां वा एषा दिग्यत्प्राची ष० 3.1. यद्वै मनुष्याणां प्रत्यक्षन्तद् देवानां परोक्षमथ यन्मनुष्याणां परोक्षन्तद् देवानां प्रत्यक्षम् तां० 22.10.3 द्राघीयो हि देवायुषं ह्रसीयो मनुष्यायुषम् श० 7.3.1.10. देवानां वै विधामनु मनुष्याः श० 6.7.4.9 त्रयो वै देवाः। वसवो रुद्रा आदित्याः श० 4.3.5.1. एते वै त्रयो देवा यद् वसवो रुद्रा आदित्याः श० 1.3.4.12., 1.5.1.17.,1.8.3.8. त्रयस्त्रिंशद् देवताः तां० 4.4.11. त्रयस्त्रिंशद्वै देवताः तै० 1.2.2.5., 1.8.7.1., 2.7.1.3-4. त्रयस्त्रिंशद्वै सर्वा देवताः कौ० 8.6. त्रयस्त्रिंशद्वै देवाः प्रजापतिश्चतुस्त्रिंशः श० 12.6.1.37 अग्निर्वायुरादित्य एतानि ह तानि देवानां हृदयानि श० 9.1.1.23. अग्निर्वै देवानामवमो विष्णुः परमस्तदन्तरेण सर्वा अन्या देवताः ऐ० 1.1. तद्यदेतस्मिन्नाके स्वर्गे लोके देवा असीदंस्तस्माद्देवा नाकसदः श० 8.6.1.1. द्यौर्वै सर्वेषां, देवानामायतनम् श० 14.3.2.4. देवगृहा वै नक्षत्राणि तै० 15.2.6. नरो वै देवानां ग्रामः तां० 6.9.2.। यो वै देवानामात्मा श०9. 3.2.7. सर्वेषां वाऽएष भूतानां सर्वेषां देवानामात्मा यद् यज्ञः श० 14.3.2.1 विद्वांसो हि देवाः श० 3.7.3.10.। तस्मात् प्राणा देवाः, श० 7.5.1.21. प्राणा देवाः श० 6.3.1.15. चक्षुर्देवः गो० पू० 2.11. मनो देवः गो० पू० 2.10. मनो वै देववाहनं मनो हीदं मनस्विनं भूयिष्ठं वनीवाह्यते श० 1.4.3.6. वाक् चवै मनश्च देवानां मिथुनम् ऐ० 5.23. वागेव देवाः श०14.4. 3.13. वाग्देवः गो० पू० 2.10. वाग्वै देवानां पुरान्नमासीत् तै० 1.3.5.1. वागिति सर्वे देवाः जै० उ० 1.9.2. वायुर्वै देवः जै० उ० 3.4.8. यशो देवाः श० 2.1.4.9. तस्माद् (देवाः) यशः श० 3.4.2.8. देवा वै यशस्कामाः सत्रमासत तां० 7.5.6.। परोक्षकामा हि देवाः श० 6.1.1.2. ,7.4.1.10., परोक्षप्रिया इव हि देवाभवन्ति प्रत्यक्षद्विषः गो० पू० 2.21. यदु ह किं च देवाः कुर्वते स्तोमेनैव तत्कुर्वते यज्ञो वै स्तोमोयज्ञेनैव तत्कुर्वते श० 8.4.3.2. मनो ह वै देवा मनुष्यस्याजानन्ति श० 2.1.4.1., 2.4.1.11. सत्यमेव देवा अनृतं मनुष्याः श० 1.1.1.4. यज्ञेन वै तद्देवा यज्ञमयजन्त यदग्निनाऽग्निमयजन्त तेस्वर्गं लोकमायन् ऐ० 1.16. अग्निर्वै देवानां होता ऐ० 1.28., 3.14. अग्निरेव देवानां दूत आस श० 3.5.1.21. वरुणो वै देवानां राजा श० 12.8.3.10. तस्मादाहुर्विष्णुर्देवानां श्रेष्ठ इति श०14.1.1.5. रुद्रो वै ज्येष्ठश्च श्रेष्ठश्च देवानाम् कौ० 25.13. अन्नमु देवानां सोमः जै० 3.174. दिवा वै मनुष्या यज्ञेन चरन्ति नक्तं देवाः। मै० 4.5.1.

ā[1]—proximity, particle of conjunction, and comparison. from all sides

iha—here, in this universe, in manifest stage

Vakṣati—sends, sustains, conducts

Anvaya (Sequencial placement of words)

agniḥ pūrvebhir nutanair uta ṛṣibhir iḍyaḥ. sa devān ā iha vakṣati

Meaning of Mantra in different contexts :

Spiritual: (अ॒ग्निः) Brahman (ईड्यः॑) is worthy to be extolled by both (पूर्वे॑भिः) ancient (उ॒त) and (नूत॑नैः) modern (ऋषि॑भिः) seers/visionary persons. (सः) He (आ व॒क्ष॒ति॒) conducts (दे॒वान्) all illuminating natural forces (इ॒ह) here.

Scientific 1: (अ॒ग्निः) Energy (ईड्यः॑) is worthy to be extolled by both (पूर्वे॑भिः) ancient (उ॒त) and (नूत॑नैः) modern (ऋषि॑भिः) seers/visionary persons. (सः) She (आ व॒क्ष॒ति॒) sustains (दे॒वान्) all matter particles (इ॒ह) in the observer space/our universe.

Scientific 2: (अ॒ग्निः) Geothermal energy located in the centre of the earth (ईड्यः॑) is worthy to be extolled by both (पूर्वे॑भिः) ancient (उ॒त) and (नूत॑नैः) modern (ऋषि॑भिः) seers/visionary persons. (सः) She (आ व॒क्ष॒ति॒) sends (दे॒वान्) geothermal radiation (इ॒ह) here (at the surface of the earth).

Scientific 3: (अ॒ग्निः) Star/our sun (ईड्यः॑) is worthy to be extolled by both (पूर्वे॑भिः) ancient (उ॒त) and (नूत॑नैः) modern (ऋषि॑भिः) seers/visionary persons. (सः) She (आ व॒क्ष॒ति॒) sends (दे॒वान्) solar radiation (इ॒ह) here (on the surface of the earth).

---

1. अर्वागर्थे नि० 1.3. एतस्मिन्नेवार्थे (समुच्चयार्थे) देवेभ्यश्च पितृभ्य एत्याकारः नि० 1.4. उपमार्थे दृश्यते नि० 3.16. अध्यर्थे दृश्यते नि० 5.5.

Note: According to the Veda, life exists on the earth with the permutation and combination of geothermal and solar energies.

Socio-political 1: (अग्निः) A Ruler (ईड्यः) is worthy to be praised by both (पूर्वेभिः) ancient (उत) and (नूतनैः) modern (ऋषिभिः) seers/visionary persons. (सः) He (आ वक्षति) conducts (देवान्) all good rules and regulations (इह) here in the society for the co-existence of all living beings.

Socio-political 2: (अग्निः) A teacher (ईड्यः) is worthy to be praised by both (पूर्वेभिः) ancient (उत) and (नूतनैः) modern (ऋषिभिः) seers/visionary persons. (सः) He (आ वक्षति) imparts (देवान्) divine knowledge and value education (इह) here in Gurukulas (schools, colleges and universities).

Note: In the Vedic society, ruler and teacher were given utmost importance. A Ruler used to ensure good governance and justice to each and every citizen and a teacher used to impart divine knowledge and value education to each and every student without any discrimination of caste, creed, race or region. So it is wrong to say that Vedic people were primitive. They were a disciplined society governed by good rulers and led by high profile teachers.

३. अग्निना॑ र॒यिम॑श्नवत् पोष॒मेव॑ दि॒वेदि॑वे। य॒शसं॑ वी॒रव॑त्तमम्॥३॥

अ॒ग्निना॑। र॒यिम्। अ॒श्न॒वत्। पोष॑म्। एव॑। दि॒वेऽदि॑वे। य॒शस॑म्।
वी॒रव॑त्ऽतमम्

Samhitāpāṭha

agnínā rayímaśnávat póṣ̌amevá divé divé. yaśasam
vīrávattámam.

Padapāṭha

agninā. rayim. aśnavat. poṣam. eva.   dive-dive. yaśasaṁ.
vīravat-tamam.

Grammatical Notes:

अग्निना॑ (Agninā)—Inst. sing. of Agni. Bhvādigaṇa root
√aga 'to go' +ni (Uṇādi suffix)[1]. Here both root and
suffix are accented as per rule of accentuation. For
example as per rule of accentuation[2], 'a' of root 'aga'
will be accented. On the other hand 'i' of suffix 'ni'
will also be accented as per another rule of
accentuation[3]. But the main rule[4] says that, there can be
only one acute accent in one word (formed of root and
suffix).   As such, in case of two acute accents in a
word, one is destined to go. Consequently, one acute
accent has to be dropped from Agni. According to the
further rules of accentuation, the acute accent which
comes first in the process of word formation will have
to go first[5]. As such suffix accent will prevail over the
root accent. The result is Agni is accented finally on the

---

1. See *Uṇādi sūtra* (4.50) —अङ्गेर्नलोपश्च *aṅgernalopaśca*.
2. Cf. Pāṇini—धातो: - 6.1.162
3. Cf. Pāṇini—आद्युदात्तश्च- 3.1.3.
4. Cf. Pāṇini—अनुदात्तं पदमेकवर्जम्-6.1.158
5. Cf. *Vārttika*—सति शिष्टस्वरे बलायान्- Pāṇini 6.1.158

root.

There are two concepts about the formation of words. First concept, enjoyed by Etymologists like Yāska and Śākaṭāyana, is that every word is formed of roots [1]. As per this concept, Agni gets acute accent on the suffix as cited above. According to another view, held by Gargya and others, it is not necessary that all the words are fromed from roots. In case of second view also if Agni is taken one single word unbreakable into the root and suffix, it gets acute accent on its final syllable following the rule of Phiṭ sūtra [2].

र॒यिम् (Rayim)—Acc. sing. of rayi. Adādigaṇa root √ rā 'to give'+?. This origin of rayi cannot be defined under any existing system of grammar. As such, it can be regularised by adding it to Pāṇini by way of a new supplementary formula.

अ॒श्न॒व॒त् (Aśnavat)—Bhvādigaṇa root √aś 'to pervade'+leṭ lakāra (Subjunctive) third person sing. This verbal form remains unaccented being followed by non—verbal form[3] in a hemistich.

पोष॑म् (poṣam)—Acc. sing. of poṣa.Bhvādigaṇa root √ puṣa 'to strengthen'+ghañ suffix or ac suffix in nominative meaning. Being formed of 'ñit' (of which final 'ñ' is elided) suffix, it is accented on the first syllable [4]. Attributive of rayim.

ए॒व (eva)—Being a particle, it carries accent on the final

---

1. नामानि आख्यातजानीति शाकटायनो नैरुक्तसमयश्च न सर्वाणि इति गार्ग्यो वैयाकरणानाम् चैके - Nir. 1.12
2. फिषोऽन्त उदात्तः - 1
3. Cf. Pāṇini—तिङ्ङतिङः - 8.1.28
4. Cf. Pāṇini—ञ्नित्यादिर्नित्यम्- 6.1.197.

syllable[1].

दि॒वेदि॑वे (Dive—Dive)—Loc. pl. of diva. Divādigaṇa root √div 'to play', 'desire to win', 'to deal with', 'to illuminate', 'to glorify', 'to be happy', 'to be intoxicated', 'to sleep', 'to shine' and 'to go'+kvip suffix in nominative sense. Iterative or Āmreḍita compound. The second member of Āmreḍita compound remains unaccented[2].

य॒शस॑म् (Yaśasam)—yaśas+ac suffix in the sense of praise [3]. Being fromed of cit suffix (of which final 'c' is elided) it should have been finally accented[4]. But its an exception to this rule, and accented on the middle syllable. Attributive of rayim.

वी॒रव॑त्तमम् (Vīravattamam)—Vīra+matup (in the sense of praise) or vīra+tamap (superlative degree suffix). Being 'pit' (of which ending 'p' is elided), suffix remains unaccented[5]. As such 'vira' enjoys acute accent on the final syllable as per the rules of Phiṭ sūtra[6]. Attributive of rayim.

Word meanings:

Agninā[7] —Through Agni

---

1. Cf. *Phiṭ. sūtra*—एवादीनामन्तः - 80.
2. Cf. Pāṇini—अनुदात्तं च - 8.1.3.
3. See Pāṇini—*arśādibhyo'c*—5.2.127.
4. Cf. Pāṇini—चितः- 6.1.163.
5. Cf. Pāṇini—अनुदात्तौ सुप्पितौ- 3.1.4.
6. See Sāyaṇa on RV. 1.1.3
7. अग्निः कस्मादग्रणीर्भवति। अक्नोपनो भवतीति स्थौलाष्ठीविर्न क्नोपयति न स्नेहयति। त्रिभ्य आख्यातेभ्यो जायत इति शाकपूणिः। इतादक्ताद्दग्धाद्वानीतात्। स खल्वेतेरकारमादत्ते गकारमनक्तेर्वा दहतेर्वा नीः परः नि० 7.14. विराडग्निः श० 6.2.2.34. यो वै रुद्रः सो ऽग्निः श० 5.2.4.13. अग्निरेष यत्पशवः श० 6.3.2.6. अग्निर्हि देवानां पशुः ऐ० 1.15. अग्निर्वै देवानां वसिष्ठः ऐ० 1.28. शिर एवाग्निः श० 10.1.2.4. अग्निः सर्वा देवताः ऐ० 2.3. अग्नि र्वैसर्वेषां देवानामात्मा श० 14.3.2.5. आत्मैवाग्निः श० .7.1.20. अग्निर्वै देवतानां मुखं

Rayim[1]—matter, life sustaining conditions. There are two things: one is prāṇa and other is rayi. Upaniṣads describe Prāṇa as Āgneya (relating to energy) and rayi as somīya (relating to matter). Water[2], wealth[3], human beings[4], animals[5], soma[6], and vital power[7].

Aśnavat—should be received.

प्रजनयितास प्रजापति: श० 3.9.1.6. अन्नादोऽग्नि: श० 2.1.4.28. अग्निर्देवानां जठरम् तै० 2. 7.12.3. अयं वै लोकोऽग्नि: श० 14.9.1.14. संवत्सर एषोऽग्नि: श० 3.7.1.18. वागेवाग्नि: श० 3.2.2.13. तेजो वाऽअग्नि: श० 2.5.4.8. अग्निर्वै रक्षसामपहन्ता कौ० 8.4.10.3. तपो वा ऽअग्नि: श०3.4.3.2. अग्निर्वै देवानां व्रतपति: श० 1.1.1.2. अग्निर्वै मृत्यु: श० 14.6.2.10. पुरुषोऽग्नि: श० 10.4.1.6. मन एवाग्नि: श० 10.1.2.3. प्राणो वा अग्नि: श० 9.5.1.68. वीर्यं वा अग्नि: तै० 1.7.2.2. गायत्री अग्नि: श० 3.4.1.9. अग्निरेव ब्रह्म श० 10.4.1.5. पर्जन्यो वा अग्नि: श० 14.9.1.13. आयुर्वाऽग्नि: श० 6.7.3.7. अग्निमतिथिं जनानाम् तै० 2.4.3.6. अमृतो ह्यग्नि:श० 1.9.2.20. असौ वा आदित्य एषोऽग्नि: श० 3.4.1.1. अग्निवैश्वानर: ता० 13.11.23. अनूचानमाहुरग्निकल्प इति मुखं ह्येतदग्नेर्यद् ब्रह्म श० 6.1.1.10. अग्निर्वै धर्म: श० 11.6.2.2. अग्निर्वैद्रष्टा गो० उ० 2.19. प्रजापतिरग्नि: श० 6.2.1.23. अथ्नर्वैयप: श० 7.2.1.10. अग्निर्वाव पुरोहित: ऐ० 8.27. प्राणा अग्नि: श० 6.3.1.21. अग्निर् ऋषि: मै० 1.6.1. अग्नि: पशुरासीत्तमालभन्त तेनायजन्त इति च ब्राह्मणम् नि० 12.41.

1. रयि:-उदकनाम निघं० 1.12. धननाम निघं० 2.10. रयिरिति धननाम रातेर्दानकर्मण: नि० 4.17. रयिरिति मनुष्या: (उपासते) श० 10.52.20. वीर्यं वै रयि: श० 13.4.2.13.पुष्टं वै रयि: श० 2.3.4.13. पशवो वै रयि: तै० 1.4.4.9. एष वै रयिर्वैश्वानर: श० 10.6.1.5. रयि सोमो रयिपतिर्दधातु तै० 2.8.1.6.
2. *Nighaṇṭu*, 1.12;
3. Ngh. 2.10; *rayti dhananāma rāterdānakarmaṇaḥ* (Rayi is the name of wealth—spiritual, material and moral and ethical) the wrod rayi has formed of the root *rā* 'to donate'.—*Nir.* 4.17.
4. *rayiriti manuṣyāḥ* (Human—beings are also called *rayi*)—*Ś.Br.* 10.52.20
5. *paśavo vai rayiḥ* (rayi is denoted by manifest world)—*TS.* 1.4.4.1
6. *rayiṁ somam rayipatir dadhātu* (The master of *rayi* sustains rayi, the material world)—*TS.* 2.8.1.6
7. *vīryaṁ vai rayiḥ* (Physical power is verily called as *rayi*)—*Ś. Br.* 13.4.2.13

Poṣam—increasing

Eva[1]—only, and

Dive-Dive—day by day

Yaśasam—fame

Vīravattamam—full of life

Anvaya (Sequencial placement of words)

agnnā yaśasaṁ rayim aśnavat dive dive poṣam eva vīravattamam.

Meaning of Mantra in different contexts :

Spiritual: (अ॒ग्निना॑) Through Brahman His (य॒शसं॑म्) famous (र॒यिम्) creation (अ॒श्न॒व॒त्) receives (पोषं॑म्) energy (दि॒वेदि॑वे) everyday (ए॒व) and becomes (वी॒रवं॑त्तमम्) full of life.

Scientific 1: (अ॒ग्निना॑) Through energy (र॒यिम्) matter particles are created (दि॒वेदि॑वे) everyday, consequent upon which this (य॒शसं॑म्) famous observer space (अ॒श्न॒व॒त्) receives (पोषं॑म्) power, (ए॒व) and becomes (वी॒रवं॑त्तमम्) full of life.

Note: Here the mantra points out that matter is created everyday at the surface of universe through conversion of energy into matter.

Scientific 2: (अ॒ग्निना॑) Through star/sun (य॒शसं॑म्) famous earth/planet (अ॒श्न॒व॒त्) receives (र॒यिम्) life sustaining (पोषं॑म्) power (दि॒वेदि॑वे) everyday, (ए॒व) so becomes (वी॒रवं॑त्तमम्) full of life.

Scientific 3: (अ॒ग्निना॑) Through geothermal energy (य॒शसं॑म्) famous earth (अ॒श्न॒व॒त्) receives (र॒यिम्) life sustaining (पोषं॑म्) power (दि॒वेदि॑वे) everyday, (ए॒व) so becomes (वी॒रवं॑त्तमम्) full of life.

Socio-political 1: (अ॒ग्निना॑) Through a good ruler (य॒शसं॑म्) a

---

1. एव एवम् नि० 2.19

famous nation (अ॒श्न॒व॒त्) receives (र॒यिम्) prosperity and (पोष॑म्) power (दि॒वेदि॑वे) everyday, (ए॒व) and (वी॒रव॑त्तमम्) people remain full of life.

Socio-political 2: (अ॒ग्निना॑) Through a good teacher (य॒शस॑म्) a famous student (अ॒श्न॒व॒त्) receives (र॒यिम्) moral and ethical values and (पोष॑म्) power of wisdom (दि॒वेदि॑वे) everyday, (ए॒व) that make him (वी॒रव॑त्तमम्) full of life.

४. अग्ने यं यज्ञमध्वरं विश्वतः परिभूरसि। स इद्देवेषु गच्छति।।४।।

अग्ने। यम्। यज्ञम्। अध्वरम्। विश्वतः। परिऽभूः। असि। सः। इत् देवेषु। गच्छति।।

Saṁhitāpāṭha

ágne yáṁ yajñám adhvaráṁ viśvátaḥ paribhū ́rási. sá íddevéṣu gácchátí.

Padapāṭha

agne. yaṁ. yajñam. adhvaraṁ. viśvataḥ. paribhūḥ. asi. saḥ. it. deveṣu. gacchati.

Grammatical Notes

अग्ने (Agne)—Voc. sing. of Agni. Bhvādigaṇa root √aga 'to go'+ni (Uṇādi suffix).[1] Being located in the begining of a hemistich It is accented on the first syllable [2].

यम् (yam)—Acc. sing. of demonstrative pronoun 'Yad'. Being pronominal form, it carries an acute accent.

यज्ञम्[3] (yajñam) —Gen. sing. of Yajña.Bhvādigaṇa √ yaja 'to

---

1. See *Uṇādi sūtra* (4.50)—*aṅgernalopaśca*
2. Cf. Pāṇ.—आमन्त्रितस्य च - 6.1.198.
3. यज्ञः-यज्ञ नाम निघं० 3.17. यज्ञः कस्मात? प्रख्यातं यजतिकर्मेति नैरुक्ताः। याच्ञ्यो भवतीति वा यजुरुन्नो भवतीति वा बहुकृष्णाजिन इत्यौपमन्यवो यजूंष्येनं नयन्तीति वा नि० 3.19. स (सोमः) तायमानो जायते स यन् जायते तस्माद् यञ्जो यञ्जो ह वै नामैतद् यद् यज्ञ इति श० 3.9.4.23. प्राणः (यज्ञस्य) सोमः कौ० 9.6. अध्वरो वै यज्ञः श० 1.2.4.5. यज्ञो वै मखः श ०6.5.2.1. तै० 3.2.8.3. तां० 7.5.6. मख इत्येतद् यज्ञनामधेयम् गो० उ० 2.5. यज्ञो वै नमः श० 7.4.1.30, 2.4.2.24, 2.6.1.42. यज्ञो वै स्वाहाकारः श० 3.1.3.27. यज्ञो वै भुज्युः (यजु० 18.42.) यज्ञो हि सर्वाणि भूतानि भुनक्ति श० 9.4.1.11. यज्ञो भगः (यजु० 11.7.) श० 6.3.1.19. गातुं वित्त्वेति यज्ञं वित्वेत्येवैतदाह। श० 1.9.2.28, 4.4.4.13. यज्ञो वै देवानां महः श० 1.9.1.11. एष ह वै महान् देवो यद् यज्ञः गो० पू० 2.19. यज्ञो वै बृहन्विपश्चित् श० 3.5.3.12. यज्ञो वा अर्यमा तै० 2.3.5.4. यज्ञो वै तार्प्यम् तै० 1.3.7.1, 3.9.20.1. यज्ञो वैवसुः (यजु० 1.2.) यज्ञो वै श्रेष्ठतमं कर्म (यजु० 1.1.) श० 2.7.1.5. यज्ञो हि श्रेष्ठतमं

worship gods', 'to unite', 'to donate'+naṅ[1] suffix and so becomes accented on the final syllable.

अ॒ध्व॒रम् (Adhvaram)—na+dhvara (Bahuvrīhi compound).

Bhvādigaṇa root √ dhvṛ 'to kill'+ac. Being Bahuvrihi compound, it is accented exceptionally on the last syllable[2].

वि॒श्वतः॑ (Viśvataḥ)—Viśva+tasil suffix in genetive sense[3].

According to Pāṇini, a stem followed by 'lit' (of which ending 'l' is elided) suffix carries an acute accent[4]. As such it is accented on the syllable followed by 'lit' suffix.

प॒रि॒भूः (Paribhūḥ)—Prefix pari+Bhavādigaṇa root √ bhū 'to be'+kvip suffix[5]. It is accented on bhūḥ as per Pāṇini—6.2.139.[6]

असि॒ (Asi)—Adādigaṇa root √as 'to be'+loṭ lakāra (Imperative) second pers. sing. Here 'asi' is accented because it is preceded by inflected forms of 'yad' pronoun[7].

कर्म तै० 3.2.1.4. ब्रह्म यज्ञः श० 3.1.4.15. ब्रह्म हि यज्ञः श० 5.3.2.4. ब्रह्म वै यज्ञः ऐ० 7.22. एष वै प्रत्यक्षं यज्ञो यत् प्रजापतिः श० 4.3.4.3. यज्ञः प्रजापतिः श० 11.6.38. यज्ञ उ वै प्रजापतिः कौ० 10.1.13.1. तै० 3.3.7.3. एष वै यज्ञ एव प्रजापतिः श० 1.7.4.4. प्रजापति र्यज्ञःऐ० 2.17, 4.26. इन्द्रो वै यज्ञस्य देवता श० 1.4.1.33, 1.4.5.4. विष्णुर्यज्ञः गो० उ० 1. 12. तै० 3.3.7.6. यज्ञो वै विष्णुः स यज्ञः श० 5.2.3.6. स यः स विष्णुर्यज्ञः सः, स यः स यज्ञोऽसौ आदित्यः श० 14.1.1.6. विष्णुर्वै यज्ञः ऐ० 1.15. यज्ञो विष्णुः तां० 13.3.2. गो० उ० 6.7.

1. Cf. Pāṇini, 3.3.90—यज-याच-यत-विच्छ-प्रच्छ-रक्षो नङ् (*yaja-yāca-yata-viccha-praccha-rakṣo naṅ).*
2. See Pāṇ.—नञ्सुभ्याम् - 6.2.172
3. See Pāṇini—*ṣaṣṭhyā vyāśraye ca*—5.4.48
4. Cf. Pāṇini—लिति - 6.1.193
5. See Pāṇini—*kvip ca* (3.2.76)
6. गतिकारकोपपदात् कृत्।
7. Cf. Pāṇini—यद्वृत्तान्नित्यम् - 8.1.66.

सः (Saḥ)—Nom. sing. masc. of deomstrative pronoun 'Tad'. It is accented following the norms set by Phiṭ sūtra.[1]

इत्[2] (It)—A particle used in the sense of 'determination'

दे॒वेषु॑[3] (Deveṣu)—Acc. sing.of deva. Divādigaṇa root √ div

---

1. Cf. Sāyaṇa on *RV.* 1.2.1.
2. इत् पदपूरणः नि० 1.9. महान् नि० 6.1.
3. देवो दानाद्वा, दीपनाद्वा, द्योतनाद्वा, द्युस्थानो भवतीति वा। यो देवः स देवता निघं० 7.15. दिवा वै नोऽभूदिति। तद् देवानां देवत्वम् तै० 2.2.9.9. दिवा देवानसृजत नक्तमसुरान् यद्दिवा देवानसृजत तद् देवानां देवत्वम् ष० 4.1 तद् देवानां देवत्वं यद् दिवसमभिपद्यासृज्यन्त श० 11. 1.6.7. प्राचीनप्रजनना वै देवाः प्रतीचीनप्रजनना मनुष्याः श० 7.4.2.40. प्राची हि देवानां दिक् श० 1.2.5.17. देवानां वा एषा दिग्यत्प्राची ष० 3.1. यद्वै मनुष्याणां प्रत्यक्षन्तद् देवानां परोक्षमथ यन्मनुष्याणां परोक्षन्तद् देवानां प्रत्यक्षम् तां० 22.10.3.। द्राघीयो हि देवायुषं ह्रसीयो मनुष्यायुषम् श० 7.3.1.10. देवानां वै विधामनु मनुष्याः श० 6.7.4.9. त्रयो वै देवाः। वसवो रुद्रा आदित्याः श० 4.3.5.1. एते वै त्रयो देवा यद् वसवो रुद्रा आदित्याः श० 1.3.4.12., 1.5.1.17., 1.8.3.8. त्रयस्त्रिंशद् देवताः तां० 4.4.11. त्रयस्त्रिंशद्वै देवताः तै० 1.2.2.5., 1.8.7.1., 2.7.1.3-4. त्रयस्त्रिंशद्वै सर्वा देवताः कौ० 8.6. त्रयस्त्रिंशद्वै देवाः प्रजापतिश्चतुस्त्रिंशः श० 12.6.1.37. अग्निर्वायुरादित्य एतानि ह तानि देवानां हृदयानि श० 9.1.1.23. अग्निर्वै देवा नामवमो विष्णुः परमस्तदन्तरेण सर्वा अन्या देवताः ऐ० 1.1. तद्यदेतस्मिन्नाके स्वर्गे लोके देवा असीदंस्तस्माद्देवा नाकसदः श० 8.6.1.1. द्यौर्वै सर्वेष, देवानामायतनम् श० 14.3.2.4. देवगृहा वै नक्षत्राणि तै० 15.2.6. नरो वै देवानां ग्रामः तां० 6.9.2. यो वै देवानामात्मा श० 9. 3.2.7. सर्वेषां वाऽएष भूतानां सर्वेषां देवानामात्मा यद् यज्ञः श० 14.3.2.1 विद्वांसो हि देवाः श० 3.7.3.10. तस्मात् प्राणा देवाः, श० 7.5.1.21. प्राणा देवाः श० 6.3.1.15. चक्षुर्देवः गो० पू० 2.11. मनो देवः गो० पू० 2.10. मनो वै देववाहनं मनो हीदं मनस्विनं भूयिष्ठं वनीवाह्यते श० 1.4.3.6. वाक् च वै मनश्च देवानां मिथुनम् ऐ० 5.23. वागेव देवाः श० 14.4.3.13. वाग्देवः गो० पू० 2.10. वाग्वै देवानां पुरान्नमासीत् तै० 1.3.5.1. वागिति सर्वे देवाः जै० उ० 1.9.2. वायुर्वै देवः जै० उ० 3.4.8. यशो देवाः श० 2.1.4.9. तस्माद् (देवाः) यशः श० 3.4.2.8. देवा वै यशस्कामाः सत्रमासत तां० 7.5.6 परोक्षकामा हि देवाः श० 6.1.1.2., 7.4.1.10., परोक्षप्रिया इव हि देवा भवन्ति प्रत्यक्षद्विषः गो० पू० 2.21. यदु ह किं च देवाः कुर्वते स्तोमेनैव तत्कुर्वते यज्ञो वै स्तोमो यज्ञेनैव तत्कुर्वते श० 8.4.3.2. मनो ह वै देवा मनुष्यस्याजानन्ति श० 2.1.4.1., 2.4.1.11. सत्यमेव देवा अनृतं मनुष्याः श० 1.1.1.4. यज्ञेन वै तद्देवा यज्ञमयजन्त यदग्निनाऽग्निमयजन्त ते स्वर्गं लोकमायन् ऐ० 1.16. अग्निर्वै देवानां

'to play', 'desire to win', 'to deal with', 'to illuminate', 'to glorify', 'to be happy', 'to be intoxicated', 'to sleep', to shine' and 'to go' or Curādigaṇa root √div 'to crush', 'to chirp'+ac suffix[1]. Being formed of cit (of which ending 'c' is elided) suffix, it is accented on the final syllable.[2] Devam is Attributive of Agni.

ग॒च्छ॒ति॒ (Gacchati)—Bhvādigaṇa root √gam 'to go'+laṭ lakāra third pers.sing. It remains unaccented, since it is followed by a non—verbal form [3]in a hemistich.

Word meanings:

Agne[4]—(God in spiritual sense; geothermal, field and solar

होता ऐ० 1.28., 3.14. अग्निरेव देवानां दूत आस श० 3.5.1.21. वरुणो वै देवानां राजा श० 12.8.3.10. तस्मादाहुर्विष्णुर्देवानां श्रेष्ठ इति श० 14.1.1.5. रुद्रो वै ज्येष्ठश्च श्रेष्ठश्च देवानाम् कौ० 25.13.अन्नमु देवानां सोमः जै० 3.174. दिवा वै मनुष्या यज्ञेन चरन्ति नक्तं देवाः। मै० 4.5.1.

1. Cf. Pāṇ. नन्दिग्रहिपचादिभ्यो ल्यु-णिनि-अचः - 3.1.134
2. चित् स्वर, see Pāṇini—चितः - 6.1.163.
3. Cf. Pāṇini—तिङ्ङतिङः - 8.1.28
4. अग्निः कस्मादग्रणीर्भवति। अक्नोपनो भवतीति स्थौलाष्ठीविर्न क्नोपयति न स्नेहयति। त्रिभ्य आख्यातेभ्यो जायत इति शाकपूणिः। इतादक्तादुदग्धाद्वानीतात्। स खल्वेतेरकारमादत्ते गकारमनक्तेर्वा दहतेर्वा नीः परः नि० 7.14. विराडग्निः श० 6.2.2.34. यो वै रुद्रः सो ऽग्निः श० 5.2.4.13. अग्निरेष यत्पशवः श० 6.3.2.6. अग्निर्हि देवानां पशुः ऐ० 1.15. अग्निर्वै देवानां वसिष्ठः ऐ० 1.28. शिर एवाग्निः श० 10.1.2.4. अग्निः सर्वा देवताः ऐ० 2.3. अग्निर्वै सवेषां देवानामात्मा श० 14.3.2.5. आत्मैवाग्निः श० .7.1.20. अग्निर्वै देवतानां मुखं प्रजनयिता स प्रजापतिः श० 3.9.1.6. अन्नादोऽग्निः श० 2.1.4.28. अग्निर्देवानां जठरम् तै०2. 7.12.3. अयं वै लोकोऽग्निः श० 14.9.1.14. संवत्सर एषोऽग्निः श० 3.7.1.18. वागेवाग्निः श० 3.2.2.13. तेजो वाऽअग्निः श० 2.5.4.8. अग्निर्वै रक्षसामपहन्ता कौ० 8.4.10.3. तपो वाऽअग्निः श० 3.4.3.2. अग्निर्वै देवानां व्रतपतिः श० 1.1.1.2. अग्निर्वै मृत्युः श०14.6.2.10. पुरुषोऽग्निः श० 10.4.1.6. मन एवाग्निः श० 10.1.2.3. प्राणो वा अग्निः श० 9.5.1.68. वीर्य वा अग्निः तै० 1.7.2.2. गायत्री अग्निः श० 3.4.1.9. अग्निरेव ब्रह्म श० 10.4.1.5. पर्जन्यो वा अग्निः श० 14.9.1.13. आयुर्वाऽग्निः श० 6.7.3.7. अग्निमतिथिं जनानाम् तै०2.4. 3.6. अमृतो ह्यग्निः श० 1.9.2.20. असौ वा आदित्य एषोऽग्निः श० 3.4.1.1. अग्निर्वैश्वानरः ता० 13.11.23. अनूचानमाहुरग्निकल्प इति मुखं ह्येतदग्नेर्यद् ब्रह्म श० 6.1.1.10. अग्निर्वै धर्मः

energy in scientific sense; star in scientific sense; Intellectual/teacher, king/commander in Socio-political context)

yam—whom

yajñam —creation of mass energy and space, social order, education (jñāna yajña)

Adhvaram[1]—na dhvaro vidyate asya (which cannot be perished). non-violent act [2], non-annhilating, yajña[3], space[4], prāṇa (vital air). used here as an attributive of yajña

Viśvataḥ—entire, of the whole.

Paribhūḥ——pervades,

Asi—you are.

Sa—that yajña

It—surely

श० 11.6.2.2. अग्निर्वैद्रष्टा गो० उ० 2.19. प्रजापतिरग्निः श० 6.2.1.23. अग्निर्वै यमः श०7. 2.1.10. अग्निर्वाव पुरोहितः ऐ० 8.27. प्राणा अग्निः श० 6.3.1.21. अग्निर् ऋषिः मै०1.6.1. अग्निः पशुरासीत् तमालभन्त तेनायजन्त इति च ब्राह्मणम् नि० 12.41.

1. ध्वरति वधकर्मा नि० 2.19. अध्वर इति यज्ञनाम 3.17. अध्वरमिति अन्तरिक्षनाम निघं० 1.3. अध्वरे यज्ञे नि० 6.13. अध्वरेषु यज्ञेषु नि० 10.19. अध्वर इति यज्ञनाम, ध्वरति हिंसाकर्मा, तत्प्रतिषेधः नि० 1.7. अध्वरम् यज्ञम् नि० 8.6. अध्वरो वै यज्ञः श० 1.2.4.5.; 4.1.38.39.; 5.3.4.10; 3.5.3.17.; 9.2.11. यज्ञो वा अध्वरः काठ० 31.11. प्राणोऽध्वरः श० 7.3.1.5. रसोऽध्वरः श० 7.3.1.6. ते ऽसुरा अपक्रामन्तोऽब्रुवन्न वा इमे ध्वर्तवा अभवन्निति। तदध्वरस्याध्वरत्वम् क० 36.4. देवान्ह वै यज्ञेन यजमानान्त्सपत्ना असुरा दुधूर्षाञ्चक्रुः। ते दुधूर्षन्त एव न शेकुर्धूर्वितुं ते परावभूबुस्तस्माद् यज्ञोऽध्वरो नाम श० 1.4.1.40.
2. Nir. (1.7)—*dhvarati hiṁsākarmā, tat pratiṣedho'dhvaraḥ* (*dhvara* is the root signifying violence, *adhavara* is place or act where violence is prohibited).
3. *adhvaro vai yajñaḥ* (*yajña* is a non—violent action or process)—*Ś.Br.* 1.2.4.5; 4.1.38.39; 5.3.4.10; 3.5.3.17. *yajño vā adhvaraḥ*—Kāṭh.S. 31.11.
4. *advaraṁ iti antarikṣanāma* (midsphere is also known as *adhavara.*)—*Ngh.* 1.3

Deveṣu—the lighted part of universe or say starry world.
Gacchti—reaches, transforms

Anvaya (Sequencial placement of words)

ágne yáṁ adhvaráṁ yajñám viśvátaḥ paribhūr ási. sá íddevéṣu gacchati.

Meaning of Mantra in different contexts :

Spiritual: (अग्ने) O Brahman! (यज्ञम् अध्वरम्) the process of creation of cosmos (यम्) that (विश्वतः परिऽभूः असि) you are governing from all sides (सः) that process of creation (देवेषु गच्छति) culminates into the origin of all celestial bodies (इत्) in the observer space (universe).

Scientific 1: (अग्ने) O Energy! (यज्ञम् अध्वरम्) the process of creation of matter particles (यम्) that (विश्वतः परिऽभूः असि) you are leading from all sides (सः) that process of creation of matter particles (देवेषु गच्छति) culminates into the origin of all celestial bodies (इत्) in the observer space (universe).

Scientific 2: (अग्ने) O Star/sun! (यज्ञम् अध्वरम्) the process of creation of life on earth/planet (यम्) that (विश्वतः परिऽभूः असि) you are leading from all sides (सः) that process of creation of life (देवेषु गच्छति) goes till the origin of human beings (इत्) on the earth.

Socio-political 1: (अग्ने) O ruler! (यज्ञम् अध्वरम्) the process of prosperous nation building (यम्) that (विश्वतः परिऽभूः असि) you are leading from all sides, (सः) that process (देवेषु गच्छति) will result into the origin of great citizens (इत्) in the nation.

Socio-political 2: (अग्ने) O teacher! (यज्ञम् अध्वरम्) the process of knowledge proliferation (यम्) that (विश्वतः परिऽभूः असि) you are leading from all sides, (सः) that process (देवेषु गच्छति) will result into to the origin of great scholars, scientists, doctors, engineers, businessmen and other professionals (इत्) in the nation.

५. अग्निर्होता कविक्रतुः सत्यश्चित्रश्रवस्तमः। देवो देवेभिरा गमत्।।५।।

अग्निः। होता। कविऽक्रतुः। सत्यः। चित्रश्रवःऽतमः। देवः। देवेभिः। आ। गमत्।।

Saṁhitāpāṭha

agnír hótā kavíkratúḥ satyáś citrá śravástámáḥ. devó devébhir ā´ gamát.

Padapāṭha

agniḥ. hotā. kavi-kratuḥ. satyaḥ. citra śravaḥ-tamaḥ. devaḥ. devebhiḥ. ā. gamat.

Grammatical Notes:

अग्निः (Agniḥ)—Nom. sing. of Agni. Bhvādigaṇa root √aga 'to go'+ni (Uṇādi suffix)[1]. Here both root and suffix are accented as per rule of accentuation. For example as per rule of accentuation[2], 'a' of root 'aga' will be accented. On the other hand 'i' of suffix 'ni' will also be accented as per another rule of accentuation[3]. But the main rule[4] says that, there can be only one acute accent in one word (formed of root and suffix). As such, in case of two acute accents in a word, one is destined to go. Consequently, one acute accent has to be dropped from Agni. According to the further rules of accentuation, the acute accent which comes first in the process of word formation will have to go first[5]. As such suffix accent will prevail over the root accent. As as a result, Agni is accented finally on the root.

---

1. See *Uṇādi sūtra* (4.50) —अङ्गेर्नलोपश्च *aṅgernalopaśca.*
2. Cf. Pāṇini—धातोः - 6.1.162
3. Cf. Pāṇini—आद्युदात्तश्च- 3.1.3.
4. Cf. Pāṇini—अनुदात्तं पदमेकवर्जम्-6.1.158
5. Cf. *Vārttika*—सति शिष्टस्वरो बलीयान्- on Pāṇini 6.1.158

There are two concepts about the formation of words. First concept, enjoyed by etymologists like Yāska and Śākaṭāyana, is that every word is formed of roots[1]. As per this concept, Agni gets acute accent on the suffix as cited above. According to another view, held by Gargya and others, it is not necessary that all the words are fromed from roots. In case of second view also when Agni is one single word unbreakable into the root and suffix, it gets acute accent on its final syllable following the rule of Phiṭ sūtra[2].

होता॑ (Hotā)—Acc. sing. of Hotṛ. Juhotyādigaṇa root √hu 'to give and to take'+tṛn suffix in nominative sense [3]. Being formed of 'nit' suffix (of which final 'n' is elided), it is accented on the first syllable [4]. Attributive of Agni.

क॒विक्र॑तुः (Kavikratu)—{Adādigaṇa root √ku 'to produce sound'+iḥ (Uṇādi suffix)}[5]+{Tanādigaṇa root √kṛñ 'to do'+katuḥ (Uṇādi suffix) in nominative sense or passive sense}, e.g. kriyate yayā or karoti veti kratuḥ[6]. Kavi—kratu being a Bahuvrihi compound, accented on the first member.[7] Predicative of Agni

स॒त्यः (Satya)—Nom. sing. of satya. Adādigaṇa root √as 'to be'+śatṛ (present active participle)+yat in the sense of 'pertaining to'. Predicative of Agni. Hardatta [8] finds it accented on final syllable under Pāṇinian rule (5.4.66).[9]

---

1. नामानि आख्यातजानीति शाकटायनो नैरुक्तसमयश्च न सर्वाणि इति गार्ग्यो वैयाकरणानां चैके - Nir. 1.12
2. फिषोऽन्त उदात्तः -1
3. Cf. Pāṇini—तृन् - 3.2.135
4. Cf. Pāṇini—ञ्नित्यादिर्नित्यम् - 6.1.197
5. See *Uṇādi sūtra* (4.140)—*acaḥ iḥ*
6. See *Uṇādi sūtra* (1.76)—*kṛñ katuḥ*.
7. Cf. Pāṇini—बहुव्रीहौ प्रकृत्या पूर्वपदम् - 6.2.1
8. See also Sāyaṇa on *RV.* 1.5.1

(5.4.66).[1]

चित्रश्रवस्तमः (Citraśravastamaḥ)—Bahuvrīhi compound between 'citra' and 'śravastamaḥ'. {Svādigaṇa root √ciñ 'to choose'+ktraḥ Uṇādi Sūtra[2]}+{Śravas+tamap superlative suffix}. Predicative of Agni. Being a Bahuvrīhi compound, it is also accented on the first member.[3]

देवः (Devaḥ)—Acc. sing.of deva. Divādigaṇa root √div 'to play', 'desire to win', 'to deal with', 'to illuminate', 'to glorify', 'to be happy', 'to be intoxicated', 'to sleep', to shine' and 'to go' or Curādigaṇa root √div 'to crush', 'to chirp'+ac suffix[4]. Being formed of cit (of which ending 'c' is elided) suffix, it is accented on the final syllable.[5] Devam is Attributive of Agni.

देवेभिः (Devebhiḥ)—Acc. sing. of deva. Divādigaṇa root √div 'to play', 'desire to win', 'to deal with', 'to illuminate', 'to glorify', 'to be happy', 'to be intoxicated', 'to sleep', to shine' and 'to go' or Curādigaṇa root √div 'to crush', 'to chirp'+ac suffix[6]. Being formed of cit (of which ending 'c' is elided) suffix, it is accented on the final syllable.[7] Devam is Attributive of Agni.

आ (Ā)—A prefix meaning proximity, conjunction and simli. Being a prefix, it is accented on the first syllable[8].

---

1. सत्यादशपथे- 5.4.66
2. See *Uṇādi sūtra—amicimiśasibhyaḥ ktraḥ*—4.165.
3. Cf. Pāṇini—बहुव्रीहौ प्रकृत्या पूर्वपदम् - 6.2.1
4. Cf. Pāṇ. नन्दिग्रहिपचादिभ्यो ल्यु-णिनि-अचः - 3.1.134
5. See Pāṇini—चितः - 6.1.163.
6. Cf. Pāṇ. नन्दिग्रहिपचादिभ्यो ल्यु-णिनि-अचः - 3.1.134
7. चित् स्वर, see Pāṇini—चितः - 6.1.163.
8. Cf. *Phiṭ sūtra*—उपसर्गाश्चाभिवर्जम् -81.

गमत् (Gamat)—Bhvādigaṇa root √gam+loṭ lakāra third pers. sing. Sāyaṇa considers it a form of loṭ lakāra. On the other hand Swami Dayananda considers it to be the form of Luṅ lakāra. It remains unaccented, since it is followed by a non-verbal form in a hemistich[1].

Word meanings

Agniḥ[2]—God in spiritual sense; geothermal, field and solar solar energy in scientific context; star in scientific context; king, teacher, commander in figurative context.

Hotā[3]—Presenter of oblations, provider of things

---

1. Cf. Pāṇini—तिङ्ङतिङः - 8.1.28
2. अग्निः कस्मादग्रणीर्भवति। अक्नोपनो भवतीति स्थौलाष्ठीविर्न क्नोपयति न स्नेहयति। त्रिभ्य आख्यातेभ्यो जायत इति शाकपूणिः। इतादक्तादुदग्धाद्वानीतात्। स खल्वेतेरकारमादत्ते गकारमनक्तेर्वा दहतेर्वा नीः परः नि० 7.14. विराडग्निः श० 6.2.2.34. यो वै रुद्रः सो ऽग्निः श० 5.2.4.13. अग्निरेष यत्पशवः श० 6.3.2.6. अग्निर्हि देवानां पशुः ऐ० 1.15. अग्निर्वै देवानां वसिष्ठः ऐ० 1.28. शिर एवाग्निः श० 10.1.2.4. अग्निः सर्वा देवताः ऐ० 2.3. अग्नि वैं सर्वेषां देवानामात्मा श० 14.3.2.5. आत्मैवाग्निः श० .7.1.20. अग्निर्वै देवतानां मुखं प्रजनयितास प्रजापतिः श० 3.9.1.6. अन्नादोऽग्निः श० 2.1.4.28. अग्निर्देवानां जठरम् तै० 2. 7.12.3. अयं वै लोकोऽग्निः श० 14.9.1.14. संवत्सर एषोऽग्निः श० 3.7.1.18. वागेवाग्निः श० 3.2.2.13. तेजो वाऽअग्निः श० 2.5.4.8. अग्निर्वै रक्षसामपहन्ता कौ० 8.4.10.3. तपो वाऽअग्निः श०3.4.3.2. अग्निर्वै देवानां व्रतपतिः श० 1.1.1.2. अग्निर्वै मृत्युः श० 14.6.2.10. पुरुषोऽग्निः श० 10.4.1.6. मन एवाग्निः श० 10.1.2.3. प्राणो वा अग्निः श० 9.5.1.68. वीर्यं वा अग्निः तै० 1.7.2.2. गायत्री अग्निः श० 3.4.1.9. अग्निरेव ब्रह्म अग्निर्वै श०10.4.1. 5. पर्जन्यो वा अग्निः श० 14.9.1.13. आयुर्वाऽग्निः श० 6.7.3.7. अग्निमतिथिं जनानाम् तै० 2.4.3.6. अमृतोह्यग्निः श० 1.9.2.20. असौ वा आदित्य एषोऽग्निः श० 3.4.1.1.अग्निर्वैश्वानरः ता० 13.11.23. अनूचानमाहुरग्निकल्प इति मुखं ह्येतदग्नेर्यद् ब्रह्म श० 6.1.1.10. अग्निर्वै धर्मः श०11.6.2.2.अग्निर्वैद्रष्टा गो० उ० 2.19. प्रजापतिरग्निः श० 6.2.1.23. अग्निर्वै यमः श०7.2. 1.10. अग्निर्वाव पुरोहितः ऐ० 8.27. प्राणा अग्निः श० 6.3.1.21. अग्निर् ऋषिः मै० 1.6.1. अग्निः पशुरासीत् तमालभन्त तेनायजन्त इति च ब्राह्मणम् नि० 12.41.
3. होतुः-ह्वातव्यस्य नि० 4.26. होतारम् ह्वातारम् निघं० 7.15. होता-यद्वा स तत्र यथाभाजनं देवता अमुमावहामुमावहेत्यावहति तदेव होतुर्होतृत्वम् ऐ० 1.2. मध्यं वा एतद् यज्ञस्य यद्धोता तै०3.3.8.10. आत्मा वै यज्ञस्य होता कौ० 9.6. (ऋ० 6.16.10., यजु० 11.35.)

Kavikratu[1]—All knowing, producer of sound

Satya[2]—Ever-existing, truth

Citraśravastamaḥ—multifarious manifestations.

Devaḥ[3]—divine, astronomical, electronic

अग्निर्वै होताश० 1.4.1.24. अग्निर्वै देवानां होता ऐ० 1.28. अग्निर्वै होताऽधिदैवं वागध्यात्मम् श० 12.1.1.4. वाग्वै होता (यजु० 13.7.) कौ० 13.9.17.7. वाग्वै यज्ञस्य होता श० 12.8.2. 23. वाग्घोता षड्ढोतृणाम् तै० 3.12.5.2. मनो होता तै० 2.1.5.9. प्राणो वै होता ऐ० 6.8. असौ वै होता योऽसौ (सूर्य:) तपति गो० उ० 6.6. पुरुषो वाव होता गो० उ० 6.6. क्षत्रं वै होता ऐ० 6.21. संवत्सरो वै होता कौ० 29.8. हेमन्तो होता तस्माद्धेमनवषट्कृता: पशव: सीदन्ति श०11.2.7.32.होतैव भर्ग: गो० पू० 5.15. होता हि साहस्र: श० 4.5.8.12. प्राची दिग् होतु: श० 13.5.4.24.उत्तरत आयतनो वै होता तै० 3.9.5.2.

1. कवि:-मेधाविनाम निघं० 3.15. कवि: क्रान्तदर्शनो भवति, कवतेर्वा नि० 12.13. असौ वाऽदित्य: कवि: श० 6.7.2.4. ये वा अनूचानास्ते कवय: ऐ० 2.2. एते वै कवयो यदृषय: श० 1.4.2.8. ये वै तेन ऋषय: पूर्वे प्रेतास्ते वै कवय: ऐ० 6.20. शुश्रुवांसो वै कवय: तै० 3.2.2.3.ये विद्वांसस्ते कवय: श० 7.2.2.4. क्रतु:-कर्मनाम निघं० 2.1. प्रज्ञानाम निघं० 3.9.

2. सत्यम् उदकनाम निघं० 1.12. सत्यं कस्मात् सत्सु तायते सत्प्रभवं भवतीति वा नि० 3.13. सत्यम् तदेतत् त्र्यक्षरं सत्यमिति स इत्येकमक्षरमित्येकमक्षरं प्रथमोत्तमे अक्षरे सत्यं मध्यतोऽनृतम् श० 14.8.6.2. तद् यत् तत् सत्यम्। त्रयी सा विद्या श० 9.5.1.18. सत्यां वा ऋतम् श० 7.3.1.23. तै० 3.8.3.4. ऋतमिति (यजु० 12.14.) सत्यमित्येतत् श० 6.7.3.11. यो वै सधर्म: सत्यंवै तत् तस्मात् सत्यं वदन्तमाहुर्धर्मंवदतीति धर्मं वा वदन्तं सत्यं वदतीति श० 14.4.2.26. सत्यं वै सुकृतस्य लोक: तै० 3.3.6.11. एतत् खलु वै व्रतस्य रूपं यत्सत्यम् श०12.8.2.4. एकं ह वै देवा व्रतं चरन्ति सत्यमेव 3.4.2.8. एकं ह वै देवा व्रतं चरन्ति यत्सत्यं तस्मादु सत्यमेव वदेत् श० 1.1.1.4. सत्यं देवा अनृतं मनुष्या: श० 1.1.2.17.। स य: सत्यं वदति स दीक्षित: कौ०7.3. सत्ये ह्येव दीक्षा प्रतिष्ठिता भवति श० 14.6.9.24. तस्यै वाच: सत्यमेव ब्रह्म श० 2.1.4.10.सत्यं ब्रह्म श० 14.8.5.1.। तद् यत् तत् सत्यम् आप एव तदापो हि वै सत्यम् श० 7.4.1.6. सत्यं वा एतत् यद् वर्षति तै० 1.7.5.3. असावादित्य: सत्यम् तै० 2.1.11.1. तद् यत् सत्यम्। असौ स आदित्य: श० 6.7.1.2. तद् यत् तत् सत्यम्। असौ स आदित्यो य एष एतस्मिन् मण्डले पुरुष: श० 14.8.6.3. सत्यमेव य एष (आदित्य:) तपति श० 14.1.2.22. (यजु० 11.47.) सत्यं वै शुक्रम् श० 3.9.3.25. सत्यं वै हिरण्यम् गो० उ० 3.17. प्राणा वै सत्यम् श० 14.5.1.23. चक्षुर्वै सत्यम् तै० 3.3.5.2.।

3. देवो दानाद्वा, दीपनाद्वा, द्योतनाद्वा, द्युस्थानो भवतीति वा। यो देव: स देवता निघं० 7.15.। दिवा वै नोऽभूदिति। तद् देवानां देवत्वम् तै० 2.2.9.9. दिवा देवानसृजत नक्तमसुरान् यद्दिवा

Devebhiḥ[2]—Alongwith devas (Natural forces), smart means, smart official machinery

Ā[1]—proximity, particle of conjunction, and comparison, from all sides

---

देवानसृजत तद् देवानां देवत्वम् ष० 4.1.। तद् देवानां देवत्वं यद् दिवसमभिपद्यासृज्यन्त श० 11.1.6.7. प्राचीन-प्रजनना वै देवाः प्रतीचीनप्रजनना मनुष्याः श० 7.4.2.40. प्राची हि देवानां दिक्श० 1.2.5.17. देवानां वा एषा दिग्यत्प्राची ष० 3.1. यद्वै मनुष्याणां प्रत्यक्षन्तद् देवानां परो क्षमथ यन्मनुष्याणां परोक्षन्तद् देवानां प्रत्यक्षम् तां० 22.10.3. द्राघीयो हि देवायुषं ह्रसीयो मनुष्यायुषम् श० 7.3.1.10. देवानां वै विधामनु मनुष्याः श० 6.7.4.9 त्रयो वै देवाः। वसवो रुद्रा आदित्याः श० 4.3.5.1. एते वै त्रयो देवा यद् वसवो रुद्रा आदित्याः श० 1.3.4.12., 1.5.1.17.,1.8.3.8. त्रयस्त्रिंशद् देवताः तां० 4.4.11. त्रयस्त्रिंशद्वै देवताः तै० 1.2.2.5., 1.8.7. 1., 2.7.1.3-4. त्रयस्त्रिंशद्वै सर्वा देवताः कौ० 8.6. त्रयस्त्रिंशद्वै देवाः प्रजापतिश्चतुस्त्रिंशः श० 12.6.1.37. अग्निर्वायुरादित्य एतानि ह तानि देवानां हृदयानि श० 9.1.1.23. अग्निर्वै देवानामवमो विष्णुः परमस्तदन्तरेण सर्वा अन्या देवताः ऐ० 1.1. तद्यदेतस्मिन्नाके स्वर्गे लोके देवा असीदंस्तस्माद्देवा नाकसदः श० 8.6.1.1. द्यौर्वै सर्वेषां, देवानामायतनम् श० 14.3.2.4. देवगृहा वै नक्षत्राणि तै० 15.2.6. नरो वै देवानां ग्रामः तां० 6.9.2. यो वै देवानामात्मा श० 9. 3.2.7. सर्वेषां वाऽएष भूतानां सर्वेषां देवानामात्मा यद् यज्ञः श० 14.3.2.1. विद्वांसो हि देवाः श०3.7.3.10. तस्मात् प्राणा देवाः, श० 7.5.1.21. प्राणा देवाः श० 6.3.1.15. चक्षुर्देवः गो० पू० 2.11. मनो देवः गो० पू० 2.10. मनो वै देववाहनं मनो हीदं मनस्विनं भूयिष्ठं वनीवाह्यते श० 1.4.3.6. वाक् च वै मनश्च देवानां मिथुनम् ऐ० 5.23. वागेव देवाः श० 14.4.3.13. वाग्देवः गो० पू० 2.10. वाग्वै देवानां पुरान्नमासीत् तै० 1.3.5.1. वागिति सर्वे देवाः जै० उ० 1.9.2. वायुर्वै देवः जै० उ० 3.4.8. यशो देवाः श० 2.1.4.9. तस्माद् (देवाः) यशः श० 3.4 .2.8. देवा वै यशस्कामाः सत्रमासत तां० 7.5.6. परोक्षकामा हि देवाः श० 6.1.1.2., 7.4.1.10., परोक्षप्रिया इव हि देवा भवन्ति प्रत्यक्षद्विषः गो० पू० 2.21. यदु ह किं च देवाः कुर्वते स्तोमेनैवतत्कुर्वते यज्ञो वै स्तोमो यज्ञेनैव तत्कुर्वते श० 8.4.3.2. मनो ह वै देवा मनुष्यस्याजानन्ति श० 2.1.4.1., 2.4.1.11. सत्यमेव देवा अनृतं मनुष्याः श० 1.1.1.4. यज्ञेन वै तद्देवा यज्ञमयजन्त यदग्निनाऽग्निमयजन्त ते स्वर्गं लोकमायन् ऐ० 1.16. अग्निर्वै देवानां हो ता ऐ० 1.28., 3.14. अग्निरेव देवानां दूत आस श० 3.5.1.21. वरुणो वै देवानां राजा श० 12.8.3.10. तस्मादाहुर्विष्णुर्देवानां श्रेष्ठ इति श० 14.1.1.5. रुद्रो वै ज्येष्ठश्च श्रेष्ठश्च देवानाम् कौ० 25.13.अन्नमु देवानां सोमः जै० 3.174 दिवा वै मनुष्या यज्ञेन चरन्ति नक्तं देवाः मै० 4. 5.1

1. अर्वागर्थे नि० 1.3. एतस्मिन्नेवार्थे (समुच्चयार्थे) देवेभ्यश्च पितृभ्य एत्याकारः नि० 1.4. उपमार्थे दृश्यते नि० 3.16. अध्यर्थे दृश्यते नि० 5.5.

gamat—come.

Anvaya (Sequencial placement of words)

agnír hótā kaví kratuḥ satyáś citrá śravastamaḥ devó devébhir ā´ gamat.

Meaning of Mantra in different contexts :

Spiritual: (अ॒ग्निः) Brahman is (होता॑) the presenter of oblations in the process of creation. (क॒विक्र॑तुः) He is all knowing, doer of all things. (स॒त्यः) He is ultimate truth and (चि॒त्रश्र॑वस्तमः) manifests multifariously. (दे॒वः) He is divine and (आ गमत्) has descended/manifested in this unverse (दे॒वेभिः॑) along with the various devine forces (natural forces).

Scientific 1: (अ॒ग्निः) Energy is (होता॑) the presenter of oblations in the process of creation of matter particles and space. (स॒त्यः) She is ever existing. (क॒विक्र॑तुः) She produces matter in the observer space, and (चि॒त्रश्र॑वस्तमः) manifests multifariously. She is (दे॒वः) divine and (आ गमत्) has manifested in this unverse (दे॒वेभिः॑) through various stars.

Scientific 2: (अ॒ग्निः) Geothermal energy is (होता॑) the presenter of oblations in creation of biolife on the earth/planets. (स॒त्यः) She is ever-existsting and (चि॒त्रश्र॑वस्तमः) manifests multifariously (क॒विक्र॑तुः) producing volcanoes, hot water springs, movement of lithosphere plates, mid plate earthquakes, hotspots, tsunamis, mountain building and global heat flow on the surface of the earth and gems. She is (दे॒वः) divine and (आ गमत्) has permeated planets/earth (दे॒वेभिः॑) through natural nuclear reactors.

Scientific 3: (अ॒ग्निः) Star/sun is (होता॑) the presenter of oblations into the yajña of creation of biolife on the earth/planets. (स॒त्यः) It is real and **(चि॒त्रश्र॑वस्तमः)** manifests multifariously. (क॒विक्र॑तुः) It emits sounds while revolving round its galaxy. It is (देवः) luminous body and (आ गमत्) has descended on planets/earth (देवेभिः) through its radition.

Socio-political 1: (अग्निः) Ruler is (होता) the presenter of oblations into the yajña of nation building. (सत्यः) He is the true custodian of masses (चित्रश्रवस्तमः) and enacts many laws (कविक्रतुः) and undertakes various welfare projects. He should be (देवः) divinely inspired and (आ गमत्) accesible to all (देवेभिः) through his good qualities, and smart official machinery.

Socio-political 2: (अग्निः) Teacher is (होता) the presenter of oblations into Jñāna yajña (process of knowledge proliferation in society). (सत्यः) He is the true pathmaker (चित्रश्रवस्तमः) embodiment of multifarious knowledge. (कविक्रतुः) He develops various methods for imparting knowledge. He should be (देवः) divinely inspired for his cause and (आ गमत्) accesible to all seekers of knowledge (देवेभिः) through his good qualities, smart means.

Note: The above mantra states that a ruler and a teacher should be divinely inspired and accessible to the needy public and seekers through smart official machinery and means.

द्वितीय वर्ग

Second Varga

In the first Varga, The charasteristics of God, energy, geothermal energy, stars, intellectuals/teachers and rulers have been narrated. Now in the second Varga, it has been suggested that prayer done to God, maintenance of energy and environment and contribution to nation and service to learned persons never go waste. Whatever prayer is done to God, maintenance done to our energies and environment, contribution to nation, service done to the scholars and learned persons, the same reverts to us.

६. यदङ्ग दाशुषे त्वमग्ने भद्रं करिष्यसि। तवेत्तत्सत्यमङ्गिरः।।६।।

यत्। अङ्ग। दाशुषे। त्वम्। अग्ने। भद्रम्। करिष्यसि। तव। इत्। तत्। सत्यम्। अङ्गिरः।।

Saṁhitāpāṭha

yádaṅgá dāśúṣe tvám ágne bhadrám̐ kariṣyási. távéttátsatyám aṅgiráḥ.

Padapāṭha

yat. aṅga. dāśuṣe. tvam. agne. bhadram. kariṣyasi. tava. it. tat. satyam. aṅgira.

Grammatical Notes:

यत् (Yat)—Nom. acc. sing. of demonstrative pronoun 'Yad'. Being a pronominal form it is accented.

अङ्ग (Aṅga)—Aṅga is a particle. Being particle, it should have carried an acute accent on the first syllable. But exceptional rule of Phiṭ sūtra[1], makes it accented on the

1. अभ्यादित्वात् - *Phiṭ sūtra*, 81

final syllable.

दाशुषे (Dāśuṣe)—Dative sing. of dāśvān. Bhvādigaṇa root √dāśṛ 'to donate'+kvasu suffix in subjunctive sense [1]. It gets the accent on suffix [2].

त्वम् (Tvam)—Nom. sing. of second person pronoun 'Yusmad'. Being a pronominal form, it is accented.

अग्ने (Agne)—Voc. sing. of Agni Bhvādigaṇa root √aga 'to go'+ni (Uṇādi suffix).[3] Being located in the begining of a hemistich, it is accented on the first syllable[4].

भद्रम् (Bhadram)—Acc. sing. of bhadra.Bhvādigaṇa root √ bhadi meaning 'wellbeing & comfort'+Uṇādi Sūtra rak[5]. It is accented on suffix[6].

करिष्यसि (Krişyasi)—Tanādigaṇa root √dukṛñ karaṇe+loṭ lakāra (future tense) second pers. sing. Here the unaccentuation is abandoned on account of its being preceded by the form of 'yad'.[7]

तव (Tava)—Gen. sing. of second person pronoun 'Yusmad'. It is accented on the syllable preceeding 'ṅas' (gen. pl) suffix.[8]

इत् (it)—A particle used in the sense of 'determination'

तत् (tat)—Nom. acc. sing of demonstrative pronoun 'Tad'. Being a pronominal form, it is also accented.

---

1. See Pāṇini, *kvasuśca*—3.2.106; *dāśvānsāhvān-mīḍhvānśca* — 6.1.12.
2. Cf. Pāṇini—आद्युदात्तश्च-3.1.3.
3. See *Uṇādi sūtra* (4.50)—*aṅgernalopaśca*
4. Cf. Pāṇ.—आमन्त्रितस्य च-6.1.198.
5. See *ṛjrendrāgra—Uṇādi* 2.28.
6. Cf. Pāṇini—आद्युदात्तश्च-3.1.3.
7. Cf. Pāṇ.—निपातैर्यद्यदिहन्त - 8.1.30.
8. Cf. Pāṇ.—युस्मदस्मदो ङसि - 6.1.205.

सत्यम् (Satyam)—Nom. sing. of satya. Adādigaṇa root √as' to be'+śatṛ (present active participle)+yat in the sense of 'pertaining to'. Predicative of Agni. Hardatta[1] finds it accented finally under Pāṇinian rule (5.4.66).[2]

अङ्गिरः (Aṅgira)—The word aṅgir cannot be derived by the Pāṇinian system of grammar. As such it can be added to Uṇādi sutra 1.53 as : अङ्गिर इतस्योपसंख्यानं कर्त्तव्यम्। so that it may be formed from Bhvādigaṇa root √agi 'to go'+kirac (Uṇādi suffix). Being a vocative case unlocated in beginning of a hemistich, it is devoid of accent.[3]

Word meanings

Yat—whatever

Aṅga —good

Dāśuṣe[4]—giver

Tvam—you

Agne[5]—God, in spiritual sense; geothermal, field and solar

---

1. See also Sāyaṇa on RV. 1.5.1
2. सत्यादशपथे- 5.4.66
3. Cf. Pāṇ.—आमन्त्रितस्य च - 8.1.19.
4. दाशुषे दत्तवते नि० 11.11.
5. अग्निः कस्मादग्रणीर्भवति। अक्नोपनो भवतीति स्थौलाष्ठीविर्न क्नोपयति न स्नेहयति। त्रिभ्य आख्यातेभ्यो जायत इति शाकपूणिः। इतादक्ताद्दग्धाद्वानीतात्। स खल्वेतेरकारमादत्ते गकारमनक्तेर्वा दहतेर्वा नीः परः नि० 7.14. विराडग्निः श० 6.2.2.34. यो वै रुद्रः सो ऽग्निः श० 5.2.4.13. अग्निरेष यत्पशवः श० 6.3.2.6. अग्निर्हि देवानां पशुः ऐ० 1.15. अग्निर्वै देवानां वसिष्ठः ऐ० 1.28. शिर एवाग्निः श० 10.1.2.4. अग्निः सर्वा देवताः ऐ० 2.3. अग्निर्वैसर्वेषां देवानामात्मा श० 14.3.2.5. आत्मैवाग्निः श० .7.1.20. अग्निर्वै देवतानां मुखं प्रजनयितास प्रजापतिः श० 3.9.1.6. अन्नादोऽग्निः श० 2.1.4.28. अग्निर्देवानां जठरम् तै० 2. 7.12.3. अयं वै लोकोऽग्निः श० 14.9.1.14. संवत्सर एषोऽग्निः श० 3.7.1.18. वागेवाग्निः श० 3.2.2.13. तेजो वाऽअग्निः श० 2.5.4.8. अग्निर्वै रक्षसामपहन्ता कौ० 8.4.10.3. तपो वाऽअग्निः श०3.4.3.2. अग्निर्वै देवानां व्रतपतिः श० 1.1.1.2. अग्निर्वै मृत्युः श० 14.6.2.10. पुरुषोऽग्निः श० 10.4.1.6. मन एवाग्निः श० 10.1.2.3. प्राणो वा अग्निः श० 9.5.1.68.

energy in scientific sense; star in scientific sense; king, nation, teacher, commander in figurative sense.

Bhadram[1]—good

Krişyasi—will do.

Tava—yours

it[2]—verily

tat —that

Satyam[3]—truly

वीर्यं वा अग्निः तै० 1.7.2.2. गायत्री अग्निः श० 3.4.1.9. अग्निरेव ब्रह्म श० 10.4.1.5. पर्जन्यो वा अग्निः श० 14.9.1.13. आयुर्वाऽग्निः श० 6.7.3.7. अग्निमतिथिं जनानाम् तै०2.4. 3.6. अमृतो ह्यग्निःश० 1.9.2.20. असौ वा आदित्य एषोऽग्निः श० 3.4.1.1. अग्निर्वैश्वानरः ता० 13.11.23. अनूचानमाहुरग्निकल्प इति मुखं ह्येतदग्नेर्यद् ब्रह्म श० 6.1.1.10. अग्निर्वै धर्मः श० 11.6.2.2. अग्निर्वैद्रष्टा गो० उ० 2.19.प्रजापतिरग्निः श० 6.2.1.23. अग्निर्वैयमः श० 7.2.1.10. अग्निर्वावपुरोहितः ऐ० 8.27. प्राणा अग्निः श० 6.3.1.21. अग्निर् ऋषिः मै० 1.6. 1. अग्निः पशुरासीत् तमालभन्त तेनायजन्त इति च ब्राह्मणम् नि० 12.41.।

1. अयं वै लोको भद्रः ऐ० 1.13. अन्नं वै भद्रम् तै० 1.3.3.6. भद्रमेभ्योऽभूदिति कल्याणमेवैतन् मानुष्यै वाचो वदति श० 4.6.9.19. भद्रं भगेन व्याख्यातं भजनीयं भूतानामभिद्रवणीयम् भवद्रमयतीति वा भाजनवद्वा नि० 4.9. श्रीर्वै भद्रम् जै० 3.172.

2. इत् पदपूरणः नि० 1.9. महान् नि० 6.1.

3. सत्यम् उदकनाम निघं० 1.12. सत्यं कस्मात् सत्सु तायते सत्प्रभवं भवतीति वा नि० 3.13. सत्यम् तदेतत् त्र्यक्षरं सत्यमिति स इत्येकमक्षरमित्येकमक्षरं प्रथमोत्तमे अक्षरे सत्यं मध्यतोऽनृतम् श० 14.8.6.2. तद् यत् तत् सत्यम्। त्रयी सा विद्या श० 9.5.1.18. सत्यां वा ऋतम् श० 7.3.1.23. तै० 3.8.3.4. ऋतमिति (यजु० 12.14.) सत्यमित्येतत् श० 6.7.3.11. यो वै सधर्मः सत्यं वै तत् तस्मात् सत्यं वदन्तमाहुर्धर्मंवदतीति धर्मं वा वदन्तं सत्यं वदतीति श०14.4. 2.26. सत्यं वै सुकृतस्य लोकः तै० 3.3.6.11. एतत् खलु वै व्रतस्य रूपं यत्सत्यम् श० 12.8.2.4. एकंह वै देवा व्रतं चरन्ति सत्यमेव 3.4.2.8. एकं ह वै देवा व्रतं चरन्ति यत्सत्यं तस्मादु सत्यमेव वदेत्श० 1.1.1.4. सत्यं देवा अनृतं मनुष्याः श० 1.1.2.17. स यः सत्यं वदति स दीक्षितः कौ० 7.3. सत्ये ह्येव दीक्षा प्रतिष्ठिता भवति श० 14.6.9.24. तस्यै वाचः सत्यमेव ब्रह्म श० 2.1.4.10.सत्यं ब्रह्म श० 14.8.5.1. तद् यत् तत् सत्यम् आप एव तदापो हि वै सत्यम् श० 7.4.1.6. सत्यं वा एतत् यद् वर्षति तै० 1.7.5.3. असावादित्यः सत्यम् तै० 2.1.11.1. तद् यत् सत्यम्।

असौ स आदित्यः श० 6.7.1.2. तद् यत् तत् सत्यम्। असौ स आदित्यो य एष एतस्मिन्

Aṅgira—Used here as attribitive of Agni

Anvaya (Sequencial placement of words)

yad aṅgá ágne dāśúṣe tvám bhadrám̐ kariṣyási. távéttátsatyám aṅgira

Meaning of Mantra in different contexts :

Spiritual: (अंगिर! अग्ने!) O Brahman, the life force of universe! (यत्) whatever is said about you that (त्वं) you (करिष्यसि) will do (भद्रं) good (इत) verily (दाशुषे) to those who contribute positively to the nation, society or your creation, (तत्) that (अंग) indeed is (सत्यम्) true (तव) about you.

Socio-political 1: (अंगिर! अग्ने!) O ruler, the life force of a nation! (यत्) whatever is said about you that (त्वं) you (करिष्यसि) will do (भद्रं) good (इत) verily (दाशुषे) to those who contribute positively to the progress of nation, or society, (तत्) let that (अंग) indeed be (सत्यम्) true (तव) about you.

Note: The above Vedic mantra emphasizes to honour those who contribute to the progress and prosperity of a nation.

मण्डले पुरुषः श॰ 14.8.6.3. सत्यमेव य एष (आदित्यः) तपति श॰ 14.1.2.22. (यजु॰ 11 .47.)सत्यं वै शुक्रम् श॰ 3.9.3.25. सत्यं वै हिरण्यम् गो॰ उ॰ 3.17. प्राणा वै सत्यम् श॰ 14.5.1.23. चक्षुर्वै सत्यम् तै॰ 3.3.5.2.

७. उप॑ त्वाग्ने दि॒वेदि॑वे॒ दोषा॑वस्तर्धि॒या व॒यम्। नमो॒ भर॑न्त॒ एम॑सि।।७।।

उप॑। त्वा॒। अ॒ग्ने॒। दिवेऽदि॑वे॒। दोषा॑वस्तः। धि॒या। व॒यम्। नम॑ः। भर॑न्तः। आ। इ॒म॒सि॒।।

Saṁhitāpāṭha

úpa tvāgné divé dive dóṣāvástár dhiyā´ vayám. námo bháranta émasí.

Padapāṭha

upa. tvā. agne. dive-dive. doṣā-vastaḥ. dhiyā. vayam. namaḥ. bharantaḥ. ā. imasi.

Grammatical Notes:

उप॑ (Upa)—A prefix meaning closeness. Being a prefix, it accented on first syllable[1].

त्वा॒ (Tvā)—Acc. sing. enclitic form of second person pronoun 'yusmad'. Being an enclitic form, it remains unaccented.[2]

अ॒ग्ने॒ (Agne)—Voc. sing. of Agni Bhvādigaṇa root √aga 'to go'+ni (Uṇādi suffix).[3] Being located in the begining of a hemistich, it is accented on the first syllable[4].

दिवेदि॑वे॒ (Dive—dive)—Loc. pl. of diva. Divādigaṇa root √div 'to play', 'desire to win', 'to deal with', 'to illuminate', 'to glorify', 'to be happy', 'to be intoxicated', 'to sleep', 'to shine' and 'to go'+kvip suffix in nominative sense. Iterative or Āmreḍita compound. The second member of Āmreḍita compund

---

1. Cf. *Phiṭ sūtra*—उपसर्गाश्चाभिवर्जम् - (81).
2. Cf. Pāṇ.—त्वामौ द्वितीयायाः - 8.1.23
3. See *Uṇādi sūtra* (4.50)—*aṅgernalopaśca*
4. Cf. Pāṇ.—आमन्त्रितस्य च - 6.1.198.

remains unaccented[1].

दोषांवस्त: (doṣāvasta)—Copulatives or Itaretara Dvandva compound : Doṣā (night) ca vasta (day) ca. {Divādigaṇa root √duṣ 'to pollute'+āḥ ((Uṇādi suffix))}[2]+{Adādigaṇa root √vas 'to cover'+kta (Uṇādi suffix)}[3]. According to the rules of accentuation, the words of devatā dvandva compound read under kārta kaujapa group of words under Pāṇ. कार्त कौ जपादित्वात् (kārtakau japāditvāt) (6.2.37.) are allowed to enjoy their natural accent on the first member the copulative compound form of doṣāvasta may also be read among 'kārta kaujapa' group of words, so that it may also justifiably carry accent on the first syllable of the first member

धिया (Dhiyā)—Inst. sing. of dhīḥ. Bhvādigaṇa root √ dhyai 'to think'+kvip siffix [4]. Dhiyā gets accent on suffix 'ā'[5], since it enjoys monosyllabic nature when inflected in locative case.

वयम् (Vayam)—Nom. pl. of first person pronoun 'Asmad'. Being a pronoun, it remains accented.

नमः (Namaḥ)—Bhvādigaṇa root √ ṇama 'to invocate'+ghañ suffix in abstract sense. It is accented on first syllable,

---

1. Cf. Pāṇini—अनुदात्तं च - 8.1.3.
2. Note : *doṣā* cannot be derived by any apparent rule of Pāṇinian system of grammar. As such this form may be regualrised by way of a supplementary formula दुसेरपि छन्दसि वक्तव्यम् added after *Uṇādi* 4.176. - आः समिणनिकषिभ्याम्।
3. Formation of *Vastaḥ* is not governed by, Pāṇinian system of grammar. As such regularisation of this form can be done through a new aphorism वसेरुपसंख्यानं वक्तव्यम् added after *Uṇādi sūtra*, 3.89.
4. See Pāṇini—*dhyāyateḥ saṁprasāraṇaṁ ca*—3.2.178
5. Cf. Pāṇini सावेकाचस्तृतीयादविभक्तिः-6.1.168.

being enumerated among particles.[1]

भर॑न्तः (Bharanta)—Nom. acc. pl of Bharan.Bhvādigaṇa root √Bhṛñ 'to wear, to bring up'+śap [2] (infix)+śatṛ (present active participle). Śap infix being 'pit' and 'śatṛ' suffix being sārvadhātuka[3], both infix and suffix will remain unaccented. In absence of both the accents, the root accent will prevail.

आ (ā)—A prefix meaning proximity, conjunction and simli. Being a prefix, it is accented on the first syllable[4].

इ॒मसि॒ (imasi)—Laṭ lakāra (present tense) first pers. pl. e.g. ā+Adādigaṇa root √iṇ 'to go'+masi. Mas is replaced by masi according to Pāṇini[5]. It remains unaccented, since it is followed by a non—verbal form [6] in a hemistich.

Word meanings:

Upa—A prefix meaning closeness [7].

Tvā —to you

Agne —O Agni[8]

---

1. Cf. *Phiṭ sūtra*—निपाताः आद्युदात्ताः-80.
2. Being a *Bhvādigaṇa* root, it gets *śap* infix as per Pāṇ. rule कर्तरिशप् 3.8.68.
3. Cf. Pāṇ. तासि-अनुदात्तेन्ङिद्दुपदेशाल्लसार्वधातुकमनुदात्तमह्न्विङो: - 6.1.186
4. Cf. *Phiṭ sūtra*—उपसर्गाश्चाभिवर्जम् -81.
5. *idanto masi*—7.1.46
6. Cf. Pāṇini—तिङ्ङतिङः - 8.1.28
7. उप इत्युपजनम् नि० 1.3. इयं (पृथिवी) वा ऽउप श० 2.3.4.9. उप वै रथन्तरम् तां० 16.5.14.
8. अग्निः कस्मादग्रणीर्भवति। अक्नोपनो भवतीति स्थौलाष्ठीविर्न क्नोपयति न स्नेहयति। त्रिभ्य आख्यातेभ्यो जायत इति शाकपूणिः। इतादक्ताद्दग्धाद्वानीतात्। स खल्वेतेरकारमादत्ते गकारमनक्तेर्वा दहतेर्वा नीः परः नि० 7.14. विराडग्निः श० 6.2.2.34. यो वै रुद्रः सो ऽग्निः श० 5.2.4.13. अग्निरेष यत्पशवः श० 6.3.2.6. अग्निर्हि देवानां पशुः ऐ० 1.15. अग्निर्वै

Dive—dive—every day

doṣāvasta—night [1] and day; dispeller of darkness

Dhiyā[2]—in our thoughts, mind

Vayam—we

Namaḥ[3]—invocations, salutations, reverential homage.

Bharanta—perform

ā[4]**+imasi**—approach

Anvaya (Sequencial placement of words)

vayám úpa émasi tvā agne námo bháranta dhiyā ́ divé dive doṣāvástáḥ.

देवानां वसिष्ठः ऐ० 1.28. शिर एवाग्निः श० 10.1.2.4. अग्निः सर्वा देवताः ऐ० 2.3. अग्निर्वै सर्वेषां देवानामात्मा श० 14.3.2.5. अग्निर्वै देवतानां मुखं प्रजनयिता स प्रजापतिः श० 3.9.1.6. अन्नादोऽग्निः श० 2.1.4.28. अग्निर्देवानां जठरम् तै० 2.7.12.3. अयं वै लोकोऽग्निः श० 14.9.1.14. संवत्सर एषोऽग्निः श० 3.7.1.18. वागेवाग्निः श० 3.2.2.13. तेजो वाऽअग्निः श० 2.5.4.8. अग्निर्वै रक्षसामपहन्ता कौ० 8.4.10.3. तपो वाऽअग्निः श०3.4.3.2. अग्निर्वै देवानां व्रतपतिः श० 1.1.1.2. अग्निर्वै मृत्युः श० 14.6.2.10. पुरुषोऽग्निः श० 10.4.1.6. मन एवाग्निः श० 10.1.2.3. प्राणो वा अग्निः श० 9.5.1.68. वीर्य वा अग्निः तै० 1.7.2.2. गायत्रीअग्निः श० 3.4.1.9. अग्निरेव ब्रह्म श० 10.4.1.5. पर्जन्यो वा अग्निः श० 14.9.1.13. आयुर्वाऽग्निः श० 6.7.3.7. अग्निमतिथिं जनानाम् तै० 2.4.3.6. अमृतो ह्यग्निः श०1.9.2.20. असौ वा आदित्य एषोऽग्निः श० 3.4.1.1. अग्निर्वैश्वानरः ता० 13.11.23.

अनूचानमाहुरग्निकल्प इति मुखं ह्येतदग्नेर्यद् ब्रह्म श० 6.1.1.10. अग्निर्वै धर्मः श० 11.6.2.2. अग्निर्वैद्रष्टा गो० उ० 2.19. प्रजापतिरग्निः श० 6.2.1.23. अग्निर्वै यमः श० 7.2.1.10. अग्निर्वाव पुरोहितः ऐ० 8.27. प्राणा अग्निः श० 6.3.1.21. अग्निर् ऋषिः मै० 1.6.1. अग्निः पशुरासीत् तमालभन्त तेनायजन्त इति च ब्राह्मणम् नि० 12.41.

1. दोषा रात्रिनाम निघं० 1.7. दोषा-रात्रौ नि० 3.15. वस्तोः अहर्नाम निघं० 1.9. वसतोः दिवा नि० 3.15.
2. धीः कर्मनाम निघं० 2.1. प्रज्ञानाम निघं० 3.9. धियः-प्रज्ञानानि नि० 11.27.
3. नमनं नमः। नमः- अन्ननाम निघं० 2.7. वज्रनाम निघं० 2.20. अन्नं नमः श० 6.3.1.17. यज्ञो वै नमः श० 2.4.2.24.
4. अर्वागर्थे नि० 1.3. एतस्मिन्नेवार्थे (समुच्चयार्थे) देवेभ्यश्च पितृभ्य एत्याकारः नि० 1.4. उपमार्थे दृश्यते नि० 3.16. अध्यर्थे दृश्यते नि० 5.5.

Meaning of Mantra in different contexts :

Spiritual: (वयम्) We (उप इमसि) approach (त्वा) you, (अग्ने) O Brahman, (नमः भरन्तः) with reverential homage (धिया) in our thoughts/actions, (दिवे दिवे) daily, (दोषावस्तः) day and night.

Scientific: (वयम्) We (उप इमसि) utilize (त्वा) you, (अग्ने) O energy, (नमः भरन्तः) in a thoughtful manner (धिया) applying our mind, (दिवे दिवे) daily, (दोषावस्तः) day and night.

Socio-political 1: (वयम्) We the seekers of knowledge (उप इमसि) approach (त्वा) you, (अग्ने) O Āchārya, (नमः भरन्तः) with reverential homage (धिया) in our thoughts/actions, (दिवे दिवे) daily, (दोषावस्तः) day and night.

Socio-political 2: (वयम्) We the seekers of safety and security (उप इमसि) approach (त्वा) you, (अग्ने) O ruler, (नमः भरन्तः) with reverential homage (धिया) in our thoughts/actions, (दिवे दिवे) daily, (दोषावस्तः) day and night.

Note: The Veda says that one should be thankful to God for His creation, ruler for providing with safety and security and teacher for providing with knowledge and value education.

८. राजन्तमध्वराणां गोपामृतस्य दीदिविम्। वर्धमानं स्वे दमे।।८।।

राजन्तम्। अध्वराणाम्। गोपाम्। ऋतस्य। दीदिविम्। वर्धमानम्। स्वे। दमे।।

Saṁhitāpāṭha

rā´jantám ádhvarā´ṇāṁ gopā´mṛtásya
dī´divím.várdhamā´naṁ své dáme.

Padapāṭha

rājantam. adhvarāṇām. gopām. ṛtasya. dīdivim.
vardhamānam. sve. dame.

Grammatical Notes:

राजन्तम् (Rājantam)—Acc. sing. of rājan. Bhvādigaṇa root √Rājṛ 'to shine' śap (infix)+śatṛ (present actice participal suffix). 'Śap' infix being 'pit' and 'śatṛ' suffix being sārvadhātuka[1], both infix and suffix will remain unaccented. In absence of both the accent, the root accent will prevail.

अध्वराणाम् (Adhvarāṇām)—na+dhvara(Bahuvrihi compound).

Bhvādigaṇa root √ dhvṛ 'to kill'+ac. Being Bahuvrihi compound, it is accented exceptionally on the last syllable[2].

गोपाम् (Gopām)—Go+Adādigaṇa root √pā 'to protect'+kvip suffix. ?

ऋतस्य (Ṛtasya)—Gen. sing. of ṛta (Bhavādigaṇa root √ṛ 'to' move' 'to send'+kta (Uṇādi suffix). Pāṇini and his followers have failed to prescribe a direct rule to govern its formation. It can be formed from '—kta' suffix as prescribed in Uṇādi sūtra 3.89. As such it 'ṛ' can also be read along with other roots like añc, ghṛ and si in Uṇādi sūtra—3.89.

---

1. Cf. Pāṇ. तासि-अनुदात्तेन्ङिददुपदेशाल्लसार्वधातुकमनुदात्तमह्न्विङोः - 6.1.186
2. See Pāṇ.—नञसुभ्याम् - 6.2.172

दीदिविम् (Dīdivim)—Divādigaṇa root √divu 'to play', 'aspiration for winning', 'interaction' and 'illumination'+kvin (Uṇādi suffix)[1]. It is accented on the first syllable following Pāṇini's rule—अभ्यस्तानामादिः (abhyastānāmādiḥ)—6.1.189.

वर्धमानम् (Vardhamānaṁ)—Bhvādigaṇa root √vṛdhu 'to increase'+śap+śānac (present passive participle—mān). Śap infix being 'pit' and 'śatṛ' suffix being sārvadhātuka[2], both infix and suffix will remain unaccented. In absence of both the accent, the root accent will prevail.

स्वे (Sve)—A loc sing. of sva used here as a noun[3].

दमे (Dame)—Divādigaṇa root √damu 'to calm down' or 'pacify'+ghañ suffix[4]. It is accented on the first syllable after the pattern of words enumerated by Pāṇini[5] in vṛṣa group of words.

Word meanings:

Rājantam—illuminating, effulgent

Adhvarāṇām[6]—of the process of creation

Gopām[1]—sun, protector[2]

---

1. *divo dve dīrghaścābhyāsasya—Uṇādi sūtra* (4.45).
2. Cf. Pāṇ. तासि-अनुदात्तेन्ङिद्दुपदेशाल्लसार्वधातुकमनुदात्तमह्न्विङोः - 6.1.186
3. According to Pāṇini (*svamjñāti—dhanākhyāyām*—1.1.34), *sva* in the meaning of 'own' is used both as noun and pronoun.
4. See Pāṇini, *halaśca*—3.3.121.
5. Cf. Pāṇ.—वृषादीनां च - 6.1.2003.
6. ध्वरति वधकर्मा नि० 2.19. अध्वर इति यज्ञनाम 3.17. अध्वरमिति अन्तरिक्षनाम निघं० 1.3. अध्वरे यज्ञे नि० 6.13. अध्वरेषु यज्ञेषु नि० 10.19. अध्वर इति यज्ञनाम, ध्वरति हिंसाकर्मा, तत्प्रतिषेधः नि० 1.7. अध्वरम् यज्ञम् नि० 8.6. अध्वरो वै यज्ञः श० 1.2.4.5.; 4.1.38.39.; 5.3.4.10; 3.5.3.17.; 9.2.11. यज्ञो वा अध्वरः काठ० 31.11. प्राणोऽध्वरः श० 7.3.1.5. रसोऽध्वरः श० 7.3.1.6. ते ऽसुरा अपक्रामन्तोऽब्रुवन्न वा इमे ध्वर्तवा अभवन्निति। तदध्वरस्याध्वरत्वम् क० 36.4. देवान्ह वै यज्ञेन यजमानान्त्सपत्ना असुरा दुधूर्षाञ्चक्रुः। ते दुधूर्षन्त एव न शेकुर्धूर्वितुं ते पराबभूवुस्तस्माद् यज्ञोऽध्वरो नाम श० 1.4.1.40.

Ṛtasya[3]—truth[4], water[5], technical term denoting some part of universal creation[6], Brahma[7], mind[8], form of energy. cosmic law

Dīdivim—illuminator

vardhamānam—being increased, increasing, thriving powerful.

Sve—in its own

Dame[9]—dwelling, field[10]

Anvaya (Sequencial placement of words)

rājantam adhvarāṇāṁ gopām ṛtásya dīdivim své dáme várdhamānaṁ.

---

1. गोपा गोपायिता आदित्यः निघं० 3.11. एष वै गोपा य एषः (सूर्यः) तपत्येष हीदं सर्वं गोपायति श० 14.1.4.9. प्राणो वै गोपाः। स हीदं सर्वमनिपद्यमानो गोपायति जै० उ० 3.37.2. इन्द्रो वै गोपाः ऐ० 6.10. गो० उ० 2.20. अग्निर्वै देवानां गोपा ऐ० 1.28.
2. *gopā gopāyitā ādityaḥ* (The protector sun is called as gopā)—Ngh. 3.11; *eṣa vai gopā ya eṣa tapatyeṣa hidaṁ sarvaṁ gopāyati* (The sun that radiates its heat is also the protector of the creation). Ś. Br. 14.1.4.9.
3. ऋतम् उदकनाम निघं० 1.12. प्रत्यृतं भवति नि० 2.25. सत्यनाम निघं० 3.10. यज्ञस्य नि० 6.22. सत्यं वाऽऋतम् श० 6.7.3.11. ऋतमित्येष (सूर्यः) वै सत्यम् ऐ० 4.20. अग्निर्वा ऋतम् तै० 2.1.11.1. ऋतमेव परमेष्ठौ तै० 1.5.5.1. चक्षुर्वा ऋतं तस्माद्यतरो विवदमानयोराहाह मनुष्ठ्या चक्षुषादर्शमिति तस्य श्रद्दधति ऐ० 2.40. मनो वा ऋतम् जै० उ० 3.36.5. ब्रह्म वाऽअग्निर्ऋतमसावादित्यः सत्यं यदि वासावृतमयं (अग्निः) सत्यमुभयम्वेतदयमग्निः श० 6.4.4.10. ऋतनेवैनं स्वर्गं गमयन्ति तां० 18.2.9.
4. *satyaṁ vā' ṛtam* (Truth verily called as *ṛta*)—Ś.Br. 7.3.1.23.
5. Nighaṇṭu (1.12) enumerates *ṛta* in the list of water.
6. One of the technical terms of universal creation (Ngh. 5.4)
7. *Brahma vā'ṛtam*—Ś.Br.4.1.4.10.
8. *mano vā ṛtam—J. Up.* Br. 3.36.5
9. दमः गृहनाम निघं० 3.4. दम इति नियतं ब्रह्मचारिणः तै आ० 10.62.1. दमेन दान्ताः किल्विषमव धून्वन्ति तै० आ० 10.63.1. दमः शमयिता (संन्यासिनो यज्ञस्य) तै० आ० 10.64.1
10. *damaḥ gṛhanāma*—Ngh. 3.4.

Meaning of Mantra in different contexts :

Spiritual: (Let us worship Brahman) who is (राजन्तम्) the effulgent one, (गोपाम्) the protector of (अध्वराणाम्) creation and other positive acts, (दीदिविम्) illuminator of (ऋतस्य्) truth and (वर्धमानम्) who thrives (स्वे) in his own (दमे) highest dwelling place.

Scientific 1: (Let us adore energy) that which is (राजन्तम्) the radiant constituent of creation, (गोपाम्) the protector of (अध्वराणाम्) mass energy, (दीदिविम्) illuminator of (ऋतस्य्) laws sustaining the creation and (वर्धमानम्) that which thrives (स्वे) in its own (दमे) dwelling place, i.e. light space.

Scientific 2: (Let us praise geothermal energy) that which (राजन्तम्) the radiates its energy, (गोपाम्) protects (अध्वराणाम्) process of creation on the earth, (दीदिविम्) illuminates (ऋतस्य्) laws of creation and (वर्धमानम्) that which thrives (स्वे) in its own (दमे) dwelling place, i.e. womb of earth.

Scientific 3: (Let us praise star/sun) that which (राजन्तम्) the radiates its energy, (गोपाम्) protects (अध्वराणाम्) process of creation on the earth, (दीदिविम्) illuminates (ऋतस्य्) laws of creation and (वर्धमानम्) that which thrives (स्वे) in its own (दमे) dwelling place, i.e. celestial sphere.

Socio-political 1: (Let us praise ruler) who (राजन्तम्) illuminates with physical prowess; (गोपाम्) protects (अध्वराणाम्) the system of governance of a nation; (दीदिविम्) publishes (ऋतस्य्) various rules and laws to regulate the society and (वर्धमानम्) thrives (स्वे) in his own (दमे) seat.

Socio-political 2: (Let us praise teacher) who (राजन्तम्) is illuminates with knowledge, (गोपाम्) who protects (अध्वराणाम्) the system of education of a nation, (दीदिविम्) brings to light (ऋतस्य्) various theories and principles of knowedge and (वर्धमानम्) thrives (स्वे) in his own (दमे) position of teacher.

९. स नः पितेव सूनवेऽग्ने सूपायनो भव। सचस्वा नः स्वस्तये॥९॥

सः। नः। पिताऽइव। सूनवे। अग्ने। सुऽउपायनः। भव। सचस्व। नः। स्वस्तये॥

Saṁhitāpāṭha

sá naḥ pitéva sūnávé'gne sū´pāyanó bhavá. sácasvā´ náḥ svastáye.

Padapāṭha

saḥ. naḥ. pitā—iva. sūnave. agne. su—upāyanaḥ. bhava. sacasva. naḥ. svastaye.

Grammatical Notes:

सः (saḥ)—Nom. sing. masc. of deomstrative pronoun 'Tad'. It is accented following the norms set by Phiṭ sūtra.[1]

नः (naḥ)—Acc./dat./gen. pl. enclitic form of first person pronoun 'Asmad'[2]. Being an enclitic form it is not accented.[3]

पिता (Pitā)—Nom.sing. of pitṛ. Adādigaṇa root √pā 'to protect'+tṛc (Uṇādi suffix).[4] Being formed of 'cit' suffix (of which final 'c' is elided), it is accented on last syllable.

इव (iva)—A particle of comparison. Being a particle, accented on the first syllable.[5]

सूनवे (Sūnave)—Dat. sing. of Sūnu (Adādigaṇa root √ṣu 'to

---

1 Cf. Sāyaṇa on RV. 1.2.1.

2. Cf. *vahuvacanasyavasnasau*—Pāṇ. 8.1.21.

3. Cf. Pāṇ. युस्मदस्मदोः षष्ठी चतुर्थी द्वितीया स्थयोर्वान्नावौ 8.1.20.

4. Cf. *Uṇādi sūtra* नप्तृनेष्टृत्वष्टृ० 2.95.

5. Cf. *Phiṭ sūtra*—निपाताः आद्युदात्ताः - 81.

deliver' +nu (Uṇādi suffix)[1].

अग्ने (Agne)—Voc. sing. of Agni Bhvādigaṇa root √aga 'to go'+ni (Uṇādi suffix).[2] Being located in the begining of a hemistich, it is accented on the first syllable[3].

सूपायनः (Supāyanaḥ)—Su+upa+ayanḥ (Ayan=Bhavādigaṇa root √aya 'to go'+lyuṭ suffix). Supāyanaḥ is Bahuvrīhi compound, so it is accented on the final syllable as per the rule of accentuation.[4]

भव (Bhava)—Bhvādigaṇa root √bhū 'to be'. Loṭ lakāra (imperative) second pers. sing. Not accented being a verbal form preceded by a non—verbal form.[5]

सचस्व (Sacasva)—Bhvādigaṇa root √ṣaca 'to irrigate', 'to serve' 'to gather'. Loṭ lakāra (imperative) second pers. sing. According to Ngh. there is another root √sac 'to go'. Here lengthening of last vowel is according to Pāṇini—anyeṣāmpi dṛṣyate—6.3.137. Accented on root [6] being preceded by a verbal form.[7]

नः (naḥ)—Acc./dat./gen. pl. enclitic form of first person pronoun 'Asmad'[8]. Being an enclitic form it is not accented.[9]

स्वस्तये (Svastaye)—su+asti=svasti. Dat. sing.

Word meanings:

saḥ—he

---

1. Cf. *suvaḥ kit—Uṇādi* 3.35
2. See *Uṇādi sūtra* (4.50)—*aṅgernalopaśca*
3. Cf. Pāṇ. आमन्त्रितस्य च 6.1.198.
4. Cf. Pān. नञ्सुभ्याम् 6.2.172.
5. Cf. Pān. तिङ्ङतिङः 8.1.28.
6. Cf. Pān. तस्यानुदात्तेन्ङिदुपदेशाल्ल सार्वधातुकम नुदात्तमह्न्विङोः 6.1.186.
7. ibid.
8. Cf. *vahuvacanasyavasnasau*—Pāṇ. 8.1.21.
9. Cf. Pāṇ. युस्मदस्मदोः षष्ठी चतुर्थी द्वितीया स्थयोर्वान्नावौ 8.1.20.

naḥ —us
Pitā[1]—father
iva[2]—particle of comparison
Sūnave[3]—for son.
Agne[4]—O Agni

---

1. पिता पाता वा पालयिता वा नि० 4.21. पिता-गोपिता नि० 6.15. पितरः-मनुष्या वै जागरितं पितरः सुप्तम् श० 12.9.2.1. रात्रिः पितरः श० 2.1.3.1. तिर इव वै पितरो मनुष्येभ्यः श० 2. 4.22.1. पितरा नमस्याः श० 1.5.2.3. यानग्निरेव दहन्त्स्वदयति ते पितरो ऽग्निष्वात्ताः श० 2. 6.1.7. ये वा यज्वानो गृहमेधिनः। ते पितरोऽग्नष्वात्ताः तै० 1.6.9.6. अर्धमासा वै पितरोऽग्निष्वात्ताः तै० 1.6.8.3. अथ ये दत्तेन पक्वेन लोकं जयन्ति ते पितरो बर्हिषदः श० 2.6.1.7. ये वै यज्वानः, ते पितरो बर्हिषदः तै० 1.6.9.6. मासा वै पितरो बर्हिषदः तै० 1.6.8. 3. तद् ये सोमेनेजानाः। ते पितरः सोमवन्त श० 2.6.1.7. सोमप्रयाजा हि पितरः तै० 1.6.9.5. इन्दव इव हि पितरः। मन व तां० 6.9. पितृदेवत्यो वै सोमः श० 2.4.2.12. औषधिलोको वै पितरः श० 13.8.1.20. यः (अर्धमासः) अपक्षीयते स पितरः श० 2.1.3.1. अपक्षयभाजो वै पितरः कौ० 5.6. अपराह्णः पितरः श० 2.1.3.1. अन्तभाजो वै पितरः कौ० 16.8. मर्त्याः पितरः श० 2.1.3.4. अनपहतपाप्मानः पितरः श० 2.1.3.4. पितृलोकः पितरः कौ० 5.7. पितरः प्रजापतिः गो०उ०6.95. मनः पितरः श० 14.4.3.13. देवा वा एते पितरः गो० उ० 1.2 4. स्विष्टकृतो वै पितरः गो० उ० 1.25. स्वधा वै पितृणामन्नम् श० 13.8.1.4. पितरा युवाना (यजु० 15.53.) वाक् चवै मनश्च पितरो युवाना श० 8.6.3.22. प्राणो वै पिता ऐ० 2.38. एष वै पिता य एष (सूर्यः) तपति श० 14.1.4.15. असौ (द्यौः) पिता तै० 3.8.9.1. श० 13.1.6.1. एष वै पिता य एष (सूर्य) तपति श० 14.1.4.15. त्रयो वै पितरः (सोमवन्तः, बर्हिषदः, अग्निष्वात्ताः) श० 5.5.4.28. पितरा नाराशंसः काठ० 34.16. संवत्सरो वै पिता वैश्वा नरः प्रजापतिः श० 1.5.1.16.
2. इवेत्युपमार्थे नि० 1.4. इव इति पदपूरणः नि० 1.10. इवः परिभयार्थे वा नि० 9.28.
3. सूनु अपत्यनाम निघं० 2.2. सूनवः पुत्राः नि० 11.17. सूनु (यजु० 12.51.) प्रजा वै सूनुः श० 7.1.1.27.
4. अग्निः कस्मादग्रणीर्भवति। अक्नोपनो भवतीति स्थौलाष्ठीविर्न क्नोपयति न स्नेहयति। त्रिभ्य आख्यातेभ्यो जायत इति शाकपूणिः। इतादक्ताद्दग्धाद्वानीतात्। स खल्वेतेरकारमादत्ते गकारमनक्तेर्वा दहतेर्वा नीः परः नि० 7.14. विराडग्निः श० 6.2.2.34. यो वै रुद्रः सो ऽग्निः श० 5.2.4.13. अग्निरेष यत्पशवः श० 6.3.2.6. अग्निर्हि देवानां पशुः ऐ० 1.15. अग्निर्वै देवानां वसिष्ठः ऐ० 1.28. शिर एवाग्निः श० 10.1.2.4. अग्निः सर्वा देवताः ऐ० 2.3. अग्नि र्वैसर्वेषां देवानामात्मा श० 14.3.2.5. आत्मैवाग्निः श० .7.1.20. अग्निर्वै देवतानां मुखं प्रजनयि

Su—easily

Upāyanaḥ—accessible

Bhava—be

Sacasva—serve[1] to be together, to be present, bless.

naḥ—us

Svastaye [2]—for good, listed among technical terms in Ngh. (5.5).

Anvaya (Sequencial placement of words)

sa agne naḥ sūpāyano bhava piteva sūnave sūpāyano bhava. sacasvā naḥ svastaye.

Meaning of Mantra in different contexts :

Spiritual: (इव) As (पिता) father (सूपायनः भव) makes the knowledge of all good things easily accessible (सूनवे) to his son; (अग्ने!) let O Brahman! (सः नः) be to us revealer of all knowledge and (सचस्व) bless (नः) us (स्वस्तये) for our good.

Scientific 1: (इव) As (पिता) father (सूपायनः भव) is easily accessible (सूनवे) to his son; (अग्ने!) let O energy! (सः) be you (नः) to us easily accessible and (सचस्व) be present (नः) for our (स्वस्तये)

तास प्रजापतिः श० 3.9.1.6. अन्नादोऽग्निः श० 2.1.4.28. अग्निर्देवानां जठरम् तै० 2.7.12.3. अयं वै लोकोऽग्निः श० 14.9.1.14. संवत्सर एषोऽग्निः श० 3.7.1.18. वागेवाग्निः श० 3.2.2.13. तेजो वाऽअग्निः श० 2.5.4.8. अग्निर्वै रक्षसामपहन्ता कौ० 8.4.10.3. तपो वाऽअग्निः श०3.4.3.2. अग्निर्वै देवानां व्रतपतिः श० 1.1.1.2. अग्निर्वै मृत्युः श० 14.6.2.10.

पुरुषोऽग्निः श० 10.4.1.6. मन एवाग्निः श० 10.1.2.3. प्राणो वा अग्निः श० 9.5.1.68. वीर्य वा अग्निः तै० 1.7.2.2. गायत्री अग्निः श० 3.4.1.9. अग्निरेव ब्रह्म अग्निर्वै श०10.4.1.5. पर्जन्यो वा अग्निः श० 14.9.1.13. आयुर्वाऽग्निः श० 6.7.3.7. अग्निमतिथिं जनानाम् तै०2.4.3.6. अमृतोह्यग्निः श० 1.9.2.20. असौ वा आदित्य एषोऽग्निः श० 3.4.1.1. अग्निर्वैश्वानरः ता० 13.11.23. अनूचानमाहुरग्निकल्प इति मुखं ह्येतदग्नेर्यद् ब्रह्म श० 6.1.1.10. अग्निर्वै धर्मः श० 11.6.2.2. अग्निर्वैद्रष्टा गो० उ० 2.19. प्रजापतिरग्निः श० 6.2.1.23. अग्निर्वै यमः श० 7.2.1.10. अग्निर्वाव पुरोहितः ऐ० 8.27. प्राणा अग्निः श० 6.3.1.21. अग्निर् ऋषिः मै० 1.6.1. अग्निः पशुरासीत् तमालभन्त तेनायजन्त इति च ब्राह्मणम् नि० 12.41.

1. *sacasvā sevasva*—Nir. 3.21; *sacante sevante*—Nir. 7.23
2. स्वस्तीत्यविनाशिनाम। अस्तिरभिपूजितः सुअस्तीति नि० 3.22. स्वस्तये-स्वस्त्ययनाय नि० 5.27.

wellbeing.

Scientific 2: (इव) As (पिता) father (सूपायनः भव) is easily accessible (सूनवे) to his son; (अग्ने!) let O sun! (सः) be you (नः) to us easily accessible and (सचस्व) serve us (नः) for the sake of our (स्वस्तये) good.

Socio-political 1: (इव) As (पिता) father (सूपायनः भव) makes the knowledge of all good things easily accessible (सूनवे) to his son; (अग्ने!) let O teacher! (सः) be you (नः) to us revealer of all knowledge and (सचस्व) show (नः) us (स्वस्तये) right path.

Socio-political 2: (इव) As (पिता) father (सूपायनः भव) is easily accessible (सूनवे) to his son; (अग्ने!) let O ruler! (सः) be you (नः) to us easily accessible and (सचस्व) put (नः) us (स्वस्तये) on the path of wellbeing.

Note : There is an advice for kings and teachers to be easily accessible respectively to people and students to solve their problems.

After giving a small description of Agni (the energy of observer space, or geothermal energy), here VÈyu (the field energy or energy in intermediate space) is described in the following sÊkta

सूक्त - 2

ऋषि– मधुच्छन्दा वैश्वामित्र। **देवता–** १-३ वायु, ४-६ इन्द्र-वायु;

७-९ मित्रावरुण। **छन्द–** गायत्री।

Seer : Madhucchandā of Viśvāmitra

Devatā : Vāyu 1—3; Indravāyu 4—6; Mitrāvaruṇā 7—9

Chanda: Gāyatrī

The Devatā (subject matter) of below given three mantras is *Vāyu* which denotes All powerful and All pervading Brahman and *Prāṇavāyu* life energy in spiritual context; field energy in the context of cosmos and magnetosphere in context of our solar system. In Socio-political context, vāyu is represented by a ruler who reaches out to all his subjects and a teacher/scholar who reaches out to all students who wants to gain knowledge and value education. In scientific context, Vāyu is located in the *Antarikṣa loka* (intermediate space). Origin of the *Yajurveda* is assigned to 'Vāyu'.

After describing Agni (energy in observer space, i.e. our universe and geothermal energy of earth), the second form of energy is described as 'Vāyu', a field energy located in the intermediate space (between light and observer space) and between sun and earth as the magnetosphere. The *Taittiriya Upaniṣad* describes constitution of *adhiloka* as follows: *adhiloka* is constituted of earth/observer space as the first constituent, sun/light space as the second constituent, *antrikṣa* (intermediate space/magnetic sphere) as link between the two (earth and sun in context of our solar system or observer space and and light space in context of cosmos) and '*Vāyu*' (field lines) as the link maker between the two i.e. earth and sun or observer space and light space. Thus *Vāyu* here is not the 'air' but field lines or magnetic field that links the Earth and Sun in our solar system and observer space and light space at cosmic level.

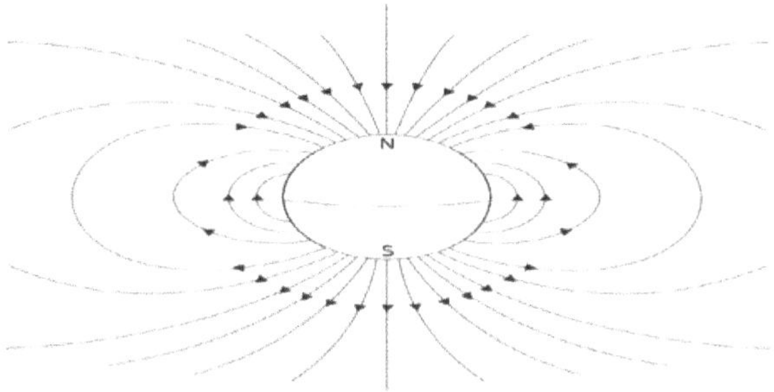

Magnetic field of earth

The magnetic field of the earth forms the magnetosphere, which deflects particles from the Solar wind. The magnetosphere shields the surface of the Earth from the charged particles of the solar wind. Magnetosphere of each and every heavenly body is generated by the plasma located as the nuclear reactor in their centre (wombs). Similarly magnetosphere of earth is generated by the plasma located as the nuclear reactor in the centre of the earth. It is compressed on the day (Sun) side due to the force of the arriving particles, and extended on the night side.

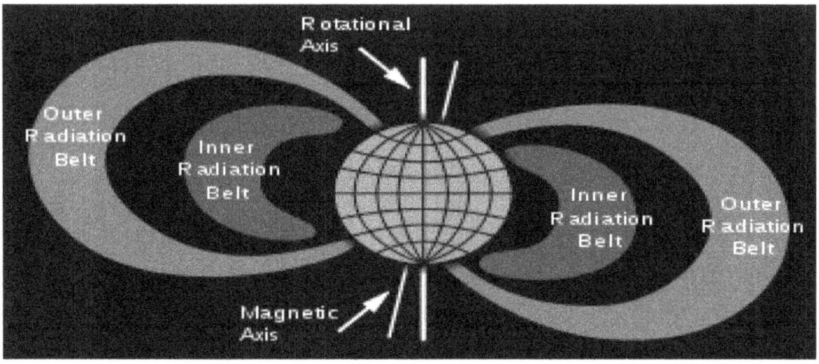

Radiation belts

The collision between the magnetic field and the solar wind forms the Radiation belt, a pair of concentric, torus[3] shaped regions of energetic charged particles. Similar radiation belts are also formed around other planets. They protect us from solar winds. It has been discovered that the Earth's atmosphere limits the belts' particles to regions above 200[3] 1,000 Kilometer. The below given *Mantras* talks about the natural phenomena discussed above in scientific context.

१०. वायवा याहि दर्शतेमे सोमा अरंकृताः।
तेषां पाहि श्रुधी हवम्।।१ ।।

वायो इति। आ। याहि। दर्शत। इमे। सोमाः। अरंऽकृताः। तेषाम्। पाहि। श्रुधि। हवम्।।

Saṁhitāpāṭha

vā´yavá yāhí dárśáteme sómā áraṅkṛ´tāḥ´. téṣāṁ pāhi śrudhī havam.

Padapāṭha

vāyo iti. ā. yāhi. darśata. ime. somāḥ. araṅkṛtāḥ. teṣām. pāhi. śrudhi. havam.

Grammatical Notes:

वायो (vāyo)—Voc. sing. of vāyu. Adādigaṇa root √vā meaning 'to move', to smell' +uṇ (Uṇādi suffix)[1]. Since this voc. is in the beginning of the hemistich, it is accented on the first syllable.[2]

आ (ā)—A prefix meaning proximity, conjunction and simli. Being a prefix, it is accented on the first syllable [3].

याहि (yāhi)—Adādigaṇa root √yā 'to make reach' +loṭ lakāra second person sing. It, being a verbal form

1. Cf. *Uṇādi sūtra* (1.1)-*kṛ-vā-pā-ji-mi-svadi-sādhi-aśūbhya.*
2. Cf. Pāṇini (6.1.192)—*āmantritasya ca.*
3. Cf. *Phiṭ sūtra*—उपसर्गाश्चाभिवर्जम् -81.

preceded by a non—verbal form, goes without accent. [1]

दृर्श॒त (darśat)—Bhvādigaṇa root √ dṛś 'to see'+atac (Uṇādi suffix)[2]. Although as per cit (having indicatory 'c') suffix 'darśata' would have been accented on the final sylable, but due to its vocative nature it has lost its accent being in the middle of the hemistich.

इ॒मे (ime)—Nom. pl. of demonstrative pronoun 'Idam'. Being a pronominal form, it bears an acute accent.

सोमा॑: (somaḥ)—Nom. pl. of soma. Bhvādigaṇa root √ṣu 'to deliver', 'to glorify' or Svādigaṇa root √ṣuñ 'to squeez' or √ṣu 'to inspire'+man (Uṇādi suffix)[3]. Due to 'nit' (having indicatory 'n') suffix, the word soma gets the accent on the first syllable[4].

अरं॑कृताः (araṅkṛtā)—Araṁ+Tanādigaṇa root √kṛ 'to do'+kta suffix. Here alaṁ has been replaced by araṁ[5] which shows that during Vedic time araṁ as well as alaṁ, both the words were in vogue in the same meaning. Attributive of soma.

तेषा॑म् (teṣām)—Gen. pl. of demonstrative pronoun 'Tad'. Being a pronominal form, it bears an acute accent.

पा॒हि (pāhi)—Adādigaṇa root √pā 'to protect'+loṭ lakāra

---

1. Cf. Pāṇ. तिङ्ङतिङः 8.1.28.
2. *bhṛ-mṛ-dṛśi-yaji-parvi-paci-ami-tami-nami-haryi-bhyo'tac—Uṇādi sutra,* 3.110.
3. *artti-stu-su-hu-sṛ-dhṛ-kṣi-kṣu-bhā-yā-vā-padi-uakṣi-nī-bhyo man-Uṇādi sutra,* 1.140.
4. Cf. Paṇini (6.1.197)—*ñnityādinityam.*
5. Note : Paṇini and his Vārtikakāras could not notice this peculiar feature and so did not formulate any rule to govern it. As such *kapilakādi gaṇa* (kapila group of words) under Pāṇini's sūtra '*kṛpo ro la*' may be supplimented with a new word 'alam', so as to regularise this Vedic vocable. Although *Niruktakāras* have identified broadly this replacement of 'l' sound by 'r' as '*ralayorabhedaḥ*'.

(imperative) second Pers. sing.

श्रुधि (śrudhi)—Bhvādigaṇa root √śru 'to hear'+loṭ lakāra (imperative) second pers. sing. Most current form is śruhi, but here in Veda śrudhi is formed with the substitution of 'hi' by 'dhi'.[1] In this hemistich one subject is followed by two roots, as such 'śrudhi' being the second one is accented even if it is not located in the beginning of the hemistich.[2]

हवंम् (havam)—Juhotyādigaṇa root √hu 'to give', 'to receive'+ap suffix [3] or Bhvādigaṇa root √hveñ 'to compete', 'to make a sound'+ap siffix in intransitive sense by vocalisation.[4] Being formed of 'pit' suffix, it is accented on the root.[5]

Word meanings:

vāyo [6] —Address to Vāyu. Vayu is located in the

---

1. Cf. Paṇini (6.4.102)—*śru—śṛṇu—pṛ—kṛ—vṛbhyaś—chandasi.*
2. Cf. Paṇ. तिङ्ङतिङः 8.1.28.
3. Cf. Pāṇini (3.3.57)—*ṛdor—ap.*
4. Cf. Pāṇini (3.3.75)—*bhāve'nupasargasya.*
5. Cf. Pāṇini (3.1.4)—*anudāttau sup—pitau.*
6. वायुः पदनाम निघं० 5.4. वायुर्वातिर्वेतेर्वास्यात् गतिकर्मणः, एतेरिति स्थौलाष्ठीविः अनर्थको
वकारः नि० 10.1. वायुः सोमस्य रक्षिता, वायुमस्य रक्षितारमाह साहचर्याद् रसहरणाद्वा नि० 11.
5. अयं वै वायुर्योऽयं पवते श० 2.6.3.7. अयं वै वायुर्योऽयं पवत ऽएष वा इदं सर्वं विविनक्ति
तयदिदं किञ्च विविच्यते श० 1.1.4.22. वातो हि वायुः श० 8.7.3.12. वायुर्वातहोमाः श० 9
.4.2.1. वायुर्वा उशन् तां० 7.5.19. वयुरनुवत्सरः तां० 17.13.17. तै० 1.4.10.1. वायुर्वै देवः
जै०उ० 3.4.8. अयं वै ब्रह्म योऽयं (वायुः) पवते श० 14.2.2.10. अयं वै पवित्र (यजु० 1.1
2.) योऽयं (वायुः) पवते श० 1.1.3.2. पवित्रं वै वायुः तै० 3.2.5.11 एतद्वै प्रजापतेः प्रत्यक्षं
रूपं यद् वायुः कौ० 19.2 यो वै वायु स इन्द्रो य इन्द्रः स वायुः श० 4.1.3.19. अयं वै वायु
र्मित्रो (यजु० 11.64.) यो ऽयं पवते श० 6.5.4.14. अयं वै यमो (यजुः० 38.9. यो ऽयं
(वायुः) पवते श० 14.2.2.11. वायुर्वै यन्ता (ऋ० 3.13.3.) वायुना हीदं यदन्तरिक्षं न समृच्
छति ऐ० 2.41 वायुर्वै प्राणाः कौ० 8.4. जै० उ० 4.22.11. वायुर्हि प्राणाः ऐ० 2.26. प्राणो
हि वायुः तां० 4.6.8. प्राणो वै वायुः कौ० 5.8 वायुर्मे प्राणे श्रितः तै० 3.10.8.4. स (वायुः)
यत्पुरस्ताद् वाति।प्राण एव भूत्वा पुरस्ताद् वाति। तस्मात् पुरस्ताद् वान्तं सर्वाः प्रजाः प्रतिनन्दन्ति

intermediate space[1], vāyu is that which moves[8], vāyu is called as the protector of soma[2], field energy[3], purifier[4]

ā[5] —near[6], and'[7], particle of simili[8] and under[9]

yāhi[1] —to make us reach,

तै० 2.3.9.4. वायुर्वै प्रणीर्यज्ञानां यदा हि प्राणित्यथ यज्ञोऽ ऽथाग्निहोत्रम् ऐ० 2.34 यत्पशुपतिर्वायुस्तेन कौ० 6.4 वायुर्वाऽउग्रः श० 6.1.3.13. वायुर्वाव पुरोहितः ऐ० 8.27. वायुर्वा उपश्रोता गो० उ० 2.19. तै० 3.7.5.4. वायुरेव महः गो० पू० 5.15. वायुर्महः श० 12.3.4.8. मनो ह वायुर्भूत्वा दक्षिणातस्तस्थौ श० 8.1.1.7. इमे वै (त्रयो) लोका पूरयमेव पुरुषो योऽयं (वायुः) पवते सोऽस्यां पुरि शेते तस्मात् पुरुषः श० 13.6.2.1. अयं वै यज्ञो योऽयं (वायुः) पवते जै० उ० 3.16.1.अयमु वै यः (वायुः) पवते स यज्ञः गो० पू० 3.2. वाग्वै वायुः तै०1.8.8.1. तां० 18.8.7. वायुरस्यतरिक्षे श्रितः। दिवः प्रतिष्ठा तै० 3.11.1.9. वायुर्वै नभसस्पतिः गो० उ० 4.9. वायुर्वा अन्तरिक्षस्याध्यक्षः तै० 3.2.1.3 वायुरेव यजुः श० 10.3.5.2. वायुर्यजुर्वेदः (अजायत) श० 11.5.8.3. यजुषां वायुदैवतं तदेव ज्योतिस्त्रैष्टुभं छन्दोऽन्तरिक्षं स्थानम् गो० पू० 1.29. त्रैष्टुभो हि वायुः श० 8.7.3.12. वायुरध्वर्युः गो० पू० 1.13. वायुर्वा अध्वर्य्युः गो० पू० 2.24 एष वाऽपां रसो योऽयं पवते स एष (वायुः) सूये समाहितः सूर्यात् पवते श० 5.1.2.7 शुक्लो हि वायुः श० 6.2.2.7. तथेति वायुः पवते जै० उ० 3.6.2. अनिरुक्तो हि वायुः श० 8.7.3.12. शान्तिर्हिवायुः तां० 4.6.9. (वायोः) मेनका च सहजन्या (यजु० 15.16.)। तं (वायुं) एताः पञ्च देवता परिभ्रियन्ते विद्युद् वृष्टिश्चन्द्रमा आदित्योऽग्निः ऐ० 8.28 सोऽयं (वायुः) पुरुषेप्रविष्टस्त्रेधा विहितः प्राण उदानो व्यान इति श० 3.1.2.20.

1. *athāto madyasthānā devatāstāsāṁ vāyu prathamagāmī bhavati, vāyor vāter—vetter—vā syād—gati karmanaḥ* (vāyu is the first among the elements located in the intermediate space. The term vāyu is formed of roots 'vā' or 'vid' meaning 'to go'—*Nir.* 10.1
2. *vāyuḥ somasya rakṣitā*—Nir. 11.5
3. vāyur vā agniḥ—Ait. Br. 2.34
4. *ayaṁ vai vāyur yo ayaṁ pavate* (Vāyu is that which purifies)—Ś.Br. 2.6.3.7; pavitraṁ vai vāyu (Vāyu is purifier)—TS. 3.2.5.11
5. अर्वागर्थे नि० 1.3. एतस्मिन्नेवार्थे (समुच्चयार्थे) देवेभ्यश्च पितृभ्य एत्याकारः नि० 1.4. उपमार्थे दृश्यते नि० 3.16. अध्यर्थे दृश्यते नि० 5.5.
6. *arvāgarthe*—Nir. 1.3
7. ibid. 1.4
8. *upamārthe dṛśyate*—Nir. 3.16
9. *adhyarthe dṛśyate*—Nir. 5.5

darśat—the means of seeing, pleasant to behold, handsome. Attributive of Vāyu.

ime—These

soma [2] —Material world, spiritual knowledge, +electric charge, that which is squeezed or inspired, herbs [3], moon[4], meals for Devas [5], paśu (particle)[6], coagulated butter (curd) [7], ruler [1], prāṇa [2], defending power [3],

---

1. याति गतिकर्मा निघं० 2.14.
2. सोम-ओषधिः सोमः सुनोतेर्यदेनमभिषुण्वन्ति नि० 11.2. सोमः-स्वा वै मऽएषेति तस्मात्सोमो नाम श० 3.9.4.22. सत्यं (वै) श्रीर्ज्योतिः सोमः श० 5.1.2.10. श्रीर्वै सोमः श० 4.1.3.9. सोमो राजा राजपतिः तै० 2.5.7.3. असौ वै सोमो राजा विचक्षणश्चन्द्रमाः कौ० 4.4. सोमो राजाचन्द्रमाः श० 10.4.2.1. चन्द्रमा वै सोमः कौ० 16.5. वृत्रो वै सोम आसीत् श०3.4.3.13.। संवत्सरो वै सोमो राजा कौ० 7.10. सोमो हि प्रजापतिः श० 5.1.5.26. सोमो वैष्णवो राजेत्याह तस्याप्सरसो विशः श० 13.4.3.8. जुष्टा विष्णव इति। जुष्टा सोमायेत्येवैतदाह (विष्णुः-सोमः) श० 3.2.4.12. तद् यदेवेदं क्रीतो विशतीव तदु हास्य (सोमस्य) वैष्णवं रूपम् कौ० 8.2. सोमोवै पवमानः श० 2.2.3.22. एष (वायुः) वै सोमस्योद्गीथो यत्पवते तां० .6.18. तस्मात् सोमं सर्वेभ्यो देवेभ्यो जुह्वति तस्मादाहुः सोमः सर्वा देवता इति श० 1.6.3.21. सोमो वाऽइन्द्रः श० 2.2.3.23. सोमो रात्रिः श० 3.4.4.15. सोम एव सवृत इति गो० उ० 2.24. सोमो वै चतुर्होता तै० 2.3.1.1. सोमो वै पर्णः श० 6.5.1.1. सोमो वै पलाशः कौ० 2.2. पशुर्वै प्रत्यक्षं सोमः श०5.1.3.7. सोम एवैव प्रत्यक्षं यत्पशुः कौ० 12.6. पशवः सोमोः राजा तै० 1.4.7.6. सोमो वै दधि तै० 1.4.7.6. एष वै यजमानो यत्सोमः तै० 1.3.3.5. द्यावापृथिव्योर्वा एष गर्भो यत्सोमो राजा ऐ० 2.26. क्षत्रं सोमः ऐ० 2.38. यशो वै सोमः श० 4.2.4.9. यशो (ऋ० 10.72.10.) वै सोमो राजा ऐ० 1.13.। प्राणः सोमः श० 7.3.1.2.। रसः सोमः श० 7.3.1.3.। तस्मात् सोमोराजा सर्वाणि नक्षत्राण्युपैति प० 3.12.। तै० 1.1.3.10. अन्तरिक्षदेवत्यो हि सोमः गो० उ० 2.4. गिरिषु हि सोमः श० 3.3.4.7. घ्नन्ति खलु वाऽएतत्सोमं यदभिषुण्वन्ति तै०2.2.8.1. सोमो राजा मृगशीर्षेण आगन् श० 3.1.2.2. सोमवीरुधां पते तै० 3.11.4.1.। आपः सोमः सुतः श०7.1.1.22. आपो ह्येतस्य (सोमस्य) लोकः श० 4.4.5.21.। पुमान् वै सोमः स्त्री सुरा तै० 1.3.3.4.।
3. Oṣadhi somaḥ sunoter yad enam abhiṣuṇvanti. Nir. 11.2
4. *somo rājā chandramāḥ*—Ś.Br. 10.4.2.1; *chandramā vai somaḥ*—Kau. Br. 16.5
5. *etad vai devānāṁ paramam annam yat somaḥ*—TS. 1.3.3.2
6. *paśrvai pratyakṣaṁ somaḥ*—Ś.Br. 5.1.3.7
7. *somo vai dadhi (electrically charged particles are*—TS. 1.4.7.6

intellectual[4], essence[5], located in intermediate space[6], soma was brought from light space by gāyatri[7]

araṅkṛtāḥ—glorious, decorated, beautifully placed

teṣām—these or from them

pāhi—protect

śrudhi—hear[8]

havam—sound of invocation, request, prayer

Anvaya (Sequencial placement of words)

darśata vā´yo ā´ yāhi imé sómāḥ áraṅkṛ´tā´ḥ téṣām pāhi śrudhí hávam.

Meaning of Mantra in different contexts :

Spiritual: (वायो) All pervading and All powerful God, (दर्शत) pleasant to behold, (आ याहि) reveal your self. (इमे) These (सोमाः) material worlds (अरंकृताः) have been beautifully placed by you. (पाहि) Protect (तेषाम्) them. (श्रुधि) Hear (हवम्) our invocations.

Scientific 1: (वायो) Field energy! (दर्शत) pleasant to behold, (आ याहि) come to the observer space. (इमे) These (सोमाः) matter particles in observer space (अरंकृताः) are electrically charged. (पाहि) Protect (तेषाम्) them, as they are very significant for the sustenance of our universe. (श्रुधि) Hear (हवम्) our invocations.

Note : The above mantra talks about the energy transferring from light space via intermediate space to the observer space in the form of matter particles. In fact, every where in universe, the process of creation and annihilation of particles is going on all the times. New particles keep on taking place old particles, creating an illusion of permanency. Process of creation starts in light space

---

1. *somo vai rājā*—A.Br. 1.13
2. *prāṇaḥ somaḥ*—Ś. Br. 7.3.1.2
3. *kṣatraṁ somaḥ*—A.Br. 2.38
4. *somo vai brāhmaṇaḥ*—Tāṇḍ. Br. 23.16.5
5. *rasaḥ somaḥ*—Ś.Br. 7.3.1.3
6. *antarikṣa devatyo hi somaḥ—Go. Br.* Second part, 2.4
7. *divi soma āsīt. taṁ gāyatrī āharat—TS.* 1.1.3.10
8. *śrudhi śṛṇu*—Nir. 10.2

(*Dyau loka*). There is a continuous interaction between light space and observer space (*bhūmi loka*) with energy changing into particles and particles changing into energy. Energy change into a pair of matter and anti matter, and when a particle and anti particle collide, they change into energy. For the maintenace of universe, the excess of matter over anti matter is essential. That is why, the seer prays for the protection of soma (electrically charged matter particles).

Scientific 2: (वायो) Magnetosphere of the earth! (दर्शत) pleasant to behold, (आ याहि) bring on the earth solar radiation useful for our sustenance. (इमे) These (सोमाः) matter particles on the earth (अरंकृताः) are electrically charged. (पाहि) Protect (तेषाम्) them, as they are very significant for our sustenance on earth. (श्रुधि) Hear (हवम्) our invocations.

Socio-political 1: (दर्शत वायो) O Handsome ruler capable of reaching out to his masses! (आ याहि) procures us the best infrastructure and facilities. Let (इमे) these (सोमाः) material facilities (अरंकृताः) be orderly placed. (पाहि) Maintain and protect (तेषाम्) them, as they are very significant for our progress. (श्रुधि) Listen to (हवम्) our prayers.

Socio-political 2: (दर्शत वायो) O glorious teacher! capable of reaching out to his students! (आ याहि) procures the best spiritual and scientific knowledge. So that (इमे) these (सोमाः) students (अरंकृताः) are adorned with knwledge. (पाहि) Protect (तेषाम्) them, as they are going to be as asset for the nation. (श्रुधि) Do, listen to (हवम्) our requests.

११. वायं उक्थेभिर्जरन्ते त्वामच्छा जरितारः। सुतसोमा अहर्विदः।।२।।

वायो इति। उक्थेभिः। जरन्ते। त्वाम्। अच्छ। जरितारः। सुतऽसोमाः।
अहऽर्विदः।।

Saṁhitāpāṭha

vāya ukthebhir jaratante tvām acchā jaritāraḥ suta-somā ahar vidaḥ.

Padapāṭha

vāyo iti . ukthebhiḥ. jaratante. tvām. acchā. jaritāraḥ. suta-somāḥ. ahar-vidaḥ.

Grammatical Notes:

वायो (vāyo)—Loc. sing. of vāyu. Adādigaṇa root √vā meaning 'to move', to smell' +uṇ (Uṇādi suffix)[1]. Since this voc. is in the beginning of the hemistich, it is accented on the first syllable.[2]

उक्थेभिः (ukthebhiḥ)—Inst. pl. of uktha. Adādigaṇa root √vac 'to speak'+thak (Uṇādi suffix)[3].

जरन्ते (jaratante)—Divāgaṇa root √jṛ 'deterioration of age', 'to worship'. Laṭ lakāra (present tense) first pers. pl. Being a verbal form, preceded by non—verbal form it loses its accent.

त्वाम् (tvām)—Acc. sing. of second person pronoun 'Yusmad'. Being a pronominal form it bears acute accent.

अच्छा (accha)—A particle (nipāt). Last syllable elongated.[4]

---

1. Cf. *Uṇādi sūtra* (1.1)-*kṛ-vā-pā-ji-mi-svadi-sādhi-aśūbhya.*
2. Cf. Pāṇini (6.1.192)—*āmantritasya ca.*
3. Cf. *Uṇādi sūtra* (2.7)—*pā-tṛ-tudi-vaci-rici-sici-bhyas thak.*
4. Cf. Pan. 6.1.136—निपातस्य च

Being a praticle, it is accented on the first syllable.[1]

जुरितार॑ः (jaritārah)—Divādigaṇa root √ jṛ 'deterioration of age, 'to worship' +tṛc suffix in nominative case.

सुतसो॑माः (suta—somāḥ)—Being a Bahuvrīhi compound of suta and soma, accent is on the first member[2]. Suta is formed of Svādigaṇa root √ṣuñ 'to squeez' +kta primary verbal derivative (past passive participle). It gets accent on suffix 3. Soma is formed ofBhvādigaṇa root √ṣu 'to deliver' +man (Uṇādi suffix)[4].

अ॒ह॒र्वि॑दः (ahar—vidaḥ)—Ahan+Tudādigaṇa root √vidlṛ 'to receive'+kvip suffix. First syllable of the second member is accented owing to the 'pit' suffix (suffix having indicatory 'p')[5].

Word meanings:

vāyo[6]—O Vāyu, vayu is located in the intermediate space[1],

---

1. See *Phiṭ sūtra* (80)— निपाता आद्युदात्ताः
2. Cf. Pāṇ. 6.2.1—बहुव्रीहौ प्रकृत्या पूर्वपदम्
3. Cf. Pāṇini, 3.1.3—आद्युदात्तश्च
4. Cf. *Unādisūtra* (1.140)
अर्त्ति-स्तु-सु-हु-सृ-धृ-क्षि-क्षु-भा-या-वा-पदि-यक्षि-नीभ्यो मन्।
5. Cf. Pāṇ. 3.1.4—अनुदात्तौ सुप्पितौ।
6. वायुः पदनाम निघं० 5.4. वायुर्वातेर्वेतेर्वास्यात् गतिकर्मणः, एतेरिति स्थौलाष्ठीविः अनर्थको वकारः नि० 10.1. वायुः सोमस्य रक्षिता, वायुमस्य रक्षितारमाह साहचर्याद् रसहरणाद्वा नि० 11. 5. अयं वै वायुर्योऽयं पवते श० 2.6.3.7. अयं वै वायुर्योऽयं पवत ऽएष वा इदं सर्वं विविनक्तियदिदं किञ्च विविच्यते श० 1.1.4.22. वातो हि वायुः श० 8.7.3.12. वायुर्वातहोमा : श० 9.4.2.1. वायुर्वा उशन् तां० 7.5.19. वयुरनुवत्सरः तां० 17.13.17. तै० 1.4.10.1. वायुर्वै देवः जै०उ० 3.4.8. अयं वै ब्रह्म योऽयं (वायुः) पवते श० 14.2.2.10. अयं वै पवित्र (यजु०1.12.) योऽयं (वायुः) पवते श० 1.1.3.2. पवित्रं वै वायुः तै० 3.2.5.11 एतद्वै प्रजापतेः प्रत्यक्षं रूपं यद् वायुः कौ० 19.2 यो वै वायु स इन्द्रो य इन्द्रः स वायुः श० 4.1.3. 19. अयं वै वायुर्मित्रो (यजु० 11.64.) यो ऽयं पवते श० 6.5.4.14. अयं वै यमो (यजुः० 38.9. यो ऽयं (वायुः) पवते श० 14.2.2.11. वायुर्वै यन्ता (ऋ० 3.13.3.) वायुना हीदं यदन्तरिक्षं न समृच्छति ऐ० 2.41 वायुर्वै प्राणाः कौ० 8.4. जै० उ० 4.22.11. वायुर्हि प्राणाः

space[1], vāyu is that which moves[8], vāyu is called as the protector of soma[2], field energy[3], purifier[4]

ukthebhiḥ[5]—stotras, prayers

ऐ० 2.26. प्राणो हि वायुः तां० 4.6.8. प्राणो वै वायुः कौ० 5.8 वायुर्मे प्राणे श्रितः तै० 3.10. 8.4. स (वायुः)यत्पुरस्ताद् वाति।प्राण एव भूत्वा पुरस्ताद् वाति। तस्मात् पुरस्ताद् वान्तं सर्वाः प्रजाः प्रतिनन्दन्ति तै० 2.3.9.4. वायुर्वै प्रणीर्यज्ञानां यदा हि प्राणित्यथ यज्ञोऽ ऽथाग्निहोत्रम् ऐ० 2.34 यत्पशुपतिर्वायुस्तेन कौ० 6.4 वायुर्वाऽउग्रः श० 6.1.3.13. वायुर्वाव पुरोहितः ऐ० 8.27. वायुर्वा उपश्रोता गो० उ० 2.19. तै० 3.7.5.4. वायुरेव महः गो० पू० 5.15. वायुर्महः श० 12.3.4.8. मनो ह वायुर्भूत्वा दक्षिणातस्तस्थौ श० 8.1.1.7. इमे वै (त्रयो) लोका पूरयमेव पुरुषो योऽयं (वायुः) पवते सोऽस्यां पुरि शेते तस्मात् पुरुषः श० 13.6.2.1. अयं वै यज्ञो योऽयं (वायुः) पवते जै० उ० 3.16.1. अयमु वै यः (वायुः) पवते स यज्ञः गो० पू० 3.2. वाग्वै वायुः तै० 1.8.8.1. तां० 18.8.7. वायुरस्यतरिक्षे श्रितः। दिवः प्रतिष्ठा तै० 3.11.1.9. वायुर्वै नभसस्पतिः गो० उ० 4.9. वायुर्वा अन्तरिक्षस्याध्यक्षः तै० 3.2.1.3 वायुरेव यजुः श० 10.3.5.2. वायुर्यजुर्वेदः (अजायत) श० 11.5.8.3. यजुषां वायुर्देवतं तदेव ज्योतिस्त्रैष्टुभं छन्दोऽन्तरिक्षं स्थानम् गो० पू० 1.29. त्रैष्टुभो हि वायुः श० 8.7.3.12. वायुरध्वर्युः गो० पू० 1.13. वायुर्वा अध्वर्य्युः गो० पू० 2.24 एष वाऽपां रसो योऽयं पवते स एष (वायुः) सूये समाहितः सूर्यात् पवते श० 5.1.2.7 शुक्लो हि वायुः श० 6.2.2.7. तथेति वायुः पवते जै० उ० 3.6.2. अनिरुक्तो हि वायुः श० 8.7.3.12. शान्तिर्हि वायुः तां० 4.6.9. (वायोः) मेनका च सहजन्या (यजु० 15.16.)। तं (वायुं) एताः पञ्च देवता परिभ्रियन्ते विद्युद् वृष्टिश्चन्द्रमा आदित्योऽग्निः ऐ० 8.28 सोऽयं (वायुः) पुरुषेऽन्त प्रविष्टस्त्रेधा विहितः प्राण उदानो व्यान इति श० 3.1.2.20.

1. *athāto madyasthānā devatāstāsāṁ vāyu prathamagāmī bhavati, vāyor vāter-vetter-vā syād-gati karmanaḥ* (*vāyu* is the first among the elements located in the intermediate space. The term vāyu is formed of roots '*vā*' or '*vid*' meaning 'to go'—*Nir.* 10.1
2. *vāyuḥ somasya rakṣitā*—Nir. 11.5
3. *vāyur vā agniḥ*—Ait. Br. 2.34
4. *ayaṁ vai vāyur yo ayaṁ pavate* (*Vāyu* is that which purifies)—Ś.Br. 2.6.3.7; *pavitraṁ vai vāyu* (Vāyu is purifier)—TS. 3.2.5.11
5. प्राण उ एवोक्तस्यान्नमेव थं तदुक्थम् श० 10.4.1.23; एष (अग्निः)उ एवोक्तस्यैतदन्नं तदुक्थम् श०10.4.1.4; आदित्यो वा उक्। तस्य चन्द्रमा एव थम् श०10.6.2.9; वागुक्थम् ष० 1.5; अन्नम् उक्थानि कौ०11.8 प्रजा वा उक्थानि तै० 1.8.7.2; पशव उक्थानि ऐ० 4.1;12; गो०उ० 6.7; अन्तरिक्षम् उक्थेन (अभ्यजयन्) ता० 9.2.9.

jaratante [1]—laud, praise

tvām—to you

accha—virtually

jaritāraḥ [2]—fans, scholars

suta-somāḥ—who have acquired knowledge

ahar-vidaḥ—cosmologists, scientists, or a person well versed with the knowledge of creation.

Anvaya (Sequencial placement of words)

vāyo aharvidaḥ sutasomā jaritāraḥ tvām ukthebhiḥ acchā jarante.

Meaning of Mantra in different contexts :

Spiritual: (वायो) O All powerful and All pervading Brahman! (जरितारः) the seers, (अहर्विदः) who have the knowledge of your creation, (जरन्ते) laud (त्वाम्) you (अच्छा) virtually (उक्थेभिः) with stotras (सुतसोमाः) seeking bliss of your realisation.

Scientific 1: (वायो) O field energy! (जरितारः) the learned astrophysicists, (अहर्विदः) who understand the secret of creation, (जरन्ते) laud (त्वाम्) you (अच्छा) virtually (उक्थेभिः) with stotras (सुतसोमाः) mindful of your filteration into the observer space.

Note: The energy particles abide in light space. From where they get filtered into the intermediate space converting into field particles and thence into the observer space converting into matter particles. On being filtered into the observer space as matter particles, they are called suta-soma or filtered matter particles.

Scientific 2: (वायो) O Magnetosphere of earth! (जरितारः) the learned astrophysicists, (अहर्विदः) who understand your secret, (जरन्ते) laud (त्वाम्) you (अच्छा) virtually (उक्थेभिः) with stotras (सुतसोमाः) mindful of your capability to filter down the useful solar radiation in the atmosphere of the earth.

Socio-political 1: (वायो) O ruler capable of reaching the

---

1. जरा स्तुतिर्जरते: स्तुतिकर्मण: नि० 10.8; जरते अर्चतिकर्मा निघं० 3.14

2. जरिता स्तोतृनाम् नि० 3.16; यजमानो जरिता ऐ० 3.38.

masses! (जरितारः) your fans, (अहर्विदः) who know your qualities, (जरन्ते) speakes highly (त्वाम्) of you (अच्छा) virtually (उक्थेभिः) showering praises (सुतसोमाः) since you have produced a good infrastructure in the nation.

Socio-political 2: (वायो) O teacher capable of reaching all students who need you! (जरितारः) your fans, (अहर्विदः) who know your qualities, (जरन्ते) speakes highly (त्वाम्) of you (अच्छा) virtually (उक्थेभिः) showering praises (सुतसोमाः) since you have produced high profile students.

१२. वायो॒ तव॑ प्रपृञ्च॒ती धेना॑ जिगाति दा॒शुषे॑। उ॒रू॒ची सोम॑पीतये॥३॥

वा॒यो॒ इति॑। तव॑। प्र॒ऽपृ॒ञ्च॒ती। धेना॑। जि॒गा॒ति॒। दा॒शुषे॑। उ॒रू॒ची। सोम॑ऽपीतये

Saṁhitāpāṭha

vāyo tava prapṛñcatī dhenā jigāti dāśuṣe. urūcī somapītaye.

Padapāṭha

vāyo iti. tava. pra-pṛñcatī. dhenā. jigāti. dāśuṣe. urūcī. somapītaye.

Grammatical Notes:

वा॒यो (vāyo)—Loc. sing. of vāyu. Adādigaṇa root √vā meaning 'to move', to smell'+uṇ (Uṇādi suffix)[1]. Since this voc. case is in the beginning of the hemistich, it is accented on the first syllable.[2]

तव॑ (tava)—Gen. sing. of second person pronoun 'Yusmad'. It is accented on the syllable preceeding 'ṅas' (gen. pl) suffix.[3]

प्र॒पृ॒ञ्च॒ती (pra—pṛñcatī)—Pra+pṛñcatī (Rudhādigaṇa root √pṛcī 'to contact'+present active participle śatṛ. It is accented on suffix.[4]

धेना॑ (dhenā)—Bhvādigaṇa root √dheṭ 'to drink'+naḥ (Uṇādi suffix).[5]

जि॒गा॒ति॒ (jigāti)—Juhotyādigaṇa root √gā 'to praise'+laṭ lakāra third person sing.

---

1. Cf. *Uṇādi sūtra* (1.1)-*kṛ-vā-pā-ji-mi-svadi-sādhi-aśūbhya.*
2. Cf. Pāṇini (6.1.192)—*āmantritasya ca.*
3. Cf. Pāṇ.—युस्मदस्मदो ङसि - 6.1.205.
4. Cf. Pāṇini, 3.1.3—आद्युदात्तश्च।
5. Cf. *Uṇādi Koṣa*, 3.11— धेट इच्च।

दा॒शुषे॑ (dāśuṣe)—Dative sing. of dāśvān. Bhvādigaṇa root √dāśṛ 'to donate'+kvasu suffix in subjunctive sense[1]. It gets the accent on suffix[2].

उ॒रू॒ची (urūcī)—Uru+Bhavādigaṇa root √añcu 'to move, to worship'+kvin suffix.[3] Here 'a' of 'ac' is elided and ṅip suffix is added to 'c', so that it becomes 'ci'. the last syllable of preceding 'uru' is prolonged.[4]

सोम॑पीतये (somapītaye)—Soma+Bhvadigaṇa root √pā 'to drink'+feminine suffix ktin. 'Ā' of 'pā' converts into 'i' under the force of Pāṇini (6.4.66).[5]

Word meanings:

vāyo [6] —Address to Vāyu. Vāyu is located in the

---

1. See Pāṇini, *kvasuśca*—3.2.106; *dāśvān-sāhvān-mīḍhvānśca* 6.1.12.
2. Cf. Pāṇini—आद्युदात्तश्च-3.1.3.
3. Cf. Pāṇini (3.2.59)— ऋत्विग्दधृक्स्रग्दिगुष्णिगञ्चुयुजिक्रुञ्चां च।
4. Cf. Pāṇini—6.1.106—वा छन्दसि।
5. घुमास्थागापाजहातिसां हलि -6.4.66.
6. वायुः पदनाम निघं० 5.4. वायुर्वातेर्वेतेर्वास्यात् गतिकर्मणः, एतेरिति स्थौलाष्ठीविः अनर्थको वकारः नि० 10.1. वायुः सोमस्य रक्षिता, वायुमस्य रक्षितारमाह साहचर्याद् रसहरणाद्वा नि० 11. 5. अयं वै वायुर्योऽयं पवते श० 2.6.3.7. अयं वै वायुर्योऽयं पवत ऽएष वा इदं सर्वं विविनक्ति तयदिदं किञ्च विविच्यते श० 1.1.4.22. वातो हि वायुः श० 8.7.3.12. वायुर्वातहोमाः श० 9 .4.2.1. वायुर्वा उशन् तां० 7.5.19. वयुरनुवत्सरः तां० 17.13.17. तै० 1.4.10.1. वायुर्वै देवः जै०उ० 3.4.8. अयं वै ब्रह्म योऽयं (वायुः) पवते श० 14.2.2.10. अयं वै पवित्र (यजु० 1.1 2.) योऽयं (वायुः) पवते श० 1.1.3.2. पवित्रं वै वायुः तै० 3.2.5.11 एतद्वै प्रजापतेः प्रत्यक्षं रूपं
   यद् वायुः कौ० 19.2 यो वै वायु स इन्द्रो य इन्द्रः स वायुः श० 4.1.3.19. अयं वै वायुर्मित्रो (यजु० 11.64.) यो ऽयं पवते श० 6.5.4.14. अयं वै यमो (यजुः० 38.9. यो ऽयं (वायुः) पवते श० 14.2.2.11. वायुर्वै यन्ता (ऋ० 3.13.3.) वायुना हीदं यदन्तरिक्षं न समृच्छति ऐ० 2.41 वायुर्वै प्राणाः कौ० 8.4. जै० उ० 4.22.11. वायुर्हि प्राणाः ऐ० 2.26. प्राणो हि वायुः तां० 4.6.8. प्राणो वै वायुः कौ० 5.8 वायुर्मे प्राणे श्रितः तै० 3.10.8.4. स (वायुः)यत्पुरस्ताद् वाति।प्राण एव भूत्वा पुरस्ताद् वाति। तस्मात् पुरस्ताद् वान्तं सर्वाः प्रजाः प्रतिनन्दन्ति तै० 2.3. 9.4. वायुर्वै प्रणीर्यज्ञानां यदा हि प्राणित्यथ यज्ञोऽ ऽथाग्निहोत्रम् ऐ० 2.34 यत्पशुपतिर्वायुस्तेन

intermediate space[1], vāyu is that which moves[8], vāyu is called as the protector of soma[2], field[3], purifier[4], All pervading God, king, teacher.

tava—your

pra-pṛñcatī—vigourusly expanding, vast encompassing, reflecting every thing

dhenā[5]—mass energy, speech, Vedic knowledge

jigāti[6]—reach, praise

dāśuṣe[1]—giver, one who gives effect to something, to

कौ० 6.4 वायुर्वाऽउग्रः श० 6.1.3.13. वायुर्वाव पुरोहितः ऐ० 8.27. वायुर्वा उपश्रोता गो० उ० 2.19. तै०3.7.5.4. वायुरेव महः गो० पू० 5.15. वायुर्महः श० 12.3.4.8. मनो ह वायुर्भूत्वा दक्षिणातस्तस्थौ श० 8.1.1.7. इमे वै (त्रयो) लोका पूरयमेव पुरुषो योऽयं (वायुः) पवते सोऽस्यां पुरि शेते तस्मात् पुरुषः श० 13.6.2.1. अयं वै यज्ञो योऽयं (वायुः) पवते जै० उ० 3.16.1. अयमु वै यः (वायुः) पवते स यज्ञः गो० पू० 3.2. वाग्वै वायुः तै० 1.8.8.1. तां० 18.8.7. वायुरस्यतरिक्षेश्रितः। दिवः प्रतिष्ठा तै० 3.11.1.9. वायुर्वै नभसस्पतिः गो० उ० 4.9. वायुर्वा अन्तरिक्षस्याध्यक्षःतै० 3.2.1.3 वायुरेव यजुः श० 10.3.5.2. वायुर्यजुर्वेदः (अजायत) श० 11.5.8.3. यजुषां वायुदैवतं तदेव ज्योतिस्त्रैष्टुभं छन्दोऽन्तरिक्षं स्थानम् गो० पू० 1.29. त्रैष्टुभो हि वायुः श० 8.7.3.12.वायुरध्वर्युः गो० पू० 1.13. वायुर्वा अध्वर्य्युः गो० पू० 2.24 एष वाऽपां रसो योऽयं पवते स एष (वायुः) सूये समाहितः सूर्यात् पवते श० 5.1.2.7 शुक्ल हि वायुः श० 6.2.2.7. तथेति वायुः पवते जै० उ० 3.6.2. अनिरुक्तो हि वायुः श० 8.7.3.1 2. शान्तिर्हि वायुः तां० 4.6.9. (वायोः) मेनका च सहजन्या (यजु० 15.16.)। तं (वायुं) एताः पञ्च देवता परिभ्रियन्ते विद्युद् वृष्टिश्चन्द्रमा आदित्योऽग्निः ऐ० 8.28 सोऽयं (वायुः) पुरुषेऽन्त प्रविष्टस्त्रेधा विहितः प्राण उदानो व्यान इति श० 3.1.2.20.

1. *athāto madyasthānā devatāstāsāṁ vāyu prathamagāmī bhavati, vāyor vāter-vetter-vā syād-gati karmanaḥ* (vāyu is the first among the elements located in the intermediate space. The term 'vāyu' is formed of roots '*vā*' or '*vid*' meaning 'to go'—*Nir.* 10.1
2. *vāyuḥ somasya rakṣitā*—Nir. 11.5
3. vāyur vā agniḥ—Ait. Br. 2.34
4. *ayaṁ vai vāyur yo ayaṁ pavate* (Vāyu is that which purifies)—Ś.Br. 2.6.3.7; *pavitraṁ vai vāyu* (Vāyu is purifier)—TS. 3.2.5.11
5. धेना वाङ्नामसु पठितम् निघं० 1.11; धेना दधातेः नि० 6.17 अन्नं वै धेना श० 7.5.2.11
6. जिगाति गतिकर्मा निघं० 2.14.

impart

urūcī—many, vast, large scale

somapītaye—to imbibe knowledge, to absorb charged particles from solar wind, to convert into charged matter particles सोमपीतये सोमपानाय नि० 9.37

Anvaya (Sequencial placement of words)

vāyo tava pṛpṛñcati urūci dhenā somapītaye dāśuṣe jigāti.

Meaning of Mantra in different contexts :

Spiritual: (वायो) All powerfull and All Pervading Brahman! (तव) your (धेना) Vedic speech, (प्रपृंचती) reflecting (उरूची) vast knowledge of all sciences and all objects (जिगाति) be revealed to the gaze of a person (सोमपीतये) who wants to imbibe the knowledge and (दाशुषे) impart it further to the deserving persons.

Scientific 1: (वायो) Intermediate space! (तव) your (प्रपृंचती) vigorously expanding (धेना) mass energy (जिगाति) enters (उरूची) the observer space (सोमपीतये) to get converted into positively charged matter particles (दाशुषे) to induce negatively charged particles.

Note: The mantra says that mass energy in intermediate space is known as *dhenā* and the mass energy in the observer space is known as *soma*. *Soma* is also the positively charged particles that exist with *agni* (negatively charged anti-particles) in observer space. That is why the Vedic seers call that the entire universe as outcome of the combination of *agni* and *soma*. Here one thing may also be known that light space, intermediate space (the interface between earth/observer space and sun/light space) and observer space are perforated one. Only all three together make space complete without holes. Particles in observer space can be thought of as condensation of energy. Particles in observer space were given the name *Paśu* because they could be seen.

Scientific 2: (वायो) Magnetosphere of Earth! (तव) your (प्रपृंचती) vast encompassing (धेना) field (जिगाति) goes to (उरूची)

---

1. दाशुषे दत्तवते नि० 11.11.

solar winds (सोमपीतये) to absorb soma (charged particles from solar wind) (दाशुषे) to give birth to radiation belt around the earth.

Socio-political 2: (वायो) Ruler, accessible by all! (तव) your (प्रपृंचती) all encompassing (धेना) orders (जिगाति) should reach (उरूची) the entire public (सोमपीतये) to enjoy prosperity and (दाशुषे) to contribute further for the progess or nation.

Socio-political 2: (वायो) Teacher, accessible by all! (तव) your (धेना) speech (प्रपृंचती) full of all types of knowledge (जिगाति) should reach (उरूची) to all students (सोमपीतये) who wants to seek knowledge and (दाशुषे) and pass it on further.

The Devata (subject matter) of below given three mantras is Indra-vāyu. This dual deity represents the dual characteristics of Brahman, i.e. All powerful and All pervading. It also represent prāṇavāyu (life energy) and mind in spiritual context. In scientific context, it represents electromagnetic force operating at the surface of the universe. It also represents collison taking place between the magnetosphere and the solar winds at the surface of the earth. In Socio-political context this dual deity represents king and commander, teacher and preacher. Astronomically, this dual deity is also located in the *Antarikṣa loka* (intermediate space).

After describing 'Vāyu' separately, Vāyu in the company of Indra is dealt with in the following three mantras. Both Vāyu (magnetic force) and Indra (electric force) are the forces of expansion of universe.

१३. इन्द्रवायू इमे सुता उप प्रयोभिरा गतम्।
इन्दवो वामुशन्ति हि।।४।।

इन्द्रवायू इति। इमे। सुताः। उप। प्रयःऽभिः। आ। गतम्। इन्दवः। वाम्। उशन्ति। हि।।

Saṁhitāpāṭha

indravāyū ime sutā upa prayobhiḥ āgatam. indavo vām uṣanti hi.

Padapāṭha

indravāyū iti. ime. sutāḥ. upa. prayḥ-abhiḥ. āḥ. gatam. indava. vām. uśanti. hi.

Grammatical Notes:

इन्द्रवायू (indravāyū)—Voc. du. Devatā dvandva compound.

{Bhavādigaṇa root √idi 'to prosper' + ran (Uṇādi

suffix)[1]}+{Divādigaṇa root vā 'to move', 'to smell'+U (Uṇādi suffix)[2]}. Being vocative form in the beginning of hemistich, it is accented on the first syllable.[3]

इमे (ime)—Nom. pl. masc. of demonstrative pronoun 'Idam'. Being a pronominal form, it bears an acute accent.

सुताः (sutāḥ)—Nom. pl. of suta. Svādigaṇa root √ṣuñ 'to press' or Bhvādigaṇa root √ṣu 'to squeez'+kta suffix.

उप (upa)—A prefix meaning closeness. Being a particle, accented on first syllable according to the rule of accentution.[4]

प्रयोभिः (prayobhiḥ)—Inst. pl. of prayan. Krayādigaṇa root √ prīñ 'to satisfy', 'to attract'+asun (Uṇādi suffix).[5] It gets 'nit' accent on the first syllable following Pāṇinian rule.[6]

आ (ā)—A prefix meaning proximity, conjunction and simli. Being a prefix, it is accented on the first syllable[7].

गतम् (gatam)—Bhvādigaṇa root √gamlṛ 'to go'+loṭ lakāra (imperative mood) second person dual number. Unaccented being preceded by non-verbal form.[8]

इन्दव (indava)—Rudhādigaṇa root √undi 'to drinch'+un

---

1. Cf. *Uṇādi* 'ऋज्रेन्द्राग्रवज्र०' 2.28.
2. Cf. *Uṇādi* 'कृवापाजि०' 1.1.
3. Cf. Pāṇini—आमन्त्रितस्य च - 61.198.
4. Cf. *Phiṭ* rule—उपसर्गश्चाभिवर्जम् - (81)
5. Cf. *Uṇādi* सर्वधातुभ्योऽसुन् -4.190.
6. ञ्नित्यादिर्नित्यम् - 6.1.197
7. Cf. *Phiṭ sūtra*—उपसर्गाश्चाभिवर्जम् -81.
8. Cf. Pāṇ.—तिङ्ङतिङः - 8.1.28

(Uṇādi suffix).[1] Being formed of 'nit' suffix, it gets an accent on the first syllable as as per rule of accentution.[2]

वा॒म् (vām)—Acc./dat./gen. pl. enclitic form of second person pronoun 'Yusmad'. Being enclitic form it loses its accent.[3]

उ॒शन्ति॑ (uśanti)— Adādigaṇa root √ vaśa 'to interest'+laṭ lakāra third person plural. Although it is destined to have lost its accent, but since it is followed by 'hi', it retains its accent.[4]

हि (hi)—'Hi' is a particle. Being a particle it carries accent.[5]

Word meanings:

इन्द्र॑वायू[6] (indravāyū)—Address to Indra—vāyu. God endowed endowed with the qualities of Indra (All powerfulness) and Vāyu (All pervasiveness), mind and life energy, electromagnetic force of the universe (according to Yāska, Indra and Vāyu both are located in the intermediate field), magnetosphere of earth and solar winds, king and commander, teacher and preacher.

इ॒मे (ime)—these

सु॒ताः (sutāḥ)—produced, pressed, squeezed

---

1. 'उन्देरिच्चादेः' उ० 1.12.
2. Cf. Pāṇ. ञ्नित्यादिर्नित्यम् - 6.1.197.
3. Cf. Pāṇ. युस्मदस्मदोः षष्ठी-चतुर्थी-द्वितीया-स्थयोर्वान्नावौ 8.1.20.
4. Cf. Pāṇ. हि च 8.1.34.
5. Cf. Phiṭ निपाताः आद्युदात्ताः 80.
6. वायुः पदनाम निघं० 5.4. वायुर्वातिर्वेतेर्वा स्यात् गतिकर्मणः, एतेरिति स्थौलाष्ठीविः अनर्थको वकारः नि० 10.1. वायुः सोमस्य रक्षिता, वायुमस्य रक्षितारमाह साहचर्याद् रसहरणाद्वा नि० 11. 5. अयं वै वायुर्योऽयं पवते श० 2.6.37.

उप॑ (upa)—closeness[1]

उप इत्युपजनम् नि० 1.3. इयं (पृथिवी) वा ऽउप श० 2.3.4.9. उप वै रथन्तरम् तां० 16.5.14.

प्रयो॑भिः (prayobhiḥ)—material stuff of universe, i.e. mass energy of universe, food stuff.

आ (ā)—proximity, conjunction and simli[2].

ग॒त॒म् (gatam)—come, make reach, procure

इन्द॑व (indava)—electricity, electric charge, charged particles[3]

वा॒म् (vām)—to both of you

उ॒शन्ति॑ (uśanti)—evince interest, want, make known

हि (hi)—since, because

Anvaya (Sequencial placement of words)

indravāyū ime sutā prayobhiḥ upa ā gatam. hi indavo vām uṣanti.

Meaning of Mantra in different contexts :

इन्द्र॑वायू॒ इति॑। इ॒मे। सु॒ताः। उप॑। प्रय॑ःऽभिः। आ। ग॒त॒म्। इन्द॑व। वा॒म्। उ॒शन्ति॑। हि॥

Spiritual: (इन्द्रवायू) O All powerful and All pervading Brahman, (इमे) these worlds in observer space are (सुताः) created by you. (उपागतम्) Provide us (प्रयोभिः) with all objects of use and enjoyments in the universe. (इन्दवः) All these objects of use and

---

1. उप इत्युपजनम् नि० 1.3. इयं (पृथिवी) वा ऽउप श० 2.3.4.9. उप वै रथन्तरम् तां० 16.5.14.

2. अर्वागर्थे नि० 1.3. एतस्मिन्नेवार्थे (समुच्चयार्थे) देवेभ्यश्च पितृभ्य एत्याकारः नि० 1.4. उपमार्थे दृश्यते नि० 3.16. अध्यर्थे दृश्यते नि० 5.5.

3. इन्दुः-उदक नाम निघं० 1.12. यज्ञनाम निघं० 3.17. पदनाम निघं० 5.4. इन्दुरिन्धेरुनत्तेर्वा नि० 10.41. सोमो वाऽइन्दुः श० 2.2.3.23. सोमो वै राजेन्दुः ऐ० 1.29.

enjoyment (हि) only (उशन्ति) reflects upon or points out (वाम्) to your above cited two qualities.

Scientific 1: (इन्द्रवायू) O electro-magnetic force operating in the universe! (इमे) these matter particles are (सुताः) created because of you (since you helped in the expansion of universe). (उपागतम्) You both come to us (प्रयोभिः) with this stuff of creation. (इन्दवः हि) Only these electrically charged particles (उशन्ति) induce (वाम्) both- electricity and magnetism.

Note: Both electricity and magneticism or electromagnetic force is a force of repulsion or expansion.They expand the universe to allow more and more generation of matter particles.

Scientific 2: Here Indra refers to the solar wind and Vāyu to the field of earth. So, the meaning would go like this. (इन्द्रवायू) O solar wind and field lines of Earth! (इमे) these radiation belts are (सुताः) created by you. (उपागतम्) You provide us (प्रयोभिः) with these protective radiation belts, (हि) Because, (इन्दवः) the electrically charged particles in the atmosphere of the earth (उशन्ति) require (वाम्) you both.

१४. वायविन्द्रश्च चेतथः सुतानां वाजिनीवसू।
तावा यातमुप द्रवत्।।५।।

वायो इति। इन्द्रः। च। चेतथः। सुतानाम्। वाजिनीऽवसू इति। तौ। आ।
यातम्। उप। द्रवत्।।

Saṁhitāpāṭha

vāyavndraḥ ca cetathaḥ sutānām vājinīvasū. tau āyātam upa dravat

Padapāṭha

vāyo iti. indraḥ. ca. cetathaḥ. sutānām. vājinī—vasū iti. tau. ā. yātam. upa. dravat.

Grammatical Notes:

वायो (vāyo)—Voc. sing. of vāyu. Adādigaṇa root √vā meaning 'to move', 'to smell'+uṇ (Uṇādi suffix)[1]. Since this voc. form is in the beginning of the hemistich, it is accented on the first syllable.[2]

इन्द्रः (indraḥ)—Voc. sing. of Indra. Bhvādigaṇa root √idi 'to prosper'+ran (Uṇādi suffix).[3] 'Nit' suffix (of which final 'n' is elided) makes it accented on the first syllable[4].

च (ca)— A particle used in the sense of togetherness, conjunction. It remains unaccented as per rules of accentuation.[5]

चेतथः (cetathaḥ)—Bhvādigaṇa root √cit 'to be conscious'+laṭ lakāra (present tense) second person

---

1. Cf. *Uṇādi sūtra* (1.1)*kṛ-vā-pā-ji-mi-svadi-sādhi-aśūbhya.*
2. Cf. Pāṇini (6.1.192)—*āmantritasya ca.*
3. Cf. *Uṇādi.* ऋज्रेन्द्राग्रवज्र० - 2.28.
4. Cf. Pāṇ. ञ्नित्यादिर्नित्यम् - 6.1.197
5. Cf. *Phiṭ sūtra*—चादयोऽनुदात्ताः - 84.

dual. Here laṭ lakāra is used in the sense of loṭ lakāra (imperative mood). It remains unaccented being preceded by a non-verbal form.[1]

सुतानाम् (sutānām)—Gen. pl. of suta. Svādigaṇa root √ ṣuñ 'to press', 'to squeez' or Bhvāgigaṇa root √ ṣu 'to deliver', 'to prosper'+kta primary suffix.

वाजिनीवसू (vājinī-vasū)—Voc. dual. {vāja+ini 'in the sense of praise'+fem. suffix ṅīp or Bhvādigaṇa root √vaja 'to go'+ṇini suffix in the meaning of 'same nature'+fem. suffix ṅīp}+{Bhvādigaṇa root √vas 'to reside'+u (Uṇādi suffix)[2]}. As voc. case, it remains unaccented being in the middle of hemistich.[3]

आ (ā)—A prefix meaning proximity, conjunction and simli. Being a prefix, it is accented on the first syllable[4].

यातम् (yātam)—Adādigaṇa root √yā 'to go', 'to send'+leṭ lakāra (subjunctive) second person dual. It remains unaccented being preceded by a non-verbal form.[5]

उप (upa)—A prefix meaning closeness. Being a prefix, it is accented on the first syllable.[6]

द्रवत् (dravat)—Bhvādigaṇa root dru 'to move'+śatṛ (present active participle suffix). It is enumerated among the 26 names denoting 'quickness'. It is accented on the final syllable as per Phiṭ sūtra.[7]

---

1. Cf. Pāṇ.—तिङ्ङतिङः - 8.1.28
2. Cf. Uṇādi. शृस्वृस्निहि० - 1.10
3. Cf. Pāṇ.—आमन्त्रितस्य च - 8.1.19.
4. Cf. *Phiṭ sūtra*—उपसर्गाश्चाभिवर्जम् -81.
5. Cf. Pāṇ.—तिङ्ङतिङः - 8.1.28.
6. Cf. *Phiṭ sūtra*—उपसर्गश्चाभिवर्जम् - 81.
7. फिषोऽन्त उदात्तः -1

Word meanings:

वायो (vāyo)—Address to Vāyu. All pervading God, Life force, inhalation, field, magnetic force, teacher, king[1].

1. वायुः पदनाम निघं० 5.4. वायुर्वातिर्वेतेर्वास्यात् गतिकर्मणः, एतेरिति स्थौलाष्ठीविः अनर्थको वकारः नि० 10.1. वायुः सोमस्य रक्षिता, वायुमस्य रक्षितारमाह साहचर्याद् रसहरणाद्वा नि० 11. 5. अयं वै वायुर्योऽयं पवते श० 2.6.3.7. अयं वै वायुर्योऽयं पवत ऽएष वा इदं सर्वं विविनक्ति तयदिदं किञ्च विविच्यते श० 1.1.4.22. वातो हि वायुः श० 8.7.3.12. वायुर्वातहोमाः श० 9 .4.2.1. वायुर्वा उशन् तां० 7.5.19. वयुरनुवत्सरः तां० 17.13.17. तै० 1.4.10.1. वायुर्वै देवः जै०उ० 3.4.8. अयं वै ब्रह्म योऽयं (वायुः) पवते श० 14.2.2.10. अयं वै पवित्र (यजु०1.12) योऽयं (वायुः) पवते श० 1.1.3.2. पवित्रं वै वायुः तै० 3.2.5.11 एतद्वै प्रजापतेः प्रत्यक्षं रूपं यद् वायुः कौ० 19.2 यो वै वायु स इन्द्रो य इन्द्रः स वायुः श० 4.1.3. 19. अयं वै वायुर्मित्रो(यजु० 11.64.) यो ऽयं पवते श० 6.5.4.14. अयं वै यमो (यजु0 38. 9. यो ऽयं (वायुः) पवते श० 14.2.2.11. वायुर्वै यन्ता (ऋ० 3.13.3.) वायुना हीदं यदन्तरिक्षं न समृच्छति ऐ० 2.41 वायुर्वै प्राणाः कौ० 8.4. जै० उ० 4.22.11. वायुर्हि प्राणाः ऐ० 2.26. प्राणो हि वायुः तां० 4.6.8. प्राणो वै वायुः कौ० 5.8 वायुर्मे प्राणे श्रितः तै० 3.10.8.4. स (वायुः)यत्पुरस्ताद् वाति।प्राण एव भूत्वा पुरस्ताद् वाति। तस्मात् पुरस्ताद् वान्तं सर्वाः प्रजाः प्रतिनन्दन्ति तै० 2.3.9.4. वायुर्वै प्रणीर्यज्ञानां यदा हि प्राणित्यथ यज्ञोऽ ऽथाग्निहोत्र मृऐ० 2.34 यत्पशुपतिर्वायुस्तेन कौ० 6.4 वायुर्वाऽउग्रः श० 6.1.3.13. वायुर्वाव पुरोहितः ऐ० 8.27. वायुर्वा उपश्रोता गो० उ० 2.19. तै० 3.7.5.4. वायुरेव महः गो० पू० 5.15. वायुर्महः श० 12.3.4.8. मनो ह वायुर्भूत्वा दक्षिणातस्तस्थौ श० 8.1.1.7. इमे वै (त्रयो) लोका पूरयमेव पुरुषो योऽयं (वायुः) पवते सोऽस्यां पुरि शेते तस्मात् पुरुषः श० 13.6.2.1. अयं वै यज्ञो योऽयं (वायुः) पवते जै० उ० 3.16.1. अयमु वै यः (वायुः) पवते स यज्ञः गो० पू० 3.2. वाग्वै वायुः तै० 1.8.8.1. तां० 18.8.7. वायुरस्यन्तरिक्षे श्रितः। दिवः प्रतिष्ठा तै० 3.11.1.9. वायुर्वै नभसस्पतिः गो० उ० 4.9. वायुर्वा अन्तरिक्षस्याध्यक्षः तै० 3.2.1.3 वायुरेव यजुः श०10. 3.5.2. वायुर्यजुर्वेदः (अजायत) श० 11.5.8.3. यजुषां वायुर्दैवतं तदेव ज्योतिस्त्रैष्टुभं छन्दोऽन्तरिक्षं स्थानम् गो० पू० 1.29. त्रैष्टुभो हि वायुः श० 8.7.3.12. वायुरध्वर्युः गो० पू० 1.13. वायुर्वा अध्वर्य्युः गो० पू० 2.24 एष वाऽपां रसो योऽयं पवते स एष (वायुः) सूर्ये समाहितः सूर्यात् पवते श० 5.1.2.7 शुक्लो हि वायुः श० 6.2.2.7. तथेति वायुः पवते जै० उ० 3.6.2. अनिरुक्तो हि वायुः श० 8.7.3.12. शान्तिर्हिवायुः तां० 4.6.9. (वायोः) मेनका च सहजन्या (यजु० 15.16.)। तं (वायुं) एताः पञ्च देवता परिभ्रियन्ते विद्युद् वृष्टिश्चन्द्रमा आदित्योऽग्निः ऐ० 8.28 सोऽयं (वायुः) पुरुषेऽन्त प्रविष्टस्त्रेधा विहितः प्राण उदानो व्यान इतिश० 3.1.2.20.

इन्द्रः (indraḥ)—Address to Indra. God, elecric force, solar wind, king, mind, teacher [1]

च (ca)—together, and [2]

चेतथः (cetathaḥ)—know, conscious of, make known

सुतानाम् (sutānām)—produced, pressed, squeezed [3], electric charge, food stuff, matter

वाजिनीवसू (vājinī—vasū)—Address to vājinī—vasū,[4] abiding in the system, in the process.

आ (ā)—proximity, conjunction and simli [5].

यातम्[6] (yātam)—come, send.

उप (upa)— closeness [7]

---

1. इन्द्रः पदनाम निघं० 5.4. इन्द्रः-इरां दृणातीति वा इरां ददातीति वा, इरां दधातीति वा। इरां दारयत इति वा। इरां धारयत इति वा। इन्दवे द्रवतीति वा। इन्दौ रमत इति वा। इन्धे भूतानीति वा। 'तद्यदेनं प्राणैः समैन्धंस्तदिन्द्रस्येन्द्रत्वमिति विज्ञायते।' इदं करणादित्याग्रायणः। इदं दर्शनादित्यौपमन्यवः। इन्दतेर्वैश्वर्यकर्मणः। इन्दञ्छत्रूणां दारयिता वा द्रावयिता वा। आदरयिता च यज्वनाम् नि० 10.8. एष वै शुक्रो य एष (सूर्यः) तपत्येष (सूर्यः) उ एवेन्द्रः श० 4.5.5.7, 4.5.9.4.। अथ यः स इन्द्रोऽसौ स आदित्यः श० 8.53.2. यो वै वायुः स इन्द्रो य इन्द्रः स वायुः श० 4.1.3.19. स योऽयं मध्ये प्राणः। एष एवेन्द्रस्तानेष प्राणान्मध्यत इन्द्रियैणैन्द्ध तस्मादिन्ध इन्धो ह वै तमिन्द्र इत्याचक्षते परोऽक्षम् श० 6.1.1.2. हृदयमेवेन्द्रः श० 12.9.1.15. यन्मनः स इन्द्रः गो० उ० 4.11. मन एवेन्द्रः श० 12.9.1.13. इन्द्रो वै यजमानः श०2.1.2.11 क्षत्रियो यदुच यजमानः श० 5.3.5.27. एन्द्रो वै राजन्य तै० 3.8.23.2. इन्द्रः क्षत्रम् श० 10.4. 1.5. वीर्यं वा इन्द्रः तां० 9.7.5, 8. इन्द्रो यज्ञस्य नेता श० 4.1.2.15.
2. च समुच्चयार्थे नि० 1.4.
3. सुतस्य अभिषुतस्य नि० 13.6. सुतेषु सोमेषु नि० 5.22. सुतः, सुतम् इत्यन्ननामानी निघं० 2.7.
4. वाजिनी उषोनाम निघं० 1.8.
5. अर्वागर्थे नि० 1.3. एतस्मिन्नेवार्थे (समुच्चयार्थे) देवेभ्यश्च पितृभ्य एत्याकारः नि० 1.4. उपमार्थे दृश्यते नि० 3.16. अध्यर्थे दृश्यते नि० 5.5.
6. याति गतिकर्मा निघं० 2.14.
7. उप इत्युपजनम् नि० 1.3. इयं (पृथिवी) वा ऽउप श० 2.3.4.9. उप वै रथन्तरम् तां० 16.5.

द्रवत् (dravat)—It is enumerated among 26 names denoting 'quickness'[1].

Anvaya (Sequencial placement of words)

vājinīvasū vāyavndraḥ ca sutānām cetathaḥ. tau dravat upa āyātam

Meaning of Mantra in different contexts :

Spiritual: (वायविन्द्रश्च) Prāṇa and mind (वाजिनीवसू) abiding in the body (चेतथः) are aware (सुतानाम्) of the sense and motor organs created in it. (तौ) Both (आयातम्) should come together (उपद्रवत्) quickly for cessation of desires and attaining Mokṣa.

Scientific 1: (वायविन्द्रश्च) Magnetic force and electric force (वाजिनीवसू) abiding in the process of creation (चेतथः) are aware (सुतानाम्) of electric charge produced owing to anhilation and of matter and antimatter particles. (तौ) Both (आयातम्) should come together (उपद्रवत्) quickly for the expansion of universe.

Note : According to the Vedas, Indra (electric force) and Vāyu (magnetic force) are the forces of repulsion. They are the main factors behind the expansion of universe. In fact the duo *Vāyavindra* are nothing but the electromagnetic force of the observer space.

Scientific 2: (वायविन्द्रश्च) Geomagnetic field lines of earth and solar winds (वाजिनीवसू) abiding at the surface of magnetosphere (चेतथः) are aware (सुतानाम्) of origin of radition belts (तौ) Both (आयातम्) should come together (उपद्रवत्) quickly to create these radiation belts around earth as our protective shields.

Socio-political 1: (वायविन्द्रश्च) The ruler and the commander (वाजिनीवसू) abiding in the state (चेतथः) should be aware (सुतानाम्) of the activities of people (तौ) Both (आयातम्) should work together (उपद्रवत्) quickly to safeguard the interest of the public.

Socio-political 2: (वायविन्द्रश्च) The teacher and preacher (वाजिनीवसू) abiding in the nation (चेतथः) should be aware (सुतानाम्)

14.

1. द्रवदिति शीघ्रनामसु पठितम्, निघं० 2.15, 125.

of young talent in the country (तौ) Both (आयातम्) should work together (उपद्रवत्) quickly to protect this talent through good teachings and preachings.

१५. वायविन्द्रश्च सुन्वत आ यातमुप निष्कृतम्।
मक्ष्वि१त्था धिया नरा।। ६।।

वायो इति। इन्द्रः। च। सुन्वतः। आ। यातम्। उप। निःऽकृतम्। मक्षु। इत्था। धिया। नरा।।

Saṁhitāpāṭha

vāyavindraś ca sunvata ā yātam upa niṣ-kṛtam. makṣ-vitthā dhiyā narā.

Padapāṭha

vāyo iti. indraḥ. ca. sunvataḥ. ā. yātam. upa. niḥ-kṛtam. makṣu. itthā. dhiyā. narā.

Grammatical Notes:

वायो (vāyo)—Voc. sing. of vāyu. Adādigaṇa root √vā meaning 'to move', to smell'+uṇ (Uṇādi suffix)[1]. Since this voc. is in the beginning of the hemistich, it is accented on the first syllable.[2]

इन्द्रः (indraḥ)—Voc. sing. of Indra.Bhvādigaṇa root √idi 'to prosper'+ran (Uṇādi suffix).[3] 'Nit' suffix (of which final 'n' is elided) makes it accented on the first syllable[4].

च (ca.)—A particle used in the sense of togetherness, conjunction. It remains unaccented as per rules of accentuation.[5]

सुन्वतः (sunvataḥ)—Gen.pl. of sunvan. Svādigaṇa root √ṣuñ 'to squeez'+śatṛ (present active participle suffix). It is

1. Cf. *Uṇādi sūtra* (1.1)*kṛ-vā-pā-ji-mi-svadi-sādhi-aśūbhya.*
2. Cf. Pāṇini (6.1.192)—*āmantritasya ca.*
3. Cf. *Uṇādi.* ऋज्रेन्द्राग्रवज्र० - 2.28.
4. Cf. Pāṇ. ञ्नित्यादिर्नित्यम् - 6.1.197
5. Cf. *Phiṭ sūtra*—चादयोऽनुदात्ताः - 84.

accented on the inflectional ending.[1]

आ (ā)—A prefix meaning proximity, conjunction and simli. Being a prefix, it is accented on the first syllable[2].

याृतम् (yātam)—Adādigaṇa root √yā 'to go', 'to send'+leṭ lakāra (subjunctive) second person dual. It remains unaccented being preceded by a non-verbal form.[3]

उप (upa)— A prefix meaning closeness. Being a prefix, it is accented on the first syllable.[4]

निष्कृतम् (niṣkṛtam)—Nis+Tanādigaṇa root √ḍukṛṅ 'to do'+ kta suffix. 'Ṛ' of 'niṣkṛt' is accented as per rule of accentuation[5].

मक्षु (makṣu)—Makṣu is enumerated in the list of names denoting 'quickness'. It also gets accent on the final syllable as per Phiṭ sūtra.[6]

इत्था (itthā)—Demonstrative pronoun Idam+thāl suffix in the sense of ' because of'.[7]

धिया (dhiyā)—Inst. sing. of dhīḥ. Bhvādigaṇa root √ dhyai 'to think'+kvip siffix[8]. Dhiyā gets accent on its suffix 'ā', since it is monosyllabic when inflected in locative

---

1. Cf. Pāṇini—शतुरनुमो नद्यजादि - 6.1.173
2. Cf. *Phiṭ sūtra*—उपसर्गाश्चाभिवर्जम् -81
3. Cf. Pāṇ.—तिङ्ङतिङः - 8.1.28.
4. Cf. *Phiṭ sūtra*—उपसर्गश्चाभिवर्जम् - 81.
5. Cf. Pāṇ.—गतिकारकोपपदात्कृत्-6.2.139.
6. फिषोऽन्त उदात्तः - 1
7. Cf. Pāṇ.था हेतौ च च्छन्दसि' अ० 5.3.26. According to Pāṇ. एतेतौ च रथोः'

   - 5.3.4 '*idam*' is repalced by '*it*' when followed by 'thā' suffix.
8. See Pāṇini—*dhyāyateḥ saṁprasāraṇaṁ ca*—3.2.178

case[1].

न॒रा (narā)—Voc. dual of nara. Here dual voc. suffix 'au' is replaced by 'ā'[2]. Being a voc. form not located in the beginning of the hemistich, it loses its accent[3].

Word meanings:

वा॒यो (vāyo)—Address to Vāyu (All pervading God, life force, inhalation, field, magnetic force, teacher, king)[4]

---

1. Cf. Pāṇini—सावेकाचस्तृतीयादविभक्तिः -6.1.168.
2. See Pāṇ. सुपां सुलुग्० 7.1.39.
3. Cf. Pāṇ. आमन्त्रितस्य च - 8.1.19.
4. वायुः पदनाम निघं० 5.4. वायुर्वातिर्वेतेर्वास्यात् गतिकर्मणः, एतेरिति स्थौलाष्ठीविः अनर्थको वकारः नि० 10.1. वायुः सोमस्य रक्षिता, वायुमस्य रक्षितारमाह साहचर्याद् रसहरणाद्वा नि० 11. 5. अयं वै वायुर्योऽयं पवते श० 2.6.3.7. अयं वै वायुर्योऽयं पवत ऽएष वा इदं सर्वं विविनक्तियदिदं किञ्च विविच्यते श० 1.1.4.22. वातो हि वायुः श० 8.7.3.12. वायुर्वातहोमा : श० 9.4.2.1. वायुर्वा उशन् तां० 7.5.19. वयुरनुवत्सरः तां० 17.13.17. तै० 1.4.10.1. वायुर्वै देवः जै०उ० 3.4.8. अयं वै ब्रह्म योऽयं (वायुः) पवते श० 14.2.2.10. अयं वै पवित्र (यजु० 1.12.) योऽयं (वायुः) पवते श० 1.1.3.2. पवित्रं वै वायुः तै० 3.2.5.11 एतद्वै प्रजापतेः प्रत्यक्षं रूपं यद् वायुः कौ० 19.2 यो वै वायु स इन्द्रो य इन्द्रः स वायुः श० 4.1.3. 19. अयं वै वायुर्मित्रो (यजु० 11.64.) यो ऽयं पवते श० 6.5.4.14. अयं वै यमो (यजुः० 3 8.9. यो ऽयं (वायुः) पवते श० 14.2.2.11. वायुर्वै यन्ता (ऋ० 3.13.3.) वायुना हीदं यदन्तरिक्षं न समृच्छति ऐ० 2.41 वायुर्वै प्राणाः कौ० 8.4. जै० उ० 4.22.11. वायुर्हि प्राणाः ऐ० 2.26. प्राणो हि वायुः तां० 4.6.8. प्राणो वै वायुः कौ० 5.8 वायुर्मे प्राणे श्रितः तै० 3.10. 8.4. स (वायुः)यत्पुरस्ताद् वाति।प्राण एव भूत्वा पुरस्ताद् वाति। तस्मात् पुरस्ताद् वान्तं सर्वाः प्रजाः प्रतिनन्दन्ति तै० 2.3.9.4. वायुर्वै प्रणीर्यज्ञानां यदा हि प्राणित्यथ यज्ञोऽथाग्निहोत्रम् ऐ० 2. 34 यत्पशुपतिर्वायुस्तेन कौ० 6.4 वायुर्वाऽउग्रः श० 6.1.3.13. वायुर्वाव पुरोहितः ऐ० 8.27. वायुर्वाउपश्रोता गो० उ० 2.19. तै० 3.7.5.4. वायुरेव महः गो० पू० 5.15. वायुर्महः श०12.3. 4.8. मनो ह वायुर्भूत्वा दक्षिणातस्तस्थौ श० 8.1.1.7. इमे वै (त्रयो) लोका पूरयमेव पुरुषो योऽयं (वायुः) पवते सोऽस्यां पुरि शेते तस्मात् पुरुषः श० 13.6.2.1. अयं वै यज्ञो योऽयं (वायुः) पवते जै० उ० 3.16.1. अयमु वै यः (वायुः) पवते स यज्ञः गो० पू० 3.2. वाग्वै वायुः तै० 1.8.8.1. तां० 18.8.7. वायुरस्यन्तरिक्षे श्रितः। दिवः प्रतिष्ठा तै० 3.11.1.9. वायुर्वै नभसस्पतिः गो० उ० 4.9. वायुर्वा अन्तरिक्षस्याध्यक्षः तै० 3.2.1.3 वायुरेव यजुः श०10.3.5.2. वायुर्यजुर्वेदः (अजायत) श० 11.5.8.3. यजुषां वायुदैवतं तदेव ज्योतिस्त्रैष्टुभं छन्दोऽन्तरिक्षं स्था

इन्द्रः (indraḥ) —Address to Indra (God, electric charge, king, mind, teacher [1])

च (ca.)—together, and

सुन्वतः (sunvataḥ)—one who produces, presses, propels or squeezes, one who acts.

आ (ā)—proximity, conjunction and simli[2].

यातम् (yātam)—to go, to send[3]

उप (upa)— close[4]

नम् गो०पू० 1.29. त्रैष्टुभो हि वायुः श० 8.7.3.12. वायुरध्वर्युः गो० पू० 1.13. वायुर्वा अध्वर्य्युः गो०पू० 2.24 एष वाऽपां रसो योऽयं पवते स एष (वायुः) सूये समाहितः सूर्यात् पवते श० 5.1.2.7 शुक्लो हि वायुः श० 6.2.2.7. तथेति वायुः पवते जै० उ० 3.6.2. अनिरुक्तो हि वायुः श० 8.7.3.12. शान्तिर्हि वायुः तां० 4.6.9. (वायोः) मेनका च सहजन्या (यजु० 15.16.)। तं(वायुं) एताः पञ्च देवता परिम्रियन्ते विद्युद् वृष्टिश्चन्द्रमा आदित्योऽग्निः ऐ० 8.28 सोऽयं (वायुः) पुरुषेऽन्त प्रविष्टस्त्रेधा विहितः प्राण उदानो व्यान इति श०3.1.2.20.

1. इन्द्रः पदनाम निघं० 5.4. इन्द्रः-इरां दृणातीति वा इरां ददातीति वा, इरां दधातीति वा। इरां दारयत इति वा। इरां धारयत इति वा। इन्दवे द्रवतीति वा। इन्दौ रमत इति वा। इन्धे भूतानीति वा। 'तद्यदेनं प्राणैः समैन्धंस्तदिन्द्रस्येन्द्रत्वमिति विज्ञायते।' इदं करणादित्याग्रायणः। इदं दर्शनादित्यौपमन्यवः। इन्दतेर्वैश्वर्यकर्मणः। इन्दञ्छत्रूणां दारयिता वा द्रावयिता वा। आदरयिता च यज्वनाम् नि० 10.8. एष वै शुक्रो य एष (सूर्यः) तपत्येष (सूर्यः) उ एवेन्द्रः श० 4.5.5.7, 4.5.9.4. अथ यः स इन्द्रोऽसौ स आदित्यः श० 8.5.3.2. यो वै वायुः स इन्द्रो य इन्द्रः स वायुः श० 4.1.3.19. स योऽयं मध्ये प्राणः। एष एवेन्द्रस्तानेष प्राणान्मध्यत इन्द्रियैणैन्द्ध तस्मादिन्ध इन्धो ह वै तमिन्द्र इत्याचक्षते परोऽक्षम् श० 6.1.1.2. हृदयमेवेन्द्रः श० 12.9.1.15. यन्मनः सइन्द्रः गो० उ० 4.11. मन एवेन्द्रः श० 12.9.1.13. इन्द्रो वै यजमानः श० 2.1.2.11 क्षत्रियो यदुच यजमानः श० 5.3.5.27. एन्द्रो वै राजन्य तै० 3.8.23.2. इन्द्रः क्षत्रम् श० 10.4. 1.5. वीर्यं वा इन्द्रः तां० 9.7.5, 8. इन्द्रो यज्ञस्य नेता श० 4.1.2.15.

2. अर्वागर्थे नि० 1.3. एतस्मिन्नेवार्थे (समुच्चयार्थे) देवेभ्यश्च पितृभ्य एत्याकारः नि० 1.4. उपमार्थे दृश्यते नि० 3.6. अध्यर्थे दृश्यते नि० 5.5.

3. याति गतिकर्मा निघं० 2.14.

4. उप इत्युपजनम् नि० 1.3. इयं (पृथिवी) वा ऽउप श० 2.3.4.9. उप वै रथन्तरम् तां० 16.5.14.

नि॒ष्कृ॒तम् (niṣkṛtam)—physical body, purified, produced, pressed[1]

म॒क्षु (makṣu)—quickly[2]

इ॒त्था (itthā)—in the like manner, truly[3]

धि॒या (dhiyā)—with the action, intelligence[4]

न॒रा (narā)— Prāṇavāyu (life energy) and mind

Anvaya (Sequencial placement of words)

vāyavindraḥ ca niṣkṛtam sunvata upa ā yātam. narā dhiyā makṣu itthā.

Meaning of Mantra in different contexts :

Spiritual: (वायविन्द्रश्च) Prāṇa (life energy) and mind (मक्षु) quickly (उपायातम्) occupied (निष्कृतम्) the physical body formed as a result of sanskaras of the past life (इत्था) with the purpose of sustaining it. (नरा) Both Prāṇavāyu and mind (सुन्वतः) propels the body (धिया) by providing it power of action and thought.

Scientific: (वायविन्द्रश्च) Electromagnetic force (मक्षु) quickly (उपायातम्) enters (निष्कृतम्) into the charged particles produced from energy (इत्था) with the purpose of sustaining this universe. (नरा) Both electric and magnetic forcces (सुन्वतः) propels the body of universe (धिया) intelligently.

The Devata (subject matter) of below given mantras is Mitra and Varuṇa. In scientific sense, Mitra represents the positive charge of the universe and Varuṇa the negative charge of the universe. Mitra may also be

---

1. यद्वै निष्कृतं तत्संस्कृतम् ऐ० आ० 1.1.4
2. मक्ष्विति क्षिप्रनामसु पठितम् निघं० 2.15, 1.2.6. मक्षु क्षिप्रनाम निघं० 2.15.
3. इत्था सत्यनाम, निघं० 3.10. पदनाम निघं० 4.2. इत्था-अमुत्र नि० 4.25.
4. धीः कर्मनाम निघं० 2.1. प्रज्ञानाम निघं० 3.9. धियः-प्रज्ञानानि नि० 11.27.

known as positively charged particle and Varuṇa as negatively charged particles. Mitra also represents hydrogen and Varuna oxygen. In spiritual sense, Mitra is the representative of prāṇa vāyu (inhalation) and Varuṇ the apāna vāyu (exhalation). In Socio-political sense, Mitra is a teacher and Varuṇa is a king.

१६. मि॒त्रं हु॑वे पू॒तद॑क्षं॒ वरु॑णं च रि॒शाद॑सम्।
धि॒यं घृ॒ताचीं॑ सा॒ध॑न्ता॥७॥

मि॒त्रम्। हु॒वे॒। पू॒तऽद॑क्षम्। वरु॑णम्। च॒। रि॒शाद॑सम्। धि॒यम्। घृ॒ताचीं॑म्।
सा॒ध॑न्ता॥

Saṁhitāpāṭha

mitraṁ huve pūta-dakshaṁ varuṇaṁ ca riśādasam dhiyaṁ ghṛtācīṁ sādhantā.

Padapāṭha

mitram. huve. pūta-dakṣam. varuṇam. ca. riśādasam. dhiyam. ghṛtācīm. sādhantā.

Grammatical Notes:

मि॒त्रम् (mitram)—Bhvādigaṇa root √ñimidā 'to oil'+ktra (Uṇādi suffix).[1] Being a masculine form, it is finally accented as per rule of prātipadika accent.

हु॒वे॒ (huve)—Bhvādigaṇa root √hveñ 'to compete', 'to make sound'+laṭ lakāra first person sing.or Juhotyādigaṇa root √hu 'to donate', 'to receive'+laṭ lakāra first person sing. Being a verbal form preceded by a non—verbal form, it loses its accent.[2]

पू॒तद॑क्षम् (pūta-dakṣam)—Bahuvrīhi compound. {Krayādigaṇa root √puñ 'to purify'+kta suffix}+Bhvādigaṇa root

---

1. Cf. Uṇādi. अमिचिमिशसिभ्यः क्त्र: - 4.164.
2. Cf. Pāṇ. तिङ्ङतिङः - 8.1.28.

√dakṣa 'to increase', 'to hasten' or √dakṣa 'to move', 'to rule'+ac suffix in nom. case or ghañ suffix in abstract sense}. 'Pūta' gets suffix accent.[1] Being a Bahuvrīhi compound, it gets natural accent on the first member.[2] As such 'pūtadakṣa' is accented on the first member.

वरुणम् (varuṇam)—Svādigaṇa root √vṛñ 'to adopt'+unan (Uṇādi suffix).[3] Being formed of 'nit' suffix (of which final 'n' is elided), it is accented on the first syllable.[4]

च (ca)—A particle used in the sense of togetherness, conjunction. It remains unaccented as per rules of accentuation.[5]

रिशादसम् (riśādasam)—{Adādigaṇa root √riśa 'to injure'+ka[6]}+{ Divādigaṇa root √dasu 'to ruin'+kvip suffix} or {Adādigaṇa root √ad 'to eat'+asun (Uṇādi suffix)}[7]. Here riśa carries accent on suffix[8], adaḥ is also accented on the first syllable, being formed of 'nit' suffix. Under the circumstances in the compound word 'riśādasaḥ' (riśa+ādasaḥ), both 'a' (final of 'riśa' and initial of 'adasaḥ') are accented. According to the rule of accentuation[9], when an acute accent is followed by another acute accent, both combine into one. As such euphonically prolonged 'ā' in 'riśādasaḥ' will have an acute accent.

1. Cf. Pāṇ. आद्युदात्तश्च - 3.1.3
2. Cf. Pāṇ. बहुव्रीहौ प्रकृत्या पूर्वपदम्- 6.2.1
3. Cf. *Uṇādi* कृवृदारिभ्य उनन् - 3.53
4. Cf. Pāṇ. ञ्नित्यादिर्नित्यम् - 6.1.197.
5. Cf. *Phiṭ sūtra*—चादयोऽदनुदात्ताः - 84.
6. Cf. Pāṇ. इगुपधज्ञा प्रीकिरः क - 3.1.135
7. Cf. Uṇādi. सर्वधातुभ्योऽसुन् - 4.190
8. Cf. Pāṇ. आद्युदातश्च - 3.1.3.
9. Cf. Pāṇ. एकादेश उदात्तेनोदात्तः - 8.2.5.

धियम् (dhiyam)—Acc. sing. of dhī. Bhvādigaṇa root √ dhyai 'to seek concern'+kvip[1]. It carries accent on its nominal root.

घृताचीम् (ghṛtācīm)—Acc. sing. of ghṛtācī. {Juhotyādigaṇa root √ghṛ 'to leak', 'to shine',+kta (Uṇādi suffix) [2] }+{Bhvādigaṇa root√ añcu 'to go', 'to worship'+kvin suffix[3]}+nīp fem. suffix.[4] It is accented accented on final syllable of first member ghṛta.[5]

साधन्ता (sādhantā)—Nom. dual of sādhayan. Svādīgaṇa root √sādha 'to be successful'+ṇic+śatṛ (present active participle)+'ṅip' fem. suffix. The dual inflectional ending 'an' is replaced by 'ā'.[6]

Word meanings:

मित्रम्[7] (mitram)—life energy called prāṇa vāyu (inhalation), (inhalation), protons, hydrogen, geothermal radiation

---

1. Cf. *Vārttika*—ध्यायतेः संप्रसारणं च - Pāṇ. 3.2.178.
2. Cf. *Uṇādi* अञ्जि धृसिभ्यः क्तः - 3.89.
3. Cf. Pāṇ. ऋत्विग्दधृकस्रग्दिगु० - 3.2.59.
4. Cf. *Vārttika*—अञ्चतेश्चोपसंख्यानम् - Pāṇ. 4.1.6.
5. Cf. Pāṇ चौ - 6.1.222.
6. Cf. Pāṇ. सुपां सुलुक्० - 7.1.39.
7. मित्रः पदनाम निघं० 5.4. मित्रः-मित्रः प्रमीतेस्त्रायते। सम्मिन्वानो द्रवतीति वा। मेदयतेर्वा नि० 10.21. सर्वस्य ह्येव मित्रो मित्रम् श० 5.3.2.7. मित्र! सत्यानामधिपतये! तै० 3.11.4.1. ब्रह्मैव मित्रः श० 4.1.4.1. मित्रः क्षत्रं क्षत्रपतिः श० 11.4.3.11. प्राणो वै मित्र श० 6.5.1.5. अयं वै वायुर्मित्रो योऽयं पवते श० 6.5.7.14. अहर्मित्रः तां० 25.10.10. यः (अर्द्धमासः) आपूर्य्यते स मित्रः तां० 25.10.10. यो (अर्धमासः)ऽपक्षीयते स मित्रः श० 2.4.4.28. मित्रेणैव यज्ञस्य स्विष्टं शमयति तै० 1.2.5.3. प्राणो मित्रम् जै० उ० 3.3.6. मित्रः क्षीरश्रीः (सोमः) तै०सं० 4.4.9.1. मित्रमहः मै० 1.8.9. मित्रो वै यज्ञस्य शान्तिः काठ० 35.19. मित्रो वै शिवो देवानाम् तै० सं० 5.1.6.1. य (अर्द्धमासः) आपूर्यते स मित्रः तां० 25.10.10. वो (अर्धमासः) ऽपक्षीयते स मित्रः श० 2.4.4.18. सत्यं वै मित्रः मै० 4.3.9

हुवे (huve) —call, accomplish, invoke[1]

पूतदक्षम् (pūta—dakṣam)—pure minded, possessing pure power[2], refining agent

वरुणम् [3] (varuṇam)—Life energy called apāna vāyu, electrons, solar radiation, oxygen

Note : Varuṇa has always been equated with agni and mitra with soma. Varuṇa represents solar radiation.

Mitra and Varuṇa have been shown in Vedas as having

---

1. हुवे आह्वये नि० 11.31. हुवेम ह्वयेम नि० 10.28
2. दक्षः बलनाम निघं० 2.9. आदित्यो दक्ष इत्याहुः नि० 11.20. दक्षाय अपत्याय नि० 11.30. दक्षो ह वै पार्वतिरेतेन यज्ञेनेष्ट्वा सर्वान् कामानाप कौ० 4.4. स (प्रजापतिः) वै दक्षो नाम श० 2.4.4.2. अथ यदस्मै तत्समृध्यते स दक्षः श० 4.1.4.1. वरुणो दक्षः श० 4.1.4.1. प्राणा वै दक्षाः। जै० 1.151. दक्षश्च मे बलं च मे (यज्ञेन कल्पताम्) तै० सं० 4.7.1.2.
3. वरुणे वृणोतीति सतः नि० 10.3. वरुणः पदनाम निघं० 5.4. (आपः) यच्च वृत्वाऽतिष्ठंस्तद्वरुणोऽभवत्तं वा एतं वा वरणं सन्तं वरुण इत्याचक्षते परोक्षेण। परोक्षप्रिया इव हि देवा भवन्ति प्रत्यक्षद्विषः गो० पू० 1. वरुणो वै जम्बुकः (यजु० 25.9.) श० 13.3.6.5. तै० 3.9.15.3. रात्रिर्वरुणः ऐ० 4.10. ता० 28.10.10. वारुणी रात्रिः तै० 1.7.10.1. यः प्राणः स वरुणः गो० उ० 4.11. यो वै वरुणः सोऽग्निः श० 5.2.4.13. यो वा ऽग्निः स वरुणस्तदप्येत दृऋषिणोक्तं त्वमग्ने वरुणो जायसे यदिति ऐ० 6.26. अथ यत्रैतत् प्रदीप्ततरो भवति तर्हि हैष (अग्निः) भवति वरुणः श० 2.3.2.10. स यदग्निर्घोरसंस्पर्शस्तदस्य वारुणं रूपम् ऐ० 3.4. वारुण्यो वाऽएष योऽग्निना श्रृतोऽथैष मित्रो य ऊष्मणा श्रृतः श० 5.3.2.8. यः (अर्द्धमासः) अपक्षीयते स वरुणः तां० 25.10.10. यः (अर्द्धमासः) एवापूर्यते स वरुणः श० 2.4.4.28. क्लोमा वरुणः श० 12.9.1.15. श्रीर्वै वरुणः कौ० 18.9. द्यावापृथिवी वै मित्रावरुणयोः प्रियं धाम तां० 14.2.4. अयं वै (पृथिवी) लोको मित्रोऽसौ (द्युलोकः) वरुणः श० 12.9.2.12. व्यानो वरुणः श० 12.9.1.16. अपानो वरुणः श० 8.4.2.6. योनिरेव वरुणः श० 12.9.1.17. वरुणो दक्षः श० 4.1.4.1. वरुण एव सविता जै० उ० 4.27.3. स वा एषो (सूर्यः) ऽपः प्रविश्य वरुणो भवति कौ० 18.9. वरुण आदित्यैः (व्यद्रवत्) ऐ० 1.24. वरुण आदित्यैः (व्यद्रवत्) श० 3.4.2.1. संवत्सरो वरुणः श० 4.4.5.18. संवत्सरो हि वरुणः श० 4.1.4.10. क्षत्रं वरुणः श० 4.1.4.1. गो० उ० 6.7. क्षत्रं वै वरुणः वरुणो वै देवानां राजा श०12.8.3.10 वारुणो वै पाशः तै० 3.3.10.1. श० 6.7.3.8. वारुण्या वा ऽएता ओषधयो याः कृष्टे जायन्ते श० 5.3.3.8.

opposite nature. According to TS (2.1.7), Mitra is day (solar radiation) and Varuṇa is night (geothermal radiation). Varuṇa is called night and by this his black or dark colour is stressed. In Vedas, black is the colour of negative electric charge and electron also carries negative electric charge. Śatapatha Br. (5.2.5.17) says that everything that is black belongs to Varuṇa. Varuṇa is described as firm on following the laws (RV. 1.25.8). Electron is also very finicky about maintaining the laws. It is because of maintaining an orderly universe that Varuṇa was elevated to the position of supreme deity by Iranians.

च॒ (ca)—together, and[1]

रि॒शाद॑सम् (riśādasam)—destroyer of harmful ones, or destroyer of enemies.[2]

धिय॑म् (dhiyam)—intelligence, action, process[3]

घृ॒ताची॑म्[4] (ghṛtācīm)—waters

साध॑न्ता (sādhantā)—to do, to perform, to attain perfection

Anvaya (Sequencial placement of words)

mitram huve pūtadakṣam, varuṇam ca riśādasaḥ, dhiyaṁ ghṛtācīṁ sādhantā.

Meaning of Mantra in different contexts :

Spiritual: (घृताचीं साधन्ता) To achieve life energy and

1. च समुच्चयार्थे नि० 1.4.
2. रिशादसः-रेशयदासिनः नि० 6.14.
3. धीः कर्मनाम निघं० 2.1. प्रज्ञानाम निघं० 3.9. धियः-प्रज्ञानानि नि० 11.27. वाग्वै धीः श० 4.2.4.13.
4. घृताची रात्रिनाम निघं० 1.7. धृतमित्युदकनाम निघं० 1.12. धृताच्यसि जुहूर्नाम्ना श० 1.3.4.14. धृताच्यसि ध्रुवा नाम्ना श० 1.3.4.14 घृताच्यस्युपभृदनाम्ना श० 1.3.4.14. स्रुग् घृताचीरिति स्रुचश्चैतद् वेदिश्चाहघृताची-स्रुक् श० 9.2.3.17. वाग्वै धीर्घृताची ऐ० आ० 1.1.4.

intelligence, let us (हुवे) invoke /perfect (मित्रम्) *prāṇa vāyu* or inhalation which (पूतदक्षम्) purifies and strengthens the body (वरुणं च) and *apāna vāyu* or exhalation which (रिशादसम्) removes all harmful viruses from the body through (धियम्) prāṇāyāma.

Scientific 1: (घृताचीं साधन्ता) To create mass energy in observer space, let us (हुवे) invoke and (धियम्) process (मित्रम्) protons or particles having +ve charge which (पूतदक्षम्) provide creation with strength (वरुणं च) and electrons or particles having negative charge which (रिशादसम्) remove harmful forces.

Scientific 2: (घृताचीं साधन्ता) For creation to take place on the earth, we (हुवे) invoke and (धियम्) process (पूतदक्षम्) purifying (मित्रम्) solar radiation (वरुणं च) and magnetosphere of the earth that (रिशादसम्) protects from harmful solar radiation.

Note: The temperature on earth is the outcome of the permutation and combination of both the radiations.

Scientific 3: (घृताचीं साधन्ता) To form waters, (हुवे) let us take (धियम्) and process (पूतदक्षम्) pure (मित्रम्) hydrogen (वरुणं च) and oxygen (रिशादसम्) that eats away or rusts all the base metals.

Socio-political 1 : (घृताचीं साधन्ता) For the prosperity of nation, (हुवे) let us call upon (मित्रम्) teachers/intellectuals (पूतदक्षम्) who provide us with pure knowledge (वरुणं च) and king (रिशादसम्) who protects us from bad and harmful elements located inside and outside the country (धियम्) to work together.

Note: For the prosperity of nation, rulers and intellectuals should work together.

१७. ऋतेन मित्रावरुणावृतावृधावृतस्पृशा। क्रतुं बृहन्तमाशाथे।।८।।

ऋतेन। मित्रावरुणौ। ऋतऽवृधौ। ऋतस्पृशा। क्रतुम्। बृहन्तम्। आशाथे।।

Saṁhitāpāṭha

ṛtena mitrāvaruṇau ṛtā-vṛdhau ṛta-spṛśā. kratuṁ bṛhantam āśāthe.

Padapāṭha

ṛtena. mitrāvaruṇau. ṛta-vṛdhau. ṛtaspṛśā. kratum. bṛhantam. āśāthe.

Grammatical Notes:

ऋतेन (ṛtena)—Although the derivation of 'ṛta' is no directly governed by Pāṇinian system of grammar, it may be derived from Bhvādigaṇa root √ṛ 'to go', 'to send'+kta suffix. As such the root 'ṛ' may be added to Uṇādi-अञ्चिधृसिभ्यः क्तः - 3.89., with the help of new supplementary formula as, उरपि वक्तव्यम्. Ṛta has been enumerated in the list of ghṛta group of words in Phiṭ sūtra. As such it carries accent on the final syllable. [1]

मित्रावरुणौ (mitrāvaruṇau)—Voc. dual of Mitrāvarūna. Devatā Dvandva compound of Mitra & Varuṇa. Final 'a' of Mitra is substituted by 'ā'.[2] A vocative case, being located in the middle of a hemistich, remains unaccented.[3]

ऋतावृधौ (ṛtā-vṛdhau) —Voc. dual of ṛtāvṛdha. {Bhvādigaṇa root √ṛ 'to go', 'to send'+kta (Uṇādi suffix)}+{Bhvādigaṇa root √vṛdhu 'to increase'+kvip suffix in the sense of 'making'}. For example, 'ṛtavṛdhau' will mean making waters/process of creation to increase.

---

1. Cf. *Phiṭ sūtrā* - घृतादीनां च - 21.
2. Cf. Pāṇ. देवता द्वन्द्वे च - 6.3.26.
3. Cf. Pāṇ. आमन्त्रितस्य च -8.1.19.

'A' of ṛta is prolonged into 'ā'.[1] Attributive of Mitrāvaruṇa.

ऋतस्पृशा (ṛtaspṛśā)—Voc. dual of ṛtaspṛśa. {Bhvādigaṇa root √ṛ 'to go', 'to send'+kta (Uṇādi suffix)}+{Tudādigaṇa root √spṛśa 'to touch'+kvip}. 'Au' of 'ṛtasparśa' is prolonged into 'ā'.[2] Attributive of Mitrāvaruṇa.

क्रतुम् (kratum)—Taṇādigaṇa root √kṛñ 'to do'+'ktuḥ'. (Uṇādi suffix) in the nom. or instrumental sense.[3] It carries accent on its suffix.[4]

बृहन्तम् (bṛhantam)—Acc. dual. of Bṛhan. Bhvādigaṇa root √bṛh 'to increase'+śatṛ (present active participle) or atiḥ (Uṇādi suffix) in the sense of present active participle.[5] Attributive of kratum.

आशाथे (āśāthe)—Ā+svādigaṇa root √aśuṅ 'to pervade', 'to condense'+liṭ lakāra second person dual number. The actually inflected form is 'ānaśāthe', but here 'n' is elided in case of Veda.[6]

Word meanings:

ऋतेन (ṛtena)[7]— with matter particles, with mind

---

1. Cf. Pāṇ. अन्येषामपि दृश्यते - 6.3.137.
2. Cf. Pāṇ सुपां सुलुक्० - 7.1.39.
3. Cf. *Uṇādi* कृञः कतुः - 1.76.
4. Cf. Pāṇ. आधुदास्तश्च - 3.1.3.
5. Cf. Uṇādi - वर्तमाने पृषद्बृहत्० - 2.84.
6. Cf. Pāṇ. अश्नोतेश्च - 7.4.72.
7. ऋतम् उदकनाम निघं० 1.12. प्रत्यृतं भवति नि० 2.25. सत्यं वाऽऋतम् श० 6.7.3.11. ऋतमित्येष (सूर्यः) वै सत्यम् ऐ० 4.20. अग्निर्वा ऋतम् तै० 2.1.11.1. ऋतमेव परमेष्ठौ तै० 1.5.5.1. मनो वा ऋतम् जै० उ० 3.36.5. ब्रह्म वा ऽअग्निर्ऋतमसावादित्यः सत्यं यदि वासावृतमयं (अग्निः) सत्यमुभयम्वेतदयमग्निः श० 6.4.4.10. ऋतनेवैनं स्वर्गं गमयन्ति तां० 18.2.9.

मित्रावरुणौ (mitrāvaruṇau)—Address to Mitrāvarūna.

Inhalation and exhalation, particles having+ve and—ve charge.

मित्रावरुणा-मित्रावरुणौ नि० 11.23. प्राणापानौ मित्रावरुणौ तां० 6.10.5. प्राणो वै मित्रोऽपानो वरुणा श० 8.4.2.6. प्राणोदानौ वै मित्रावरुणौ श० 1.8.3.12. अहोरात्रौ वै मित्रावरुणौ तां० 25.10.10. अथैतावेवमासौ मित्रावरुणौ, य एवापूर्यते स वरुणो योऽपक्षीयते स मित्रः श० 2.4.4.18. बाहू वै मित्रावरुणौ श० 5.4.1. 35. द्यावापृथिवी वै मित्रावरुणयोः प्रियं धाम तां० 14.2.40 गोसंस्तवौ वै मित्रावरुणौ कौ० 18.13. चक्षुश्च मनश्च मैत्रावरुणः काठ० 27.5. मनो मैत्रावरुणः श०12.8.2.23. यज्ञो वै मैत्रावरुणः कौ० 13.2.

ऋतावृधौ (ṛtā-vṛdhau)[1]—Attributive of Mitrāvaruṇa. Augmentors

ऋतस्पृशा (ṛtaspṛśā)—Attributive of Mitrāvaruṇa. Dispensers

क्रतुम् (kratum)[2]—process of creation, act

बृहन्तम् (bṛhantam)[3]—Attributive of kratum. Vast

आशाथे (āśāthe)—pervaded

Anvaya (Sequencial placement of words)

ṛtāvṛdhau ṛtaspṛśā mitrāvaruṇau bṛhantam kratum āśāthe ṛtena

Meaning of Mantra in different contexts :

Spiritual : (मित्रावरुणौ) Prāṇa Vāyu and Apāna Vāyu of the

---

1. ऋतावृध्-सत्यवृधो वा यज्ञवृधो वा नि० 12.33.
2. क्रतुं कर्म वा प्रज्ञां वा नि० 2.28. क्रतुः-कर्मनाम निघं० 2.1. प्रज्ञानाम निघं० 3.9. क्रतुना कर्मणा नि० 10.10. कृत्वे अपत्याय नि० 11.27. स यदेव मनसाऽकामयतऽइदं मे स्यादिदं कुर्वीयेति स एव क्रतुः श० 4.1.4.1. क्रतुर्मनोजवः श० 3.3.4.7. हृत्सु ह्यसं क्रतुर्मनोजवः प्रविष्टः श० 3.3.4.7. क्रतुं दक्षं वरुण सं शिशाधि ऋ० 8.42.3 इति वीर्यं प्रज्ञानं वरुण सं शिशाधीति ऐ० 1.13. मित्र एव क्रतुः श० 4.1.4.1.
3. बृहन् एष ते शुक्रो य एष (सूर्यः) तपत्येष उ ऽएव बृहन् श० 4.5.9.6.

body are (ऋतावृद्धौ) augmentors and (ऋतस्पृशौ) dispensers of life energies. They (आशाथे) have pervaded the (बृहन्तम्) vast (क्रतुम्) creation of animate life (ऋतेन) alongwith mind.

Scientific 1: (मित्रावरुणौ) Positively charged energy particles and negatively charged particles are (ऋतावृद्धौ) augmentors and (ऋतस्पृशौ) dispensers of matter and anti-matter particles. They (आशाथे) have pervaded the (बृहन्तम्) vast (क्रतुम्) process of creation (ऋतेन) alongwith laws underlying it.

Scientific 2: (मित्रावरुणौ) Mitra and Varuṇa are (ऋतावृद्धौ) augmentors and (ऋतस्पृशौ) dispensers of rain. They (आशाथे) have pervaded the (बृहन्तम्) vast (क्रतुम्) process of rain-formation and anti-rain (ऋतेन) alongwith laws underlying it.

Note: Co-ordination of both the elements in a particular ratio stimulates rain. See for more detail author's work '*Vedic Meteorology*'.

Scientific 3: (मित्रावरुणौ) solar radiation and geothermal radiation are (ऋतावृद्धौ) augmentors and (ऋतस्पृशौ) dispensers of radiation belts around the earth. They (आशाथे) have pervaded the (बृहन्तम्) vast (क्रतुम्) process of formation of radiation belts (ऋतेन) alongwith laws underlying it.

Socio-political 1: (मित्रावरुणौ) Ruler and commander are (ऋतावृद्धौ) augmentors and (ऋतस्पृशौ) dispensers of governance in the nation. They (आशाथे) have pervaded the (बृहन्तम्) vast (क्रतुम्) socio-political system (ऋतेन) alongwith rules and laws to regulate it.

Socio-political 2: (मित्रावरुणौ) Teacher and preacherare (ऋतावृद्धौ) augmentors and (ऋतस्पृशौ) dispensers of knowledge and awareness in the nation. They (आशाथे) have pervaded the (बृहन्तम्) vast (क्रतुम्) system of educational (ऋतेन) alongwith moral and ethical values to maintain it.

१८. कवी नो मित्रावरुणा तुविजाता उरुक्षया।
दक्षं दधाते अपसम्।।९।।

कवी। नः। मित्रावरुणा। तुविऽजातौ। उरुऽक्षया। दक्षम्। दधाते। अपसम्।।

Saṁhitāpāṭha

kavī no mitrāvaruṇā tuvi-jātā uru—kṣayā. dakṣaṁ dadhāte apasam.

Padapāṭha

kavī. naḥ. mitrāvaruṇā. tuvi-jātau. uru-kṣayā. dakṣam. dadhāte. apasam.

Grammatical Notes:

कवी (kavī)—Nom./acc. dual of kavi. Adādigaṇa root √ ku 'to make sound'+iḥ (Uṇādi suffix).[1] It carries an accent on suffix.[2]

नः (naḥ) —Acc./dat./gen. pl. enclitic form of first person pronoun 'Asmad'. Being an enclitic form, it is not accented.[3]

मित्रावरुणा (mitrāvaruṇā) —Nom. dual of Mitrāvaruṇa. Devatā Dvandva compound of Mitra and Varuṇa. Final 'a' of mitra is substituted by 'ā'.[4] Final 'au' of 'mitrāvaruṇau' is replaced by 'ā'.[5] Mitra carries accent on nominal stem and Varuṇa is accented on the first syllable, being formed of 'nit' suffix.

तुविजातौ (tuvi—jātau)—Nom. dual of compound form of tuvijāta or (Tuvi+jāta). Tuvi+Divādigaṇa root √ janī

1. Cf. Unādi अचइः - 4.139.
2. Cf. Pāṇ. आद्युदात्तश्च - 3.1.3.
3. Cf. Pāṇ. युस्मदस्मदोः षष्ठी चतुर्थी द्वितीया स्थयोर्वान्नावौ 8.1.20.
4. Cf. Pāṇ. देवता द्वन्द्वे च - 6.3.26.
5. Cf. Pāṇ - सुपां सुलुक्० - 7.1.39.

'to take birth', 'to appear'+kta suffix. It has its final syllable of the second member accented.[1]

उरुक्षया (uru-kṣayā)—Nom. dual of compound form of urukṣ

aya or (uru+kṣaya). Uru+Tudādigaṇa root √ kṣi 'to dwell', 'to move'+ghaḥ suffix in locative sense.[2] According to the Pāṇini rule 3.3.118., it should have received accent on suffix. Other way round, it should have been accented finally. But another aphorism of Pāṇini[3] makes it accented on the first syllable if the meaning of kṣaya is 'dwelling'. According to the above aphorism, had the meaning of kṣaya been 'destruction', it would have been accented on suffix or last syllable.

दक्षम् (dakṣam)—Bhvādigaṇa root √dakṣa 'to increase', 'to

hasten' orBhvādigaṇa root √dakṣa 'to move', 'to rule' or 'to prosper'+ghañ or an suffix. In case of both suffixes (one being ñit, and another being 'nit'), it carries accent on first syllable.

दधाते (dadhāte)—Juhotyādigaṇa root √dhāñ 'to sustain', 'to

bring up', 'to tone up'+loṭ lakāra (present tense) third person dual number. Being a verbal form preceded by a non—verbal form, it loses its accent.[4]

अपसम् (apasam)—Svādigaṇa root √āplṛ 'to pervade'+asun

(Uṇādi suffix)[5]. Being formed of 'nit' suffix, it should have been accented on first syllable (or root syllable)[6], but this is an exception to the rule of 'nit' accentuation. As such this exceptional case of accentuation be added to the basic rule of Pāṇ. 6.1.197. by way of a new Vārttika (suplimentary formula) as अपसो अपवादत्वेनुपसंख्येयम्।

---

1. Cf. Pāṇ. समास्य - 6.1.223.
2. Cf. Pāṇ. पुसि संज्ञायां घः प्रायेण - 3.3.118.
3. क्षयो निवासे - 6.1.201.
4. Cf. Pāṇ. तिङ्ङतिङः - 8.1.28.
5. Cf. Uṇādi sātra - आप कर्माख्यायां ह्रस्वो नुट् च वा - 4.208.
6. Cf. ञ्नित्यादिर्नित्यम् - 6.1.197.

Word meanings:

क॒वी (kavī) [1]—Intelligent, sapient

न॒: (naḥ) — us, universe

मि॒त्रावरु॑णा (mitrāvaruṇā)[2]—inhalation and exhalation, +ve and -ve charge, hydrogen and oxygen, solar and geothermal radiations

तु॒वि॒जा॒तौ (tuvi-jātau[3]—Attributive of Mitrāvaruṇau. Beneficial to many

उ॒रु॒क्षया॑ (uru-kṣayā)—Attributive of Mitrāvaruṇau. Refuge of multitudes

दक्ष॑म् (dakṣam)[4]—Strength

द॒धा॒ते॒ (dadhāte)—Boost, increase, give, prosper

---

1. कविः-मेधाविनाम निघं:० 3.15 कविः क्रान्तदर्शनो भवति, कवतेर्वा नि० 12.13. असौ वाऽदित्यः कविः श० 6.7.2.4. ये वा अनूचानस्ते कवयः ऐ० 2.2. एते वै कवयो यदृषयः श० 1.4.2.8. ये वै तेन ऋषयः पूर्वे प्रेतास्ते वै कवयः ऐ० 6.20. शुश्रुवांसो वै कवयः तै० 3. 2.2.3 ये विद्वांसस्ते कवयः श० 7.2.2.4

2. मित्रावरुणा-मित्रावरुणौ नि० 11.23. प्राणापानौ मित्रावरुणौ तां० 6.10.5. प्राणो वै मित्रोऽपानो वरुणः श० 8.4.2.6. प्राणोदानौ वै मित्रावरुणौ श० 1.8.3.12. अहोरात्रौ वै मित्रावरुणौ तां० 25.10.10. अथैतावेवमासौ मित्रावरुणौ, य एवापूर्यते स वरुणो योऽपक्षीयते स मित्रः श०2.4.4. 18.बाहू वै मित्रावरुणौ श० 5.4.1.35. द्यावापृथिवी वै मित्रावरुणयोः प्रियं धाम तां० 14.2.40 गोसंस्तवौ वै मित्रावरुणौ कौ० 18.13. चक्षुश्च मनश्च मैत्रावरुणः काठ० 27.5. मनोमैत्रावरुणः श० 12.8.2.23. यज्ञो वै मैत्रावरुणः कौ० 13.2.

3. तुवीति बहुनामसु पठितम्, निघं० 3.1, 12.9. तुविजातः बहुजातः नि० 12.36.

4. दक्षतेः समर्द्धयतिकर्मणः (नि० 1.7.) दक्षः बलनाम निघं० 2.9. आदित्यो दक्ष इत्याहुः नि० 11.20. दक्षाय अपत्याय नि० 11.30. दक्षो ह वै पार्वतिरेतेन यज्ञेनेष्ट्वा सर्वान् कामानाप कौ 4.4. स (प्रजापतिः) वै दक्षो नाम श० 2.4.4.2. क्रतुं दक्षं वरुण संशिशाधि (ऋ० 8.42.3)इति वीर्यं प्रज्ञानं वरुण संशिशाधीति ऐ० 1.13. स्वैर्दक्षैर्दक्षपितेह सीदेति। स्वेन वीर्येणेह सीदेत्येतत्श० 4.1.4.1. वरुणो दक्षः श० 4.1.4.1. प्राणा वै दक्षाः। जै० 1.151. दक्षश्च मे बलं च मे (यज्ञेन कल्पताम्) तै० सं० 4.7.1.2.

अपसम् (apasam) 1—work, matter, rainwaters, radiation belts

Anvaya (Sequencial placement of words)

kavī mitrāvaruṇā naḥ dakṣam apasam dadhāte tuvijātā urukṣ ayā.

Meaning of Mantra in different contexts :

Spiritual: (कवी) Sapient (मित्रावरुणा) inhalation and exhalation (दधाते) increase (नः) our (दक्षम्) efficiency and power to (अपसम्) work. They are (तुविजाता) beneficial to all, and (उरुक्षया) refuge of multitudes.

Scientific: (कवी) Sapient (मित्रावरुणा) positively charged particles and negatively charged particles (दधाते) increase (दक्षम्) efficiency and power of (अपसम्) matter over anti-matter (नः) in our universe. They are (तुविजाता) beneficial to all, and (उरुक्षया) refuge of multitudes.

Note : According to Vedas, every where in universe, the process of creation and annhilation of matter and anti-matter is going on all the time. If the matter and antimatter are in equal proportion, they both annhilate each other and there cannot be any creation. For the creation to take place and persist, the increase of matter over antimatter is must. That is why, the seer wants to increase the power of matter over antimatter and this is possible only through the Mitra and Varuṇa, the positively and negatively charged particles of the universe.

Scientific 2: (कवी) Sapient (मित्रावरुणा) somīya element or *āpastattva/* hydrogen and āgneya element/ jyotiṣ tattva/oxygen (दधाते) increase (दक्षम्) power of (अपसम्) rainformation (नः) in our atmosphere. They are (तुविजाता) beneficial to all, and (उरुक्षया) refuge of multitudes.

Scientific 3: (कवी) Sapient (मित्रावरुणा) solar radiation and geothermal raditon of the earth (दधाते) increase (दक्षम्) efficiency

---

1. अप इत्युदकनाम निघं० 1.12. कर्मनाम निघं० 2.1. अपो यत्कर्म नि० 7.27. अपः प्रजननकर्म नि० 11.31.

of (नः अपसम्) our magnetosphere/radiation belts. They are (तुविजाता) beneficial to all, and (उरुक्षया) refuge of multitudes.

Socio-political 1: (कवी) Intelligent (मित्रावरुणा) ruler and commander (दधाते) increase (दक्षम्) efficiency and power of (अपसम्) working (नः) of our officials. They do undertake projects (तुविजाता) to benefit all. They are (उरुक्षया) refuge of multitudes.

Socio-political 2: (कवी) Intelligent (मित्रावरुणा) teacher and preacher (दधाते) increase (दक्षम्) efficiency and power of (अपसम्) working (नः) of our students. They undertake teaching and preaching (तुविजाता) for the benefit of all. They are (उरुक्षया) refuge of multitudes.

सूक्त - 3

ऋषि– मधुच्छन्दा वैश्वामित्र। **देवता–** १-३ अश्विनीकुमार, ४-६ इन्द्र,

७-९ विश्वेदेवा, १०-१२ सरस्वती। **छन्द–** गायत्री।

The Devatā (subject matter) of below given three mantras is *Aśvinau.* In spiritual sense, Aśvinau represents left and right nasal breathings. In scientific sense, they represent, two poles (negative and positive poles or north and south poles) of universe, earth and a magnet. They also represent the duo of observer space and light space. The sun and moon are also represented by Aśvinau. In Socio-political sense, they represent couples, like teacher and his spouse, king and queen, doctor and his spouse etc.

१९. अश्विना यज्वरीरिषो द्रवत्पाणी शुभस्पती। पुरुभुजा चनस्यतम्।।१।।

अश्विना। यज्वरीः। इषः। द्रवत्ऽपाणी। शुभः। पती इती। पुरुऽभुजा। चनस्यतम्।।

Saṁhitāpāṭha

aṣvinā yajvarīr-iṣo dravat-pāṇī śubhas-patī. puru-bhujā canasyatam

Padapāṭha

aṣvinā. yajvarīḥ. iṣaḥ. dravat-pāṇī. śubhaḥ-patī. puru-bhujā. canasyatam.

Grammatical Notes:

अश्विना (aṣvinā)—Voc. dual of Aśvin. Aśva+ini suffix in the sense of matup (possession). It may also variously be derived from Svādigaṇa root aśūṅ 'to pervade'+viniḥ. It, being voc. case located in the beginning of hemistich, is accented on the first syllable.

यज्वरीः (yajvarīḥ)—Bhvādigaṇa root √yaja 'to worship

gods', 'to combine', 'to donate'+vanip or ṅvanip[1]+ṅīp fem. suffix [2] 'N' is replaced by 'P'. Both suffixes being 'pit', go without accent. [3] As such the root accent prevails.

इषः (iṣaḥ)—Acc. pl. of 'iṣa'. Tudadigaṇa root √iṣu 'to desire' or Divādigaṇa root iṣa 'to go'+kvip. Being formed of 'pit' suffix (whose final 'p' is elided), it is accented on the first syllable (root syllable).

द्रवत्पाणी (dravat-pāṇī)—Voc. dual of dravatpāṇī. Compound of dravat & pāṇī. {Bhvādigaṇa root √dru 'to go'+śatṛ (present active participle form}+{Bhavādigaṇa root √ paṇa 'to interact', 'to behave'+iṇa (Uṇādi suffix). [4] Attibutive of Aśvinau.

शुभः (śubhas)—Gen. sing. of śubha. Bhvādigaṇa root √śubha or śumbha 'to illumine'+kvip in the sense of 'pertaining to'. Being formed of 'pit' suffix, it is accented on the first syllable (root syllable). [5]

पती (patī)—Voc. dual of pati. Adādigaṇa root √pā 'to protect'+ḍati (Uṇādi suffix)[6] or Bhvādigaṇa root √pati 'to go'+in (Uṇādi suffix). Being vocative case not located in the beginning of a hemistich, it goes without accent. [7]

पुरुभुजा (puru—bhujā)—Voc. dual of purubhuja. Puru+Rudhādigaṇa root √bhuja 'to bring up', 'to feed'+kvip suffix. The voc. dual suffix 'au' is replaced

---

1. Cf. Pāṇ. सुयजोर्ङ्वनिप् - 3.2.103.
2. Cf. Pāṇ. वनो रच - 4.1.7.
3. Cf. Pāṇ. अनुदात्तौ सुप्पितौ - 3.1.4.
4. Cf. *Uṇādi* - पशिपणाय्योरुडाय लुकौ च - 4.133.
5. Cf. Pāṇ. अनुदात्तौ सुप्पितौ - 3.1.4.
6. Cf. *Uṇādi* - पातेर्डतिः 4.57.
7. Cf. आमन्त्रितस्य च ' 8.1.19.

by 'ā'.[1] Being a vocative case in the beginning of a hemistich, it is accented on the initial syllable.[2]

च॒न॒स्यत॑म् (canasyatam)—Bhvādigaṇa root √cāyṛ 'to worship'+asun (Uṇādi suffix)[3] +kyac denominative suffix in the sense of 'desire'[4]+loṭ lakāra (imperative) second person dual number. All denominative suffixes are taken in grammar as root suffixes.[5] That is why being a denominative stem, 'canasya' is inflected in loṭ lakāra.

Word meanings:

अश्वि॑ना[6] (aṣvinā)—Address to Aśvinau. Observer and light light space, two poles of a magnet, male and female, breathings of left and right nostrils,

यज्व॑री॒: (yajvarīḥ) —executor of yajña, instrumental for the execution of yajña

इष॑:[7] (iṣaḥ)—stuff of universe (mass energy), food, progeny

द्रव॑त्पाणी[8] (dravat-pāṇī)—Address to dravatpāṇī. Attributive

---

1. Cf. Pāṇ. सुपां सुलुक् - 7.1.39.
2. Cf. Pāṇ. आमन्त्रितस्य च - 6.1.198.
3. Cf. *Uṇādi sūtra* चायतेरन्ने ह्रस्वश्च - 4.207.
4. Cf. Pāṇ सुपः आत्मनः क्यच् - 3.1.8.
5. Cf. Pāṇ सनाद्यन्ताः धातवः 3.1.32.
6. अश्विनौ (द्यावापृथिव्यौ) यद् व्यश्नुवाते सर्वं रसेनान्यो ज्योतिषान्यः नि० 12.1. इमे ह वै द्यावापृथिवी प्रत्यक्षमश्विनाविमे हीदᳪ सर्वमश्नुवातां पुष्करस्रजावित्यग्निरेवास्यै (पृथिव्यै) पुष्करमादित्योऽमुष्यै (दिवे) श० 4.1.5.16. श्रोत्रे अश्विनौ श० 12.9.1.13. नासिके अश्विनौ श० 12.9.1.14. तद् यो ह वा ऽइमौ पुरुषाविवाक्ष्योः। एतावेवाश्विनौ श० 12.9.1.12. अश्विनावध्वर्यू ऐ० 1.18 मुख्यौ वा ऽश्विनौ (यज्ञस्य) श० 4.1.5.19. अश्विनाविव रूपेण (भूयासम्) मं० 2.4.14. वसन्तग्रीष्मावेवाश्विभ्याम् (अवरुन्धे) श० 12.8.2.34.
7. इषम् अन्ननाम निघं० 2.7. इष अद्भिः सह नि० 10.26. प्रजा वाऽइषः श० 1.7.3.14. अन्नं वाऽ इषम् कौ० 28.5. अयं वै लोक इषमिति ऐ० 6.7.
8. पाणिः पणायतेः पूजाकर्मणः अगृह्य पाणी देवान् पूजयन्ति नि० 2.26 पाणी वै गभस्ती

epithet of Aśvinau. Swift running sun—rays, swift hands.

शुभः (śubhas)—good , auspicious

शुभस्पती (patī)—Address to śubhaspatī. Atributive epithet of Aśvinau, protector, lord

पुरुभुजा (puru—bhujā)—Address to Purubhujā. Attributive of Aśvinau. long armed, great consumers

चनस्यतम् (canasyatam)—accept, desire to consume (food, or stuff of universe)

Anvaya (Sequencial placement of words)

asvinā canasyatam iṣaḥ yajvarī dravatpāṇī śubhaspatī purubhujā.

Meaning of Mantra in different contexts :

Spiritual: (अश्विनौ) breathing of left and right nostrils are (पुरुभुजा) great consumers. They (चनस्यतम्) consume (इषः) the food taken by human-beings. They (यज्वरीः) execute the metabolism of the body. (द्रवत्पाणी) They are swift in their movements, and (शुभस्पती) protector of the good health.

Scientific 1: (अश्विनौ) The polar regions of the earth are (पुरुभुजा) great consumers. They (चनस्यतम्) consume (इषः) high speed particles-electrons and protons from sun. They are instrumental in (यज्वरीः) executing auroral lights. (द्रवत्पाणी) They have swift movements, and (शुभस्पती) protector of the good.

Scientific 2: (अश्विनौ) Two poles of our universe are (पुरुभुजा) great consumers. They (चनस्यतम्) consume (इषः) the food stuff of universe, i.e. mass energy of universe. They are instrumental in (यज्वरीः) executing the process of creation in our universe. (द्रवत्पाणी) They have swift movements, and (शुभस्पती) protector of the good.

श० 4.1.1.9.

Socio-political: (अश्विनौ) Male and female partners are (पुरुभुजा) great consumers. They (चनस्यतम्) consume (इषः) the food. They are instrumental in (यज्वरीः) executing or extending the process of progeny. (द्रवत्पाणी) They have swift movements, and (शुभस्पती) lord of auspicious act of progenation.

Here the Veda highlights the male and female members are are instrumental for progenation.

२०. अश्विना पुरुदंससा नरा शवीरया धिया। धिष्ण्या वनतं गिरः।।२।।

अश्विना। पुरुऽदंससा। नरा। शवीरया। धिया। धिष्ण्या। वनतम्। गिरः।।

Saṁhitāpāṭha

aśvinā purudansasā narā śavīrayā dhiyā. dhiṣṇyā vanataṁ giraḥ.

Padapāṭha

aśvinā. purudansasā. narā. śavīrayā. dhiyā. dhiṣṇyā. vanatam. giraḥ.

Grammatical Notes:

अश्विना (aśvinā)— Voc. dual of Aśvin. Aśva+ini suffix in the sense of matup (possession). It may also variously be derived from Svādigaṇa root aśūṅ 'to pervade'+viniḥ. It, being voc. case located in the beginning of hemistich, is accented on the first syllable.

पुरुदंससा (purudansasā)—Compound of puru and dansas. Voc. dual of purudansas. {Juhotyādigaṇa root √pṛ 'to bring up', 'to fill up'+kuḥ (Used suffix)[1] }+ {Curādigaṇa root √dasi 'to see', 'to bite'+ghañ suffix in the instrumental sense[2]}. Voc. dual 'au' is replaced by 'ā'[3].

नरा (narā)—Voc. dual of nara. Bhvādigaṇa root √ṇīñ 'to carry', 'to send'+ṛ (Uṇādi suffix).[4] Nom. dual 'au' is replaced by 'ā '[5]

शवीरया (śavīrayā)—Inst. sing. of śavīrā. Bhvādigaṇa root

1. Cf. *Uṇādi sūtra*—पृभिदिव्यधि० - 1.23
2. Cf. Pāṇ. हलश्च -3.3.121
3. Cf. Pāṇ. सुपां सुलुक्० 7.1.39
4. Cf. Pāṇ. नयतेर्डिच्च -2.100
5. Cf. Pāṇ. सुपां सुलुक्० 7.1.39

√śava 'to go' or √śu 'to go'+īran (Uṇādi suffix) [1]+ṭāp fem. suffix. Being formed of 'nit' suffix, it is accented on the first syllable.[2] Attributive of dhiyā.

धि॒या (dhiyā)—Inst. sing. of dhīḥ. Bhvādigaṇa root √dhyai 'to think'+kvip siffix[3]. Dhiyā gets accent on its suffix 'ā', since it is monosyllabic when inflected in locative case.[4]

धिष्ण्या॑ (dhiṣṇyā)—Voc. dual. of dhiṣṇyā. Juhotyādigaṇa root √dhiṣ+kanin suffix.[5] Being formed of 'nit' suffix, it is accented on the first syllable.[6]

वन॑तम् (vanatam)—Bhvādigaṇa root √vana 'to divide'+loṭ (imperative) second person dual. Nom. or Bhvādigaṇa root √vana 'to divide'+śatṛ (present active participle). Acc. sing. In the former case śap (infix of Bhvādigaṇa) being 'pit' [7] and loṭ second person dual being sārvadhāuka, lose their accent. Under the circumstances, root accent will prevail. In the second case also śatṛ suffix, being sārvadhātuka, loses its accent[8] and the root suffix prevails.

गिर॑ः (giraḥ)—Nom. pl. of gi. Tudādigaṇa root √ gṛ 'to gulp' or 'to swallow' or Krayādigaṇa root √gṛ 'to make sound'+kvip suffix. 'Sup' suffixes (nominal suffixes) are never accented, as such only the root accent will prevail leading it to be accented on the first syllable.

---

1. Cf. Pāṇ. कृ-शृ-पृ-कटि-पटि-शौटिभ्य ईरन् - 4.31
2. Cf. Pāṇ. ञ्नित्यादिर्नित्यम् - 6.1.197
3. See Pāṇini—*dhyāyateḥ samprasāraṇaṁ ca*—3.2.178
4. Cf. Pāṇini—सावेकाचस्तृतीयादविभक्तिः -6.1.168.
5. Cf. *Uṇādi.* धृषेधिषः च संज्ञायाम् - 2.83
6. Cf. Pāṇ. ञ्नित्यादिर्नित्यम् - 6.1.197
7. Cf. Pāṇ. अनुदात्तौ सुप्पितौ - 3.1.4
8. Cf. Pāṇ. तास्यनुदात्तेन्ङिदुपदेशाल्लसार्वधातुकमहन्विङोः - 6.1.186

Word meanings:

अश्विना[1] (aśvinā)— Address to Aśvinau.

पुरुदंससा[2] (purudansasā)—Address to purudansasau. Attributive of Aśvinā. manifold effects, movements

नरा (narā) —Attributive of Aśvinā, carrier, sender

शवीरया (śavīrayā)—fast, with unobstructed movement

धिया[3] (dhiyā)—intelligently, carefully

धिष्ण्या[4] (dhiṣṇyā)—Attributive of Aśvinā, accelerator of metabolism.

वनतम् (vanatam)—receive, accept, enjoy, practised

गिरः[5] (giraḥ)—speech, total mass energy of universe, progeny

Anvaya (Sequencial placement of words)

aśvinā giraḥ śavīrayā dhiyā vanatam purudansasā narā dhiṣ ṇyā.

Meaning of Mantra in different contexts :

Spiritual: (अश्विना) O left and right nostril- breathings, i.e. anuloma and viloma prāṇāyāma), you (पुरुदंससा) create multiple

---

1. अश्विनौ (द्यावापृथिव्यौ) यद् व्यश्नुवाते सर्वं रसेनान्यो ज्योतिषान्यः नि० 12.1. इमे ह वै द्यावापृथिवी प्रत्यक्षमश्विनाविमे हीदꣳ सर्वमश्नुवातां पुष्करस्रजावित्यग्निरेवास्यै (पृथिव्यै) पुष्करमादित्योऽमुष्यै (दिवे) श० 4.1.5.16. श्रोत्रे अश्विनौ श० 12.9.1.13. नासिके अश्विनौ श० 12.9.1.14. तद् यो ह वा ऽइमौ पुरुषाविवाक्ष्योः। एतावेवाश्विनौ श० 12.9.1.12. अश्विनावध्वर्यू ऐ० 1.18 मुख्यौ वा ऽश्विनौ (यज्ञस्य) श० 4.1.5.19.। अश्विनाविव रूपेण (भूयासम्) मं० 2.4.14. वसन्तग्रीष्मावेवाश्विभ्याम् (अवरुन्धे) श० 12.8.2.34.
2. दंसस् कर्मनाम निघं० 2.1. पुरुबहुनाम निघं० 3.1.
3. धीः कर्मनाम निघं० 2.1. प्रज्ञानाम निघं० 3.9. धियः-प्रज्ञानानि नि० 11.27.
4. भ्रातृव्यायतनं धिष्ण्याः मै० 3.3.2. मित्रावरुणौ धिष्ण्येभिः मै० 1.9.2. काठ० 9.10
5. गी वाङ् नाम निघं० 1.11. वाग्वै गीः श० 7.2.2.4. विशो गिरः श० 3.6.1.24.।

healng effects on the body (शवीरया) very fast. You (नरा) carry the (गिरः) bio-energy to all parts of the body.You are (धिष्ण्या) accelerator of the metabolism of the body. both anuloma and viloma prāṇāyāma should be (वनतम्) practised (धिया) carefully.

Here the Vedic mantra is pointing out to the significance of *anuloma* and *viloma prāṇāyāma. Anuloma* and *viloma prāṇāyama* promotes physical health.

Scientific 1: (अश्विना) O two poles of magnetic universe, you (पुरुदंससा) exert multiple effects on the body of universe (शवीरया) very fast. You (नरा) carry the (गिरः) mass energy to all parts of the universe. You are (धिष्ण्या) accelerator of the process of creation. (वनतम्) You process mass energy (धिया) very intelligently.

Scientific 2: (अश्विना) O the polar regions of the earth, you (पुरुदंससा) exert multiple effects on the body of earth (शवीरया) very fast. You (नरा) carry the (गिरः) geothermal energy to all parts of the earth. You are (धिष्ण्या) accelerator of the process of creation on the earth. You (वनतम्) receive high speed particles (electrons and protons) from sun (धिया) with great intelligence.

Socio-political 1: (अश्विना) O couple! you (पुरुदंससा) have a lot of role in shaping a society (शवीरया) at fast pace. You are (नरा) a carrier of (गिरः) good customs and ideals in the society. You are (धिष्ण्या) accelerator of the process of progenation on the earth. You (वनतम्) act (धिया) carefully (because you will be followed by the future generations).

२१. दस्रा॑ युवाक॑वः सुता नास॑त्या वृक्तब॑र्हिषः।
आ या॑तं रुद्रवर्तनी।।३।।

दस्रा॑। युवाक॑वः। सुताः। नास॑त्या। वृक्तब॑र्हिषः। आ। या॒त॒म्।
रु॒द्र॒व॒र्त॒नी।।

Saṁhitāpāṭha

dasrā yuvākavaḥ sutā nāsatyā vṛkta-barhiṣaḥ. āyātaṁ rudravartanī.

Padapāṭha

dasrā. yuvākavaḥ. sutāḥ. nāsatyā. vṛkta-barhiṣaḥ. ā. yātam. rudravartanī.

Grammatical Notes:

दस्रा॑ (dasrā)—Voc. dual of dasra. Divādigaṇa root √ dasu 'to destroy'+rak (Uṇādi suffix)[1]. Nom. dual 'au' is replaced by 'ā '[2]. Being a voc. case in the beginning of the hemistich, it is accented[3].

युवाक॑वः (yuvākavaḥ) —Adādigaṇa root √yu 'to mix and unmix'+kākuḥ suffix [4]. It is accented on the suffix [5], so so 'ā' gets acute accent. Attributive of sutāḥ.

सुताः (sutāḥ)—Nom. pl. of suta. Svādigaṇa root √ṣu 'to squeez' 'to press' or Bhvādigaṇa root √ṣu 'to deliver' 'to prosper'+kta (primary suffix) [6] or kta (Uṇādi suffix). It gets acute accent on suffix, so accented on

1. Cf. *Uṇādi sūtra*—स्फायितञ्जिवश्चि० - 2.13
2. Cf. Pāṇ. सुपां सुलुक्० 7.1.39
3. Cf. Pāṇ. आमन्त्रितस्य च - 6.1.198
4. Cf. *Uṇādi sūtra*—कठिकषिभ्यां काकुः - 3.77
5. Cf. Pāṇ. आद्युदात्तश्च - 3.1.3
6. Cf. Pāṇ. क्तक्तवतु निष्ठा -1.1.26

the last syllable.[1]

नास॑त्या (nāsatyā)—Voc. dual of nāsatya. 'Na' and 'astya' are compunded here.[2] Due to its being a voc. case in the beginning of the hemistich, it is accented on the first syllable.[3]

वृ॒क्तब॑र्हिषः (vṛkta-barhiṣaḥ)—A Bahuvrīhi compound of Vṛkta and Barhi. {Adādigaṇa root √vṛjī 'to be devoid of' +kta[4]}+{Bhvādigaṇa root √bṛhi 'to grow/ increase' +isiḥ (Uṇādi suffix)[5]}. Being a Bahuvrīhi compound, its first member retains its natural accent. First member 'vṛkta', being formed of kta suffix, will get its suffixal accent on suffix 'kta'. Attributive of sutāḥ.

आ (ā)—A prefix meaning proximity, conjunction and simli. Being a prefix, it is accented on the first syllable[6].

या॒त॒म् (yātam)—Adādigaṇa root √yā 'to go', 'to send'+leṭ lakāra (subjunctive) second person dual. It remains unaccented being preceded by a non—verbal form.[7]

रु॒द्र॒व॒र्त॒नी॒ (rudravartanī)—Rudra and vartani are compounded. Voc. dual of rudravartani. Adādigaṇa root √ rudir 'to shed tears'+ṇic+rak (Uṇādi suffix)[8]}+{Bhvādigaṇa root √vṛtu 'to be'+aniḥ (Uṇādi suffix)[9]}. It,being a voc. case not located in the beginning of a hemistich,

---

1. Cf. Pāṇ. आद्युदात्तश्च - 3.1.3
2. Cf. Pāṇ. नभ्राण्नपात्० - 6.3.75.
3. Cf. Pāṇ. आमन्त्रितस्य च - 6.1.198
4. Cf. Pāṇ. क्तक्तवतु निष्ठा -1.1.26
5. Cf. *Uṇādi sūtra*—बृंहेर्नलोपश्च - 2.109
6. Cf. *Phiṭ sūtra*—उपसर्गाश्चाभिवर्जम् -81.
7. Cf. Pāṇ.—तिङ्ङतिङः - 8.1.28.
8. Cf. *Uṇādi sūtra*—रोदेर्णिलुक् च - 2.22
9. Cf. *Uṇādi sūtra*—वृतेश्च- 2.108

goes without accent. [1]

Word meanings:

दस्रा[2] (dasrā)—Address to dasra, south pole

युवाकवः(yuvākavaḥ)—Attributive of sutāḥ. Combineable & non—combineable, never mixing with each other,

सुताः[3] (sutāḥ) —produced, pressed, squeezed

नासत्या[4] (nāsatyā)—Address to nāsatyā. North pole

वृक्तबर्हिषः[5] (vṛkta-barhiṣaḥ)—Attributive of sutāḥ. Charged particles, physical body, earth

आ[6] (ā)—proximity, conjunction and simli.

यातम्[7] (yātam)—come here

रुद्रवर्तनी (rudravartanī)—Address to Rudravartanī. Part of Rudras, radiation pressure, plate tectonic activities, following the path of warriors.

Anvaya (Sequencial placement of words)

dasrā nāsatyā rudravartanī yuvākavaḥ vṛkta barhiṣaḥ sutā āyātam.

Meaning of Mantra in different contexts :

---

1 Cf. Pāṇ. आमन्त्रितस्य च - 8.1.19

2. दस्रौ दर्शनीयौ नि० 6.26.

3. सुतस्य अभिषुतस्य नि० 13.6. सुतेषु सोमेषु नि० 5.22. सुतः, सुतम् इत्यन्ननामनी निघं० 2.7.

4. नासत्यौ चाश्विनौ, सत्यावेव नासत्यावित्यौर्णानाभः, सत्यस्य प्रणीता रावित्याग्रायणः नि० 6.13.

5. बर्हिष्-बर्हिः अन्तरिक्षनाम निघं० 1.3. उदकनाम निघं० 1.12. पदनाम निघं० 5.2. वृक्तबर्हिषः ऋत्विङ्नाम निघं० 3.18.

6. अर्वागर्थे नि० 1.3. एतस्मिन्नेवार्थे (समुच्चयार्थे) देवेभ्यश्च पितृभ्य एत्याकारः नि० 1.4. उपमार्थे दृश्यते नि० 3.16. अध्यर्थे दृश्यते नि० 5.5.

7. याति गतिकर्मा निघं० 2.14.

Spiritual: (दस्रा) O Right (नासत्या) and left breathings! you are (रुद्रवर्तनी) parts of 11 Rudras (10 prāṇas and a mind), you (युवाकवः) never mix with each other, (आ यातम्) occupy (वृक्तबर्हिषः) these physical bodies (सुताः) made for you.

Scientific: (दस्रा) O magnetic south pole (नासत्या) and north pole of earth! you are (रुद्रवर्तनी) keep reversing/changing places, but (युवाकवः) never meet with each other. (आ यातम्) You occupy (वृक्तबर्हिषः) these celestial bodies (सुताः) made for you.

२२. इन्द्रायाहि चित्रभानो सुता इमे त्वायवः।
अण्वीभिस्तना पूतासः।।४।।

इन्द्र। आ। याहि। चित्रभानो। सुताः। इमे। त्वायवः। अण्वीभिः।
तना। पूतासः।।

Saṁhitāpāṭha

indrā-yāhi citra-bhāno sutā ime tvāyavaḥ. aṇvībhis-tanā pūtāsaḥ.

Padapāṭha0

indra. ā. yāhi. citrabhāno. sutāḥ. ime. tvāyavaḥ. aṇvībhiḥ. tanā. pūtāsaḥ.

Grammatical Notes:

इन्द्र (indra)—Voc. sing. of Indra. Bhvādigaṇa root √idi 'to prosper'+ran (Uṇādi suffix).[1] 'Nit' suffix (of which final 'n' is elided) makes it accented on the first syllable[2].

आ (ā)—A prefix meaning proximity, conjunction and simli. Being a prefix, it is accented on the first syllable[3].

याहि (yāhi)—Adādigaṇa root √yā 'to make reach'+loṭ lakāra second person sing. It, being a verbal form preceded by a non-verbal form, goes without accent.[4]

चित्रभानो (citrabhāno)—Voc. sing. of citrabhānu. {Svādigaṇa root √ciñ 'to choose'+ktra (Uṇādi suffix)[5]}+

1. Cf. *Uṇādi.* ऋज्रेन्द्राग्रवज्र० - 2.28.
2. Cf. Pāṇ. ञ्नित्यादिर्नित्यम् - 6.1.197
3. Cf. *Phiṭ sūtra*—उपसर्गाश्चाभिवर्जम् -81.
4. Cf. Pāṇ. तिङ्ङतिङः 8.1.28.
5. Cf. *Uṇādi sūtra* - अनिचिमिशसि भ्यः क्त्रः - 4.164.

{Adādigaṇa root √bhā 'to shine'+nu (Uṇādi suffix)[1]}. It, being a vocative case not located in the beginning of a hemistich, receives no accent.

सुताः (sutāḥ)—Nom. pl. of suta. Svādigaṇa root √ ṣu 'to squeez' 'to press' or Bhvādigaṇa root √ṣu 'to deliver' 'to prosper'+kta (primary suffix)[2] or kta (Uṇādi suffix). It gets acute accent on suffix, so accented on the last syllable.[3]

इमे (ime)—Nom. pl. of demonstrative pronoun 'Idam'. Being a pronominal form, it is accented.

त्वायवः (tvāyavaḥ)—Nom. pl. of tvāyu. Second person pronoun 'Yusmad'[4]+kyac denominative suffix[5] in the sense of 'desire'+u suffix.[6] It is accented on suffix 'u'[7]. According to Swami Dayananda, it is a combination of 'Yusmad'+āyaus'.[8]

अण्वीभिः (aḥvībhiḥ)—Inst. pl. of aṇvī. Bhvādigaṇa root √ aṇ 'to make sound'+u Unādi suffix[9]+ṅīṣ[10] >ṅīn. Being formed of 'nit' suffix, it is accented on the first syllable.[11]

---

1. Cf. *Uṇādi sūtra* - दाभाभ्यां नुः - 3.32.
2. Cf. Pāṇ. क्तक्तवतु निष्ठा -1.1.26
3. Cf. Pāṇ. आद्युदात्तश्च - 3.1.3
4. According to Pāṇini, when '*Yusmad*' is followed by a suffix, it transforms into 'tva'. See Pāṇ प्रत्ययोत्तर पदयोश्च 7.2.98.
5. Cf. Pāṇ सुप आत्मनः क्यच् - 3.1.8.
6. Cf. Pāṇ क्याच्छन्दसि - 3.2.170.
7. Cf. Pāṇ आद्युदांत्तश्च 3.1.3.
8. *Adādigaṇa* root √*iṣa* 'to go'+*uṇ* suffix.
9. Cf. *Uṇādi sūtra* धान्ये नित् - 1.9. Note : This *sūtra* describes it to be '*nit*' so that it may be accented on the first syllable.
10. Cf. Pāṇ वोतोगुणवचनात् - 4.1.44.
11. Cf. Pāṇ ञ्नित्यादिर्नित्यम् - 6.1.197.

तना॑ (tanā)—According to Sāyaṇa, it is a particle meaning 'always' and being a particle, it carries accent on the first syllable. But according to Swami Dayananda, it is formed of Svadigaṇa root √tanu 'to expand'+an (Uṇādi suffix). In case of Swami Dayananda also, 'tanā', being formed of 'nit' suffix, gets accent on first syllable and would signify the 'expansion'.

पू॒तास॑: (pūtāsaḥ)—Nom. pl. of pūta. Krayādigaṇa root √puñ 'to purify'+kta. Here pl. ending -as (Pāṇ.-jas) is replaced by-āsas (Pāṇ. -asuk)[1]

Word meanings:

इन्द्र॑ (indra)—Address to Indra. God, electric force, solar winds, teacher2

आ (ā) —proximity, conjunction and simli[3].

या॒हि॒ (yāhi)—come[4]

चि॒त्र॒भा॒नो॒[1] (citrabhāno)—Address to Citrabhāno. Attributive

---

1. Primary suffix.
2. इन्द्रः पदनाम निघं० 5.4. इन्द्रः-इरां दृणातीति वा इरां ददातीति वा, इरां दधातीति वा। इरां दारयत इति वा। इरां धारयत इति वा। इन्दवे द्रवतीति वा। इन्दौ रमत इति वा। इन्धे भूतानीति वा। 'तद्यदेनं प्राणैः समैन्धंस्तदिन्द्रस्येन्द्रत्वमिति विज्ञायते।' इदं करणादित्याग्रायणः। इदं दर्शनादित्यौपमन्यवः। इन्दतेर्वैश्वर्यकर्मणः। इन्दञ्छत्रूणां दारयिता वा द्रावयिता वा। आदरयिता च यज्वनाम् नि० 10.8. एष वै शुक्रो य एष (सूर्यः) तपत्येष (सूर्यः) उ एवेन्द्रः श० 4.5.5.7, 4.59.4. अथ यः स इन्द्रोऽसौ स आदित्यः श० 8.53.2. यो वै वायुः स इन्द्रो य इन्द्रः स वायुः श० 4.1.3.19. स योऽयं मध्ये प्राणः। एष एवेन्द्रस्तानेष प्राणान्मध्यत इन्द्रियैणैन्द्ध तस्मादिन्ध इन्धो ह वै तमिन्द्र इत्याचक्षते परोऽक्षम् श० 6.1.1.2. हृदयमेवेन्द्रः श० 12.9.1.15. यन्मनः स इन्द्रः गो० उ० 4.11. मन एवेन्द्रः श० 12.9.1.13. इन्द्रो वै यजमानः श०2.1.2.11 क्षत्रियो यदु च यजमानः श० 5.3.5.27.एन्द्रो वै राजन्य तै० 3.8.23.2. इन्द्रः क्षत्रम् श०10.4.1 .5. वीर्यं वा इन्द्रः तां० 9.7.5, 8.इन्द्रो यज्ञस्य नेता श० 4.1.2.15.
3. अर्वागर्थे नि० 1.3. एतस्मिन्नेवार्थे (समुच्चयार्थे) देवेभ्यश्च पितृभ्य एत्याकारः नि० 1.4. उपमार्थे दृश्यते नि० 3.16. अध्यर्थे दृश्यते नि० 5.5.
4. याति गतिकर्मा निघं० 2.14.

of Indra. Of wonderful splendour .

सुताः[2] (sutāḥ)—offerings, expressed

इमे (ime)—these

त्वायवः (tvāyavaḥ)—for you

अण्वीभिः[3] (aṇvībhiḥ)—by all means, fingers, matter particles, charged particles, electric current

तना[4] (tanā)—always, expansion, food stuff, stuff of universe

पूतासः (pūtāsaḥ)—pure, fine tuned

Anvaya (Sequencial placement of words)

citrabhāno indra āyāhi ime aṇvībhiḥ sutā pūtāsaḥ tanā tvāyavaḥ.

Meaning of Mantra in different contexts :

Spiritual: (इन्द्र) O' Brahman! (चित्रभानो) of wonderful splendor (आयाहि), you reveal yourself to us. (इमे) These worlds (सुताः) created (अण्वीभिः) by matter particles (पूतासः) are fine tuned (त्वायवः) by you (तना) for life to flourish.

Scientific 1: (इन्द्र) O' electric force! (चित्रभानो) of wonderful splendor (त्वायवः) you (आयाहि) occupy the observer space. (इमे) These worlds (सुताः) created (अण्वीभिः) by matter particles (पूतासः) are fine tuned (तना) for life to flourish.

Note: electric force is exerted by the charged particles. This electric force help expansion of universe.

Scientific 2: (इन्द्र) O' solar radiation (चित्रभानो) of wonderful splendor! (त्वायवः) you (आयाहि) come to the earth. (इमे) These solar winds (सुताः) are filtered and (पूतासः) fine tuned by (तना) vast

---

1. भानुः-अहर्नाम निघं० 1.9.
2. सुतस्य अभिषुतस्य नि० 13.6. सुतेषु सोमेषु नि० 5.22. सुतः, सुतम् इत्यन्ननामनी निघं० 2.7.
3. अङ्गुलिभिः 20.87.। 'अण्व्यः' पठितम् निघं० 2.5.
4. तना धननाम निघं० 2.10.

magnetosphere of earth generated by (अण्वीभिः) electric currents caused by heat escaping from the core of the earth.

Socio-political: (इन्द्र) O' ruler or teacher (चित्रभानो) of wonderful splendor! (आयाहि), you should be approachable by public/students. (इमे) These (सुताः) people/students (पूतासः) pure at heart (तना) always need (त्वायवः) you (अण्वीभिः) by all means.

Note : The mantra says that the people or students are always in need for a good leader or a good guide/ Guru.

२३. इन्द्रायाहि धियेषितो विप्रंजूतः सुतावंतः।
उप ब्रह्माणि वाघतः।।५।।

इन्द्र। आ। याहि। धिया। इषितः। विप्रऽजूतः। सुतऽवंतः। उप।
ब्रह्माणि। वाघतः।।

Saṁhitāpāṭha

indrā-yāhi dhiyeṣito viprajūtaḥ sutāvataḥ. upa brahmāṇi vāghataḥ.

Padapāṭha

indra. āyāhi. dhiyā. iṣitaḥ. viprajūtaḥ. suta-vataḥ. upa. brahmāṇi. vāghataḥ.

Grammatical Notes:

इन्द्र (indra)—Voc. sing. of Indra. Bhvādigaṇa root √idi 'to prosper'+ran (Uṇādi suffix).[1] 'Nit' suffix (of which final 'n' is elided) makes it accented on the first syllable[2].

आ (ā)—A prefix meaning proximity, conjunction and simli. Being a prefix, it is accented on the first syllable[3].

याहि (yāhi)—Adādigaṇa root √yā 'to make reach'+loṭ lakāra second person sing. It, being a verbal form preceded by a non—verbal form, goes without accent.[4]

धिया (dhiyā) —Inst. sing. of dhīḥ. Bhvādigaṇa root √ dhyai 'to think'+kvip siffix[5]. Dhiyā gets accent on its suffix 'ā' as per Pāṇini सावेकाचस्तृतीयादविभक्तिः -6.1.168., since it is

---

1. Cf. *Uṇādi.* ऋज्रेन्द्राग्रवज्र० - 2.28.
2. Cf. Pāṇ. ञ्नित्यादिर्नित्यम् - 6.1.197
3. Cf. *Phiṭ sūtra*—उपसर्गाश्चाभिवर्जम् -81.
4. Cf. Pāṇ. तिङ्ङतिङः 8.1.28.
5. See Pāṇini—*dhyāyateḥ saṁprasāraṇaṁ ca*—3.2.178

monosyllabic when inflected in locative case.

इषितः (iṣitaḥ)—Divādigaṇa root √iṣa 'to go'+kta. [1] It carries accent on suffix, making iṣitaḥ accented on the final syllable.[2]

विप्रजूतः (viprajūtaḥ)—{Bhvādigaṇa root √vap 'to seed'+ran (Uṇādi suffix)[3]}+{Sautra root √jū 'to speed', 'to go'.[4]+kta[5]}. According to Pāṇini[6], a nominal stem ending with instrumental case suffix followed by a past passive participle, gets its natural accent on first member and the first member 'vipra' is accented on the first syllable being formed of 'nit' suffix.

सुतावतः (suta—vataḥ)—Gen. sing. of sutavān. Svādigaṇa root √suñ 'to squeeze', 'to press'+kta (Uṇādi suffix)+matup. Matup, being pit remains unaccented [7], under the circumstances, suffixal accent on suffix—kta prevails.

उप (upa)—A prefix meaning closeness. Being a prefix, it is accented on the first syllable.[8]

ब्रह्माणि (brahmāṇi)—Nom. pl. of Brahma. Bhvādigaṇa root √bṛhi 'to increase'+manin (Uṇādi suffix).[9] It is accented on the first syllable.[10]

वाघतः (vāghataḥ)—Nom. pl. of vāghat. It is accented on

---

1. Cf. Pāṇ क्तक्तवतु निष्ठा - 1.1.26.
2. Cf. Pāṇ आद्युदात्तश्च - 3.1.3.
3. Cf. *Uṇādi sūtra* - ऋज्रेन्द्राग्रवज्रविप्र० - 2.186.
4. Cf. Pāṇ जुचङ्क्रम्यदन्द्रम्यसृगृधिज्वलशुचलषपतपदः - 3.2.150.
5. Past passive participle.
6. See तृतीया कर्मणि - 6.2.48.
7. Cf. Pāṇ अनुदात्तौ सुप्पितौ - 3.1.4.
8. Cf. *Phiṭ sūtra*—उपसर्गश्चाभिवर्जम् - 81.
9. Cf. Pāṇ बृंहेर्नोऽच्च - 4.146.
10. Cf. *Phiṭ sūtra* नब्विषयस्यानिसन्तस्य - 26.

nominal stem.[1] Its derivation is not known to the ancient commentators. This word is difficult to be derived with known material of Pāṇinian system of grammar.

Word meanings:

इन्द्र[2] (indra)—God, electric force of universe, solar winds, king, teacher

आ[3] (ā) —proximity, conjunction and simli.

याहि[4] (yāhi) —be accesible

धिया[5] (dhiyā)—by actions, charged particles, pure knowledge

इषितः (iṣitaḥ)—attainable

विप्रजूतः (viprajūtaḥ)—scholars, scientists

सुतावतः (sutā-vataḥ)—experts of material sciecnes, charged

---

1. See Sāyaṇa *RV.* 1.3.5.
2. इन्द्रः पदनाम निघं० 5.4. इन्द्रः-इरां दृणातीति वा इरां ददातीति वा, इरां दधातीति वा। इरां दारयत इति वा। इरां धारयत इति वा। इन्दवे द्रवतीति वा। इन्दौ रमत इति वा। इन्धे भूतानीति वा। 'तद्यदेनं प्राणैः समैन्धंस्तदिन्द्रस्येन्द्रत्वमिति विज्ञायते।' इदं करणादित्याग्रायणः। इदं दर्शनादित्यौपमन्यवः। इन्दतेर्वैश्वर्यकर्मणः। इन्दञ्छत्रूणां दारयिता वा द्रावयिता वा। आदरयिता च यज्वनाम् नि० 10.8. एष वै शुक्रो य एष (सूर्यः) तपत्येष (सूर्यः) उ एवेन्द्रः श० 4.5.5.7, 4.5.9.4. अथ यः स इन्द्रोऽसौ स आदित्यः श० 8.53.2. यो वै वायुः स इन्द्रो य इन्द्रः स वायुः श० 4.1.3.19. स योऽयं मध्ये प्राणः। एष एवेन्द्रस्तानेष प्राणान्मध्यत इन्द्रियैणैन्द्ध तस्मादिन्ध इन्धो ह वै तमिन्द्र इत्याचक्षते परोऽक्षम् श० 6.1.1.2. हृदयमेवेन्द्रः श० 12.9.1.15. यन्मनः स इन्द्रः गो० उ० 4.11. मन एवेन्द्रः श० 12.9.1.13. इन्द्रो वै यजमानः श०2.1.2.11 क्षत्रियो यदु च यजमानः श० 5.3.5.27. एन्द्रो वै राजन्य तै० 3.8.23.2. इन्द्रः क्षत्रम् श०10.4. 1.5. वीर्यं वा इन्द्रः तां० 9.7.5,8. इन्द्रो यज्ञस्य नेता श० 4.1.2.15.
3. अर्वागर्थे नि० 1.3. एतस्मिन्नेवार्थे (समुच्चयार्थे) देवेभ्यश्च पितृभ्य एत्याकारः नि० 1.4. उपमार्थे दृश्यते नि० 3.16. अध्यर्थे दृश्यते नि० 5.5.
4. याति गतिकर्मा निघं० 2.14.
5. धीः कर्मनाम निघं० 2.1. प्रज्ञानाम निघं० 3.9. धियः-प्रज्ञानानि नि० 11.27.

particles

उप॑[1] (upa)—close

ब्रह्मा॑णि[2] (brahmāṇi)—knowers of Vedas

वा॒घतः॑ [3] (vāghataḥ)— experts of the science of Yajña intellectuals, spiritualists

Anvaya (Sequencial placement of words)

indra dhiyeṣito viprajūtaḥ sutāvataḥ brahmāṇi vāghataḥ upa āyāhi.

Meaning of Mantra in different contexts :

Spiritual : (इन्द्र) O' Brahman, you are (इषितः) attainable (धिया) by good actions and pure knowledge. (आ याहि) You are accessible (ब्रह्माणि) to knower of Vedas, (विप्रजूतः) scholars, (वाघतः) spiritualists/intellectuals (सुतावतः) and experts of the science of Yajña.

Scientific 1: (इन्द्र) O' electricity! (ब्रह्माणि) the knower of Vedas, (विप्रजूतः) scholars, (वाघतः) experts in the science of yajña (सुतावतः) and experts of material sciences (इषितः) have liking for you. (आ याहि) You are produced by them (धिया) by various actions and knowledge.

Scientific 2: (इन्द्र) O' electric force of universe, you are (इषितः) generated (धिया) by charged particles (आ याहि) You are known by (ब्रह्माणि) the knower of Vedas, (विप्रजूतः) scholars, (वाघतः) experts in the science of yajña (सुतावतः) and experts of material sciences.

Socio-political 1: (इन्द्र) O' ruler! you are (इषितः) liked by

1. उप इत्युपजनम् नि० 1.3. इयं (पृथिवी) वा ऽउप श० 2.3.4.9. उप वै रथन्तरम् तां० 16.5.14.
2. ब्रह्म उदकनाम निघं 1.12. अन्ननाम निघं० 2.7. धननाम निघं० 2.10. ब्रह्मा सर्वविद्यः सर्वं वेदितुमर्हति। ब्रह्मा परिवृढः श्रुततो ब्रह्मा परिवृढं सर्वतः नि० 1.8. ब्रह्माणि कर्माणि नि० 12.34.
3. वाघतः मेधाविनाम निघं० 3.15. ऋत्विङ्नाम निघं० 3.18. वाघतः वोढारो मेधाविनो वा नि० 11.16.

(ब्रह्माणि) the knower of Vedas, (विप्रजूत:) scholars, (वाघत:) experts in the science of yajña (सुतावत:) and experts of material sciences. (आ याहि) You become accessible to them (धिया) by various means.

Socio-political 2: (इन्द्र) O' teacher! you are (इषित:) liked by those (ब्रह्माणि) who want to know the Vedas, (विप्रजूत:) want to become scholars, (वाघत:) want to be experts in the science of yajña (सुतावत:) and experts of material sciences. (आ याहि) You become accessible to them (धिया) by your action.

Note: Vedas directs the kings and teachers to be easily accessible to scholars, scientists and spriritualists.

२४. इन्द्रायाहि तूतुजान उप ब्रह्माणि हरिवः।
सुते दधिष्व नश्चनः।।६।।

इन्द्र। आ। याहि। तूतुजानः। उप। ब्रह्माणि। हरिवः। सुते।
दधिष्व। नः। चनः।।

Saṁhitāpāṭha

indra āyāhi tūtujāna upa brahmāṇi harivaḥ. sute dadhiṣ va naś-canaḥ.

Padapāṭha

indra. ā. yāhi. tūtujāna. upa. brahmāṇi. harivaḥ. sute. dadhiṣva. naḥ. canaḥ.

Grammatical Notes:

इन्द्र (indra)—Voc. sing. of Indra. Bhvādigaṇa root √idi 'to prosper'+ran (Uṇādi suffix).[1] 'Nit' suffix (of which final 'n' is elided) makes it accented on the first syllable[2].

आ (ā)—A prefix meaning proximity, conjunction and simli. Being a prefix, it is accented on the first syllable[3].

याहि (yāhi)—Adādigaṇa root √yā 'to make reach'+loṭ lakāra second person sing. It, being a verbal form preceded by a non-verbal form, goes without accent.[4]

तूतुजानः (tūtujāna)—Bhvādigaṇa root √tuja 'violence'+kānac suffix [5] (past perfect participle) added to the perfect

1. Cf. *Uṇādi.* ऋज्रेन्द्राग्रवज्र० - 2.28.
2. Cf. Pāṇ. ञ्नित्यादिर्नित्यम् - 6.1.197
3. Cf. *Phiṭ sūtra*—उपसर्गाश्चाभिवर्जम् -81.
4. Cf. Pāṇ. तिङ्ङतिङः 8.1.28.
5. Cf. Pāṇ लिटः कानज्वा - 3.2.106.

stem of the root. Being reduplicated [1], it is accented on the first syllable.[2]

उप (upa)—A prefix meaning closeness. Being a prefix, it is accented on the first syllable.[3]

ब्रह्माणि (brahmāṇi)—Nom. pl. of Brahma. Bhvādigaṇa root √bṛhi 'to increase'+manin (Uṇādi suffix).[4] It is accented on the first syllable.[5]

हरिवः (harivaḥ)—Voc. sing. of hariva. 'Hari+matup'. Here 'm' of matup is replaced by vatup[6] making it Harivan. Final 'n' of Harivan is substituted by 'ru'>'r'[7] and 'r' becomes voiceless spirtant (:). Being a a voc. case not located in beginning of a hemistich, it remains un—accented.[8]

सुते (sute)—Nom. dual of suta. Svādigaṇa root√ṣu 'to squeez' 'to press' or Bhvādigaṇa root √ṣu 'to deliver' 'to prosper'+kta (primary suffix)[9] or kta (Uṇādi suffix). It gets acute accent on suffix, so accented in the last syllable.[10]

दधिष्व (dadhiṣva)—Juhotyādigaṇa root √ dhāñ 'to sustain', 'to bring up'+loṭ lakāra (imperative) second person sing. Here second person ending '—thas' transforms

1. See Pāṇ तुजादीनां दीर्घोऽभ्यासस्य - 6.1.7.
2. Cf. Pāṇ अभ्यस्तानामादिः - 6.1.189.
3. Cf. *Phiṭ sūtra*—उपसर्गश्चाभिवर्जम् - 81.
4. Cf. Pāṇ बृहेर्नोऽच्च - 4.146.
5. Cf. *Phiṭ sūtra* नब्विषयस्यानिसन्तस्य - 26.
6. Cf. Pāṇ. छन्दसीरः।
7. Cf. Pāṇ. मतुवसो रु संबुद्धौ छन्दसि - 8.3.1.
8. Cf. Pāṇ. आमन्त्रितस्य च० 8.1.19.
9. Cf. Pāṇ. क्तक्तवतु निष्ठा -1.1.26
10. Cf. Pāṇ. आद्युदात्तश्च - 3.1.3

into '-se'[1] and final 'e' of '-se' becomes 'va'[2] leading the formation as 'dadhiṣva' in place 'dadhithaḥ' or 'dadhiṣe'. It, being a verbal form preceded by a non-verbal form, remains un-accented.[3]

नः (naḥ)—Acc./dat./gen. pl. enclitic form of first person pronoun 'Asmad'[4]. Being an enclitic form it is not accented.[5]

चनः (canaḥ)—Bhādigaṇa root √cāyṛ 'to worship'+asun (Uṇādi suffix).[6] Being formed of 'nit' suffix, it is accented on the first syllable.[7]

Word meanings:

इन्द्र[8] (indra)—Address to Indra. Brahman, mind, electric force, solar winds, teacher, king

---

1. Cf. Pāṇ. थासः से - 3.4.80.
2. Cf. Pāṇ. सवाभ्यां वामौ - 3.4.91.
3. Cf. Pāṇ. तिङ्ङतिङः - 8.1.28.
4. Cf. *vahuvacanasyavasnasau*—Pāṇ. 8.1.21.
5. Cf. Pāṇ. युस्मदस्मदोः षष्ठी चतुर्थी द्वितीया स्थयोर्वान्नावौ 8.1.20.
6. Cf. *Unādi sūtra* चायते रन्ने ह्रस्वश्च - 4.201.
7. Cf. Pāṇ. ञ्नित्यादिर्नित्यम् - 6.1.197.
8. इन्द्रः पदनाम निघं० 5.4. इन्द्रः-इरां दृणातीति वा इरां ददातीति वा, इरां दधातीति वा। इरां दारयत इति वा। इरां धारयत इति वा। इन्दवे द्रवतीति वा। इन्दौ रमत इति वा। इन्धे भूतानीति वा। 'तद्यदेनं प्राणैः समैन्धंस्तदिन्द्रस्येन्द्रत्वमिति विज्ञायते।' इदं करणादित्याग्रायणः। इदं दर्शनादित्यौपमन्यवः। इन्दतेर्वैश्वर्यकर्मणः। इन्दञ्छत्रूणां दारयिता वा द्रावयिता वा। आदरयिता च यज्वनाम् नि० 10.8. एष वै शुक्रो य एष (सूर्यः) तपत्येष (सूर्यः) उ एवेन्द्रः श० 4.5.5.7, 4.5.9.4. अथ यः स इन्द्रोऽसौ स आदित्यः श० 8.5.3.2. यो वै वायुः स इन्द्रो य इन्द्रः स वायुः श० 4.1.3.19. स योऽयं मध्ये प्राणः। एष एवेन्द्रस्तानेष प्राणान्मध्यत इन्द्रियैणैन्द्ध तस्मादिन्ध इन्धो ह वै तमिन्द्र इत्याचक्षते परोऽक्षम् श० 6.1.1.2. हृदयमेवेन्द्रः श० 12.9.1.15. यन्मनः स इन्द्रः गो० उ० 4.11. मन एवेन्द्रः श० 12.9.1.13. इन्द्रो वै यजमानः श०2.1.2.11 क्षत्रियो यदु च यजमानः श० 5.3.5.27. एन्द्रो वै राजन्य तै० 3.8.23.2. इन्द्रः क्षत्रम् श० 10. 4.1.5. वीर्यं वा इन्द्रः तां० 9.7.5, 8. इन्द्रो यज्ञस्य नेता श० 4.1.2.15.

आ[1] (ā) —proximity, conjunction and simli

याहि[2] (yāhi) —come

तूतुजानः[3] (tūtujāna)—quickly

उप[4] (upa)—close

ब्रह्माणि[5] (brahmāṇi)—praise, prayers, stotra

हरिवः (harivaḥ)—Address to Hariva. sun, possessed of rays

सुते[6] (sute)—charged particles, food stuff

दधिष्व[7] (dadhiṣva)—receive, hold, accept, attend

नः (naḥ)—to us, our, for us

चनः[8] (canaḥ)—oblations, electric force, food stuff, mass energy

Anvaya (Sequencial placement of words)

harivaḥ indra brahmāṇi upa āyāhi tūtujāna sute naḥ canaḥ dadhiṣva.

Meaning of Mantra in different contexts :

---

1. अर्वागर्थे नि० 1.3. एतस्मिन्नेवार्थे (समुच्चयार्थे) देवेभ्यश्च पितृभ्य एत्याकारः नि० 1.4. उपमार्थे दृश्यते नि० 3.16. अध्यर्थे दृश्यते नि० 5.5.
2. याति गतिकर्मा निघं० 2.14.
3. तूतुजानः क्षिप्रनाम निघं० 2.15. तूतुजानः त्वरमाणः नि० 6.20.
4. उप इत्युपजनम् नि० 1.3. इयं (पृथिवी) वा ऽउप श० 2.3.4.9. उप वै रथन्तरम् तां० 16.5.14.
5. ब्रह्म उदकनाम निघं 1.12. अन्ननाम निघं० 2.7. धननाम निघं० 2.10. ब्रह्मा सर्वविद्यः सर्वं वेदितुर्महति। ब्रह्मा परिवृढः श्रुतुतो ब्रह्मा परिवृढं सर्वतः नि० 1.8. ब्रह्माणि कर्माणि नि० 12.34.
6. सुतस्य अभिषुतस्य नि० 13.6. सुतेषु सोमेषु नि० 5.22. सुतः, सुतम् इत्यन्ननामनी निघं० 2.7.
7. दधिषे धत्सव निघं० 5.25.
8. चनः अन्ननाम नि० 6.15.

Scientific: (इन्द्र) O' electric force! (हरिवः) possessed of aśva particle (उप आयाहि) get generated in the observer space (तुतुजानः) quickly (दधिष्व) to receive (नः) our (ब्रह्माणि) praise. (चनः) Electric force acts (सुते) between electrically charged particles.

Note: Electric force depend upon the magnitude of electric charge. Greater the charge, larger the force. In other words, it can be said that electric force can act between the electrically charged particles only. Aśva is a electrically charged particle (quark), so Indra is called as possessed of aśvas. Some other mantras call soma as the semen of strong aśva particle which explicitly points out that electric charge is distributed all over the aśva particles. Electric force work against the contraction and helps the expansion of the universe.

After dealing Agni, energy of observer space, Vayu, energy of the intermediate space is also dealt with. Vāyu in fact, acted as an interface between light space and observer space during the origin of observer space from light space. Indra, the electric force that helped the expansion of the observer space after its origin from light space was dealt with susequently. Meantime Vāyu-Indra and Indra-Vāyu as dual deities are also described keeping in view of their combine role in the origin and expansion of the observer space from light space. All other deities located between observer space and light space have been mentioned as Viśvedevāḥ. The Devatā (subject matter) of below given three mantras is Viśvedevāḥ. In spiritual sense, Viśvedevāḥ represents all life energies and sense organs. In scientific sense, they represent, matter particles born of energy as its condensed from. In scientific sense, all celestial bodies are Viśvedevāḥ. In Socio-political sense, all scholars are known as Viśvedevāḥ.

२५. ओमासश्चर्षणीधृतो विश्वे देवास आ गत।

दाश्वांसो दाशुषः सुतम्।।७।।

ओमासः। चर्षणिऽधृतः। विश्वे। देवासः। आ। गत। दाश्वांसः।
दाशुषः। सुतम्।।

Saṁhitāpāṭha

omāsaś-carṣaṇī-dhṛto viśve-devāsa āgata. dāśvānso dāśuṣaḥ sutam.

Padapāṭha

omāsaḥ. carṣaṇī-dhṛtaḥ. viśve. devāsaḥ. ā.gata. dāśvānsaḥ. dāśuṣaḥ. sutam.

Grammatical Notes:

ओमासः (omāsaḥ)—Voc. pl. masc. of Oma. Bhvādigaṇa

root √ava 'to protect'+man Unādi suffix.[1] Here the normal pl. ending-as (or Pāṇ.-jas) is replaced by '-āsas' (or Pāṇ-asuk).[2] Being a voc. form in the beginning of the hemistich, it is accented on the initial syllable.[3]

चर्षणीधृतः (carṣaṇī-dhṛtaḥ)—Voc. pl. masc. of carṣṇīdhṛta. {Bhvādigaṇa root √kṛṣa 'to plough'+ani (Uṇādi suffix)[4]}+{Bhvādigaṇa root √dhṛñ 'to sustain'+kvip}. Being a voc. form not located in the beginning of a hemistich, it goes without accent.[5]

विश्वे (viśve)—Voc. pl. of viśva. Tudādigaṇa root √viśa 'to enter'+kvan (Uṇādi suffix).[6] It is accented on the first syllable, being a voc. form located in the beginning of hemistich.[7] It will also be accented on the initial syllable. It will also be accented on the first syllable, being formed of 'nit' suffix.

देवासः (devāsaḥ)—Acc. sing. of deva. Divādigaṇa root √div 'to play', 'desire to win', 'to deal with', 'to illuminate', 'to glorify', 'to be happy', 'to be intoxicated', 'to sleep', to shine' and 'to go' or Curādigaṇa root √div 'to crush', 'to chirp'+ac suffix[8]. Here the normal pl.

---

1. Cf. *Uṇādi sūtra* अविसिविसिशुषिभ्यः कित् - 1.144.
2. Cf. Pāṇ. आज्जेसरसुक् - 7.1.50.
3. Cf. Pāṇ. आमन्त्रितस्य च० - 6.1.198.
4. The word *carṣṇi* cannot be derived with help of any rule given in Pāṇinian system of grammar. But it can be formed with *-ani* suffix added after root √*kṛṣa*. *Uṇādi sūtra*—कृषेरादेश्च घः -2.106 forms a word '*dharṣaṇī*' from root √*kṛṣa* substituting initial '*k*' by '*dh*'. Similarly, we can regularlise this peculiar form '*carṣaṇī*' with the help of a new supplementry formula—कृषेरादेश्च चः added after *Unādi Sūtra* 1.106.
5. Cf. Pāṇ. आमन्त्रितस्य च०-8.1.19.
6. Cf. *Uṇādi sūtra* अशुप्रुषिलिटि कणि० - 1.151.
7. Cf. Pāṇ. आमन्त्रितस्य च० 6.1.198.
8. Cf. Pāṇ. नन्दिग्रहिपचादिभ्यो ल्यु-णिनि-अचः - 3.1.134

ending -as (Pāṇ -jas) is substituted with -asas (Pāṇ -asuk).[1] Being a voc. form not located in the beginning of a hemistich, it goes without accent.[2]

आ (ā)—A prefix meaning proximity, conjunction and simli. Being a prefix, it is accented on the first syllable[3].

ग॒त॒ (gata)—Bhvādigaṇa root √gam 'to go'+loṭ lakār second person pl. Being a verbal form preceded by a non—verbal form, it goes without accent.[4]

दा॒श्वांसः॑ (dāśvānsaḥ)—Nom. pl. of dāśvān. Bhvādigaṇa root √dāśṛ 'to donate'+kvasu suffix (past perfect particple) added to the perfect stem of the root.[5] It is accented on the suffix.[6]

दा॒शुषः॑ (dāśuṣaḥ)—Nom. pl. of dāśuṣa. Bhvādigaṇa root √dāśṛ 'to donate'+kvasu suffix (past perfect participle) added to the perfect stem of the root.[7] As per Pāṇini-vasoḥ saṁprasāraṇam[8] 'dāś+vas+śas' becomes 'daśuṣ ah'. It is also accented on the suffix. Note : dāśvāṅsaḥ and dāśuṣaḥ are one and the same form wearing different looks .

सु॒तम् (sutam)—Acc. sing. of suta. Svādigaṇa root √ṣu 'to squeez' 'to press' orBhvādigaṇa root √ṣu 'to deliver' 'to prosper'+kta (primary suffix) [9]or kta (Uṇādi suffix). Its Its gets acute accent on suffix, so accented on the last

---

1. Cf. Pāṇ. आज्जसेरसुक् - 7.1.50.
2. Cf. Pāṇ. आमन्त्रितस्य च० 8.1.19.
3. Cf. *Phiṭ sūtra*—उपसर्गाश्चाभिवर्जम् -81.
4. Cf. Pāṇ. तिङ्ङतिङः - 8.1.28.
5. Cf. Pāṇ. क्वसुश्च - 3.2.107.
6. Cf. Pāṇ. आद्युदात्तश्च - 3.1.3.
7. Cf. Pāṇ. क्वसुश्च - 3.2.107.
8. 6.4.131.
9. Cf. Pāṇ. क्तक्तवतु निष्ठा -1.1.26

syllable.[1]

Word meanings:

ओमा॑सः[2] (omāsaḥ)—Address to Om. Life energies, charged particles, technical term used in the process of creation.

च॒र्ष॒णी॒धृ॒तः[3] (carṣaṇī-dhṛtaḥ)—Address to Carṣaṇīdhṛta. Protection

विश्वे॑[4] (viśve) —Address to Viśva. All

दे॒वा॒सः[5] (devāsaḥ)—life energies, matter particles, luminary

---

1. Cf. Pāṇ. आद्युदात्तश्च - 3.1.3
2. ओमासः पदनाम निघं० 4.3. ओमासः अवितारो वा ऽवनीया वा नि० 12.40
3. चर्षणिधृतः-मनुष्यधृतः नि० 12.40.
4. यद्वै विश्वं सर्व तत् श० 3.1.2.11. तदन्नं वै विश्वम्प्राणो मित्रम् जै० उ० 3.3.6
5. देवो दानाद्वा, दीपनाद्वा, द्योतनाद्वा, द्युस्थानो भवतीति वा। यो देवः स देवता निघं० 7.15. दिवा वै नोऽभूदिति। तद् देवानां देवत्वम् तै० 2.2.9.9. दिवा देवानसृजत नक्तमसुरान् यद्दिवा देवानसृजत तद् देवानां देवत्वम् ष० 4.1. तद् देवानां देवत्वं यद् दिवसमभिपद्यासृज्यन्त श० 11.1.6.7. प्राचीनप्रजनना वै देवाः प्रतीचीनप्रजनना मनुष्याः श० 7.4.2.40. प्राची हि देवानां दिक् श० 1.2.5.17. देवानां वा एषा दिग्यत्प्राची ष० 3.1. यद्वै मनुष्याणां प्रत्यक्षन्तद् देवानां परोक्षमथ यन्मनुष्याणां परोक्षन्तद् देवानां प्रत्यक्षम् तां० 22.10.3. द्राघीयो हि देवायुषं ह्रसीयो मनुष्यायुषम् श० 7.3.1.10. देवानां वै विधामनु मनुष्याः श० 6.7.4.9. त्रयो वै देवाः। वसवो रुद्रा आदित्याः श० 4.3.5.1. एते वै त्रयो देवा यद् वसवो रुद्रा आदित्याः श० 1.3.4.12., 1.5.1.17., 1.8.3.8. त्रयस्त्रिंशद् देवताः तां० 4.4.11. त्रयस्त्रिंशद्वै देवताः तै० 1.2.2.5., 1.8.7.1., 2.7.1.3-4. त्रयस्त्रिंशद्वै सर्वा देवताः कौ० 8.6. त्रयस्त्रिंशद्वै देवाः प्रजापतिश्चतुस्त्रिंशः श० 12.6.1.37. अग्निर्वायुरादित्य एतानि ह तानि देवानां हृदयानि श० 9.1.1.23. अग्निर्वै देवानामवमो विष्णुः परमस्तदन्तरेण सर्वा अन्या देवताः ऐ० 1.1. तद्यदेतस्मिन्नाके स्वर्गे लोके देवाअसीदंस्तस्माद्देवा नाकसदः श० 8.6.1.1. द्यौर्वै सर्वेषां, देवानामायतनम् श० 14.3.2.4. देवगृहा वै नक्षत्राणि तै० 15.2.6. नरो वै देवानां ग्रामः तां० 6.9.2. यो वै देवानामात्मा श० 9. 3.2.7. सर्वेषां वाऽएष भूतानां सर्वेषां देवानामात्मा यद् यज्ञः श० 14.3.2.1. विद्वांसो हि देवाः श०3.7.3.10.। तस्मात् प्राणा देवाः, श० 7.5.1.21. प्राणा देवाः श० 6.3.1.15. चक्षुर्देवः गो०पू० 2.11. मनो देवः गो० पू० 2.10. मनो वै देववाहनं मनो हीदं मनस्विनं भूयिष्ठं वनीवा ह्यते श० 1.4.3.6. वाक् च वै मनश्च देवानां मिथुनम् ऐ० 5.23. वागेव देवाः श० 14.4.3.1 3.

bodies, scholars

आ[1] (ā)—proximity, conjunction and simli.

ग॒त॒ (gata)—come

दा॒श्वांसः (dāśvānsaḥ)—persons, observer space, living beings[2]

दा॒शुषः[3] (dāśuṣaḥ)—human beings, universe

सु॒तम्[4] (sutam)—condensed form, elevated

Anvaya (Sequencial placement of words)

viśvedevāsa āgata dāśuṣaḥ sutam. omāsaḥ carṣaṇīdhṛto dāśvānsaḥ.

Meaning of Mantra in different contexts :

वाग्देवः गो० पू० 2.10. वाग्वै देवानां पुरान्नमासीत् तै० 1.3.5.1. वागिति सर्वे देवाः जै०उ० 1. 9.2. वायुर्वै देवः जै० उ० 3.4.8.। यशो देवाः श० 2.1.4.9. तस्माद् (देवाः) यशः श० 3.4. 2.8. देवा वै यशस्कामाः सत्रमासत तां० 7.5.6. परोक्षकामा हि देवाः श०6.1.1.2., 7.4.1.10., परोक्षप्रिया इव हि देवा भवन्ति प्रत्यक्षद्विषः गो० पू० 2.21. यदु ह किं च देवाः कुर्वते स्तोमेनैव तत्कुर्वते यज्ञो वै स्तोमो यज्ञेनैव तत्कुर्वते श० 8.4.3.2. मनो ह वै देवा मनुष्यस्याजानन्ति श० 2.1.4.1., 2.4.1.11. मनो देवा मनुष्यस्याजानन्ति श० 3.4.2.6. सत्यमेवदेवा अनृतं मनुष्याः श० 1.1.1.4. यज्ञेन वै तद्देवा यज्ञमयजन्त यदग्निनाऽग्निमयजन्त ते स्वर्गं लोकमायन् ऐ० 1.16. अग्निर्वै देवानां होता ऐ० 1.28., 3.14. अग्निरेव देवानां दूत आस श० 3.5.1.21. वरुणो वै देवानां राजा श० 12.8.3.10. तस्मादाहुर्विष्णुर्देवानां श्रेष्ठ इति श०14.1.1.5. रुद्रो वै ज्येष्ठश्च श्रेष्ठश्च देवानाम् कौ० 25.13. अन्नमु देवानां सोमः जै० 3.174. दिवा वै मनुष्या यज्ञेन चरन्ति नक्तं देवाः मै० 4.5.1.

1. अर्वागर्थे नि० 1.3. एतस्मिन्नेवार्थे (समुच्चयार्थे) देवेभ्यश्च पितृभ्य एत्याकारः नि० 1.4. उपमार्थे दृश्यते नि० 3.16. अध्यर्थे दृश्यते नि० 5.5.
2. दाश्वांसः दत्तवन्तः नि० 12.40. यजमानो वै दाश्वान् श० 2.3.4.38.
3. दाशुषे दत्तवते नि० 11.11.
4. सुतस्य अभिषुतस्य नि० 13.6. सुतेषु सोमेषु नि० 5.22. सुतः, सुतम् इत्यन्ननामनी निघं० 2.7.

Spiritual: (विश्वेदेवासः) All life energies (आगत) reach (दाश्वांसः) human beings (दाशुषः) to give them (सुतम्) power. They are (ओमासः) protectors and (चर्षणिधृतः) sustainer of human beings.

Scientific 1: (विश्वेदेवासः) All matter particles (आगत) come to this observer space (दाशुषः) to give it (सुतम्) power. These charged particles are (ओमासः) the protector and (चर्षणिधृतः) sustainer of our universe.

Scientific 2: (विश्वेदेवासः) All celestial bodies (आगत) reach us through the light reflected by them. They (दाशुषः) give (दाश्वांसः) living beings (सुतम्) life energies and (ओमासः) act as protective shields and (चर्षणिधृतः) and help sustenance of life on the earth.

Socio-political 1: (विश्वेदेवासः) All scholars (आगत) should come forward (दाशुषः) to give (सुतम्) knowledge to (दाश्वांसः) people in the nation. They are (ओमासः) the custodian of (चर्षणिधृतः) and sustainer of humanity.

२६. विश्वे॑ दे॒वासो॑ अ॒प्तुर॑: सु॒तमा ग॑न्त॒ तूर्ण॑यः।
उ॒स्रा इ॑व॒ स्वस॑राणि॥८॥

विश्वे॑। दे॒वास॑:। अ॒प्तुर॑:। सु॒तम्। आ। ग॒न्त॒। तूर्ण॑यः।
उ॒स्राःऽइ॑व। स्वस॑राणि॥

Saṁhitāpāṭha

viśve devāso apturaḥ sutam āganata tūrṇayaḥ. usrā iva svasarāṇi.

Padapāṭha

viśve. devāsaḥ. apturaḥ. sutam. ā. ganata. tūrṇayaḥ. usrāḥ-iva. svasarāṇi.

Grammatical Notes:

विश्वे[1] (viśve)—Voc. pl. of viśva. Tudādigaṇa root √viśa 'to enter'+kvan (Uṇādi suffix).[2] It is accented on the first syllable, being a voc. form located in the beginning of hemistich.[3] It will also be accented on the initial syllable, being formed of 'nit' suffix.

दे॒वा॒सः (devāsaḥ)—Voc. pl. of deva. Acc. pl. nominal suffix -jas is replaced by -asuk.[4] Divādigaṇa root √ div 'to play', 'desire to win', 'to deal with', 'to illuminate', 'to glorify', 'to be happy', 'to be intoxicated', 'to sleep', to shine' and 'to go' or Curādigaṇa root √div 'to crush', 'to chirp'+ac suffix[5]. Being a voc. form not located in the beginning of a hemistich, it loses its

1. यद्वै विश्वं सर्वं तत् श० 3.1.2.11. तदन्नं वै विश्वम्प्राणो मित्रम् जै० उ० 3.3.6.
2. Cf. *Uṇādi sūtra* अशुप्रुषिलिटि कणि० - 1.151.
3. Cf. Pāṇ. आमन्त्रितस्य च० 6.1.198.
4. Cf. Pāṇ. आज्जसेरसुक् - 7.1.50
5. Cf. Pāṇ. नन्द्ग्रहिपचादिभ्यो ल्यु-णिनि-अचः - 3.1.134

accent.[1]

अप्तुरः (apturaḥ) —Apa+Juhotyādigaṇa root √tura 'to hasten'+kvip suffix [2]. It will receive accent on the second member, first member being a prefix.[3]

सुतम् (sutam)—Acc. sing. of suta. Svādigaṇa root √ ṣu 'to squeez' 'to press' orBhvādigaṇa root √ṣu 'to deliver' 'to prosper'+kta (primary suffix) [4]or kta (Uṇādi suffix). Its gets acute accent on suffix, as such acented on the last syllable.[5]

आ (ā)—A prefix meaning proximity, conjunction and simli. Being a prefix, it is accented on the first syllable[6].

गन्त (ganata)—Bhvādigaṇa root √gam 'to go'+loṭ lakāra second person pl. It, being a verbal form preceded by a non-verbal form, goes without accent.[7]

तूर्णयः (tūrṇayaḥ)—Bhvādigaṇa root √ñtvirā 'to be in confusion'+niḥ (Uṇādi suffix) [8]. 'Tva' of 'tvira' transforms into 'tu'[9]. Being formed of 'ñit' suffix, it is accented on the first syllable.

उस्रा इव (usrāḥ-iva)—Bhvādigaṇa root √vas 'to dwell'+rak (Uṇādi suffix) [10] +iva. As per rules of accentuation, when a nominal stem is compounded with iva, it retains

---

1. Cf. Pāṇ. आमन्त्रितस्य च० 6.1.198
2. Cf. Pāṇ. क्विप् च - 3.2.76
3. Cf. Pāṇ. गतिकारकोपपदात्कृत् - 6.2.139
4. Cf. Pāṇ. क्तक्तवतु निष्ठा -1.1.26
5. Cf. Pāṇ. आद्युदात्तश्च - 3.1.3
6. Cf. *Phiṭ sūtra*—उपसर्गाश्चाभिवर्जम् -81.
7. Cf. Pāṇ. तिङ्ङतिङः - 8.1.28
8. Cf. *Uṇādi sūtra*—वहिश्रिश्रुयुद्रुग्लाहात्वरिभ्यो नित् - 4.51.
9. Cf. Pāṇ. ज्वरत्वर० - 6.4.20
10. Cf. *Uṇādi sūtra*—ज्वरत्वर० - 6.4.20

its case ending and carries its accent [1].

स्वसराणि (svasarāṇi)—Bahuvrīhi compound of sva+sarāṇi (Bhvādigaṇa root √sṛ 'to move'+ac suffix[2]). Being a Bahuvrīhi compound, it carries the natural accent on the first member. The first member, sva, being a particle, is accented on the first syllable[3].

Word meanings:

विश्वे (viśve)—Address to Viśva,i.e all

यद्वै विश्वं सर्व तत् श० 3.1.2.11. तदन्नं वै विश्वम्प्राणो मित्रम् जै० उ० 3.3.6.।

देवासः[4] (devāsaḥ)—Address to devas. Life energies, matter

---

1. Cf. *Vārttika* No. 2 in Mahābhāṣya—इवेन विभक्त्यलोपः पूर्वपदप्रकृतिस्वरत्वं च- on Pāṇ. 2.1.4
2. Cf. Pāṇ. नन्दीग्रहिपचादिभ्यो ल्युणिन्यचः - 3.1.134
3. Cf. *Phiṭ sūtra*—निपाता आद्युदात्ताः - 80
4. देवो दानाद्वा, दीपनाद्वा, द्योतनाद्वा, द्युस्थानो भवतीति वा। यो देवः स देवता निघं० 7.15. दिवा वै नोऽभूदिति। तद् देवानां देवत्वम् तै० 2.2.9.9. दिवा देवानसृजत नक्तमसुरान् यद्दिवा देवानसृजत तद् देवानां देवत्वम् ष० 4.1. तद् देवानां देवत्वं यद् दिवसमभिपद्यासृज्यन्त श० 11.1.6.7. प्राचीनप्रजनना वै देवाः प्रतीचीनप्रजनना मनुष्याः श० 7.4.2.40. प्राची हि देवानां दिक् श० 1.2.5.17. देवानां वा एषा दिग्यत्प्राची ष० 3.1. यद्वै मनुष्याणां प्रत्यक्षन्तद् देवानां परोक्षमथ यन्मनुष्याणां परोक्षन्तद् देवानां प्रत्यक्षम् तां० 22.10.3. द्राघीयो हि देवायुषं ह्रसीयो मनुष्यायुषम् श० 7.3.1.10. देवानां वै विधामनु मनुष्याः श० 6.7.4.9. त्रयो वै देवाः। वसवो रुद्रा आदित्याः श० 4.3.5.1. एते वै त्रयो देवा यद् वसवो रुद्रा आदित्याः श०1.3.4.12, 1.5.1.17., 1.8.3.8. त्रयस्त्रिंशद् देवताः तां० 4.4.11. त्रयस्त्रिंशद्वै देवताः तै० 1.2.2.5., 1.8.7.1., 2.7.1.3-4. त्रयस्त्रिंशद्वै सर्वा देवताः कौ० 8.6. त्रयस्त्रिंशद्वै देवाः प्रजापतिश्चतुस्त्रिंशः श० 12.6.1.37. अग्निर्वायुरादित्य एतानि ह तानि देवानां हृदयानि श० 9.1.1.23. अग्निर्वै देवा नामवमो विष्णुः परमस्तदन्तरेण सर्वा अन्या देवताः ऐ० 1.1. तद्यदेतस्मिन्नाके स्वर्गे लोके देवा असीदंस्तस्माद्देवा नाकसदः श० 8.6.1.1. द्यौर्वै सर्वेषां, देवानामायतनम् श० 14.3.2.4. देवगृहा वै नक्षत्राणि तै० 1.5.2.6. नरो वै देवानां ग्रामः तां० 6.9.2. यो वै देवानामात्मा श० 9.3.2.7. सर्वेषां वाऽएष भूतानां सर्वेषां देवानामात्मा यद् यज्ञः श० 14.3.2.1. विद्वांसो हि देवाः श० 3.7.3.10.। तस्मात् प्राणा देवाः, श० 7.5.1.21. प्राणा देवाः श० 6.3.1.15. चक्षुर्देवः गो०

particles, scholars, luminary bodies.

अ॒प्तुरः॑[1] (apturaḥ) —charged particles, life energies, heavenly bodies, scholars, rulers

सु॒तम्[2] (sutam)—body, observer space, people, stuff of universe

आ[3] (ā)—proximity, conjunction and simli.

ग॒न्त॒ (ganata)—come

तू॒र्ण॑यः[4] (tūrṇayaḥ)—swift moving

उ॒स्रा इ॑व[5] (usrāḥ—iva)—sun rays

पू० 2.11. मनो देवः गो० पू० 2.10. मनो वै देववाहनं मनो हीदं मनस्विनं भूयिष्ठं वनीवाह्यते श० 1.4.3.6. वाक् च वै मनश्च देवानां मिथुनम् ऐ० 5.23. वागेव देवाः श० 14.4.3.13. वाग्देवः गो० पू० 2.10. वाग्वै देवानां पुरान्नमासीत् तै० 1.3.5.1. वागिति सर्वे देवाः जै० उ० 1.9.2. वायुर्वै देवः जै० उ० 3.4.8.। यशो देवाः श० 2.1.4.9. तस्माद् (देवाः) यशः श० 3.4.2.8. देवा वै यशस्कामाः सत्रमासत तां० 7.5.6. परोक्षकामा हि देवाः श० 6.1.1.2., 7.4.1.10., परोक्षप्रिया इव हि देवा भवन्ति प्रत्यक्षद्विषः गो० पू० 2.21. यदु ह किं च देवाः कुर्वते स्तोमेनैव तत्कुर्वते यज्ञो वै स्तोमो यज्ञेनैव तत्कुर्वते श० 8.4.3.2. मनो ह वै देवा मनुष्यस्याजानन्ति श० 2.1.4.1., 2.4.1.11. मनो देवा मनुष्यस्याजानन्ति श० 3.4.2.6. सत्यमेव देवाअनृतं मनुष्याः श० 1.1.1.4. यज्ञेन वै तद्देवा यज्ञमयजन्त यदग्निनाऽग्निमयजन्त ते स्वर्गं लोकमायन् ऐ० 1.16. अग्निर्वै देवानां होता ऐ० 1.28., 3.14. अग्निरेव देवानां दूत आस श० 3.5.1.21. वरुणो वै देवानां राजा श० 12.8.3.10. तस्मादाहुर्विष्णुर्देवानां श्रेष्ठ इति श० 14.1.1.5. रुद्रो वै ज्येष्ठश्च श्रेष्ठश्च देवानाम् कौ० 25.13. अन्नमु देवानां सोमः जै० 3.174. दिवा वै मनुष्या यज्ञेन चरन्ति नक्तं देवाः मै० 4.5.1.

1. अप इति निघण्टौ कर्मनाम, उदकनाम च।
2. सुतस्य अभिषुतस्य नि० 13.6. सुतेषु सोमेषु नि० 5.22. सुतः, सुतम् इत्यन्ननामनी निघं० 2.7.
3. अर्वागर्थे नि० 1.3. एतस्मिन्नेवार्थे (समुच्चयार्थे) देवेभ्यश्च पितृभ्य एत्याकारः नि० 1.4. उपमार्थे दृश्यते नि० 3.16. अध्यर्थे दृश्यते नि० 5.5.
4. तूर्णिः क्षिप्रनाम निघं० 2.15. तूर्णिः कर्म नि० 7.27. सर्व ह्येष पाप्मानं तरति तस्मादाह तूर्णिर्हव्यवाडिति श० 1.4.2.12. वायुर्वै तूर्णिर्वायुर्हीदं सर्व सद्यस्तरति यदिदं किञ्चं ऐ० 2.34. तूर्णिर्हव्यवाडित्याह, सर्वं ह्येष (अग्निः) तरति तै० सं० 2.5.9.3.
5. उस्रा रश्मिनाम निघं० 1.5. गोनाम निघं० 2.11.

स्वसराणि[1] (svasarāṇi)—The one who has its own sara (sun) i.e. day.

Anvaya (Sequencial placement of words)

viśvedevāsḥ sutam āganata apturaḥ tūrṇayaḥ. usrā iva svasarāṇi.

Meaning of Mantra in different contexts :

Spiritual : (विश्वेदेवासः) All life energies (आगन्त) come to the body on its birth. (अप्तुरः) These life energies are (तूर्णयः) swift moving and provide (सुतम्) power and intellect to the physical bodies, (इव) just like (उस्रा) sun rays to the (स्वसराणि) days.

Scientific 1: (विश्वेदेवासः) All matter particles (आगन्त) come to this observer space as condensed from of energy. (अप्तुरः) These charged particles are (तूर्णयः) swift moving and provide (सुतम्) power to Indra (electric force), (इव) just like (उस्रा) sun rays to (स्वसराणि) the days.

Scientific 2: (विश्वेदेवासः) All lumanry bodies in the heaven (आगन्त) reach us through the light reflected by them. (अप्तुरः) These bodies are (तूर्णयः) moving around dtheir sources and provide (सुतम्) various energies for the sustenance of life on the earth, (इव) just like (उस्रा) sun rays to (स्वसराणि) the days.

Socio-political 1: (विश्वेदेवासः) All scholars/rulers (आगन्त) should come to the aid of people/student in need. (अप्तुरः) They (तूर्णयः) should move swiftly from one place to another place daily to enlighten/help the people in need, (इव) just like (उस्रा) sun rays to (स्वसराणि) the days

---

1. स्वसराणि अहर्नाम निघं० 1.9. गृहनाम निघं० 3.4. पदनाम निघं० 4. स्वसराणिस्वसराण्यहानि भवन्ति स्वयं सारिण्यपि वा। स्वरादित्यो भवति स एनानि सारयति नि० 5.4.

२७. विश्वे देवासो अस्रिध एहिमायासो अद्रुहः।
मेधं जुषन्त वह्नयः।।९।।

विश्वे। देवासः। अस्रिधः। एहिऽमायासः। अद्रुहः। मेधम्।
जुषन्त। वह्नयः।।

Saṁhitāpāṭha

viśve devāso asridha ehimāyāso adruhaḥ. medham juṣ anta vahnayaḥ.

Padapāṭha

viśve. devāsaḥ. asridhaḥ. ehimāyāsḥ. adruhaḥ. medham. juṣanta. vahnayaḥ.

Grammatical Notes:

विश्वे[1] (viśve)—Voc. pl. of viśva. Tudādigaṇa root √ viśa 'to enter'+kvan (Uṇādi suffix).[2] It is accented on the first syllable, being a voc. form located in the beginning of hemistich.[3] It is also be accented on the first syllable, being formed of 'nit' suffix.

देवासः (devāsaḥ)—Voc. pl. of deva. Acc. pl. nominal suffix jas is replaced by asuk.[4]. Divādigaṇa root √div 'to play', 'desire to win', 'to deal with', 'to illuminate', 'to glorify', 'to be happy', 'to be intoxicated', 'to sleep', to shine' and 'to go' or Curādigaṇa root √div 'to crush', 'to chirp'+ac suffix[5]. Being a voc. form located in the beginning of hemistich, it is accented on the initial

1. यद्वै विश्वं सर्व तत् श० 3.1.2.11. तदन्नं वै विश्वम्प्राणो मित्रम् जै० उ० 3.3.6.
2. Cf. *Uṇādi sūtra* अशुप्रुषिलिटि कणि० - 1.151.
3. Cf. Pāṇ. आमन्त्रितस्य च० 6.1.198.
4. Cf. Pāṇ. आज्जसेरसुक् - 7.1.50
5. Cf. Pāṇ. नन्दिग्रहिपचादिभ्यो ल्यु-णिनि-अचः - 3.1.134

syllable.[1]

अस्रिधः (asridhaḥ)—Bahuvrīhi compund of Nañ+sridhaḥ (Root √sridha 'to ruin', 'to exploit'+kvip[2]). Sāyaṇa derives sridhaḥ from root √sridha. Swami Dayananda also accept this derivation of Sāyaṇa. But it may be informed that this root is not registered in Dhātupāṭha of Pāṇini. Being a Bahuvīhi compound in the company of Nañ, it carries an accent on the second member (srídhaḥ).[3]

एहिमायासः (ehimāyāsḥ)—Bahuvrīhi compound of ehi+māyāsaḥ. {Ā+Bhvādigaṇa root √īha 'to act'+in (Uṇādi suffix)[4] or Ā+Adādigaṇa root √iṇa 'to go'+loṭ lakāra second person sing.}+{Adādigaṇa root √mā 'to measure'+ya (Uṇādi suffix)[5]}. Here also fem. pl. ending -as (Pāṇ.-jas) is replaced by-āsas (Pāṇ. asuk) like the one in devasaḥ etc. Being a Bahuvrīhi compound, it is accented on its first member and the first member, being formed of 'nit' suffix, is accented on the first sullable[6]. As such ehimāyāsaḥ is accented on the first syllable 'e' of the first member 'ehi'.

अद्रुहः (adruhaḥ)—Bahuvrīhi compund of Nañ+druhaḥ (Divādigaṇa root √druha 'violence',+kvip[7]). Being a Bahuvrīhi compound in the company of Nañ, it carries an accent on the second member (druḥ).[8]

---

1. Cf. Pāṇ. आमन्त्रितस्य च - 8.1.19
2. Cf. *Varttika* No. 9 in *Mahābhāṣya*—संपदादिभ्यः क्विप् - on Pāṇ. 3.3.108
3. Cf. Pāṇ. नञ्सुभ्याम् - 6.2.172.
4. Cf. *Uṇādi sūtra*—सर्वधातुभ्योऽसुन् - 4.190
5. Cf. *Uṇādi sūtra*—मा छाशसिभ्यो यः - 4.109
6. Cf. Pāṇ. बहुव्रीहि प्रकात्या पूर्वपदम् - 6.2.1
7. Cf. *Varttika* No. 9 in *Mahābhāṣya*—संपदादिभ्यः क्विप् - on Pāṇ. 3.3.108
8. Cf. Pāṇ. नञ्सुभ्याम् - 6.2.172.

मेधम् (medham)—Bhvādigaṇa root √medhṛ 'to meet, 'confluence',+ghañ in the accusative sense). It, being formed of 'ñit' suffix, is accented on the initial syllable[1].

जुषन्त (juṣanta)—Tudāgaṇa root √juṣī 'to love' 'to serve',+laṅ lakāra (imperfect) third person pl.). Here 'aṭ' augment is dropped[2]. Laṅ lakāra (imperfect) is used used to denote loṭ lakāra (imperative)[3]. Being a verbal form preceded by a non-verbal form, it goes without accent.

वह्नयः (vahnayaḥ)—Bhvādigaṇa root √vaha 'to reach, 'to send',+niḥ (Uṇādi suffix)[4]. It, being formed of 'nit' suffix, is accented on the initial syllable[5].

Word meanings:

विश्वे[6] (viśve)—Address to Viśva. All

देवासः[7] (devāsaḥ)—Address to Devas. Life energies, matter

---

1. Cf. Pāṇ. ञ्नित्यादिर्नित्यम् - 6.1.197
2. Cf. Pāṇ. बहुलं छन्दस्यमाङ् योगे - 6.4.75
3. Cf. Pāṇ. छन्दसि लुङ्लङ्लिटः - 3.4.6ण
4. Cf. *Uṇādi sūtra*—वहि श्रिश्रुयुद्रुग्लाहात्वरिभ्यो नित् - 4.51
5. Cf. Pāṇ. ञ्नित्यादिर्नित्यम् - 6.1.197
6. यद्वै विश्वं सर्वं तत् श० 3.1.2.11. तदन्नं वै विश्वम्प्राणो मित्रम् जै० उ० 3.3.6.
7. देवो दानाद्वा, दीपनाद्वा, द्योतनाद्वा, द्युस्थानो भवतीति वा। यो देवः स देवता निघं० 7.15. दिवा वै नोऽभूदिति। तद् देवानां देवत्वम् तै० 2.2.9.9. दिवा देवानसृजत नक्तमसुरान् यद्दिवा देवानसृजत तद् देवानां देवत्वम् ष० 4.1. तद् देवानां देवत्वं यद् दिवसमभिपद्यासृज्यन्त श० 11.1.6.7. प्राचीनप्रजनना वै देवाः प्रतीचीनप्रजनना मनुष्याः श० 7.4.2.40. प्राची हि देवानां दिक् श० 1.2.5.17. देवानां वा एषा दिग्यत्प्राची ष० 3.1. यद्वै मनुष्याणां प्रत्यक्षन्तद् देवानां परोक्षमथ यन्मनुष्याणां परोक्षन्तद् देवानां प्रत्यक्षम् तां० 22.10.3. द्राघीयो हि देवायुषं ह्रसीयो मनुष्यायुषम् श० 7.3.1.10. देवानां वै विधामनु मनुष्याः श० 6.7.4.9. त्रयो वै देवाः। वसवो रुद्रा आदित्याः श० 4.3.5.1. एते वै त्रयो देवा यद् वसवो रुद्रा आदित्याः श० 1.3.4.12., 1.5.1.17., 1.8.3.8. त्रयस्त्रिंशद् देवताः तां० 4.4.11. त्रयस्त्रिंशद्वै देवताः तै० 1.2.2.5.,

particles, scholars, heavenly bodies

अस्रिधः (asridhaḥ) —decay, harm

एहिमायासः (ehimāyāsḥ)—life energies

अद्रुहः (adruhaḥ)—without confliction, without annhilating

मेधम्[1] (medham)—physical body, matter

जुषन्त[2] (juṣanta)—operate, dwell

वह्नयः[1] (vahnayaḥ)—carrier

1.8.7.1., 2.7.1.3-4. त्रयस्त्रिंशद्वै सर्वा देवताः कौ० 8.6. त्रयस्त्रिंशद्वै देवाः प्रजापतिश्चतुस्त्रिंशः श० 12.6.1.37. अग्निर्वायुरादित्य एतानि ह तानि देवानां हृदयानि श० 9.1.1.23. अग्निर्वै देवा नामवमो विष्णुः परमस्तदन्तरेण सर्वा अन्या देवताः ऐ० 1.1. तद्यदेतस्मिन्नाके स्वर्गे लोके देवा असीदंस्तस्माद्देवा नाकसदः श० 8.6.1.1. द्यौर्वै सर्वेषां, देवानामायतनम् श० 14.3.2.4. देवगृहा वै नक्षत्राणि तै० 15.2.6. नरो वै देवानां ग्रामः तां० 6.9.2. यो वै देवानामात्मा श० 9. 3.2.7. सर्वेषां वाऽएष भूतानां सर्वेषां देवानामात्मा यद् यज्ञः श० 14.3.2.1. विद्वांसो हि देवाः श० 3.7.3.10.। तस्मात् प्राणा देवाः, श० 7.5.1.21. प्राणा देवाः श० 6.3.1.15. चक्षुर्देवः गो० पू० 2.11. मनो देवः गो० पू० 2.10. मनो वै देववाहनं मनो हीदं मनस्विनं भूयिष्ठं वनीवाह्यते श० 1.4.3.6. वाक् च वै मनश्च देवानां मिथुनम् ऐ० 5.23. वागेव देवाः श० 14.4.3.13. वाग्देवः गो० पू० 2.10. वाग्वै देवानां पुरान्नमासीत् तै० 1.3.5.1. वागिति सर्वे देवाः जै० उ० 1.9.2. वायुर्वै देवः जै० उ० 3.4.8.। यशो देवाः श० 2.1.4.9. तस्माद् (देवाः) यशः श० 3. 4.2.8. देवा वै यशस्कामाः सत्रमासत तां० 7.5.6. परोक्षकामा हि देवाः श० 6.1.1.2., 7.4.1. 10., परोक्षप्रिया इव हि देवा भवन्ति प्रत्यक्षद्विषः गो० पू० 2.21. यदु ह किं च देवाः कुर्वते स्तोमेनैव तत्कुर्वते यज्ञो वै स्तोमो यज्ञेनैव तत्कुर्वते श० 8.4.3.2. मनो ह वै देवा मनुष्यस्याजानन्ति श० 2.1.4.1., 2.4.1.11. मनो देवा मनुष्यस्याजानन्ति श० 3.4.2.6. सत्यमेव देवा अनृतं मनुष्याः श० 1.1.1.4. यज्ञेन वै तद्देवा यज्ञमयजन्त यदग्निनाऽग्निमयजन्त ते स्वर्गं लोकमायन् ऐ० 1.16. अग्निर्वै देवानां होता ऐ० 1.28., 3.14. अग्निरेव देवानां दूत आस श० 3.5.1.21. वरुणो वै देवानां राजा श० 12.8.3.10. तस्मादाहुर्विष्णुर्देवानां श्रेष्ठ इति श० 14.1.1.5. रुद्रो वै ज्येष्ठश्च श्रेष्ठश्च देवानाम् कौ० 25.13. अन्नमु देवानां सोमः जै०3.174. दिवा वै मनुष्या यज्ञेन चरन्ति नक्तं देवाः मै० 4.5.1.

1. मेधः यज्ञनाम निघं० 3.17. धननाम निघं० 2.10. मेधायेत्यन्नायेत्येतत् श० 7.5.2.32. सर्वेषां वा ऽएष पशूनां मेधौ यद् ब्रीहियवौ श० 3.8.3.1. मेदो वै मेधः श० 3.8.4.6. पशुर्वै मेधः ऐ० 2.6. मेधो वा एष पशूनां यत् पुरोडाशः कौ० 10.5. मेधो वा आज्यम् तै० 3.9.12.1
2. जुषते कान्तिकर्मा निघं० 2.6.

Anvaya (Sequencial placement of words)

viśvedevāsaḥ medham juṣanta asridhaḥ ehimāyāsaḥ adruhaḥ vahnayaḥ.

Meaning of Mantra in different contexts :

Spiritual :(विश्वेदेवासः) All life energies (जुषन्त) operate from this physical body (अस्रिधः) without doing any harm to it. (एहिमायासः) These life energies should support (मेधम्) this body and (वह्नयः) carrier of energy to every part of body (अद्रुहः) without conflicting with each other.

Scientific 1: (विश्वेदेवासः) May all particles (जुषन्त) dwell in observer space (अस्रिधः) without being harmed by their anti-particles. (एहिमायासः) These particles should support (मेधम्) this universe and become (वह्नयः) carrier of it (अद्रुहः) without being annihilated by each other .

Note : According to the Veda, our universe is matter dominated. If the matter and antimatter is in equal proportion, they will annhilate each other converting into energy and there will be no scope for the creation. As such the seer in his transcendental stage prays that all particles should not get annhilated by their anti-particles, but some of them must survive to sustain this universe.

Scientific 2: (विश्वेदेवासः) All luminary bodies should operate in this universe (अस्रिधः) without doing any harm to it. (एहिमायासः) These luminary bodies should support (मेधम्) this earth (वह्नयः) in supporting life (अद्रुहः) without conflicting with each other.

Socio-political 1: (विश्वेदेवासः) All scholars should operate **in the nation** (अस्रिधः) without harming the interests of students. (एहिमायासः) They should support (मेधम्) the intectaul activities (वह्नयः) and carry this tradition further (अद्रुहः) without conflicting with each other.

Socio-political 2: (विश्वेदेवासः) All rulers should operate in a

---

1. वह्निः अश्वनाम निघं० 1.14. वह्नि वोळ्हा नि० 3.4. वह्निम् पुत्रम् नि० 3.6. वह्नयः-वोढारः नि० 8.3. वह्निर्वा अनड्वान् तै० 1.1.6.10. वह्निर्होता तै० सं० 2.2.10.5. वह्निर सि हव्यवाहनः मै० 1.2.12. काठ० 2.13. वह्निना हि तत्र गच्छति यत्र जिगमिषति जै० 2.99.

state (अस्रिधः) without harming the interests of publci. (एहिमायासः) They should support (मेधम्) the common cause (वह्नयः) for the survival of humanity (अद्रुहः) without conflicting with each other.

After assigning the role of Viśvedevas, now the seer takes up the issue of Sarasvati. Sarasvati represents the spiritual knowledge in spiritual sense. In scientific sense, Sarasvati represents mass energy in the intermediate space. Sarasvati is the flow of rain waters. In Socio-political sense, Sarasvati represents ladies endowed with spiritual knowledge.

२८. पावका नः सरस्वती वाजेभिर्वाजिनीवती।

यज्ञं वष्टु धियावसुः ॥१०॥

पावका। नः। सरस्वती। वाजेभिः। वाजिनीऽवती। यज्ञम्। वष्टु।

धियाऽवसुः॥

Saṁhitāpāṭha

pāvakā naḥ sarasvatī vājebhir vājinīvatī. yajñam vaṣṭu dhiyāvasuḥ.

Padapāṭha

pāvakā. naḥ. sarasvatī. vājebhiḥ. vājinī—vatī. yajñam. vaṣṭ u. dhiyāvasuḥ.

Grammatical Notes:

पावका (pāvakā)—Bhvādigaṇa root √pūṅ 'to purify'+ṇvul in the nominative sense+ṭāp fem. suffix. It may also be formed as the compund of pāva+ka, e.g. {Bhvādigaṇa root √pūṅ 'to purify'+ghañ}+{Bhvādigaṇa root √kai 'to produce sound'+ka suffix[1]}+ ṭāp. Generally, in case of -ṭāp, 'a' of 'pāvakā' is substituted with 'i' thus making the fem. form as 'pāvikā'. But in the Veda, 'i' substitution is not allowed [2]. In the second case nominal stem being followed by a word ending with a primary suffix (kṛdanta) gets accent on the primary derivative. As such 'pāvakā' is accented on the final syllable.

---

1. Cf. Pāṇ. आतोऽनुपसर्गे कः - 3.2..3
2. Cf. *Vārttika*—पावकादीनां छन्दस्युपसंख्यानम् - on Pāṇ. 7.3.45.

नः (naḥ) —Acc./dat./gen. pl. enclitic form of first person pronoun 'Asmad'[1]. Being an enclitic form it is not accented.[2]

सरस्वती (sarasvatī)—Bhvādigaṇa root √sṛ 'to go'+asun suffix [3] +matup in the sense of 'praise' and 'abundance'+ṅīp fem. suffix. Here 'saras', being formed of 'nit suffix, gets accent on the first syllable[4]. Rests '-matup' and '-ṅīp' being 'pit' (of which 'p' is elided), remains unaccented.

वाजेभिः (vājebhiḥ)—Inst. pl. of vāja. Bhvādigaṇa root √vaja 'to go'+ghañ suffix. It is accented on the first syllable, being read in the list of 'vṛṣa' group of words.[5]

वाजिनीवती (vājinī-vatī)—vāja+ni suffix[6]+matup>vatup[7]+ ṅīp fem. suffix. 'Matup' and 'ṅīp' suffixes being 'pit' remain unaccented. In this situation, vājini, being formed of 'nit' suffix, carries accent.[8]

यज्ञम् (yajñam)—Acc. sing. of Yajña. Bhvādigaṇa √yaja 'to worship gods', 'to unite', 'to donate'+naṅ[9] suffix. It receives accent on suffix, so becomes accented on the final syllable.

वष्टु (vaṣṭu)—Adādigaṇa root √vaśa 'to wish'+loṭ third person sing. Being a verbal form preceded by a non-

---

1. Cf. *vahuvacanasyavasnasau*—Pāṇ. 8.1.21.
2. Cf. Pāṇ. युस्मदस्मदोः षष्ठी चतुर्थी द्वितीया स्थयोर्वान्नावौ 8.1.20.
3. Cf. Pāṇ. सर्वधातुभ्योऽसुन् - 4.190
4. Cf. Pāṇ. ञ्नित्यादिर्नित्यम् - 6.1.197
5. Cf. Pāṇ. वृषादीनां च - 6.1.203.
6. Cf. Pāṇ. अतइनिठनौ - 5.2.115.
7. Cf. Pāṇ. छन्दसीरः - 8.2.15.
8. Cf. Pāṇ. ञ्नित्यादिर्नित्यम् - 6.1.197.
9. Cf. Pāṇini, 3.3.90—यज-याच-यत-विच्छ-प्रच्छ-रक्षो नङ् (*yaja-yāca-yata-viccha-praccha-rakṣo naṅ).*

verbal form, it goes without accent [1].

धि॒यावसुः (dhiyāvasuḥ)—Bhuvrīhi compound between 'dhī' and 'vasu'. The third case ending 'ā' is not elided in the compound formation. {Bhvādigaṇa root √dhyai 'to have concern'+kvip [2] }+{Bhvādigaṇa root √vasa 'to dwell'+u (Uṇādi suffix)[3]. In the loc. pl. 'dhīṣu' 'dhi', being a monosyllabic stem before the loc. pl. case ending, 'su' is accented on the third case ending 'ā' [4]. Being a Bahuvrīhi compound, the accent on the first member well prevail [5] and so first member of the compound 'dhiyā' well be accented on its third case ending 'ā'.

Word meanings:

पा॒व॒का (pāvakā)—purifier

न॒ः (naḥ) —us

सर॑स्वती[6] (sarasvatī)—mass energy in the intermediate space, space, learned ladies.

वाजे॑भिः[7] (vājebhiḥ)—matter

---

1. Cf. Pāṇ. तिङ्ङतिङः - 8.1.28.
2. Cf. Pāṇ. ध्यायतेः सम्प्रसारणं च - 3.2.178.
3. Cf. *Uṇādi sūtra* शृस्वृस्निहित्रप्यसि वसि० - 1.10.
4. Cf. Pāṇ. तृतीया दि विभक्तिः - 6.1.162.
5. Cf. Pāṇ. बहुब्रीहौ प्रकृत्या पूर्वपदम् - 6.2.1.
6. सरस्वती-सरस् इत्युदकनाम सर्त्तेस्तुदवती नि० 9.26. सरस्वती वाङ्नाम निघं० 1.11. सरस्वत्यः नदीनाम निघं० 1.13. सरः वाङ्नाम निघं० 1.11 वाक् सरस्वती श० 7.5.1.32. वाग्वै सरस्वती कौ० 5.2. तां० 6.7.7. श० 2.5.4.6. तै० 1.3.4.5. गो० उ० 1.120. वाग्वै सरस्वती पवीरवी ऐ० 3.37. वागेव सरस्वती ऐ० 2.24. वाग्धि सरस्वती ऐ० 3.2. जिह्वा सरस्वती श० 12.9.1.14. (यजु० 38.2.) सरस्वती हि गौः श० 14.2.1.7. अमावस्या वै सरस्वती गो० उ० 1.12. योषा वै सरस्वती वृषा पूषा श० 2.5.1.11. एषा वा अपां पृष्ठं यत् सरस्वती तै० 1.8.5.5.
7. वाजः अन्ननाम निघं० 2.7. बलनाम निघं० 2.9. वाजेभिरन्नैः नि० 11.26. अन्नं वै वाजः तै० 1.3.6.2. श० 5.1.4.3. ता० 13.9.13. अन्नं वाजः श० 5.1.1.16. अन्नं वै वाजः श० 1.4.1.9. वीर्यं वै वाजः श० 3.3.4.7. ओषधयः खलु वै वाजः तै० 1.3.7.1. वाजो वै

वा॒जिनी॑वती (vājinī-vatī)—possessed of matter-antimatter, food

य॒ज्ञम्[1] (yajñam)—process of creation of matter particles.

व॒ष्टु[2] (vaṣṭu)—fruition

धि॒याव॑सुः[3] (dhiyāvasuḥ)—intelligent action

Anvaya (Sequencial placement of words)

pāvakā sarasvatī vājebhiḥ vājinīvatī naḥ yajñam dhiyāvasuḥ vaṣṭu.

पशवः ऐ० 5.8. वाजो वै स्वर्गो लोकः तां० 18.7.12. गो० उ० 5.8. वाग्वै वाजस्य प्रसवः तै० 1.3.2.5. सोमो वै वाजः मै० 4.5.4. सर्वः सोमं पिपासति वाजः ह गच्छति मै० 1.11.5. अमृतोऽन्नं वै वाज जै० 2.193.

1. यज्ञः कस्मात? प्रख्यातं यजतिकर्मेति नैरुक्ताः। याच्ञ्यो भवतीति वा यजुरुन्नो भवतीति वा बहुकृष्णाजिन इत्यौपमन्यवो यजूंष्येनं नयन्तीति वा नि० 3.19. स (सोमः) तायमानो जायते स यन् जायते तस्माद् यज्ञो ह वै नामैतद् यद् यज्ञ इति श० 3.9.4.23. प्राणः (यज्ञस्य) सोमः कौ० 9.6. अध्वरो वै यज्ञः श० 1.2.4.5. यज्ञो वै मखः श० 6.5.2.1. तै० 3.2.8.3. तां० 7.5.6. मख इत्येतद् यज्ञनाम वेयम् गो० उ० 2.5. यज्ञो वै नमः श० 7.4.1.30,2.4.2.24, 2.6.1.42. यज्ञो वै स्वाहाकारः श० 3.1.3.27. यज्ञो वै भुज्युः (यजु० 18.42.) यज्ञो हि सर्वाणि भूतानि भुनक्ति श० 9.4.1.11. यज्ञो भगः (यजु० 11.7.) श० 6.3.1.19. गातुं वित्त्वेति यज्ञं वित्वेत्येवैतदाह। श० 1.9.2.28, 4.4.4.13. यज्ञो वै देवानां महः श० 1.9.1.11. एष ह वै महान् देवो यद् यज्ञः गो० पू० 2.19. यज्ञो वै बृहन्विपश्चित् श० 3.5.3.12. यज्ञो वा अर्यमा तै० 2.3.5.4. यज्ञो वै तार्प्यम् तै० 1.3.7.1, 3.9.20.1. यज्ञो वै वसुः (यजु० 1.2.) यज्ञो वै श्रेष्ठतमं कर्म (यजु० 1.1.) श० 2.7.1.5. यज्ञो हि श्रेष्ठतमं कर्म तै० 3.2.1.4. ब्रह्म यज्ञः श० 3.1.4.15. ब्रह्म हि यज्ञः श० 5.3.2.4. ब्रह्म वै यज्ञः ऐ० 7.22. एष वै प्रत्यक्षं यज्ञो यत् प्रजापतिः श० 4.3.4.3. यज्ञः प्रजापतिः श० 11.6.38. यज्ञ उ वै प्रजापतिः कौ० 10.1.13.1. तै० 3.3.7.3. एष वै यज्ञ एव प्रजापतिः श० 1.7.4.4. प्रजापतिर्यज्ञः ऐ० 2.17, 4.26. इन्द्रो वैयज्ञस्य देवता श० 1.4.1.33, 1.4.5.4. विष्णुर्यज्ञः गो० उ० 1.12. तै० 3.3.7.6. यज्ञो वै विष्णुः स यज्ञः श० 5.2.3.6. स यः स विष्णुर्यज्ञः सः, स यः स यज्ञोऽसौ आदित्यः श० 14.1.1.6. विष्णुर्वै यज्ञः ऐ० 1.15. यज्ञो विष्णुः तां० 13.3.2. गो० उ० 6.7.
2. वष्टि कान्तिकर्मा निघं० 2.6.
3. धियावसुः कर्मवसुः नि० 11.26. धीः कर्मनाम निघं० 2.1. प्रज्ञानाम निघं० 3.9. वसु रात्रिनाम निघं० 1.7. धननाम निघं० 2.10. वाग् वै धियावसुः ऐ०आ० 1.1.4

Meaning of Mantra in different contexts :

Spiritual : (सरस्वती) Sarasvati (वाजिनीवती), the possessor of the spiritual knowledge, is (पावका) the purifier of body and mind. (वाजेभिः) Through the food of spiritual knowledge, it leads our mind (धियावसुः) to perform intelligent acts i.e. acts of altruistic welfare and make (यज्ञम्) Brahma yajña (jñāna yajña) (वष्टु) a success.

Note: The mantra says that the actual knowledge leads one towards acts of altruistic welfare and not to act in self interest.

Scientific 1: (सरस्वती) Mass energy in the intermediate space is (वाजिनीवती) possessor of matter and antimatter. It is (पावका) the fine tuner of the matter in observer space. It leads (यज्ञम्) the yajña of creation of matter in the observer space (वष्टु) to the successful end.

Scientific 2: (सरस्वती) Rainy waters in the our atmosphere are (वाजिनीवती) possessor of the seeds of grains and vegetations. They are (पावका) purifier. They help (वष्टु) flourish (यज्ञम्) bio-life on the earth .

Note : Rainy waters were the only source of water on the earth in the beginning of its history. Now, also rainy waters play a pivotal role in flourishing vegetations on the earth.

Socio-political 1: (सरस्वती) Learned ladies (वाजिनीवती) possessed of good Sanskāras (पावका) fine tune (यज्ञम्) the family and lead it (वष्टु) to the successful end

२९. चोदयित्री सूनृतानां चेतन्ती सुमतीनाम्। यज्ञं दधे सरस्वती।।११।।

चोदयित्री। सूनृतानाम्। चेतन्ती। सुऽमतीनाम्। यज्ञम्। दधे। सरस्वती।।

Saṁhitāpāṭha

codayitrī sūnṛtānām cetantī sumatīnām. yajñaṁ dadhe sarasvatī.

Padapāṭha

codayitrī. sūnṛtānām. cetantī. sumatīnām. yajñam. dadhe. sarasvatī.

Grammatical Notes:

चोदयित्री (codayitrī)—Curādigaṇa root √cud 'to grind'+ṇic suffix+tṛc in the nom. sense+ṅip fem. suffix[1]. 'Codayitra', being formed of 'cit' (of which 'c' is elided') suffix, gets accent on the final syllable[2].

सूनृतानाम् (sūnṛtānām) —Gen. pl. of sunṛta. Su+ūn 'to decrease'+kvip[3].

चेतन्ती (cetantī) —Bhvādigaṇa root √ citi 'to cognize'+śatṛ (present active participle)+ṅīp fem. suffix.

सुमतीनाम् (sumatīnām)—Gen. pl. of sumati.

Su+Divādigaṇa root √ mana 'to know'+ktin suffix[4]+matup. In sumatinām, gen. pl. case ending 'nām' is accented, since ,as per rules of

---

1. Cf. Pāṇ. ऋन्नेभ्यो ङीप् - 4.1.5.
2. Cf. Pāṇ. चितः - 6.1.163.
3. Cf. Pāṇ. क्विप् च - 3.2.76. Note : The root √ *ūn* is not listed in the 'dhātupātha' of Pāṇini. But Sāyaṇa mentions it. Swami Dayananda also accepts the existence of this root.
4. Cf. Pāṇ. मन्त्रेवृषेपचमन विद भूवीरा उदात्तः - 3.3.93.

accentuation, [1]'matup' is preceded by a short vowel 'i' of 'mati'.

य॒ज्ञम् (yajñam)—Acc. sing. of Yajña. Bhvādigaṇa √ yaja 'to worship gods', 'to unite', 'to donate'+naṅ[2] suffix and so becomes accented on the final syllable.

द॒धे (dadhe)—Juhotyādigaṇa root √ dhāñ 'to sustain', 'to bring up'+liṭ lakāra (perfect tense) third person sing.

सर॑स्वती (sarasvatī)—Bhvādigaṇa root √sṛ 'to go'+asun suffix [3] +matup in the sense of 'praise' and 'abundance'+ṅīp fem. suffix. Here 'saras', being formed of 'nit' suffix, gets accent on the first syllable[4]. Rests '—matup' and '—ṅīp' being 'pit' (of which 'p' is elided), remains unaccented.

Word meanings:

चो॒द॒यि॒त्री (codayitrī)—to inspire

सू॒नृता॑नाम्[5] (sūnṛtānām) —good speech

चेत॑न्ती (cetantī) —to instruct

सु॒म॒ती॒नाम्[6] (sumatīnām)—genius, intellectuals, children

य॒ज्ञम्[7] (yajñam)—life of human beings, process of creation,

1. Cf. Pāṇ. नामन्यतरस्याम् - 6.1.177.
2. Cf. Pāṇini, 3.3.90—यज-याच-यत-विच्छ-प्रच्छ-रक्षो नङ् (*yaja-yāca-yata-viccha-praccha-rakṣo naṅ).*
3. Cf. Pāṇ. सर्वधातुभ्योऽसुन् - 4.190
4. Cf. Pāṇ. ञ्नित्यादिर्नित्यम् - 6.1.197
5. सूनृता उषो नाम निघं० 1.8. अन्ननाम निघं० 2.7. वाङ्नाम निघं० 11.11
6. मतयः मेधाविनाम निघं० 3.15.
7. यज्ञः कस्मात? प्रख्यातं यजतिकर्मेति नैरुक्ताः। याच्ञ्यो भवतीति वा यजुरुन्नो भवतीति वा बहुकृष्णाजिन इत्यौपमन्यवो यजूंष्येनं नयन्तीति वा नि० 3.19. स (सोमः) तायमानो जायते स यन् जायते तस्माद् यञ्जो यञ्जो ह वै नामैतद् यद् यज्ञ इति श० 3.9.4.23. प्राणः (यज्ञस्य) सोमः कौ० 9.6. अध्वरो वै यज्ञः श० 1.2.4.5. यज्ञो वै मखः श० 6.5.2.1. तै० 3

process of life, household life.

द॒धे (dadhe)—to sustain

सर॑स्वती[1] (sarasvatī)—spiritual knowledge, mass energy of the intermediate space, rainmakers, learned lady, speech.

Anvaya (Sequencial placement of words)

sarasvatī yajñam dadhe sūnṛtānām codayitrī sumatīnām cetantī

Meaning of Mantra in different contexts :

Spiritual: (सरस्वती) The knowledge (दधे) sustains (यज्ञम्) life of a human beings. (चोदयित्री) It inspires and (चेतन्ती) awakens

---

.2.8.3. तां० 7.5.6. मख इत्येतद् यज्ञनाम वेयम् गो० उ० 2.5. यज्ञो वै नमः श० 7.4.1.30, 2.4.2.24, 2.6.1.42. यज्ञो वै स्वाहाकारः श० 3.1.3.27. यज्ञो वै भुज्युः (यजु० 18.42.) यज्ञो हि सर्वाणि भूतानि भुनक्ति श० 9.4.1.11. यज्ञो भगः (यजु० 11.7.) श० 6.3.1.19. गा तुं वित्त्वेति यज्ञं वित्त्वेत्येवैतदाह श० 1.9.2.28, 4.4.4.13. यज्ञो वै देवानां महः श० 1.9.1.11. एष ह वै महान् देवो यद् यज्ञः गो० पू० 2.19. यज्ञो वै बृहन्विपश्चित् श० 3.5.3.12. यज्ञो वा अर्यमा तै० 2.3.5.4. यज्ञो वै तार्प्यम् तै० 1.3.7.1, 3.9.20.1. यज्ञो वै वसुः (यजु० 1.2.) यज्ञो वै श्रेष्ठतमं कर्म (यजु० 1.1.) श० 2.7.1.5. यज्ञो हि श्रेष्ठतमं कर्म तै० 3.2.1.4. ब्रह्म यज्ञः श० 3.1.4.15. ब्रह्म हि यज्ञः श० 5.3.2.4. ब्रह्म वै यज्ञः ऐ० 7.22. एष वै प्रत्यक्षं यज्ञो यत् प्रजापतिः श० 4.3.4.3. यज्ञः प्रजापतिः श० 11.6.38. यज्ञ उ वै प्रजापतिः कौ० 10.1.13 .1. तै० 3.3.7.3. एष वै यज्ञ एव प्रजापतिः श० 1.7.4.4. प्रजापतिर्यज्ञः ऐ० 2.17, 4.26. इन्द्रो वै यज्ञस्य देवता श० 1.4.1.33, 1.4.5.4. विष्णुर्यज्ञः गो० उ० 1.12. तै० 3.3.7.6. यज्ञो वै विष्णुः स यज्ञः श० 5.2.3.6. स यः स विष्णुर्यज्ञः सः, स यः स यज्ञोऽसौ आदित्यः श० 14.1.1.6. विष्णुर्वै यज्ञः ऐ० 1.15. यज्ञो विष्णुः तां० 13.3.2. गो० उ० 6.7.

1. सरस्वती-सरस् इत्युदकनाम सर्त्तेस्तुदवती नि० 9.26. सरस्वती वाङ्नाम निघं० 1.11. सरस्वत्यः नदीनाम निघं० 1.13. सरः वाङ्नाम निघं० 1.11 वाक् सरस्वती श० 7.5.1.32. वाग्वै सरस्वती कौ० 5.2. तां० 6.7.7. श० 2.5.4.6. तै० 1.3.4.5. गो० उ० 1.120. वाग्वै सरस्वती पवीरवी ऐ० 3.37. वागेव सरस्वती ऐ० 2.24. वाग्धि सरस्वती ऐ० 3.2. जिह्वा सरस्वती श० 12.9.1.14. (यजु० 38.2.) सरस्वती हि गौः श० 14.2.1.7. अमावस्या वै सरस्वती गो० उ० 1.12. योषा वै सरस्वती वृषा पूषा श० 2.5.1.11. एषा वा अपां पृष्ठं यत् सरस्वती तै० 1.8.5.5.

(सुमतीनाम्) good minds or intellectuals (सूनृतानाम्) and good speakers.

Scientific 1: (सरस्वती) Mass energy of the intermediate space (दधे) sustains (यज्ञम्) the process of creation of matter and anti matter in the observer space. (चोदयित्री) It inspires (चेतन्ती) the minds (सुमतीनाम्) of intellectuals and (सूनृतानाम्) good speakers to narrate its properties.

Scientific 2: (सरस्वती) The rainy waters (दधे) sustain (यज्ञम्) the process of life on the earth. (चोदयित्री) They inspire (चेतन्ती) the minds (सुमतीनाम्) of intellectuals and (सूनृतानाम्) good speakers to speak highly of them.

Socio-political 1: (सरस्वती) A learned lady (दधे) is the mainstay of (यज्ञम्) household life. (चोदयित्री) They are inspiration behind (चेतन्ती) awakening (सुमतीनाम्) of good minds or intellectuals (सूनृतानाम्) and good speakers.

३०. म॒हो अर्ण॑: सर॑स्वती॒ प्र चे॑तयति के॒तुना॑।

धियो॒ विश्वा॑ वि रा॑जति॥१२॥

म॒ह:। अर्ण॑:। सर॑स्वती। प्र। चे॒त॒य॒ति। के॒तुना॑। धिय॑:। विश्वा॑:।

वि। रा॒ज॒ति॥

Samhitāpāṭha

maho ārṇaḥ sarasvatī pracetayati ketunā. dhiyo viśvā vi rājati.

Padapāṭha

mahaḥ. ārṇaḥ. sarasvatī. pra. cetayati. ketunā. dhiyaḥ. vishvāḥ. vi. rājati.

Grammatical Notes:

म॒ह: (mahaḥ)—Bhvādigaṇa root √maha 'to worship'+ati suffix[1]. 'T' of 'mahat' changes into 's'. It is accented on the suffix syllable[2].

अर्ण॑: (ārṇaḥ)—Bhvādigaṇa root √ṛ 'to go', 'to send'+asun & (Uṇādi suffix)[3]. Being formed of 'ṇit' suffix, it is accented on the first syllable[4].

सर॑स्वती (sarasvatī)—Bhvādigaṇa root √sṛ 'to go'+asun suffix[5] +matup in the sense of 'praise' and 'abundance'+ṅīp fem. suffix. Here 'saras', being formed of 'ṇit suffix, gets accent on the first syllable[6]. Rests '-matup' and '—ṅīp' being 'pit' (of which 'p' is elided), remains unaccented.

---

1. Cf. *Uṇādi* suffix वर्तमाने पृषद्बृहन्महत्॰ – 284.
2. Cf. Pāṇ. आद्युदात्तश्च – 3.1.3.
3. Cf. *Uṇādi sūtra* उदके नुद् च – 4.196.
4. Cf. Pāṇ. ञ्नित्यादिर्नित्यम् – 6.1.197.
5. Cf. Pāṇ. सर्वधातुभ्योऽसुन् – 4.190
6. Cf. Pāṇ. ञ्नित्यादिर्नित्यम् – 6.1.197

प्र (pra)—A Prefix. Being a prefix, it is accented on the first syllable[1].

चेतयति (cetayati)—Bhvādigaṇa root √ citi 'to be aware or conscious'+ṇic+laṭ lakāra (present tense) third person sing. Being a verbal form preceded by non—verbal form, it loses its accent[2].

केतुना (ketunā)—Inst. sing. of ketu.Bhvādigaṇa root √ cāyṛ 'to woship'+tu (Uṇādi suffix)[3] or Bhavādigana root √kita 'to reside' 'to remove ailment'+u Uèādi suffix. It is accented on suffix[4].

धियः (dhiyaḥ)—Bhvādigaṇa root √dhyai 'to seek concern'+kvip[5]. It carries accent on its nominal root.

विश्वाः (viśvāḥ)—Voc. pl. of viśva. Tudādigaṇa root √ viśa 'to enter'+kvan (Uṇādi suffix).[6] It is accented, being a voc. form located in the beginning of hemistich.[7] Its accent is on the initial syllable, being formed of 'nit' suffix.

वि (vi)—A Prefix. Being a prefix, it is accented on the first syllable[8].

राजति (rājati)—Bhvādigaṇa root √ rājṛ 'to shine'+laṭ lakāra (present tense) third person sing. Being a verbal form, preceded by a non-verbal form, it loses its accent.

Word meanings:

---

1. Cf. *Phiṭ sūtra* उपसर्गाश्चाभिवर्जम् - 81.
2. Cf. Pāṇ. तिङ्ङतिङः - 8.1.28.
3. Cf. *Uṇādi sutra* चायः की - 1.74.
4. Cf. Pāṇ. आद्युदात्तश्च 3.1.3.
5. Cf. *Vārttika*—ध्यायतेः संप्रसारणं च - Pāṇ. 3.2.178.
6. Cf. *Uṇādi sūtra* अशुप्रुषिलिटि कणि० - 1.151.
7. Cf. Pāṇ. आमन्त्रितस्य च० 6.1.198.
8. Cf. *Phiṭ sūtra* उपसर्गश्चाभिवर्जम् - 81.

म॒हः[1] (mahaḥ)—vast, abundance

अर्णः[2] (ārṇaḥ) —ocean of knowledge, abundance

सर॑स्वती[3] (sarasvatī) —Vedic speech, flow of mass energy in the intermediate space

प्र[4] (pra)—A prefix

चे॒त॒य॒ति॒ (cetayati)—to make known, nourish

के॒तुना॑[5] (ketunā)—through knowledge or through Intelligent action

धियः॑[6] (dhiyaḥ)—intelligent factor, mind

विश्वाः॑[1] (vishvāḥ)—all

---

1. महः उदकनाम निघं० 1.12. महन्नाम् निघं० 3.3. महो महतः नि० 9.25. पशवो वै महस्तस्माद् यस्यैते बहवो भवन्ति भूयिष्ठमस्यकुले महीयन्ते श० 11.8.1.3. यज्ञो वै देवानां महः श० 1.9.1.11. अध्वर्युरेव महः गो० पू० 5.15. यजुर्वेदो मह० श० 12.3.4.9. वायुर्महः श० 12.3.4.8. प्राणो महः श० 12.3.4.10. प्रतीच्येव महः गो० पू० 5.15. सुवर्गो वै लोको महः तै० 3.8.18.5. रुद्र एव महः गो० पू० 5.15. ग्रीष्म एव महः गो० पू० 5.15. त्रिष्टुभं महः गो० पू० 5.15. पंचदश एव महः गो० पू० 5.15.
2. अर्णः उदक नाम निघं० 1.12. अर्णा नदीनाम निघं० 1.13.
3. सरस् इत्युदकनाम सर्त्तेस्तुदवती नि० 9.26. सरस्वती वाङ्नाम निघं० 1.11. सरस्वत्यः नदीनाम निघं० 1.13. सरः वाङ्नाम निघं० 1.11 वाक् सरस्वती श० 7.5.1.32. वाग्वै सरस्वती कौ० 5.2. तां० 6.7.7. श० 2.5.4.6. तै० 1.3.4.5. गो० उ० 1.120. वाग्वै सरस्वती पवीरवी ऐ० 3.37. वागेव सरस्वती ऐ० 2.24. वाग्धि सरस्वती ऐ० 3.2. जिह्वा सरस्वती श० 12.9.1.14. (यजु० 38.2.) सरस्वती हि गौः श० 14.2.1.7. अमावस्या वै सरस्वती गो० उ० 1.12. योषा वै सरस्वती वृषा पूषा श० 2.5.1.11. एषा वा अपां पृष्ठं यत् सरस्वती तै० 1.8.5.5.
4. प्र परेत्यस्य प्रातिलोम्यम् नि० 1.3. प्रेव नश्यसि पराचीव नश्यसि नि० 9.28. अन्तरिक्षं वै प्र ऐ० 2.41. प्राणो वै प्र ऐ० 2.40.
5. केतुः प्रज्ञानाम निघं० 3.9. केतुना कर्मणा प्रज्ञया वा नि० 11.27. केतव रश्मयः नि० 12.15. केतुं प्रज्ञानम् नि० 12.7.
6. धीः कर्मनाम निघं० 2.1. प्रज्ञानाम निघं० 3.9. धियः-प्रज्ञानानि नि० 11.27. वाग्वै धीः श० 4.2.4.13.

वि[2] (vi)—A prefix

रा॒ज॒ति॒[3] (rājati)—nourish, enlightens, to bring into existence

Anvaya (Sequencial placement of words)

sarasvatī ketunā maho ārṇaḥ pracetayati visvā dhiyaḥ virājati.

Meaning of Mantra in different contexts :

Spiritual :(सरस्वती) The Vedic speech (प्र चेतयति) makes known (महो अर्णः) the vast ocean of knowledge. (विराजति) It enlightens/nourish (धियः) the mind (विश्वा) of all seekers (केतुना) through knoweldge.

Scientific 1: (सरस्वती) The flow of mass energy in the intermediate space (प्र चेतयति) produces (महो अर्णः) the vast ocean of matter particles in the observer space. (विश्वा विराजति) It makes everything in the observer space shine with (धियः) the factor of intelligence or smartness (केतुना) through intelligent action.

Note: The Veda wants to say that our universe is smart or an intelligent universe.

Scientific 2: (सरस्वती) Rainy waters puring down on the earth (प्र चेतयति) nourish (महो अर्णः) vast oceans. (केतुना) It is because of them, (विश्वा) the entire (धियः) life on the earth (विराजति) flourish.

Socio-political: (सरस्वती) A learned lady in the society (प्र चेतयति) awakens the (महो अर्णः) vast ocean of masses. (केतुना) It is because of their knowledge and action that (विश्वा) the entire wolrd may (विराजति) flourish with (धियः) lintelligent people.

Note: Veda emphasizes upon education of ladies. Educated ladies can transform the whole world.

---

1. यद्वै विश्वं सर्वं तत् श० 3.1.2.11. तदन्नं वै विश्वम्प्राणो मित्रम् जै० उ० 3.3.6.
2. वि इत्येकीभावस्य प्रातिलोम्यम् नि० 1.3.
3. राजति ऐश्वर्यकर्मा निघं० 2.21.

ANUVĀKA II

सूक्त - 4

ऋषि– मधुच्छन्दा वैश्वामित्र। देवता– इन्द्र। छन्द– गायत्री।

३१. सुरूपकृत्नुमूतये सुदुघामिव गोदुहे। जुहूमसि द्यविद्यवि।।१।।

सुरूपऽकृत्नुम्। ऊतये। सुदुघाम्ऽइव। गोदुहे। जुहूमसि। द्यविऽद्यवि।।

Saṁhitāpāṭha

surūpa-kṛtnum ūtaye sudughāmiva goduhe juhūmasi dyavi-dyavi.

Padapāṭha

surūpa-kṛtnum. ūtaye. sudughām-iva. goduhe. juhūmasi. dyavi-dyavi.

Grammatical Notes:

सुरूपकृत्नुम् (surūpa-kṛtnum)—Surūpa+Tanādigaṇ root √kṛñ 'to do'+ktnu (Uṇādi suffix) [1]. Being a compound, it receives accent on the last syllable [2].

ऊतये (ūtaye)—Bhvādigaṁa root √ava 'to protect', 'to move', 'to shine' 'to love', 'to enter', 'to hear', 'to request', 'to donate' 'to share', 'to increase'+ktin suffix[3]. Ktin suffix being accented, ūtaye receives an acute accent on the middle syllable.

सुदुघामिव (sudughām—iva) —Su+Adādigaṇa root √duha 'to fill up'+kap suffix. 'Ha' is replaced by 'gha'[4]+ṭāp fem. suffix+iva. '-Kap', being 'pit', goes without

---

1. Cf. *Uṇādi sūtra* कृहनिभ्यां क्तनुः -3.30.
2. Cf. Pāṇ. समासस्य - 6.1.223.
3. Cf. Pāṇ. ऊति-यूति-जूति-सति-हेति कीर्तयश्च - 3.3.97.
4. Cf. Pāṇ. दुहः कप् घश्च - 3.2.70.

accent. Under the circumstances root suffix on 'duh' will prevail. Compound form 'su-dughām—iva' has composition of three words. In case of the composition of first two words 'su-dughām', the accent will switch over to 'dughām', because as per rule of accentuation, if a primary derivative 'dughām' is preceded by a prefix 'su', the accent will switch over to the primary derivative in case the relationship between them is of determinative (Tatpuruṣa) nature[1]. Again, in case of composition of last two words 'dughām+iva', the rule of accentuation says that if a word is compounded with 'iva', it will retain its case ending as well as accent[2]. In both situations 'dughā' will receive accent.

गोदुहे (goduhe)—Go+Adādigaṇa root √duha 'to fill up'+kvip[3]. It will also receive accent on the second member 'duha', a primary derivative, preceded by 'go' in the relationship of Tatpuruṣa (determinative) compound[4].

जुहूमसि (juhūmasi)—Bhvādigaṇa root √hveñ 'to compete', 'to produce sound'+laṭ lakāra (present tense) first person pl. Here personal ending -mas, converts into -masi[5]. It, being a verbal form in the beginning of a hemistich, is accented.

द्यविद्यवि (dyavi—dyavi)—Loc. sing. of dyo. Bhvādigaṇa root √dyut 'to shine'+ḍoḥ Uṇādī suffix. Here 'dyavi' is repeated[6]. The second member will be called

---

1. Cf. Pāṇ. गतिकारकोपपदात् कृत् - 6.2.139.
2. Cf. *Vārttika* इवेन विभक्त्यलोपः पूर्वपदप्रकृति स्वरत्वं च - *Mahābhāṣya* on Pāṇ. 2.1.4
3. Cf. Pāṇ सत्सूद्विष० - 3.2.61.
4. Cf. Pāṇ. गति कारकोपपदात् कृत् - 6.2.139.
5. Cf. Pāṇ इदन्तो मसि - 7.1.46.
6. Cf. Pāṇ. नित्यवीप्सयोः 8.1.4.

Āmreḍita[1], and so will lose its accent[2]. The first member 'dyavi' will receive its accent on nominal stem.

Word meanings:

सुरूपकृत्नुम्[3] (surūpa-kṛtnum)—Effulgent God, luminous electric force, a teacher having a luminous aura, a ruler shining with physical prowess.

ऊतये[4] (ūtaye) —for protection

सुदुघामिव (sudughām-iva)—good milch cow

गोदुहे (goduhe)—milk

जुहूमसि (juhūmasi)—remember

द्यविद्यवि[5] (dyavi—dyavi)—daily

Anvaya (Sequencial placement of words)

surūpa kṛtnum ūtaye dyavi dyavi sudughāmiva goduhe juhūmasi.

Meaning of Mantra in different contexts :

Spiritual: We (द्यवि द्यवि) daily (जुहूमसि) invoke/ remember (सुरूपकृत्नुम) the effulgent Brahman (ऊतये) for our protection, (इव) just like (सुदुघाम्) a good milch-cow is remembered (गोदुहे) for the milk.

Scientific 1: We (द्यवि द्यवि) daily (जुहूमसि) remember (सुरूपकृत्नुम) the luminous electric force (ऊतये) for the protection

---

1. Cf. Pāṇ. तस्यपरमाम्रेडितम् - 8.1.2.
2. Cf. Pāṇ. अनुदात्तं च - 8.1.3.
3. योऽयमनिरुक्तः प्राणः स सुरूपकृत्नुः कौ० 16.4.
4. ऊतिरवनात् निघं० 5.3. ऊती ऊत्या च पथा (च) नि० 12.21. ऊतयः खलु वै ता नाम याभिर्देवा यजमानस्य हवमायन्ति। ये वै पन्थानो या सुतयस्ता वा ऊतयस्त उ एवैतत् स्वर्गयाणा यजमानस्य भवन्ति ऐ० 1.2.
5. द्यविद्यवि अहर्नाम निघं० 1.9. द्युरित्यह्नो नामधेयम्, द्योतत इति सतः नि० 1.6. द्युभिः-अहोभि नि० 6.1.

of our universe, (इव) just like (सुदुघाम्) a good milch-cow is remembered (गोदुहे) for the milk.

Scientific 2: We (द्यवि द्यवि) daily (जुहूमसि) remember (सुरूपकृत्नुम) the luminous sun for (ऊतये) the protection of our life on the earth, (इव) just like (सुदुघाम्) a good milch-cow is remembered (गोदुहे) for the milk.

Socio-political 1: We (द्यवि द्यवि) daily (जुहूमसि) remember (सुरूपकृत्नुम) the teacher having a luminous aura around his face (ऊतये) for protecting us with knowledge, (इव) just like (सुदुघाम्) a good milch-cow is remembered (गोदुहे) for the milk.

Socio-political 2: We (द्यवि द्यवि) daily (जुहूमसि) remember (सुरूपकृत्नुम) a ruler shining with physical prowess (ऊतये for giving us protection (economic, political and social), (इव) just like (सुदुघाम्) a good milch-cow is remembered (गोदुहे) for the milk.

३२. उप नः सवनागहि सोमस्य सोमपाः पिब।
गोदा इद्रेवतो मदः।।२।।

उप। नः। सवन। आ। गहि। सोमस्य। सोमऽपाः। पिब।
गोऽदा। इत्। रेवतः। मदः।।

Saṁhitāpāṭha

upa naḥ savan ā-gahi somasya somapāḥ piba. godā id-revato madaḥ.

Padapāṭha

upa. naḥ. savanā. ā. gahi. somasya. soma-pāḥ. piba. go-dā. it. revataḥ. madaḥ.

Grammatical Notes:

उप (upa)—A prefix meaning closeness. Being a prefix, it is accented on the first syllable.[1]

नः (naḥ)—Acc./dat./gen. pl. enclitic form of first person pronoun 'Asmad'[2]. Being an enclitic form it is not accented.[3]

सवन (savanā)—Bhvādigaṇa root √ ṣu 'to deliver', 'to prosper' or Svādīgaṇa root √ ṣuñ 'to sqeeze' or 'to press'+lyuṭ in the instrumental or locative sense [4]. being formed of 'lit' suffix (of which 'l' is elided) the preceding of 'lit' 'sa' is accented [5].

आ (ā)—A prefix meaning proximity, conjunction and simli.

---

1. Cf. *Phiṭ sūtra*—उपसर्गश्चाभिवर्जम् - 81.
2. Cf. *vahuvacanasyavasnasau*—Pāṇ. 8.1.21.
3. Cf. Pāṇ. युस्मदस्मदोः षष्ठी चतुर्थी द्वितीया स्थयोर्वान्नावौ 8.1.20.
4. Cf. Pāṇ. अधिकरणे ल्युट् - 3.3.117.
5. Cf. Pāṇ. लिति - 6.1.193.

Being a prefix, it is accented on the first syllable[1].

ग॒हि (gahi)—Bhvādigaṇa root √ gam+loṭ lakāra (imperative) second person sing. Being a verbal form preceded by a non-verbal form, it goes without accent[2].

सोम॑स्य (somasya)—Gen. sing. of soma. Bhvādigaṇa root √ṣu 'to deliver', 'to glorify' or Svādigaṇa root √ṣuñ 'to squeez' or √ṣu 'to inspire'+man (Uṇādi suffix)[3]. Due to 'nit' (having indicatory 'n') suffix, the word 'soma' gets accent on the first syllable[4].

सो॒म॒पा॒: (soma-pāḥ)—Voc. sing. of somapā. Soma+Adādigaṇa root √ pā 'to protect' or Bhvādigaṇa root √ pā 'to drink'+kvip suffix. Being a vocative form not located in the beginning of a hemistich, it remains unaccented[5].

पि॒ब॒ (piba)—Bhvādigaṇa root √pā 'to drink'+loṭ lakāra (imperative) second person sing. Being a verbal form preceded by a non—verbal form, it goes without an accent[6].

गो॒दा (go-dā)—Go+Juhotyādigaṇa root √ dāñ 'to donate'+kvip[7] or Go+Adādigaṇa root √ duha 'to complete'+kvip[8]. It receives suffixal accent and so accented on the last syllable[9].

---

1. Cf. *Phiṭ sūtra*—उपसर्गाश्चाभिवर्जम् -81.
2. Cf. Pāṇ. तिङ्ङतिङः 8.1.28.
3. *artti-stu-su-hu-sṛ-dhṛ-kṣi-kṣu-bhā-yā-vā-padi-uakṣi-nī-bhyo man- Uṇādi sūtra*—1.140.
4. Cf. Paṇini (6.1.197)—*ñnityādinityam.*
5. Cf. Pāṇ. आमन्त्रितस्य च - 8.1.19.
6. Cf. Pāṇ. तिङ्ङतिङः 8.1.28.
7. Cf. Pāṇ. क्विप् च - 3.2.76.
8. Cf. Pāṇ. सत्सूद्विष० 3.2.61.
9. Cf. Pāṇ. आद्युदात्तश्च - 3.1.3.

इत् (it)—A particle used in the sense of 'determination'.

रेवतः (revataḥ)—Rayi+matup in the sense of 'possession'. Matup>vatup [1]. Here suffix will be accented [2].

मदः (madaḥ)—Divādigaṇa root √ madī 'to be happy'+ap suffix [3]. 'Ap' suffix being 'pit', root syllable is accented.

Word meanings:

उप[4] (upa)—close

नः (naḥ)—us

सवन (savanā)—creation, mass energy, three periods of morning, noon and evening of creation of mass and energy (yajña).

आ[5] (ā)—proximity, conjunction and simli.

गहि (gahi)—come

सोमस्य [6] (somasya)—charged matter particles, creation,

---

1. Cf. Pāṇ. छन्दसीरः - 8.2.14.
2. Cf. Pāṇ. ह्रस्वनुडभ्यां मतुप - 6.1.176.
3. Cf. Pāṇ. मदोऽनुपसर्गे - 3.3.67.
4. उप इत्युपजनम् नि० 1.3. इयं (पृथिवी) वा ऽउप श० 2.3.4.9. उप वै रथन्तरम् तां० 16.5.14.
5. अर्वागर्थे नि० 1.3. एतस्मिन्नेवार्थे (समुच्चयार्थे) देवेभ्यश्च पितृभ्य एत्याकारः नि० 1.4. उपमार्थे दृश्यते नि० 3.16. अध्यर्थे दृश्यते नि० 5.5.
6. सोमः सुनोतेर्यदेनमभिषुण्वन्ति नि० 11.2. स्वा वै मऽएषेति तस्मात्सोमो नाम श० 3.9.4.22. सत्यं (वै) श्रीर्ज्योतिः सोमः श० 5.1.2.10. श्रीर्वै सोमः श० 4.1.3.9. सोमो राजा राजपतिः तै० 2.5.7.3. असौ वै सोमो राजा विचक्षणश्चन्द्रमाः कौ० 4.4. सोमो राजा चन्द्रमाः श०10.4. 2.1. चन्द्रमा वै सोमः कौ० 16.5. वृत्रो वै सोम आसीत् श० 3.4.3.13. संवत्सरो वै सोमो राजा कौ० 7.10. सोमो हि प्रजापतिः श० 5.1.5.26. सोमो वैष्णवो राजेत्याह तस्याप्सरसो विशः श० 13.4.3.8. जुष्टा विष्णव इति। जुष्टा सोमायेत्येवैतदाह (विष्णुः-सोमः) श० 3.2.4. 12. तद् यदेवेदं क्रीतो विशतीव तदु हास्य (सोमस्य) वैष्णवं रूपम् कौ० 8.2. सोमो वै

students, electric charge

सोमपाः (soma—pāḥ)—Address to somapā. Protector of soma (creation, students), drinker of electric charge

पिब (piba)—inbibe, consume

गोदा (go-dā)—prosperity

इत्[1] (it)—surely

रेवतः (revataḥ)—knowledge, power

मदः[2] (madaḥ)—intoxication, favour

Anvaya (Sequencial placement of words)

somapāḥ savana upa ā-gahi. revataḥ somasya piba. madaḥ naḥ godā it.

Meaning of Mantra in different contexts :

Spiritual: Brahman, (सोमपाः) the protector (सोमस्य) of

पवमानः श० 2.2.3.22. एष (वायुः) वै सोमस्योद्गीथो यत्पवते तां० .6.18. तस्मात् सोमं सर्वेभ्यो देवेभ्यो जुह्वति तस्मादाहुः सोमः सर्वा देवता इति श० 1.6.3.21. सोमो वाऽइन्द्रः श० 2.2.3.23. सोमो रात्रिः श० 3.4.4.15. सोम एव सवृत इति गो० उ० 2.24. सोमो वै चतुर्होता तै० 2.3.1.1. सोमो वै पर्णः श० 6.5.1.1. सोमो वै पलाशः कौ० 2.2. पशुर्वै प्रत्यक्षं सोमः श० 5.1.3.7. सोम एवैव प्रत्यक्षं यत्पशुः कौ० 12.6. पशवः सोमोः राजा तै० 1.4.7.6. सोमो वै दधि तै० 1.4.7.6. एष वै यजमानो यत्सोमः तै० 1.3.3.5. द्यावापृथिव्योर्वा एष गर्भो यत्सोमो राजा ऐ० 2.26. क्षत्रं सोमः ऐ० 2.38. यशो वै सोमः श० 4.2.4.9. यशो (ऋ० 10. 72.10.) वै सोमो राजा ऐ० 1.13. प्राणः सोमः श० 7.3.1.2. रसः सोमः श० 7.3.1.3. तस्मात् सोमो राजा सर्वाणि नक्षत्राण्युपैति प० 3.12. तै० 1.1.3.10. अन्तरिक्षदेवत्यो हि सोमः गो० उ० 2.4. गिरिषु हि सोमः श० 3.3.4.7. घ्नन्ति खलु वाऽएतत्सोमं यदभिषुण्वन्ति तै० 2.2.8.1.सोमो राजा मृगशीर्षेण आगन् श० 3.1.2.2. सोमवीरुधां पते तै० 3.11.4.1. आपः सोमः सुतः श० 7.1.1.22. आपो ह्येतस्य (सोमस्य) लोकः श० 4.4.5.21. पुमान् वै सोमः स्त्री सुरा तै० 1.3.3.4.

1. इत् पदपूरणः नि० 1.9. महान् नि० 6.1.
2. मदाय मदनीयाय जैत्राय नि० 4.8. यो वा ऋचि मदो यः सामन्नसो वै सः श० 4.3.2.5. रसो वै मदः जै० 1.215.

creation, (उपागहि) manifest here. (नः) Make us (पिब) imbibe (सवन) the knowledge of this creation (Veda). (मदः) The bliss of this knowledge (इत्) be surely (गोदा) for our prosperity and (रेवतः) power.

Scientific 1: Electric force, (सोमपाः) the drinker (सोमस्य) of electric charge (उपागहि) comes in the observer space (सवन) through rich electirc charge. It (पिब) consumes electirc charge and (मदः) gets intoxicated which is for (नः) our (गोदा) prosperity and (रेवतः) power.

Note :Mantra says that Indra is repulsive electric force of nature which is created due to (soma) rich electric charge in nature. This phenomenon is figuratively decribed as intoxication of Indra by drinking of soma. This intoxication of Indra is for the prosperity and power of observer space. As Indra as the repulsive electric force helps expansion of the universe.Expansion signifies the sustenance of the universe and contraction signifies its collapse.

Scientific 2: Sun, (सोमपाः) the protector of (सोमस्य) this creation on our earth, (उपागहि) be present in this world for (नः) us (पिब) to enjoy (सवन) your sunlight. (मदः) Your favour (इत्) is surely meant (गोदा) for our prosperity and (रेवतः) nourishment.

Socio-political 1: Teacher, (सोमपाः) the custodian of (सोमस्य) younger generation in the nation, (उपागहि) be present in the nation for (नः) us (पिब) to enjoy (सवन) education/ knowledge. (मदः) Your favour (इत्) is surely meant (गोदा) for our prosperity and (रेवतः) power.

३३. अथा ते अन्तमानां विद्याम सुमतीनाम्।
मा नो अतिख्य आगहि।।३।।

अथ। ते। अन्तमानाम्। विद्याम। सुमतीनाम्। मा। नः। अति। ख्यः। आ। गहि।।

Saṁhitāpāṭha

athā te antamānāṁ vidyāma sumatinām. mā no atikhya āgahi.

Padapāṭha

atha. te. antamānām. vidyāma. sumatinām. mā. naḥ. ati. khyaḥ. ā. gahi.

Grammatical Notes:

अथ (atha)—A particle meaning (afterwards). The final 'a' of 'atha' is prolonged[1]. Being a particle, it is accented on the initial syllable[2].

ते (te)—Gen. sing. enclitic form of second person pronoun 'Yusmad'. Being an enclitic form, it goes without accent [3].

अन्तमानाम् (antamānām) —{Anta + ṭhan [4]} + tamap (superlative degree suffix)[5]. 'T' of 'tamap' is elided[6]. 'Tamap', being 'pit', remains unaccented. As a result, the accent will go on the first syllable of 'anta', being formed of 'nit' suffix.

---

1. Cf. Pāṇ. निपातस्य च - 6.3.136
2. Cf. Phiṭ. Sūtra—निपाताः आद्युदात्ताः - 80
3. Cf. Pāṇ. युस्मदस्मदोः षष्ठी चतुर्थी द्वितीया स्थयोर्वान्नावौ 8.1.20.
4. Cf. Pāṇ. अत इनिठनौ - 5.2.115
5. Cf. Pāṇ. अतिशायने मतुप् - 5.3.55
6. Cf. *Vārttika*— तमे तादेश्च -on Pāṇ.—6.4.149

वि॒द्याम॑ (vidyāma)—Adādigaṇa root √ vid 'to know'+liṅ lakāra (subjunctive mood) first person pl. Being in the beginning of hemistich, it gets an accent [1].

सु॒म॒ती॒नाम् (sumatinām)—Gen. pl. of sumati.

Su+Divādigaṇa root √ mana 'to know'+ktin suffix [2]+matup. In sumatinām, gen. pl. case ending 'nām' will be accented, since as per rules of accentuation, [3]'matup' is preceded by a short vowel of 'mati'.

मा (mā)—Particle of Negation. Being a particle, it is accented on the first syllable [4].

न॒: (naḥ)—Acc./dat./gen. pl. enclitic form of first person pronoun 'Asmad' [5]. Being an enclitic form it is not accented. [6]

अति॑ (ati)—Ati is a particle. Being a particle, it is accented on the first syllable [7].

ख्य॒: (khyaḥ)—Adādigaṇa root √khā 'to narrate' luṅ lakāra (aorist) second person sing. Being a verbal form preceded by a non—verbal form, it is not accented [8].

आ (ā)—A prefix meaning proximity, conjunction and simli. Being a prefix, it is accented on the first syllable [9].

ग॒हि॒ (gahi)—Bhvādigaṇa root √ gam+loṭ lakāra (imperative)

---

1. Cf. Pāṇ. तिङ्ङतिङः - 8.1.28.
2. Cf. Pāṇ. मन्त्रेवृषेपचमन-विद-भूवीरा उदात्तः - 3.3.93.
3. Cf. Pāṇ. नामन्यतरस्याम् - 6.1.177.
4. Cf. *Phiṭ sūtra*—निपाताः आद्युदात्ताः - 80
5. Cf. *vahuvacanasyavasnasau*—Pāṇ. 8.1.21.
6. Cf. Pāṇ. युस्मदस्मदोः षष्ठी चतुर्थी द्वितीया स्थयोर्वान्नावौ 8.1.20.
7. Cf. *Phit sūtra* निपाताः आद्युदात्ताः - 80.
8. Cf. Pāṇ तिङ्ङतिङः 8.1.28.
9. Cf. *Phiṭ sūtra*—उपसर्गाश्चाभिवर्जम् -81.

second person sing. Being a verbal form preceded by a non—verbal form, it goes without accent [1].

Word meanings:

अथ॑ (atha)—afterwards

ते॒ (te) —you

अन्त॑मानाम् (antamānām) —closeness अन्तमानाम् अन्तिकनाम निघं० 2.16

वि॒द्याम॑ (vidyāma)—realise, recognise

सु॒म॒ती॒नाम् (sumatinām)—high spirited yogis, Vedic cosmologists, intelligent students

मा (mā)—Negation, don't

नः॒ (naḥ)—to us

अति॑ख्य॒ः (atikhyaḥ)—pass by, overlook

आग॒हि॒ (āgahi)—come, reveal, known

Anvaya (Sequencial placement of words)

athā antamānāṁ sumatinām te vidyāma. mā no atikhya. āgahi.

Meaning of Mantra in different contexts :

Spiritual: Brahman! (विद्याम) we know (ते) you (सुमतीनाम्) in the company of high profile yogis who have realised you and (अथ) afterwards (अन्तमानाम्) living close to you. (आगहि) Reveal yourself to (नः) us. (मा) Don't (अतिख्य) overlook us.

Scientific 1: Electric force! ! (विद्याम) we know you through (सुमतीनाम्) high profile yogis who discovered you and (अथ) afterwards (अन्तमानाम्) observing your behavior closely. (आगहि) Be known to (नः) us. (मा) Don't (अतिख्य) overlook us.

Scientific 2: Sun! (विद्याम) we know your properties through

---

1. Cf. Pāṇ. तिङ्ङतिङः 8.1.28.

(सुमतीनाम्) scholars (अथ अन्तमानाम्) observing your behavior closely. (आगहि) Come to light up this world. (मा) Don't (अतिख्य) ignore (नः) us.

Socio-political: Teacher! (विद्याम) we could recognise you through (सुमतीनाम्) your intelligent (अथ अन्तमानाम्) students. (आगहि) Come to enlighten (नः) us with the knowledge. (मा) Don't (अतिख्य) ignore us.

३४. परेहि विग्रमस्तृतमिन्द्रं पृच्छा विपश्चितम्।
यस्ते सखिभ्य आ वरम्।।४।।

परा। इहि। विग्रम्। अस्तृतम्। इन्द्रम्। पृच्छ। विपःऽचितम्।
यः। ते। सखिभ्यः। आ। वरम्।।

Saṁhitāpāṭha

parehi vigram-astṛtam indram pṛcchā vipaścitam. yaste sakhibhya ā varam.

Padapāṭha

parā. ihi. vigram. astṛtam. indram. pṛccha. vipaḥ—citam. yaḥ. te.sakhibhyaḥ. ā. varam.

Grammatical Notes:

परा (parā)—Being a particle, it is accented on the first syllable [1].

इहि (ihi)—Adādigaṇa root √iṇ 'to go'+loṭ lakāra (imperative mood) second person sing. Being a verbal form preceded by a non—verbal form, it is accented [2].

विग्रम् (vigram)—Compound between vi+nāsikā. Nāsikā is replaced by 'graḥ' [3]. It is accented on the first syllable, just like the words read in the list of 'vṛṣa' group of words [4].

अस्तृतम् (astṛtam)—Nañ+stṛta (Negative determinative compound). We don't find any verbal root to form stṛta. But Yāska forms it from the root √ stṛ 'to kill'+kta suffix.

---

1. Cf. Phit sūtra - निपाताः आद्युदात्ताः - 80.
2. Cf. Pāṇ. तिङ्ङतिङः 8.1.28.
3. Cf. *Vārttika* वेर्ग्रो वक्तव्यः - 5.4.119.
4. Cf. Pāṇ. वृषादीनाम् - 6.1.203.

इन्द्रम् (indram)—Acc. sing. of Indra. Bhvādigaṇa root √idi 'to prosper'+ran (Uṇādi suffix).[1] 'Nit' suffix (of which final 'n' is elided) makes it accented on the first syllable[2].

पृच्छ (pṛccha)—Tudādigaṇa root √ praccha 'to be curious'+loṭ lakāra (imperative) second person sing.

विपश्चितम् (vipaś—citam)—{Vi+Adādigaṇa root √pā 'to protect'+kaḥ suffix[3]}+{Bhvādigaṇa root √ ati 'to be conscious'+kvip}+{Bhvādigaṇa root √citī 'to be conscious of'+kvip}.

यः (yaḥ)—Nom. sing. masc. of demonstrative Pronoun 'Yad'. Being a pronominal form, it is accented.

ते (te)—Dat. gen. sing. enclitic form of second person pronoun 'Yusmad'[4]. Being an enclitic form, it is not accented[5].

सखिभ्यः (sakhibhyaḥ)—Dat. pl. of sakhi.

Samāna+Adādigaṇa root √ khyā 'to state'+iṇ (Uṇādi suffix)[6]. Here 'samāna' is substituted by 's'[7].

आ (ā)—A prefix meaning proximity, conjunction and simli. Being a prefix, it is accented on the first syllable[8].

वरम् (varam)—Svādigaṇa root √ vṛñ 'to choose'+ap suffix[9].

---

1. Cf. *Uṇādi*. ऋज्रेन्द्राग्रवज्र० - 2.28.
2. Cf. Pāṇ. ञ्नित्यादिर्नित्यम् - 6.1.197
3. Cf. Pāṇ. आतश्चोपसर्गे - 3.1.136.
4. Cf. Pāṇ. तेमयावेकवचनस्य - 8.1.22.
5. Cf. Pāṇ. युस्मदस्मदोः षष्ठी चतुर्थी द्वितीया स्थयोर्वान्नावौ - 8.1.20.
6. Cf. *Uṇādi sūtra* - समाने ख्यः स चोदात्तः 3.137.
7. Cf. Pāṇ. समानस्य छन्दस्यमूर्द्धप्रभृत्युदर्केषु - 6.3.84.
8. Cf. *Phiṭ sūtra*—उपसर्गाश्चाभिवर्जम् -81.

suffix[1]. Here 'ap' suffix is not accented being 'pit'. So the root accent on 'va' will prevail [2].

Word meanings:

परा[3] (parā)—close

इहि (ihi) —go

विग्रम् (vigram)—Attributive of Indra. Allknowing, Intelligent

अस्तृतम् (astṛtam)—Attributive of Indra. Non-violent

इन्द्रम्[4] (indram)—God, scholar

पृच्छ (pṛccha)—pray, ask

विपश्चितम्[5] (vipaś-citam)—Attributive of Indra. All knowing, expert

यः (yaḥ)—what is

ते (te)—your

---

1. Cf. Pāṇ. ग्रहवृद्धनिश्चि - 3.3.58.
2. Cf. Pāṇ. आद्युदात्तश्च - 3.1.3.
3. प्रपरेत्यस्य प्रातिलोम्यं प्राहुः नि० 10.3.; 3.49.
4. इन्द्रः पदनाम निघं० 5.4. इन्द्रः-इरां दृणातीति वा इरां ददातीति वा, इरां दधातीति वा। इरां दारयत इति वा। इरां धारयत इति वा। इन्दवे द्रवतीति वा। इन्दौ रमत इति वा। इन्धे भूतानीति वा। 'तद्यदेनं प्राणैः समैन्धंस्तदिन्द्रस्येन्द्रत्वमिति विज्ञायते।' इदं करणादित्याग्रायणः। इदं दर्शनादित्यौपमन्यवः। इन्दतेर्वैश्वर्यकर्मणः। इन्दञ्छत्रूणां दारयिता वा द्रावयिता वा। आदरयिता च यज्वनाम् नि० 10.8. एष वै शुक्रो य एष (सूर्यः) तपत्येष (सूर्यः) उ एवेन्द्रः श० 4.5.5. 7, 4.5.9.4. अथ यः स इन्द्रोऽसौ स आदित्यः श० 8.5.3.2. यो वै वायुः स इन्द्रो य इन्द्रः स वायुः श० 4.1.3.19. स योऽयं मध्ये प्राणः। एष एवेन्द्रस्तानेष प्राणान्मध्यत इन्द्रियैणैन्द्ध तस्मादिन्ध इन्धो ह वै तमिन्द्र इत्याचक्षते परोऽक्षम् श० 6.1.1.2. हृदयमेवेन्द्रः श० 12.9.1.15. यन्मनः स इन्द्रः गो० उ० 4.11. मन एवेन्द्रः श० 12.9.1.13. इन्द्रो वै यजमानः श० 2.1.2.11 क्षत्रियो यदु च यजमानः श० 5.3.5.27. एन्द्रो वै राजन्य तै० 3.8.23.2. इन्द्रः क्षत्रम् श० 10.4.1.5. वीर्यं वा इन्द्रः तां० 9.7.5, इन्द्रो यज्ञस्य नेता श० 4.1.2.15.
5. विपश्चित् मेधाविनाम निघं० 3.15. यज्ञो वै बृहन् विपश्चित् श० 3.5.3.12.

सखिभ्यः[1] (sakhibhyaḥ)—for friends

आ[2] (ā)—proximity, conjunction and simli.

वरम्[3] (varam)—good

Anvaya (Sequencial placement of words)

parehi indram vigram astṛtam vipaścitam. yas te sakhibhya ā varam pṛccha.

Meaning of Mantra in different contexts :

Spiritual: (परेहि) Go close to (इन्द्रम्) the Brahman, (विपश्चितम्) who is very intelligent, (अस्तृतम्) non-violent and (विग्रम्) all knowing. (पृच्छ) Pray to him (यः) for what (वरम्) is good for (ते) your (सखिभ्यः) friends.

Note : Here the mantra says to look after the interest of those who are friendly to you and never harbor ill-will against you.

Socio-political: (परेहि) Go close to (इन्द्रम्) scholar (विपश्चितम्) who is very intelligent, (अस्तृतम्) non-violent and (विग्रम्) learned. (पृच्छ) Ask him (यः) what (वरम्) is good for (ते) your (सखिभ्यः) friends.

---

1. सखायः समानख्यानाः नि० 7.30. सखायः सप्तपदा अभूम तै० 3.7.7.11
2. अर्वागर्थे नि० 1.3. एतस्मिन्नेवार्थे (समुच्चयार्थे) देवेभ्यश्च पितृभ्य एत्याकारः नि० 1.4. उपमार्थे दृश्यते नि० 3.16. अध्यर्थे दृश्यते नि० 5.5.
3. वरो वरयितव्यो भवति नि० 1.7. वर इव वै स्वर्गो लोकः जै० 2.99. वरो न प्रतिगृह्यः तै० सं० 7.1.6.5. सर्वं वै वरः श० 2.2.1.4

३५. उत ब्रुवन्तु नो निदो निरन्यतश्चिदारत। दधाना इन्द्र इद्दुवः।।५।।

उत। ब्रुवन्तु। नः। निदः। निः। अन्यतः। चित्। आरत। दधानाः।
इन्द्रे। इत्। दुवः।।

Saṁhitāpāṭha

uta bruvantu no nido niranyataścidārata. dadhānā indra idduvaḥ.

Padapāṭha

uta. bruvantu. naḥ. nidaḥ. niḥ.anyataḥ. cit. ārata. dadhānāḥ. indre. it. duvaḥ.

Grammatical Notes:

उत (uta)—A particle. According to the rule of accentuations, it should have been accented on the first syllable[1], but it is not so. Pāṇini has read several particles in the group of 'svara' particles (svrādigaṇa) as accented on final syllable under his aphorism—स्वरादीनिपातमव्ययम् - 1.1.37. But he makes no mention of 'uta' among such particles. As such 'uta' may also be added to the list of particles mentioned in svrādigaṇa as—उत छन्दसि। Its accent on final syllable is also governed by Phiṭ sūtra 2.

ब्रुवन्तु (bruvantu)—Adādigaṇa root √brūñ 'to speak' + loṭ lakāra (imperative) third person pl.

नः (naḥ) —Acc./dat./gen. pl. enclitic form of first person pronoun 'Asmad'[3]. Being an enclitic form it is not accented.[4]

---

1. Cf. *Phiṭ sūtra*—निपाताः आद्युदात्ताः - ८०.

2. एवादीनामन्तः (evādinām—antaḥ) -82.

3. Cf. *vahuvacanasyavasnasau*—Pāṇ. 8.1.21.

4. Cf. Pāṇ. युस्मदस्मदोः षष्ठी चतुर्थी द्वितीया स्थयोर्वान्नावौ 8.1.20.

निदः (nidaḥ)—Bhvādigaṇa root √ṇidi 'back biting'+kvip suffix.-Kvip, being 'pit', remains unaccented. As such the root suffix prevails [1].

निः (niḥ)—

अन्यतः (anyataḥ)—Anyataḥ+tasi (representing all case endings).

चित् (cit)—Bhvādigaṇa root √citī 'to be conscious of' +kvip

आरत (ārata)—Ā+Juhotyādigaṇa root √ṛ to go'+luṅ (aorist) lakāra second person pl. in the sense of loṭ lakāra (imperative) [2]. Being a verbal form preceded by a non—verbal form, it goes without accent [3].

दधानाः (dadhānāḥ)—Juhotyādigaṇa root √(ḍu)dhāñ 'to sustain, 'to bring up'+śānac (-ān, present active participle)+ṭāp fem. suffix. Suffix being 'cit', should have been accented finally, but due to reduplication, it is accented initially [4].

इन्द्रे (indre)—Loc. sing. of Indra. Bhvādigaṇa root √idi 'to prosper'+ran (Uṇādi suffix).[5] 'Nit' suffix (of which final 'n' is elided) makes it accented on the first syllable[6].

इत् (it)—A particle used in the sense of 'determination'

दुवः (duvaḥ)—√Duva 'to serve'+kvip suffix. This root is not traceable to any of the list of roots furnished by Pāṇini and his followers. This root has been quoted by

1. Cf. Pāṇ. आद्युदात्तश्च - 3.1.3
2. Cf. Pāṇ. छन्दसि लुङ्लङ्लिटः-3.4.6
3. Cf. Pāṇ. तिङ्ङतिङः - 8.1.28
4. Cf. Pāṇ. अभ्यस्तानामादिः - 6.1.189
5. Cf. *Uṇādi.* ऋज्रेन्द्राग्रवज्र० - 2.28.
6. Cf. Pāṇ. ञ्नित्यादिर्नित्यम् - 6.1.197

Yāska[1]. According to Sāyaṇa, its accent on first syllable is governed by Phiṭ sūtra [2].

Word meanings:

उ॒त[3] (uta)—only

ब्रु॒व॒न्तु (bruvantu)—teach

न॒: (naḥ) —us

नि॒दः[4] (nidaḥ)—non-believers, atheists

निः[5] (niḥ)—determinative sense

अ॒न्यतः (anyataḥ)—other place

चि॒त्[6] (cit)—surely

आ॒र॒त (ārata)—go

दधानाः (dadhānāḥ)—to do

इन्द्रे[7] (indre)—God

1. *Nighaṇṭu*—3.5
2. Cf. *Phiṭ sūtra*—नब्विषयस्यानिसन्तस्य - 26
3. उत अपि नि० 1.6. च नि० 10.27.
4. निदः-अभिनिन्दितारम् नि० 10.42.
5. निश्चिताऽर्थे 1.22.10. नित्यम् 1.52.15. नितरां कियायोगे 1.8.2. सदैव, आर्याभि० 1.16, ऋ० 1.3.10.14. नीचैः 27.4
6. अथापि पशुनामेह भवत्युदात्तः चिदसि मनांसि धीरसि चितास्त्वयि भोगाः, चेतयस इति वा नि 5. चित् मर्मणि नि०6.33
चिदित्येषोऽनेककर्मा। आचार्यश्चिदिदं ब्रयादिति पूजायाम्। दधिचिदित्युपमार्थे कुल्माषाश्चिदाहरेत्यवकुत्सिते नि० 1.4.
7. इन्द्रः पदनाम निघं० 5.4. इन्द्रः-इरां दृणातीति वा इरां ददातीति वा, इरां दधातीति वा। इरां दारयत इति वा। इरां धारयत इति वा। इन्दवे द्रवतीति वा। इन्दौ रमत इति वा। इन्धे भूतानीति वा। 'तद्यदेनं प्राणैः समैन्धंस्तदिन्द्रस्येन्द्रत्वमिति विज्ञायते।' इदं करणादित्याग्रायणः। इदं दर्शनादित्यौपमन्यवः। इन्दतेर्वैश्वर्यकर्मणः। इन्दञ्छत्रूणां दारयिता वा द्रावयिता वा। आदरयिता च यज्वनाम् नि० 10.8. एष वै शुक्रो य एष (सूर्यः) तपत्येष (सूर्यः) उ एवेन्द्रः श० 4.5.5.7,

इत्[1] (it)—surely

दुवः[2] (duvaḥ)—worship

Anvaya (Sequencial placement of words)

indre duvaḥ dadhānā uta naḥ bruvantu. nidaḥ it anyataś cid nir ārata.

Meaning of Mantra in different contexts :

Socio-politiccal Context: The scholars/teachers, (इन्द्रे दुवः दधानाः) who are doing 'duvas' (prayers) or worship of Brahman, (उत) should only (ब्रुवन्तु) teach (नः) us. (निद्) The non-believers should (चित्) surely (आरत) go (निरन्यत्) to some other place.

Note : The Vedic mantra emphasizes that non-believers cannot be the teachers or spiritual guides.It should be noted that the Urdu word 'duā' meaning 'prayer' is formed of the Vedic word 'duva'.

4.5.9.4. अथ यः स इन्द्रोऽसौ स आदित्यः श० 8.5.3.2. यो वै वायुः स इन्द्रो य इन्द्रः स वायुः श० 4.1.3.19. स योऽयं मध्ये प्राणः। एषे एवेन्द्रस्तानेष प्राणान्मध्यत इन्द्रियैणैन्द्ध तस्मादिन्ध इन्धो ह वै तमिन्द्र इत्याचक्षते परोऽक्षम् श० 6.1.1.2. हृदयमेवेन्द्रः श० 12.9.1.15. यन्मनः स इन्द्रः गो० उ० 4.11. मन एवेन्द्रः श० 12.9.1.13. इन्द्रो वै यजमानः श०2.1.2.11 क्षत्रियो यदु च यजमानः श० 5.3.5.27. एन्द्रो वै राजन्य तै० 3.8.23.2. इन्द्रः क्षत्रम् श०10.4. 1.5. वीर्यं वा इन्द्रः तां० 9.7.5, 8. इन्द्रो यज्ञस्य नेता श० 4.1.2.15.

1. इत् पदपूरणः नि० 1.9.
2. दुवस्यति परिचरणकर्मा निघं० 3.5.

३६. उत नः सुभगाँ अरिर्वोचेयुर्दस्म कृष्टयः।
स्यामेदिन्द्रस्य शर्मणि।।६।।

उत। नः। सुभगान्। अरिः। वोचेयुः। दस्म। कृष्टयः। स्याम। इत्।
इन्द्रस्य। शर्मणि।।

Saṁhitāpāṭha

uta naḥ subhagān arir-voceyur-dasma kṛṣṭayaḥ.
syāmedindrasya śarmaṇi.

Padapāṭha

uta. naḥ. subhagān. ariḥ. voceyuḥ.dasma. kṛṣṭayaḥ. syāma. it. indrasya. śarmaṇi.

Grammatical Notes:

उत (uta)—A particle. According to the rule of accentuations, it should have been accented on the first syllable [1], but it is not so. Pāṇini has read several particles in the group of 'svara' particles (svrādigaṇa) as accented on final syllable under his aphorism—स्वरादीनिपातमव्ययम् (svarādī-nipātam-avyayam -1.1.37. But he makes no mention of 'uta' among such particles. As such 'uta' may also be added to the list of particles mentioned in svrādigaṇa as—उत छन्दसि (uta chandasi). Its accent on final syllable is also governed by Phiṭ sūtra—एवादीनामन्तः (evādinām—antaḥ) (82).

नः (naḥ)—Acc./dat./gen. pl. enclitic form of first person pronoun 'Asmad' [2]. Being an enclitic form it is not accented. [3]

---

1. Cf. *Phiṭ sūtra*—निपाताः आद्युदात्ताः - 80.
2. Cf. *vahuvacanasyavasnasau*—Pāṇ. 8.1.21.
3. Cf. Pāṇ. युस्मदस्मदोः षष्ठी चतुर्थी द्वितीया स्थयोर्वान्नावौ 8.1.20.

सुभगान् (subhagān)—Su+Bhvādigaṇa root √bhaj 'to serve'+ghaḥ suffix[1]. Being a Bahuvrīhi compound in the company of 'su', the second member 'bhaga' receives the acute accent on the first syllable[2].

अरिः (ariḥ)—Bhvādigaṇa root √ṛ 'to go', 'to send'+iḥ (Uṇādi suffix)[3]. It carries the accent on its suffix[4]. Being in the beginning of a hemistich, it is accented.

वोचेयुः (voceyuḥ)—Adādigaṇa root √vac 'to speak'+luṅ lakāra (aorist) third person pl.

दस्म (dasma)—Voc. of dasma. Divādigaṇa root √dasu 'loss'+mak (Uṇādi suffix)[5]. Being a voc. case not located in the beginning of the hemistich, it goes without accent[6].

कृष्टयः (kṛṣṭayaḥ)—Bhvādigaṇa root √ kṛṣa 'to plough'+ktic suffix[7] to denote a noun/human being. Formed of 'cit' suffix, it is accented on the last syllable[8].

स्याम (syāma)—Adādigaṇa root √as 'to be'+vidhiliṅ lakāra (subjunctive mood) first person pl. Being in the beginning of a hemistich, it is accented.

इत् (it)—A particle used in the sense of 'determination'

इन्द्रस्य (indrasya)—Gen. sing. of Indra. Bhvādigaṇa root

1. Cf. Pāṇ. पुंसि संज्ञायाम् घ प्रायेण - 3.3.118
2. Cf. Pāṇ. क्रत्वादयश्च - 6.2.118
3. Cf. *Uṇādi sūtra*—अच इः 4.139.
4. Cf. Pāṇ.—आद्युदात्तश्च - 3.1.3
5. Cf. *Uṇādi sūtra*—इषियुधीन्धिदसिश्याधूसूभ्यो मक् - 1.145
6. Cf. Pāṇ. आमन्त्रितस्य च - 8.1.19
7. Cf. Pāṇ. क्तिच्क्तौ च संज्ञायाम्- 3.3.174
8. Cf. Pāṇ. चितः - 6.1.163

√idi 'to prosper'+ran (Uṇādi suffix).[1] 'Nit' suffix (of which final 'n' is elided) makes it accented on the first syllable[2].

शर्मणि (śarmaṇi)—Nom. dual of śarman. Krayādigaṇa root

√śṛ 'meaning violence'+manin suffix[3]. Being formed of of 'nit' suffix, it is accented on the first syllable[4].

Word meanings:

उत[5] (uta)—and

नः (naḥ)—our

सुभगान्[6] (subhagān)—good

अरिः[7] (ariḥ)—enemies

वोचेयुः (voceyuḥ)—speak

दस्म (dasma)—Address to Dasma. Undestructible

कृष्टयः[8] (kṛṣṭayaḥ)—human-beings

स्याम (syāma)—to be

इत्[9] (it)—surely

---

1. Cf. *Uṇādi.* ऋज्रेन्द्राग्रवज्र० - 2.28.
2. Cf. Pāṇ. ञ्नित्यादिर्नित्यम् - 6.1.197
3. Cf. Pāṇ.—अन्येभ्योऽपि दृश्यन्ते - 3.2.75, See also *Uṇādi sūtra*—सर्वधातुभ्यो मनिन् 4.145
4. Cf. Pāṇ. ञ्नित्यादिर्नित्यम् - 6.1.197
5. उत अपि नि० 1.6. च नि० 10.27.
6. भगः धननाम निघं० 2.10. भगो भजतेः नि० 1.7.
7. अरिः अमित्र ऋच्छतेः। ईश्वरोऽप्यरिरेतस्मादेव नि० 5.7.
8. कृष्टयः-मनुष्यनाम निघं० 2.3. कृष्टीः मनुष्यजातानि नि० 10.29, 10.31. कृष्टय इति मनुष्यनाम कर्मवन्तो भवन्ति विकृष्टदेहा वा नि० 10.22.
9. इत् पदपूरणः नि० 1.9. महान् नि० 6.1.

इन्द्रस्य[1] (indrasya)—God

शर्मणि[2] (śarmaṇi)—shelter

Anvaya (Sequencial placement of words)

dasma indrasya śarmaṇi syāma. kṛṣṭayaḥ uta naḥ arir it subhagān voceyur.

Meaning of Mantra in different contexts :

Scientific Meaning: (दस्म) Undestructible Brahman! let us (स्याम) be safe (शर्मणि) under the custody (इन्द्रस्य) of Indra. (कृष्टयः) Let the human-beings (उत) and (अरिः) even our enemies (वोचेयुः) speak (सुभगान्) good about (नः) us.

Note : We are living under the shelter provided by Indra (electric force) which does not let the universe contract. Vṛtra being the surface tension of the Universe is the contracting force. Indra, being repulsive force always acts against vṛtra and neutralize it allowing the expansion of the Universe. The expanding universe is the symbol of creation and contracting universe of decreation.

Scientific Meaning 2: (दस्म) Undestructible Brahman! let us (स्याम) be safe (शर्मणि) under the custody (इन्द्रस्य) of a sun. (कृष्टयः)

---

1. इन्द्रः पदनाम निघं० 5.4. इन्द्रः-इरां दृणातीति वा इरां ददातीति वा, इरां दधातीति वा। इरां दारयत इति वा। इरां धारयत इति वा। इन्दवे द्रवतीति वा। इन्दौ रमत इति वा। इन्धे भूतानीति वा। 'तद्यदेनं प्राणैः समैन्धंस्तदिन्द्रस्येन्द्रत्वमिति विज्ञायते।' इदं करणादित्याग्रायणः। इदं दर्शनादित्यौपमन्यवः। इन्दतेर्वैश्वर्यकर्मणः। इन्दञ्छत्रूणां दारयिता वा द्रावयिता वा। आदरयिता च यज्वनाम् नि० 10.8. एष वै शुक्रो य एष (सूर्यः) तपत्येष (सूर्यः) उ एवेन्द्रः श० 4.5.5.7, 4.5.9.4. अथ यः स इन्द्रोऽसौ स आदित्यः श० 8.5.3.2. यो वै वायुः स इन्द्रो य इन्द्रः स वायुः श० 4.1.3.19. स योऽयं मध्ये प्राणः। एष एवेन्द्रस्तानेष प्राणान्मध्यत इन्द्रियेणैन्द्ध तस्मादिन्ध इन्धो ह वै तमिन्द्र इत्याचक्षते परोऽक्षम् श० 6.1.1.2. हृदयमेवेन्द्रः श० 12.9.1.15. यन्मनः स इन्द्रः गो० उ० 4.11. मन एवेन्द्रः श० 12.9.1.13. इन्द्रो वै यजमानः श० 2.1.2.11 क्षत्रियो यदु च यजमानः श० 5.3.5.27. एन्द्रो वै राजन्य तै० 3.8.23.2. इन्द्रः क्षत्रम् श० 10.4.1.5. वीर्यं वा इन्द्रः तां० 9.7.5, 8. इन्द्रो यज्ञस्य नेता श० 4.1.2.15.
2. शर्म गृहनाम निघं० 3.4. सुखनाम निघं० 3.6. शर्म शरणनाम् नि० 9.19. चर्म वाऽएतत् कृष्णास्य (मृगस्य) तन्मानुषं शर्म देवत्रा श० 3.2.1.4. (ऋ० 3.13.4.) वाग्वै शर्म ऐ० 2.40. (ऋ० 3.13.4.) अग्निर्वै शर्मण्यन्नाद्यानि यच्छति ऐ० 2.41.

Let the human-beings (उत) and (अरिः) even our enemies (वोचेयुः) speak (सुभगान्) good about (नः) us.

Socio-Political Context 1: (दस्म) Undestructible Brahman! let us (we students) (स्याम) be safe (शर्माणि) under the custody (इन्द्रस्य) of a teacher/scholar. (कृष्टयः) Let the human-beings (उत) and (अरिः) even our enemies (वोचेयुः) speak (सुभगान्) good about (नः) us.

Socio-Political Context 2: (दस्म) Undestructible Brahman! let us (we people of public) (स्याम) be safe (शर्माणि) under the custody (इन्द्रस्य) of a king. (कृष्टयः) Let the human-beings (उत) and (अरिः) even our enemies (वोचेयुः) speak (सुभगान्) good about (नः) us.

३७. एमाशुमाशवे भर यज्ञश्रियं नृमादनम्। पतयन्मन्दयत्सखम्।।७।।

आ। ईम्। आशुम्। आशवे। भर। यज्ञऽश्रियम्। नृऽमादनम्। पतयत्। मन्दयत्ऽसखम्।।

Saṁhitāpāṭha

em-āśum-āśave bhara yajña-śriyaṁ nṛmādanam. patayan-mandayat sakham.

Padapāṭha

ā. im. āśum. āśave. bhara. yajña-śriyam. nṛmādanam. patayat. mandayat-sakham.

Grammatical Notes:

आ (ā)—A prefix meaning proximity, conjunction and simli. Being a prefix, it is accented on the first syllable[1].

ईम् (im)—According to Sāyaṇa, īma is a particle representing demonstrative pronoun, idam. It seems to be an encilitc form of demonstrative pronoun' idam' and so does not carry an accent.

आशुम् (āśum)—Svādigaṇa root √aśūṅ 'to pervade', 'to condense'+uṇa (Uṇādi suffix)[2]. It receives suffixal accent [3].

आशवे (āśave)—Svādigaṇa root √aśūṅ 'to pervade', 'to condense'+uṇa (Uṇādi suffix)[4]. It is also accented on suffix [5].

भर (bhara)—Juhotyādigaṇa root √bhṛñ 'to sustain', 'to

1. Cf. *Phiṭ sūtra*—उपसर्गाश्चाभिवर्जम् -81.
2. Cf. *Uṇādi sūtra*—कृवापा० 1.1.
3. Cf. Pāṇ. आद्युदात्तश्च - 3.1.3
4. Cf. *Uṇādi sūtra*—कृवापा० 1.1.
5. Cf. Pāṇ. आद्युदात्तश्च - 3.1.3

bring up'+loṭ lakāra second person sing. Being a verbal formation preceded by a non-verbal form, it goes without accent [1].

यज्ञश्रियम् (yajña-śriyam)—Ṣaṣṭhi Tatpuruṣa (Genitive determinative) compound. It is accented on the final syllable of second member, as per general rule of compond accentuation [2].

नृमादनम् (nṛmādanam)—Gen. determinative compound (Ṣaṣṭhi Tatpuruṣa) of Nṛ+Divādigaṇa root √madi 'to be happy'+ṇic+lyuṭ suffix [3] in the instrumental or locative sense. Here 'mādana', being formed of 'lit' suffix, is accented on the first syllable 'ā'. The combine word, nṛmādana, being a determinative compound between a nominal case 'nṛ' and primary derivative 'mādana', allows its second member to retain its accent [4].

पतयत् (patayat.)—Pati+ṇic+śatṛ [5] or, according to Yāska, Bhvādigaṇa root √patlṛ 'to go'+ṇic+śatṛ. It carries suffixal accent [6].

मन्दयत्सखम् (mandayat-sakham)—Compound between mandayat {√madi 'to praise' ṇic+śatrṛ}+{sakhā}. There are two confronting views about the nature of this compound. According to Sāyaṇa, it is a loc. determinative (saptamī tatpuruṣa) compound : as 'mandayati (indre) sakhā' meaning 'friend of Indra' [7]. Indra is called 'mandayat' as he keeps every body happy. As per above cited tatpuruṣa composition,

---

1. Cf. Pāṇ. तिङ्ङतिङः - 8.1.28
2. Cf. Pāṇ. समासस्य च -
3. Cf. Pāṇ. करणाधिकरणयोश्च - 3.3.117
4. Cf. Pāṇ. गतिकारकोपपदात् कृत्- 6.2.139
5. Cf. *Vārttika* तत्करोति तदाचष्टे - on Pāṇ. 3.1.26
6. Cf. Pāṇ. आद्युदात्तश्च - 3.1.3
7. As per Pāṇ. सप्तमी शौण्डैः - 2.1.40

accent will be on the first memeber[1]. As per another view of Swami Dayananda, it is a possessive compound meaning 'who has scholar friends'. According to Bahuvrīhi composition also, it will be accented on the first member.

Word meanings:

आ[2] (ā)—proximity, conjunction and simli.

ईम्[3] (im) —electric charge, libations

आशुम्[4] (āśum) —quickly

आशवे[5] (āśave)—to God, to electric force, teacher/Guru

भर[6] (bhara)—offer

यज्ञश्रियम् (yajña-śriyam)—grace of universal creation, grace of civilised society

नृमादनम् (nṛmādanam)—exhilarator of humankind

पतयत्7 (patayat.)—master

1. In Tatpuruṣa compound, if the first member is nominal form with loc. case ending, then also first member is accented like that of Bahuvīhi (possessive) compound. See Pāṇ. तत्पुरुषे तुल्यार्थ० - 6.2.2
2. अर्वागर्थे नि० 1.3. एतस्मिन्नेवार्थे (समुच्चयार्थे) देवेभ्यश्च पितृभ्य एत्याकार: नि० 1.4. उपमार्थे दृश्यते नि० 3.16. अध्यर्थे दृश्यते नि० 5.5.
3. ईम् उदकनाम निघं० 1.12. पदपूरण: नि० 1.9. ईम् पदनाम निघं० 4.2.
4. आशु: क्षिप्रनाम, निघं० 2.15. अश्वनाम निघं० 1.14. आशु इति शु इति च क्षिप्रनामनी भवत:। नि० 6.1. आशु भार्गवं भवति तां० 14.9.9. अहर्वा एतदव्लीयत तद्देवा आशुनाभ्यधिन्वथ्ंस्तदाशोराशुत्वमु तां० 14. 9.10. आशव: क्षिप्रकारिण: नि० 9.5.
5. आशु: क्षिप्रनाम, निघं० 2.15. अश्वनाम निघं० 1.14. आशु इति शु इति च क्षिप्रनामनी भवत:। नि० 6.1. आशु भार्गवं भवति तां० 14.9.9. अहर्वा एतदव्लीयत तद्देवा आशुनाभ्यधिन्वथ्ंस्तदाशोराशुत्वमु तां० 14. 9.10. आशव: क्षिप्रकारिण: नि० 9.5.
6. भर आहर नि० 6.32.
7. पतयति गतिकर्मा निघं० 2.14.

मन्दयत्सखम् (mandayat-sakham)—friends of creation

Anvaya (Sequencial placement of words)

ā bhara āśum īm āśave. yajña-śriyam nṛmādanam patayat mandayat-sakham.

Meaning of Mantra in different contexts :

Spiritual: (आ भर) Offer (आशुम्) quickly (ईम्) these libations (ahutis) (आशवे) to Brahman, Who is (यज्ञश्रियम्) the grace of this universal creation, (नृमादनम्) the exhilarator of humankind. (पतयत्) Pervading this universe, (मन्दयत्सखम्) He brings happiness to the friends of this creation, i.e. who undertakes echo friendly activities.

Note: The mantra devides the human beings into two categories-friends of creation and foes of creation. Those who undertake echofirendly activities are the friends and those who pollute the environment are the foes of creation. The mantra clearly says that Brahman bestows happiness to those who are friends of creation.

Scientific: (ईम्) These electrical charges (आ भर) sustain (आशवे) electric force (आशुम्) quickly. (This electric force) is (यज्ञश्रियम्) the grace of expansing universe, (नृमादनम्) the exhilarator of humankind. (पतयत्) While being born in this universe, (मन्दयत्सखम्), he brings happiness to the friends of this creation.

Note : Without electric charge, the survival of electric force is not possible. Since electric force causes the expansion, the mantra calls it the grace of yajña (expanding universe).

Socio-political 1: (आ भर) Offer (आशुम्) quickly (ईम्) regards (आशवे) to the teacher, who is (यज्ञश्रियम्) the grace of this Jñāna Yajña, (नृमादनम्) the exhilarator of students. (पतयत्) Imparting knowledge, (मन्दयत्सखम्) he brings happiness to the lovers of knowledge.

३८. अस्य पीत्वा शंतक्रतो घनो वृत्राणामभवः।

प्रावो॑ वाजे॑षु वा॑जिन॑म्॥८॥

अस्य। पीत्वा। शतक्रतो॒ इति शतक्रतो। घन॒ः। वृत्राणा॒म्। अभव॒ः। प्र॒ः।

आव॒ः। वाजे॑षु। वा॑जिन॑म्॥

Saṁhitāpāṭha

*asya pītvā śatakrato ghano vṛtrāṇāmabhavaḥ. prāvo
vājeṣu vājinam.*

Padapāṭha

*asya. pītvā. śatakrato iti śatakrato. ghanaḥ. vṛtrāṇām.
abhavaḥ. pra. āvaḥ. vājeṣu. vājinam.*

Grammatical Notes:

अस्य (asya)—Gen.sing.masc. of demonstrative pronoun
'idam'. Here the gen. case ending receives   accent [1].

पीत्वा (pītvā)—Bhvādigaṇa root √pā 'to drink'+ktvā (gerund
suffix). It carries accent on suffix.

शतक्रतो॒ (śatakrato)—Voc. sing. of śatakratu.

घनः (ghanaḥ)—Adādigaṇa root √ han 'to kill' 'to
move'+ap suffix [2]+ac suffix in the sense of
possession [3]. Being formed of 'cit' suffix, it is accented
finally [4].

वृत्राणा॒म् (vṛtrāṇām)—Gen. pl. of vṛtra. Bhvādigaṇa root
√vṛtu 'to be'+rak (Uṇādi suffix) [5]+nām (gen. case

---

1. Cf. Pāṇ. ऊडिदम्पदाद्यप्पुम्रैद्युभ्यः - 6.1.171

2. Cf. Pāṇ. मूर्त्तौ धनः - 3.3.77

3. Cf. Pāṇ. अर्शआदिभ्योऽच् - 5.2.127

4. Cf. Pāṇ. चितः - 6.1.163

5. Cf. *Uṇādi sūtra*—स्फायितञ्जि॰ - 2.13

ending).

अभवः (abhavaḥ)—Bhvādigaṇa root √bhū 'to be'+loṭ lakāra (imperative) second pers. sing. Not accented being a verbal form preceded by a non—verbal form[1].

प्रः (pra)—A Prefix. Being a prefix, it is accented on the first syllable[2].

आवः (āvaḥ)—Ā+Curādigaṇa root √vṛñ 'to cover'+luṅ lakāra (aorist) second person sing.

वाजेषु (vājeṣu)—Bhvādigaṇa √vaja 'to go'+ghañ suffix. It, being formed of 'ñit' suffix, is accented on the first syllable[3].

वाजिनम् (vājinam)—vāja+ini suffix in the sense of praise+'ṅip' fem. suffix. It receives accent on the suffix 'ini'. The other formation is Bhvādigaṇa root √vaja 'to go'+ṇini+ṅip fem. suffix.

Word meanings:

अस्य (asya)—these, libations, offerings

पीत्वा (pītvā)—having imbibed, having augmented, having drunk

शतक्रतो[4] (śatakrato)—Address to śatakratu. God, electric force, teacher and ruler performer of hundreds of jobs.

घनः (ghanaḥ)—killer

वृत्राणाम्[5] (vṛtrāṇām)—bad ideas, evil habits, surface tension,

1. Cf. Pān. तिङ्ङतिङः 8.1.28.

2. Cf. *Phiṭ sūtra* उपसर्गाश्चाभिवर्जम् - 81.

3. Cf. Pāṇ. ञ्नित्यादिर्नित्यम् - 6.1.197

4. शतं दशदशतः नि० 3.10. शतम् बहुनाम निघं० 3.1. क्रतुः कर्मनाम निघं० 2.1. प्रज्ञानाम निघं० 3.9. शतक्रतुः इन्द्र आसीत् सीरपतिः शतक्रतुः तै० 2.4.8.7

5. वृत्रः मेघनाम निघं० 1.10. वृत्रं धननाम निघं० 2.10. वृत्रो वृणोतेर्वा वर्त्ततेर्वा। यदवृणोत्तद्

forces of contraction

अभवः (abhavaḥ)—became

प्रः[1] (pra)—a perfix

आवः (āvaḥ)—to protect

वाजेषु [2] (vājeṣu)—in fights, in battlefields.

वाजिनम् [3](vājinam)—universe, believers, people

Anvaya (Sequencial placement of words)

śatakrato pītvā asya abhavaḥ ghanaḥ vṛtrāṇām. pra āvaḥ vājinam vājeṣu.

Meaning of Mantra in different contexts :

Spiritual: (शतक्रतो) O Brahman, the conductor of the act of

वृत्रस्य वृत्रत्वमिति विज्ञायते। यदवर्त्तत तद् वृत्रस्य वृत्रत्वमिति विज्ञायते। यदवर्धत तद् वृत्रस्य वृत्रत्वमिति विज्ञायते नि० 2.17. तत्को वृत्रः? मेघ इति नैरुक्ताः। त्वाष्ट्रोऽसुर इत्यैतिहासिकाः नि० 2.16. वृत्रो ह वाऽइदं सर्वं वृत्वा शिश्ये। यदिदमन्तरेण द्यावापृथिवी स यदिदं सर्वं वृत्वा शिश्ये तस्माद् वृत्रो नाम श० 1.1.3.4. स यद् वर्त्तमानः समभवत् तस्माद् वृत्रः श० 1.6.3.9. तथैवैद् यजमानः पौर्णमासेनैव वृत्रं पाप्मानं हत्वापहतापाप्मैतत् कर्मारभते श० 6.2.2.19. पाप्मा वै वृत्रः श० 11.1.5.7. (यजु० 11.33) वृत्रहणं पुरन्दरमिति पाप्मा वै वृत्रः पाप्महनं पुरन्दरमित्येतत् श० 6.4.2.3. इन्द्रो वै वृत्रहा कौ० 4.3. वृत्रो वै सोम आसीत् श० 3.4.3.13. अथैष एव वृत्रो वै सोम आसीत् श० 3.4.3.13. अथैष एव वृत्रो यच्चन्द्रमाः श० 1.6.4.13. आपो ह वै वृत्रं जघ्नुस्तेनैवैतद् वीर्येणापः स्यन्दन्ते श० 3.9.4.14.

1. प्र परेत्यस्य प्रातिलोम्यम् नि० 1.3. प्रेव नश्यसि पराचीव नश्यसि नि० 9.28. अन्तरिक्षं वै प्र ऐ० 2.41. प्राणो वै प्र ऐ० 2.40.
2. वाजः अन्ननाम निघं० 2.7. बलनाम निघं० 2.9. वाजेभिरन्नैः नि० 11.26. अन्नं वै वाजः तै० 1.3.6.2. श० 5.1.4.3. ता० 13.9.13. अन्नं वाजः श० 5.1.1.16. अन्नं वै वाजाः श० 1.4.1.9. वीर्यं वै वाजाः श० 3.3.4.7. ओषधयः खलु वै वाजः तै० 1.3.7.1. वाजो वै पशवः ऐ० 5.8. वाजो वै स्वर्गो लोकः तां० 18.7.12. गो० उ० 5.8. वाग्वै वाजस्व प्रसवः तै० 1.3.2.5. सोमो वै वाजः मै० 4.5.4. सर्वं सोमं पिपासति वाजं ह गच्छति मै० 1.11.5. अमृतोऽन्नं वै वाज जै० 2.193.
3. वाजिनी उषोनाम निघं० 1.8

creation that last for hundred Brāhma years, i.e. 311 Trillion years)! (पीत्वा) having received offerings/libations of (अस्य) this seeker, (अभवः) you become (घनः) the killer (वृत्राणाम्) of his bad ideas or evil habits and (प्र आवः) protect (वाजिनम्) the seeker (वाजेषु) in the battlefield of life.

Note: The above mantra tells us that the age of one creation cycle is 100 Brāhma years, i.e. 311 Trillion years.

Scientific 2: (शतक्रतो) O Śatakratu! (Electric force, the conductor of the act of expansion of universe for 100 Brāhma years! (पीत्वा) having drunk the electric charge, (अभवः) you become (घनः) the killer (वृत्राणाम्) of forces of contraction (gravitational force of universe and surface tension of the universe. (प्र आवः) Protect (वाजिनम्) this universe (अस्य) of Brahman (वाजेषु) in the fights against the forces of contraction.

Note : Electric force is one of the most powerful fundamental force of the universe. The Veda wants to say that forces of expansion are stronger than the forces of contraction. That is why, the universe is persisting. As and when the forces of contraction will dominate over the forces of expansion, this universe will tend towards its end.

Socio-political 1: (शतक्रतो) O Śatakratu (teacher capable of teaching for hundred years)! (पीत्वा) having accepted our regards, (अभवः) you become (घनः) the killer of (वृत्राणाम्) the ignorance of seeker. (प्र आवः) Protect (वाजिनम्) seeker of (अस्य) this knowledge (वाजेषु) in the battlefield of life by providing them suitable knowledge.

Socio-political 2: (शतक्रतो) O Śatakratu (ruler, who rules for hundreds years), (पीत्वा) having augmented his power, (अभवः) you become (घनः) the killer of (वृत्राणाम्) all terrorists/ ultras in your nation. (प्र आवः) Protect (अस्य) this nation (वाजेषु) in the fights against terrorists and foes.

३९. तं त्वा वाजेषु वाजिनं वाजयामः शतक्रतो।
धनानामिन्द्र सातये।।९।।

तम्। त्वा। वाजेषु। वाजिनम्। वाजयामः। शतक्रतो इति शतक्रतो।
धनानाम्। इन्द्र। सातये।।

Saṁhitāpāṭha

taṁ tvā vājeṣu vājinaṁ vājayāmaḥ śatakrato dhamnānām—indra sātaye.

Padapāṭha

tam. tvā. vājeṣu. vājinam. vājayāmaḥ. śatakrato iti śatakrato. dhamnānām. indra. sātaye.

Grammatical Notes:

तम् (tam.)—Acc.sing.masc. of demonstrative pronoun 'Tad'. Being a pronominal form, it is accented.

त्वा (tvā)—Acc.sing. enclitic form of second person pronoun 'Yusmad'[1]. Being an enclitic form, it is not accented[2].

वाजेषु (vājeṣu) —Bhvādigaṇa √vaja 'to go'+ghañ suffix. It, being formed of 'ñit' suffix, is accented on the first sullable[3].

वाजिनम् (vājinam)—vāja+ini suffix in the sense of praise+'ṅip' fem. suffix. It receives accent on the suffix 'ini'. The other formation is Bhvādigaṇa root √vaja 'to go'+ṇini+ṅip fem. suffix.

वाजयामः (vājayāmaḥ)—Bhavādigaṇa root √vaja 'to go' (used in Curādigaṇa)+laṭ lakāra first person pl. Being located

1. Cf. Pāṇ. त्वामौ द्वितीयायाः - 8.1.23
2. Cf. Pāṇ. युस्मदस्मदोः षष्ठी-चतुर्थी.द्वितीयास्थयोर्वान्नावौ- 8.1.20
3. Cf. Pāṇ. ञ्नित्यादिर्नित्यम् - 6.1.197

in the beginning of a hemistich, it goes without accent[1].

शतक्रतो (śatakrato)—Voc. sing. of śatakratu. Being a voc. case not located in the beginning of a hemistich, it does not carry acute accent.[2]

धनानाम् (dhanānām)—Juhotyādigaṇa root √dhāñ 'to sustain', 'to bring up'+kyuḥ (Uṇādi suffix)[3].

Note : The term 'dhana' is not directly governed by the above mentioned (Uṇādi suffix), but it can indirecly be derived with (Uṇādi suffix) 'lyu' on the pattern of 'nidhana'.

इन्द्र (indra)—Voc. sing. of Indra. Bhvādigaṇa root √idi 'to prosper'+ran (Uṇādi suffix).[4] 'Being a voc. form not located in the beginning of a hemistich,it goes without accent[5].

सातये (sātaye)—Bhvādigaṇa root √ṣaṇa 'to divide'+ktin sufix. It is accented on 'ktin' suffix[6]

Word meanings:

तम् (tam.)—that, those

त्वा (tvā) —to you

वाजेषु[7] (vājeṣu) —resources

---

1. Cf. Pāṇ. तिङ्ङतिङः - 8.1.28
2. Cf. Pāṇ. आमन्त्रितस्य च - 8.1.19
3. Cf. *Uṇādi sūtra*—कृपृवृजिमन्दिनिधञः क्युः - 4.82
4. Cf. Uṇādi. ऋज्रेन्द्राग्रवज्र० - 2.28.
5. Cf. Pāṇ. आमन्त्रितस्य च - 8.1.19
6. Cf. Pāṇ.ऊति-यूति-जूति-साति-हेति-कीर्तयश्च - 3.3.97
7. वाजः अन्ननाम निघं० 2.7. बलनाम निघं० 2.9. वाजेभिरन्नैः नि० 11.26. अन्नं वै वाजः तै० 1.3.6.2. श० 5.1.4.3. ता० 13.9.13. अन्नं वाजः श० 5.1.1.16. अन्नं वै वाजाः श० 1.4.1.9. वीर्यं वै वाजाः श० 3.3.4.7. ओषधयः खलु वै वाजः तै० 1.3.7.1. वाजो वै पशवः ऐ० 5.8. वाजो वै स्वर्गो लोकः तां० 18.7.12. गो० उ० 5.8. वाग्वै वाजस्य प्रसवः तै० 1.3.

वा॒जिन॑म्[1] (vājinam)—resource

वा॒जया॑मः (vājayāmaḥ)—to thank

श॒त॒क्र॒तो॒[2] (śatakrato)—Address to Śatakratu.

धना॑नाम्[3] (dhanānām)—natural resources, material resources, knowledge, facilities

इ॒न्द्र॒ (indra)—Address to Indra. God, electric force, teacher, ruler

सा॒तये॑ (sātaye)—distribution, winning, comforts

Anvaya (Sequencial placement of words)

śatakrato indra tvā vājayāmaḥ dhanānām sātaye vājeṣu vājinam tam.

Meaning of Mantra in different contexts :

Spiritual: (इन्द्र) O Brahman, (शतक्रतो) the conductor of the act of creation that last for hundred Brāhma years, i.e. 311 Trillion years)!, (वाजयामः) we thank (त्वा) you for (सातये) gift of (धनानाम्) various natural resources in the universe. We shall use (तम्) the same (वाजिनम्) resources (वाजेषु) in the battlefield of our life.

Scientific: (इन्द्र) O electric force, (शतक्रतो) the conductor of the act of expansion of universe for 100 Brāhma years, (वाजयामः) we urge (त्वा) you for (सातये) the protection of (तम्) the charge (वाजिनम्) of (धनानाम्) matter particles (वाजेषु) in the battle against

---

25. सोमो वै वाजः मै० 4.5.4. सर्वं सोमं पिपासति वाजं ह गच्छति मै० 1.11.5. अमृतोऽन्नं वै वाज जै० 2.193.

1. वाजिनी उषोनाम निघं० 1.8.

2. शतं दशदशतः नि० 3.10. शतम् बहुनाम निघं० 3.1. क्रतुः कर्मनाम निघं० 2.1. प्रज्ञानाम निघं० 3.9. शतक्रतुः इन्द्र आसीत् सीरपतिः शतक्रतुः तै० 2.4.8.7

3. धनम् धिनोतीति सतः नि० 3.6. राष्ट्राणि वै धनानि ऐ० 8.26. तस्माद् हिरण्यं कनिष्ठं धनानाम् तै० 3.11.8.7. धनं मे शंस्य पाहि काठ० 7.3.

vṛtra, the contracting forces.

Socio-political 1: (इन्द्र) O teacher, (शतक्रतो) capable of teaching for hundreds years, (वाजयामः) we thank (त्वा) you for (सातये) the gift (धनानाम्) of knowledge you bestowed upon us. We shall use (तम्) the same (वाजिनम्) knowledge (वाजेषु) in the battlefield of our life.

Socio-political 2: (इन्द्र) O ruler, (शतक्रतो) who rules for hundreds years, (वाजयामः) we thank (त्वा) you for we thank you for (सातये) the gift (धनानाम्) of prosperity you gave us. We enjoyed (तम्) the same (वाजिनम्) prosperity (वाजेषु) in the battlefield of our life.

४०. यो रायोऽवनिर्महान्त्सुपारः सुन्वतः सखा।
तस्मा इन्द्राय गायत॥१०॥

यः। रायः। अवनिः। महान्। सुऽपारः। सुन्वतः। सखा। तस्मै। इन्द्राय।
गायत॥

Saṁhitāpāṭha

yo rāyo vanir-mahānt-supāraḥ sunvataḥ sakhā. tasmā indrāya gāyata.

Padapāṭha

yaḥ. rāyaḥ. avaniḥ.mahān. su-pāraḥ. sunvataḥ. sakhā. tasmai. indrāya. gāyata.

Grammatical Notes:

यः (yaḥ)—Nom. sing. masc. of demonstrative Pronoun 'Yad'. Beng a pronominal form, it is accented.

रायः (rāyaḥ)—Gen. sing. of rai. Adādigaṇa root √ rā 'to donate'+ghañ suffix or kvip suffix. It is accented on the gen. case ending[1].

अवनिः (avaniḥ)—Bhvādigaṇa root √ ava 'to protect', 'to go', 'to love'+iniḥ (Uṇādi suffix) [2]. It carries suffixal accent[3].

महान् (mahān)—Bhvādigaṇa root √maha 'to worship'+atiḥ (Uṇādi suffix)[4]. महान् कस्मान्

सुपारः (su-pāraḥ)—Su+pāra (Curādigaṇa root √ pāra 'to accomplish' or Juhotyādigaṇa root √ pṛ 'to bring up',

1. Cf. Pāṇ. ऊडिदम्पदाद्यप्पुम्रैद्युभ्यः - 6.1.171
2. Cf. Pāṇ. अत्तिसृधृ०-2.102.
3. Cf. Pāṇ. आद्युदात्तश्च-3.1.3
4. Cf. *Uṇādi sutra*-वर्त्तमाने पृषद्बृहन्महत्०-2.84.

'to fill up'+ac [1]. Being formed of 'cit' suffix, it is accented finally [2].

सुन्वतः (sunvataḥ)—Nom./acc. pl. of sunvan. Svādigaṇa root √ṣuñ 'to squeez'+śatṛ (present active participle suffix). It is accented on the inflectional ending.[3]

सखा (sakhā)—Nom. sing. of sakhi. Samāna+Adādigaṇa root √ khyā 'to state'+iṇ (Uṇādi suffix) [4]. Here 'samāna' is substituted by 's' [5].

तस्मै (tasmai)—Dat. sing. masc. of demonstrative pronoun 'Tad'. Being a pronominal form it is accented in the first syllable.

इन्द्राय (indrāya)—Dat. sing. of Indra. Bhvādigaṇa root √idi 'to prosper'+ran (Uṇādi suffix).[6] 'Nit' suffix (of which which final 'n' is elided) makes it accented on the first syllable [7].

गायत (gāyata)—Bhvādigaṇa root √gai 'to make sound'+loṭ lakāra second person pl. Being a verbal form preceded by a non-verbal form, it loses its accent [8].

Word meanings:

यः (yaḥ)—who

रायः (rāyaḥ) —universe, mass energy

---

1. Cf. Pāṇ. नन्दिग्रहिपचादिभ्यो ल्युणिन्यचः-3.1.134
2. Cf. Pāṇ. चितः-6.1.163
3. Cf. Pāṇini-शतुरनुमो नद्यजादि - 6.1.173
4. Cf. *Uṇādi sūtra* - समाने ख्यः स चोदात्तः 3.137.
5. Cf. Pāṇ. समानस्य छन्दस्यमूर्द्धप्रभृत्युदर्केषु - 6.3.84.
6. Cf. *Uṇādi.* ऋज्रेन्द्राग्रवज्र०-2.28.
7. Cf. Pāṇ. ञ्नित्यादिर्नित्यम्-6.1.197
8. Cf. Pāṇ. तिङ्ङतिङः - 8.1.28

अ॒वनिः॑[1] (avaniḥ) —protector

म॒हान्[2] (mahān)—great, strong

सु॒पा॒रः (su—pāraḥ)—accomplisher of all desires of seeker, swim over, win over, carry out,

सु॒न्व॒तः (sunvataḥ)—electric charge, producer, spiritualist

सखा॑[3] (sakhā)—friend

तस्मै॑ (tasmai)—that

इन्द्रा॑य[4] (indrāya)—God, electric force, teacher

गा॒य॒त॒ (gāyata)—pray
गायतीति अर्चति कर्मसु पठितम् निघं॰ 3.14

Anvaya (Sequencial placement of words)

tasmai indrāya gāyata yaḥ mahān su—pāraḥ sunvataḥ sakhā

---

1. अवनिः पृथिवीनाम निघं॰ 1.1. अवनयः अंगुलिनाम निघं॰ 2.5. अवनयो नदीनाम निघं॰ 1.13. अवनयोऽङ्गुलयोभवन्ति अवन्ति कर्माणि नि॰ 3.8
2. महान् कस्मान् मानेनान्याञ्जहातीति शाकपूणिः। महनीयो भवतीति वा नि॰ 3.13. महद्वा अन्तरिक्षम् ऐ॰ 5.18, 19.. अन्तो वै महत् ऐ॰ 5.2, 12. एष ह वै महान् देवा यद्यज्ञः गो॰ 1.2.16.
3. सखायः समानख्यानाः नि॰ 7.30. सखायः सप्तपदा अभूम तै॰ 3.7.7.11.
4. इन्द्रः पदनाम निघं॰ 5.4. इन्द्रः-इरां दृणातीति वा इरां ददातीति वा, इरां दधातीति वा। इरां दारयत इति वा। इरां धारयत इति वा। इन्दवे द्रवतीति वा। इन्दौ रमत इति वा। इन्धे भूतानीति वा। 'तद्यदेनं प्राणैः समैन्धंस्तदिन्द्रस्येन्द्रत्वमिति विज्ञायते।' इदं करणादित्याग्रायणः। इदं दर्शनादित्यौपमन्यवः। इन्दतेर्वैश्वर्यकर्मणः। इन्दञ्छत्रूणां दारयिता वा द्रावयिता वा। आदरयिता च यज्वनाम् नि॰ 10.8. एष वै शुक्रो य एष (सूर्यः) तपत्येष (सूर्यः) उ एवेन्द्रः श॰ 4.5.5.7, 4.5.9.4. अथ यः स इन्द्रोऽसौ स आदित्यः श॰ 8.5.3.2. यो वै वायुः स इन्द्रो य इन्द्रः स वायुः श॰ 4.1.3.19. स योऽयं मध्ये प्राणः। एष एवेन्द्रस्तानेष प्राणान्मध्यत इन्द्रियैणैन्द्ध तस्मादिन्ध इन्धो ह वै तमिन्द्र इत्याचक्षते परोऽक्षम् श॰ 6.1.1.2. हृदयमेवेन्द्रः श॰ 12.9.1.15. यन्मनः स इन्द्रः गो॰ उ॰ 4.11. मन एवेन्द्रः श॰ 12.9.1.13. इन्द्रो वै यजमानः श॰ 2.1.2.11 क्षत्रियो यदु च यजमानः श॰ 5.3.5.27. एन्द्रो वै राजन्य तै॰ 3.8.23.2. इन्द्रः क्षत्रम् श॰ 10.4.1.5. वीर्यं वा इन्द्रः तां॰ 9.7.5, 8. इन्द्रो यज्ञस्य नेता श॰ 4.1.2.15.

rāyaḥ avaniḥ.

Meaning of Mantra in different contexts :

Spiritual: (गायत) Pray unto (तस्मै) that (इन्द्राय) Brahman (यः) who (महान्) is great, (सुपारः) accomplisher of all desires of a seeker, (सखा) friend of a spiritualist, (अवनिः) the protector and (सुन्वतः) dispenser of (रायः) prosperity.

Scientific: (गायत) Have praise for (तस्मै) that (इन्द्राय) electric force (यः) which (महान्) is strong fundamental force of the universe, (सुपारः) helps the creation cross over the hurdles of contracting forces, (सखा) friend of maruts (radiation), (अवनिः) the protector and (सुन्वतः) deliverer of (रायः) mass energy.

Socio-political 1: (गायत) Give regard (तस्मै) to that (इन्द्राय) teacher/Guru (यः) who (महान्) is great, (सुपारः) helps us swim over the ignorance, (सखा) friend of the seeker of knowledge, (अवनिः) protector and (सुन्वतः) and one who delivers (रायः) knowledge.

Socio-political 2: (गायत) Give regard (तस्मै) to that (इन्द्राय) ruler (यः) who is (महान्) great, (सुपारः) helps us win over difficulties of life, (सखा) friend of good persons who contributes to the development of a nation or a society, (अवनिः) protector of the rights of citizens and one who (सुन्वतः) delivers (रायः) prosperity.

सूक्त - 5

ऋषि– मधुच्छन्दा वैश्वामित्र। **देवता–** इन्द्र। **छन्द–** गायत्री।

४१. आ त्वेता निषीदतेन्द्रमभि प्रगायत। सखायः स्तोमवाहसः।।१।।

आ। तु। आ। इत। नि। सीदत। इन्द्रम। अभि। प्र। गायत। सखायः। स्तोमऽवाहसः।।

Saṁhitāpāṭha

ā tvetā niṣīdata-indram-abhi pragāyata. sakhāyaḥ stomavāhasaḥ.

Padapāṭha

ā. tu. ā. it. ni. sīdata. indram. abhi. pra. gāyata. sakhāyaḥ. stoma-vāhasaḥ.

Grammatical Notes:

आ (ā)—A particle meaning proximity, conjunction and simli. Being a particle, it is accented on the first syllable[1]

तु (tu)—A particle meaning 'haste'. Being a particle, it is accented on the first syllable[2]

आ (ā) —A particle meaning proximity, conjunction and simli. Being a particle, it is accented on the first syllable[3].

इत (it)—Adādigaṇa root √iṇa 'to go'+loṭ lakāra second person pl. Being a verbal form preceded by a non-verbal form, it goes without accent[4].

---

1. Cf. *Phiṭ sūtra*—निपाताः आद्युदात्ताः - 80
2. Cf. *Phiṭ sūtra*—निपाताः आद्युदात्ताः - 80
3. Cf. *Phiṭ sūtra*—निपाताः आद्युदात्ताः - 80
4. Cf. Pāṇ. तिङ्ङतिङः - 8.1.28

नि (ni)—A particle meaning 'sure'. Being a particle, it is accented on the first syllable[1].

सीदत (sīdata)—Bhvādigaṇa root √ṣadlṛ 'to be ruined' 'to move', 'to sit'+loṭ lakāra second person pl. Here √sa becomes √sīd[2]. Being a verbal form preceded by a non—verbal form, it goes without accent[3].

इन्द्रम (indram)—Acc. sing. of Indra. Bhvādigaṇa root √idi 'to prosper'+ran (Uṇādi suffix).[4] 'Nit' suffix (of which final 'n' is elided) makes it accented on the first syllable[5].

अभि[6] (abhi)—A particle meaning 'in front of'. Being a particle, it is accented on the first syllable.[7]

प्र (pra)—A Prefix. Being a prefix, it is accented on the first syllable[8].

गायत (gāyata)—Bhvādigaṇa root √gai 'to make sound'+loṭ lakāra second person pl. Being a verbal form preceded by a non—verbal form, it loses its accent[9].

सखायः (sakhāyaḥ)—(sakhā)-Voc. pl. of sakhi.

Samāna+Adādigaṇa root √ khyā 'to state' +iṇ (Uṇādi suffix)[10]. Here 'samāna' is substituted by 's'[11]. Being

---

1. Cf. *Phiṭ sūtra*—निपाताः आद्युदात्ताः - 80
2. Cf. Pāṇ. पाघ्राध्मास्था० - 7.3.78.
3. Cf. Pāṇ. तिङ्ङतिङः - 8.1.28
4. Cf. *Uṇādi.* ऋज्रेन्द्राग्रवज्र० - 2.28.
5. Cf. Pāṇ. ञ्नित्यादिर्नित्यम् - 6.1.197
6. अभीत्याभिमुख्यम् निघं० 1.3
7. Cf. *Phiṭ sūtra*—निपाताः आद्युदात्ताः - 80
8. Cf. *Phiṭ sūtra* उपसर्गाश्चाभिवर्जम् - 81.
9. Cf. Pāṇ. तिङ्ङतिङः - 8.1.28
10. Cf. *Uṇādi sūtra* - समाने ख्यः स चोदात्तः 3.137.
11. Cf. Pāṇ. समानस्य छन्दस्यमूर्द्धप्रभृत्युदर्केषु - 6.3.84.

voc. case not located in the beginning of the hemistich, it is accented [1].

स्तोम॑वाहसः (stoma-vāhasaḥ)—Nom. pl. Compound of

Stoma+Vāhasḥ. {Adādigaṇa root √stuñ 'to extol'+man (Uṇādi suffix)[2]}+{Bhvādigaṇa root √vaha 'to send' 'to carry'+asun (Uṇādi suffix)[3]}.

Note : Sāyaṇa cite Uṇādi sūtra वहिहाधञ्भ्यश्छन्दसि - 4.222 to

govern the derivation of 'vāhasaḥ'. But the above rule of Uṇādi sūtra does not prescribe 'asun' suffix. As such this quote of the Sāyaṇa is mistaken one. 'Asun' suffix is better prescribed by the 4.190. According to Sāyaṇa, it is a Tatpuruṣa compound. He tries to determine its accent on the basis of Uṇādi sūtra. But Swami Dayananda accept it as a Bahuvrīhi (possessive) compound, because the accent is retained on the first member[4]. And first member being formed of 'nit' suffix suffix is accented on the first syllable. The view of Swami Dayananda seems to be more viable.

Word meanings:

आ[5] (ā)—proximity, conjunction and simli

तु (tu) —haste

आ[1] (ā) —proximity, conjunction and simli

इ॒त (it)— come

नि (ni)—surely

सी॒द॒त (sīdata)—sit together

---

1. Cf. Pāṇ. आमन्त्रितस्य च - 8.1.19

2 Cf. *Uṇādi sūtra*—अर्त्तिस्तुसु० - 1.140

3 Cf. *Uṇādi sūtra*—सर्वधातुभ्योऽसुन् - 4.190

4. Cf. Pāṇ. बहुव्रीहि प्रकृत्या पूर्वपदम् - 6.2.1

5. अर्वागर्थे नि० 1.3. एतस्मिन्नेवार्थे (समुच्चयार्थे) देवेभ्यश्च पितृभ्य एत्याकारः नि० 1.4. उपमार्थे दृश्यते नि० 3.16. अध्यर्थे दृश्यते नि० 5.5.

इन्द्रम[1] (indram)—electric force

अभि[2] (abhi)—in front of

प्र[3] (pra)—A prefix

गायत[4] (gāyata)—discover, find, sing

सखायः[5] (sakhāyaḥ)—scholars

स्तोमवाहसः (stoma-vāhasaḥ)—Attributive of Sakhāyaḥ. Possessed of good qualities

Anvaya (Sequencial placement of words)

stoma-vāhasaḥ sakhāyaḥ ā tu ā ni sīdata it. indram abhi pra gāyata.

Meaning of Mantra in different contexts :

Spiritual: (सखाय) Scholars (स्तोमवाहसः) possessed of good qualities (आ इत) should come here and (नि सीदत) sit together (तु) soon to (अभि प्रगायत) praise (इन्द्रम्) Brahman.

---

1. इन्द्रः पदनाम निघं० 5.4. इन्द्रः-इरा दृणातीति वा इरां ददातीति वा, इरां दधातीति वा। इरां दारयत इति वा। इरां धारयत इति वा। इन्दवे द्रवतीति वा। इन्दौ रमत इति वा। इन्धे भूतानीति वा। 'तद्यदेनं प्राणैः समैन्धंस्तदिन्द्रस्येन्द्रत्वमिति विज्ञायते।' इदं करणादित्याग्रायणः। इदं दर्शनादित्यौपमन्यवः। इन्दतेर्वैश्वर्यकर्मणः। इन्दञ्छत्रूणां दारयिता वा द्रावयिता वा। आदरयिता च यज्वनाम् नि० 10.8. एष वै शुक्रो य एष (सूर्यः) तपत्येष (सूर्यः) उ एवेन्द्रः श० 4.5.5.7, 4.5.9.4. अथ यः स इन्द्रोऽसौ स आदित्यः श० 8.5.3.2. यो वै वायुः स इन्द्रो य इन्द्रः स वायुः श० 4.1.3.19. स योऽयं मध्ये प्राणः। एष एवेन्द्रस्तानेष प्राणान्मध्यत इन्द्रियैणैन्द्ध तस्मादिन्ध इन्धो ह वै तमिन्द्र इत्याचक्षते परोऽक्षम् श० 6.1.1.2. हृदयमेवेन्द्रः श० 12.9.1.15. यन्मनः स इन्द्रः गो० उ० 4.11. मन एवेन्द्रः श० 12.9.1.13. इन्द्रो वै यजमानः श०2.1.2.11 क्षत्रियो यदु च यजमानः श० 5.3.5.27. एन्द्रो वै राजन्य तै० 3.8.23.2. इन्द्रः क्षत्रम् श०10.4. 1.5. वीर्यं वा इन्द्रः तां० 9.7.5, 8. इन्द्रो यज्ञस्य नेता श० 4.1.2.15.
2. अभीत्याभिमुख्यम् निघं० 1.3.
3. प्र परेत्यस्य प्रातिलोम्यम् नि० 1.3. प्रेव नश्यसि पराचीव नश्यसि नि० 9.28. अन्तरिक्षं वै प्र ऐ० 2.41. प्राणो वै प्र ऐ० 2.40.
4. गायतीति अर्चति कर्मसु पठितम् निघं० 3.14
5. सखायः समानख्यानाः नि० 7.30. सखायः सप्तपदा अभूम तै० 3.7.7.11.

Scientific: (सखाय) Scholars (स्तोमवाहसः) possessed of good qualities (आ इत) should come here and (नि सीदत) sit together (तु) soon to (अभि प्रगायत) praise (इन्द्रम्) electric force of the universe.

Socio-political: (सखाय) Scholars (स्तोमवाहसः) possessed of good qualities (आ इत) should come here and (नि सीदत) sit together (तु) soon to (अभि प्रगायत) praise (इन्द्रम्) Good teacher/ruler.

४२. पुरूतमं पुरूणामीशानं वार्याणाम्। इन्द्रं सोमे सचा सुते।।२।।

पुरूऽतमम्। पुरूणाम्। ईशानम्। वार्याणाम्। इन्द्रम्। सोमे। सचा। सुते।।

Saṁhitāpāṭha

purūtamaṁ purūṇāmīśānaṁ vāryāṇām. indraṁ some sacā sute.

Padapāṭha

pure-tamam. purūṇām.īśānam. vāryāṇām. indram. some. sacā. sute.

Grammatical Notes:

पुरूतमम् (purū—tamam)—Puru+Divādigaṇa root √tamu 'to desire'+ ac suffix. The suffix being 'cit', 'tama' should have been accented on the final syllable, but it is exceptionally accented on the first syllable of the suffix 'ac'[1].

पुरूणाम् (purūṇām) —Juhotyādigaṇa root √pṛ 'to bring up' 'to fill up'+kuḥ (Uṇādi suffix)[2].

ईशानम् (īśānam) —Acc. sing. of īśāna. Adadīgaṇa root √īśa 'to prosper'+śānac (present active participle). Śānac, being a sārvadhātuk suffix[3], remains unaccented, as such the root is accented.

वार्याणाम् (vāryāṇām)—Gen. sing. of vārya. Svādigaṇa root √vṛṅ 'to divide'+ṇyat suffix[4]. Being formed of '√vṛṅ+ṇyat', it is accented on the first syllable[5].

---

1. Cf. Pāṇ. परादिश्छन्दसि बहुलम् - 6.2.199.
2. Cf. *Uṇādi sūtra*—पॄभिदिव्यधि० -1.23
3. Cf. Pāṇ. तिङ्शित्सार्वधातुकम् - 3.4.113
4. Cf. Pāṇ. ऋहलोर्ण्यत् - 3.1.124
5. Cf. Pāṇ.—ईडवन्दवृशंसदुहां ण्यत् - 6.1.214

इन्द्र॑म् (indram)—Acc. sing. of Indra. Bhvādigaṇa root √idi 'to prosper'+ran (Uṇādi suffix).[1] 'Nit' suffix (of which final 'n' is elided) makes it accented on the first syllable[2].

सोमे॑ (some)—Loc. sing. of soma. Bhvādigaṇa root √ṣu 'to deliver', 'to glorify' or Svādigaṇa root √ṣuñ 'to squeez' or √ṣu 'to inspire'+man (Uṇādi suffix)[3]. Due to 'nit' (having indicatory 'n') suffix, the word soma gets the accent on the first syllable[4].

सचा॑ (sacā)—A particle meaning 'togetherness'. Being a particle, it is acented on the first syllable[5].

सु॒ते (sute)—Loc. sing. of suta. Svādigaṇa root √ ṣu 'to squeez' 'to press' or Bhvādigaṇa root √ṣu 'to deliver' 'to prosper'+kta (primary suffix)[6] or kta (Uṇādi suffix). It gets acute accent on suffix,i.e. last syllable.[7]

Word meanings:

पु॒रू॒तम॑म्[8] (purū-tamam)—many, strong

पु॒रू॒णाम्[9] (purūṇām) —many

ईशा॑नम्[10] (īśānam) —lord, master

---

1. Cf. *Uṇādi.* ऋज्रेन्द्राग्रवज्र० - 2.28.
2. Cf. Pāṇ. ञ्नित्यादिर्नित्यम् - 6.1.197
3. *artti-stu-su-hu-sṛ-dhṛ-kṣi-kṣu-bhā-yā-vā-padi-uakṣi-nī-bhyo man-Uṇādi sūtra*—1.140.
4. Cf. Paṇini (6.1.197)—*ñnityādinityam.*
5. Cf. *Phiṭ sūtra*—निपाताः आद्युदात्ताः - 80
6. Cf. Pāṇ. क्तक्तवतु निष्ठा -1.1.26
7. Cf. Pāṇ. आद्युदात्तश्च - 3.1.3
8. पुरु बहुनाम निघं० 3.1.
9. पुरु बहुनाम निघं० 3.1.
10. आदित्यो वा ऽ ईशान आदित्यो ह्यस्य सर्वस्येष्टे श० 6.1.3.17. एतान्यष्टौ (रुद्रः, सर्वशर्वः, पशुपतिः उग्रः, अशनिः, भवः, महान्देवः, ईशानः) अग्निरूपाणि। कुमारो नवमः श० 6.1.3.1

वार्याणाम्[1] (vāryāṇām)—universe, sciences

इन्द्रम् (indram)—God, electric force, teacher

इन्द्रः पदनाम निघं० 5.4. इन्द्रः-इरां दृणातीति वा इरां ददातीति वा, इरां दधातीति वा। इरां दारयत इति वा। इरां धारयत इति वा। इन्दवे द्रवतीति वा। इन्दौ रमत इति वा। इन्धे भूतानीति वा। 'तद्यदेनं प्राणैः समैन्धंस्तदिन्द्रस्येन्द्रत्वमिति विज्ञायते।' इदं करणादित्याग्रायणः। इदं दर्शनादित्यौपमन्यवः। इन्दतेर्वैश्वर्यकर्मणः। इन्दञ्छत्रूणां दारयिता वा द्रावयिता वा। आदरयिता च यज्वनाम् नि० 10.8. एष वै शुक्रो य एष (सूर्यः) तपत्येष (सूर्यः) उ एवेन्द्रः श० 4.5.5.7, 4.5.9.4. अथ यः इन्द्रोऽसौ स आदित्यः श० 8.53.2. यो वै वायुः स इन्द्रो य इन्द्रः स वायुः श० 4.1.3.19. स योऽयं मध्ये प्राणः। एष एवेन्द्रस्तानेष प्राणान्मध्यत इन्द्रियैणैन्द्ध तस्मादिन्ध इन्धो ह वै तमिन्द्र इत्याचक्षते परोऽक्षम् श० 6.1.1.2. हृदयमेवेन्द्रः श०12.9.1.15. यन्मनः स इन्द्रः गो० उ० 4.11. मन एवेन्द्रः श० 12.9.1.13. इन्द्रो वै यजमानः श० 2.1.2.11 क्षत्रियो यदु च यजमानः श० 5.3.5.27. एन्द्रो वै राजन्य तै० 3.8.23.2. इन्द्रः क्षत्रम् श० 10.4.1.5. वीर्य वा इन्द्रः तां० 9.7.5,8. इन्द्रो यज्ञस्य नेता श० 4.1.2.15.

सोमे (some)—world, electric charge, student

सोम-ओषधिः सोमः सुनोतेर्यदेनमभिषुण्वन्ति नि० 11.2. सोमः-स्वा वै मऽएषेति तस्मात्सोमो नाम श० 3.9.4.22. सत्यं (वै) श्रीर्ज्योतिः सोमः श० 5.1.2.10. श्रीर्वै सोमः श० 4.1.3.9. सोमो राजा राजपतिः तै० 2.5.7.3. असौ वै सोमो राजा विचक्षणश्चन्द्रमाः कौ० 4.4. सोमो राजा चन्द्रमाः श० 10.4.2.1. चन्द्रमा वै सोमः कौ० 16.5. वृत्रो वै सोम आसीत् श० 3.4.3.13. संवत्सरो वै सोमो राजा कौ० 7.10. सोमो हि प्रजापतिः श० 5.1.5.26. सोमो वैष्णवो राजेत्याह तस्याप्सरसो विशः श० 13.4.3.8. जुष्टा विष्णव इति। जुष्टा सोमायेत्ये वैतदाह (विष्णुः-सोमः) श० 3.2.4.12. तद् यदेवेदं क्रीतो विशतीव तदु हास्य (सोमस्य) वैष्णवं रूपम् कौ० 8.2. सोमो वै पवमानः श० 2.2.3.22. एष

8.। यदीशानोऽन्नं तेन कौ० 6.8.

1. वार्यं वृणोतेरथापि वरतमम् नि० 5.1. वार्याणाम् अश्वनाम निघं० 1.14

(वायुः) वै सोमस्योद्गीथो यत्पवते तां० .6.18. तस्मात् सोमं सर्वेभ्यो देवेभ्यो जुह्वति तस्मादाहुः सोमः सर्वा देवता इति श० 1.6.3.21. सोमो वाऽइन्द्रः श० 2.2.3.23. सोमो रात्रिः श० 3.4.4.15. सोम एव सवृत इति गो० उ० 2.24. सोमो वै चतुर्होता तै० 2.3.1.1. सोमो वै पर्णः श० 6.5.1.1. सोमो वै पलाशः कौ० 2.2. पशुर्वै प्रत्यक्षं सोमः श० 5.1.3.7. सोम एवैव प्रत्यक्षं यत्पशुः कौ० 12.6. पशवः सोमो राजा तै० 1.4.7.6. सोमो वै दधि तै० 1.4.7.6. एष वै यजमानो यत्सोमः तै० 1.3.3.5. द्यावापृथिव्योर्वा एष गर्भो यत्सोमो राजा ऐ० 2.26. क्षत्रं सोमः ऐ० 2.38. यशो वै सोमः श० 4.2.4.9. यशो (ऋ० 10. 72.10) वै सोमो राजा ऐ० 1.13. प्राणः सोमः श० 7.3.1.2.रसः सोमः श० 7.3.1.3. तस्मात् सोमो राजा सर्वाणि नक्षत्राण्युपैति प० 3.12. तै० 1.1.3.10. अन्तरिक्षदेवत्यो हि सोमः गो० उ० 2.4. गिरिषु हि सोमः श० 3.3.4.7. घ्नन्ति खलु वाऽएतत्सोमं यदभिषुण्वन्ति तै० 2.2.8.1. सोमो राजा मृगशीर्षेण आगन् श० 3.1.2.2. सोमवीरुधां पते तै० 3.11.4.1. आपः सोमः सुतः श० 7.1.1.22. आपो ह्येतस्य (सोमस्य) लोकः श० 4.4.5.21. पुमान् वै सोमःस्त्री सुरा तै० 1.3.3.4.

सचा॑ (sacā)—to be adored, to be lauded, to be induced

सु॒ते[1] (sute)—being created, initiated, produced

Anvaya (Sequencial placement of words)

some sute purū-tamam indram, purūṇām vāryāṇām īśānam, sacā.

Meaning of Mantra in different contexts :

पु॒रू॒ऽतम॑म्। पु॒रू॒णाम्। ईशा॑नम्। वार्या॑णाम्। इन्द्र॑म्। सोमे॑। सचा॑। सु॒ते।।

Spiritual: (सोमे) When this world is (सुते) created, (इन्द्रम्) Brahman, (पुरूतमम्) the great (ईशानम्) lord of (पुरूणाम्) many (वार्याणाम्) worlds (सचा) is adored.

Socio-political 1: (सोमे) When the student is (सुते) initiated

1. सुतस्य अभिषुतस्य नि० 13.6. सुतेषु सोमेषु नि० 5.22. सुतः, सुतम् इत्यन्ननामनी निघं० 2.7.

into knowledge, (इन्द्रम्) teacher/Guru, (पुरूतमम्) the great (ईशानम्) master of (पुरूणाम्) many (वार्याणाम्) sciences (सचा) is lauded.

Note : The Vedas give first and formost place to the teachers in the society. The teachers should be respected and given due credit for their contribution to the national development.

४३. स घा॑ नो॒ योग॒ आ भु॑व॒त् स रा॒ये स पुर॑न्ध्याम्।
गम॒द् वाजे॑भिरा स नः॑ ॥३॥

सः॒। घ॒। नः॒। योगे॑। आ। भु॒व॒त्। सः॒। रा॒ये। सः॒। पुर॑न्ध्याम्। गम॒त्।
वाजे॑भिः। आ। सः॒। नः॒ ॥

Samhitāpāṭha

sa gha naḥ yoge ābhuvatsa rāye sa purandhyām. gamad
vājebhirā sa naḥ.

Padapāṭha

saḥ. gha. naḥ. yoge. ā. bhuvat. saḥ. rāye. saḥ.
purandhyām. gamat. vājebhiḥ. ā. saḥ. naḥ.

Grammatical Notes:

स: (saḥ)—Nom. sing. masc. of deomstrative pronoun
'Tad'. It is accented following the norms set by Phiṭ
Sūtra.[1]

घ (gha)—A particle meaning 'determination'. It is
prolonged [2]. Being a particle, it should have been
accented on the first syllable as per rule of accentuation
registered in the Phiṭ Sūtras, but there are some
particles which are not accented. Those particles have
been listed in the list beginning with 'c'[3]. As such 'gha'
is among such particles that are not accented.
highlighted by an exceptional rule of a phiṭ sūtra.

नः (naḥ)—Acc./dat./gen. pl. enclitic form of first person
pronoun 'Asmad'[4]. Being an enclitic form it is not

---

1 Cf. Sāyaṇa on *RV*. 1.2.1.

2. Cf. Pāṇ. ऋचि तुनुघ॰ 6.3.133.

3. Cf. *Phiṭ sūtra*—चादयोऽनुदात्ताः - 84

4. Cf. *vahuvacanasyavasnasau*—Pāṇ. 8.1.21.

accented.[1]

योगे (yoge)—Rudhādigaṇa root √ yujir 'to combine', 'to unite' +ghañ suffix. Being formed of 'ñit' suffix, it is accented on the first syllable[2].
योगः-यद् योक्त्रं स योगः तै० 3.3.3.3.

आ (ā)—A prefix meaning proximity, conjunction and simli. Being a prefix, it is accented on the first syllable[3].

भुवत् (bhuvat)—Bhvādigaṇa root √ bhū 'to be' +Āśirliṅ third person sing. Being a verbal form preceded by a non—verbal form, it remains unaccented[4].

सः (saḥ)—Nom. sing. masc. of demonstrative pronoun 'Tad'. It is accented being a pronominal form following the norms set by Phiṭ sūtra.[5]

राये (rāye)— Dat. sing. of rāya. Adādigaṇa root √ rai or rā 'to donate' +ḍaiḥ (Uṇādi suffix). The dat. case ending is accented here[6].

सः (saḥ)—Nom. sing. masc. of demonstrative pronoun 'Tad'. It is accented following the norms set by Phiṭ sūtra.[7]

पुरन्ध्याम् (purandhyām)—Loc. sing. of purandhi. The derivation of this word is not known. It may be read among the list of 'Pṛṣarodara' etc. words[8]. It is accented on the first syllable. Its accentuation also

---

1. Cf. Pāṇ. युस्मदस्मदोः षष्ठी चतुर्थी द्वितीया स्थयोर्वान्नावौ 8.1.20.
2. Cf. Pāṇ. ञ्नित्यादिर्नित्यम् - 6.1.197
3. Cf. *Phiṭ sūtra*—उपसर्गाश्चाभिवर्जम् -81.
4. Cf. Pāṇ. तिङ्ङतिङः - 8.1.28
5 Cf. Sāyaṇa on *RV.* 1.2.1.
6. Cf.Pāṇ. ऊडिदंपाद्यप्पुम्रैद्युभ्यः - 6.1.171
7 Cf. Sāyaṇa on *RV.* 1.2.1.
8. Cf. Pāṇ. पृषोदरादीनि यथोपदिष्टम् - 6.3.109

cannot be defined for want of its derivation.

गमत् (gamat)—Bhvādigaṇa root √gam+loṭ lakāra third pers. sing. Sāyaṇa considers it a use of loṭ lakāra. On the other hand Swami Dayananda, considers it to be the form of luṅ lakāra (aorist). It remains unaccented, since it is followed by a non—verbal form [1]in a hemistich. Here 'a' is absent[2].

वाजेभिः (vājebhiḥ)—Inst. pl. of vāja. Bhvādigaṇa root √ vaja 'to go'+ghañ suffix. It is accented on the first syllable, being read in the list of 'vṛṣa' group of words.[3]

आ (ā)—A prefix meaning proximity, conjunction and simli. Being a prefix, it is accented on the first syllable[4].

सः (saḥ)—Nom. sing. masc. of demonstrative pronoun 'Tad'. It is accented following the norms set by Phiṭ sūtra.[5]

नः (naḥ)—Acc./dat./gen. pl. enclitic form of first person pronoun 'Asmad'[6]. Being an enclitic form it is not accented.[7]

Word meanings:

सः (saḥ)—that

घ (gha)—surely

नः (naḥ)—us

---

1. Cf. Pāṇini—तिङ्ङतिङः - 8.1.28
2. Cf. Pāṇ. बहुलं छन्दसि अमाङ्योगेऽपि - 6.4.75.
3. Cf. Pāṇ. वृषादीनां च - 6.1.203.
4. Cf. *Phiṭ sūtra*—उपसर्गाश्चाभिवर्जम् -81.
5 Cf. Sāyaṇa on RV. 1.2.1.
6. Cf. *vahuvacanasyavasnasau*—Pāṇ. 8.1.21.
7. Cf. Pāṇ. युस्मदस्मदोः षष्ठी चतुर्थी द्वितीया स्थयोर्वान्नावौ 8.1.20.

योगे (yoge)—puruṣārtha, expansion of universe, goals

आ[1] (ā)—proximity, conjunction and simli

भुवत् (bhuvat)—be

सः (saḥ)—that God, that electric force, that teacher/ruler

राये[2] (rāye)—matter particles, riches

सः (saḥ)—that God, that electric force, that teacher/ruler

पुरन्ध्याम्[3] (purandhyām)—knowledge, universe, intelligence

(आ) गमत् (gamat)—come

वाजेभिः[4] (vājebhiḥ)—food stuff of creation, matter, power, food

आ[5](ā)—proximity, conjunction and simli

सः (saḥ)—that God, that electric force, that teacher/ruler

---

1. अर्वागर्थे नि० 1.3. एतस्मिन्नेवार्थे (समुच्चयार्थे) देवेभ्यश्च पितृभ्य एत्याकारः नि० 1.4. उपमार्थे दृश्यते नि० 3.16. अध्यर्थे दृश्यते नि० 5.5.
2. रायः पशवो वै रायः श० 3.3.1.8.
3. पुरन्धिर्बहुधीः, तत्कः पुरन्धिर्भगः पुरस्तात् तस्यान्वादेश इत्येकम्। इन्द्र इत्यपरं स बहुकर्मतमः पुरां च दारयितृतमः, वरुण इत्यपरं न प्रज्ञया स्तौति नि० 6.13. पुरन्ध्या-स्तुत्या नि० 12.30. पुरन्धी-द्यावापृथिवीनाम नि० 3.30. पुरन्धिः-पदनाम निघं० 4.3. पुरन्धियोषेति, योषित्येव रूपं दधाति तस्माद्रूपिणी युवतिः प्रिया भावुका श० 13.1.9.6.
4. वाजः अन्ननाम निघं० 2.7. वलनाम निघं० 2.9. वाजेभिरन्नैः नि० 11.26. अन्नं वै वाजः तै० 1.3.6.2. श० 5.1.4.3. ता० 13.9.13. अन्नं वाजः श० 5.1.1.16. अन्नं वै वाजः श०1. 4.1.9. वीर्य वै वाजः श० 3.3.4.7. ओषधयः खलु वै वाजः तै० 1.3.7.1. वाजो वै पशवः ऐ०5.8. वाजो वै स्वर्गो लोकः तां० 18.7.12. गो० उ० 5.8. वाग्वै वाजस्व प्रसवः तै० 1.3.2. 5. सोमो वै वाजः मै० 4.5.4. सर्वः सोमं पिपासति वाजः ह गच्छति मै० 1.11.5. अमृतोऽन्नं वै वाज जै० 2.193.
5. अर्वागर्थे नि० 1.3. एतस्मिन्नेवार्थे (समुच्चयार्थे) देवेभ्यश्च पितृभ्य एत्याकारः नि० 1.4. उपमार्थे दृश्यते नि० 3.16. अध्यर्थे दृश्यते नि० 5.5.

नः (naḥ)—to us

Anvaya (Sequencial placement of words)

saḥ gha naḥ yoge ā bhuvat. saḥ purandhyām. saḥ rāye. saḥ vājebhiḥ naḥ ā gamat.

Meaning of Mantra in different contexts :

Spiritual: (सः) May that Brahman (आभुवत्) be (नः) with us (योगे) in attaining the puruṣārtha (four fold objectives: dharma, artha, kama, and mokṣa); (सः) may He be with us (पुरन्ध्याम्) in the acquisition of knowledge and intelligence; (सः) may he be with us (राये) acquiring the riches; (सः) may He (घ) surely (आगमत्) come (नः) to us (वाजेभिः) with food.

Scientific: (सः) May that Indra (electric force) (आभुवत्) be (नः) with us (योगे) in the expansion of universe; (सः) may he (पुरन्ध्याम्) sustain this universe; (सः) may he be with us (राये) in making the observer space rich with matter particles, (सः) may he (घ) surely (आगमत्) come (नः) to this universe (वाजेभिः) with lot of power to dominate the contracting forces.

Socio-political 1: (सः) May that Guru/teacher (आभुवत्) be (नः) with us (योगे) in attaining goal of life; (सः) may he be with us (पुरन्ध्याम्) in acquisition of knowledge and intelligence; (सः) may he be with us (राये) in acquiring riches; (सः) may he (घ) surely (आगमत्) train (नः) to us (वाजेभिः) with the means of living a hale and hearty life.

Socio-political 2: (सः) May that ruler (आभुवत्) be (नः) with us (योगे) in attaining goal of life; (सः) may he be with us (पुरन्ध्याम्) in sustained development; (सः) may he be with us (राये) in acquiring riches; (सः) may he (घ) surely (आगमत्) help (नः) us (वाजेभिः) with the means living a hale and hearty life.

४४. यस्यं संस्थे न वृण्वते हरीं समत्सु शत्रंवः।
तस्मा इन्द्रांय गायत।।४।।

यस्यं। संऽस्थे। न। वृण्वतें। हरी इतिं। समत्ऽसुं। शत्रंवः। तस्मैं। इन्द्रांय।गायत।।

Saṁhitāpāṭha

yasya sansthe na vṛṇvate harī samatsu śatravaḥ. tasmā indrāya gāyata.

Padapāṭha

yasya. san-sthe. na. vṛṇvate. harī iti. samat-su. śatravaḥ. tasmai. indrāya. gāyata.

Grammatical Notes:

यस्यं (yasya)—Gen. sing. masc. of demonstrative pronoun 'Yad'. Being a pronominal form, it is accented on the first syllable.

संस्थे (san—sthe)—Sam+Bhvādigaṇa root √ṣṭhā 'to stoppage of movement' +kaḥ suffix[1]. In this case 'saṁ' prefix is followed by a word ending with a primary suffix (kṛdanta), so it gets accent on the primary derivative. As such 'sansthe' is accented on the final syllable.

न (na) —'N' is a particle of negation. Being a particle, it is accented on the first syllable[2].

वृण्वतें (vṛṇvate)—Svādigaṇa root √vṛñ 'to choose'+laṭ lakāra third person sing. It carries an accent being preceded by a form of demonstrative pronoun 'yad' [3].

हरी (harī)—Bhvādigaṇa root root √hvam 'to kidnap'+in

1. Cf. Pāṇ. आतश्चोपसर्गे - 3.1.136
2. Cf. *Phiṭ sūtra* निपाताः आद्युदात्ताः - 80
3. Cf. Pāṇ. यद्वृत्तान्नित्यम् - 8.1.66

(Uṇādi suffix)[1]. Being formed of 'nit' suffix, it is accented on the first syllable[2].

स॒मत्सु॑ (samat-su)—Sam+Adādigaṇa root √ ada 'to eat'+kvip.

शत्र॑वः (śatravaḥ)—Nom./acc. pl. of śatru. Bhvādigaṇa root √śadlṛ 'to destroy'+krūn (Uṇādi suffix).[3] Being formed of 'nit' suffix, it is accented on the first syllable[4].

तस्मै॑ (tasmai)—Dat. sing. masc. of demonstrative pronoun 'Tad'. Being a pronominal form, it is accented on the first syllable.

इन्द्रा॑य (indrāya)—Dat. sing. of Indra. Bhvādigaṇa root √idi 'to prosper'+ran (Uṇādi suffix).[5] 'Nit' suffix (of which final 'n' is elided) makes it accented on the first syllable[6].

गा॒य॒त॒ (gāyata)—Bhvādigaṇa root √gai 'to make sound'+loṭ lakāra second person pl. Being a verbal form preceded by a non—verbal form, it loses its accent[7].

Word meanings:

यस्य॑ (yasya)—whose

सं॒स्थे (san-sthe)—chariot,
न[8] (na)—negation

---

1. Cf. *Uṇādi sūtra*—हृपिषिरुहिवृतिविदिच्छिदिकीर्तिभ्यश्च - 4.120
2. Cf. Pāṇ. ञ्नित्यादिर्नित्यम् - 6.1.197
3. Cf. *Uṇādi sūtra* रु-शातिभ्यां क्रुन् - 4.103.
4. Cf. Pāṇ. ञ्नित्यादिर्नित्यम् - 6.1.197
5. Cf. *Uṇādi.* ऋज्रेन्द्राग्रवज्र० - 2.28.
6. Cf. Pāṇ. ञ्नित्यादिर्नित्यम् - 6.1.197
7. Cf. Pāṇ. तिङ्ङतिङः - 8.1.28
8. भाषायामुभयमन्वध्यायम् 'नेन्द्र देवममंसत' इति प्रतिषेधीयः पुरस्तादुपचारस्तस्य यत् प्रतिषेधति। 'दुर्मदासो न सुरायाम्' इत्युपमार्थीय उपरिष्टाद् उपचारस्तस्य येनोपमिमीते नि० 1.4.

वृ॒ण्व॒ते (vṛṇvate)—withstand

हरी॒ (harī)—horses

स॒मत्सु॑[1] (samat—su)—combat

शत्र॑वः[2] (śatravaḥ)—enemies, forces of destruction, forces of contraction

तस्मै॒ (tasmai)—that

इन्द्रा॑य[3] (indrāya)—God, electric force, teacher, ruler

गा॒य॒त॒ (gāyata)—sing
गायतीति अर्चति कर्मसु पठितम् निघं० 3.14

Anvaya (Sequencial placement of words)

tasmai indrāya gāyata. samatsu śatravaḥ yasya sansthe harī na vṛṇvate.

Meaning of Mantra in different contexts :

Spiritual: (गायत) Sing praises (तस्मै) to that (इन्द्राय) Brahman, (यस्य) His (संस्थे) world is yoked (हरी) with horses of knowledge and bliss. With His help (शत्रवः) bad ideas (न) cannot (वृण्वते)

---

1. समत्सु संग्रामनाम निघं० 2.17. समदो वात्तेः, सम्मदो वा मदतेः नि० 9.17.

2. शत्रुः-शमयिता शातयिता वा नि० 2.16.

3. इन्द्रः पदनाम निघं० 5.4. इन्द्रः-इरां दृणातीति वा इरां ददातीति वा, इरां दधातीति वा। इरां दारयत इति वा। इरां धारयत इति वा। इन्दवे द्रवतीति वा। इन्दौ रमत इति वा। इन्धे भूतानीति वा। 'तद्यदेनं प्राणैः समैन्धंस्तदिन्द्रस्येन्द्रत्वमिति विज्ञायते।' इदं करणादित्याग्रायणः। इदं दर्शनादित्यौपमन्यवः। इन्दतेर्वैश्वर्यकर्मणः। इन्दञ्छत्रूणां दारयिता वा द्रावयिता वा। आदरयिता च यज्वनाम् नि० 10.8. एष वै शुक्रो य एष (सूर्यः) तपत्येष (सूर्यः) उ एवेन्द्रः श० 4.5.5.7, 4.5.9.4. अथ यः स इन्द्रोऽसौ स आदित्यः श० 8.5.3.2. यो वै वायुः स इन्द्रो य इन्द्रः स वायुः श० 4.1.3.19. स योऽयं मध्ये प्राणः। एष एवेन्द्रस्तानेष प्राणान्मध्यत इन्द्रियैणैन्द्ध तस्मादिन्ध इन्धो ह वै तमिन्द्र इत्याचक्षते परोऽक्षम् श० 6.1.1.2. हृदयमेवेन्द्रः श० 12.9.1.15. यन्मनः स इन्द्रः गो० उ० 4.11. मन एवेन्द्रः श० 12.9.1.13. इन्द्रो वै यजमानः श०2.1.2.11 क्षत्रियो यदु च यजमानः श० 5.3.5.27. एन्द्रो वै राजन्य तै० 3.8.23.2. इन्द्रः क्षत्रम् श० 10.4.1.5. वीर्यं वा इन्द्रः तां० 9.7.5, 8. इन्द्रो यज्ञस्य नेता श० 4.1.2.15.

emerge victorious (समत्सु) in the fight between bad and good ideas.

Scientific 1: (गायत) Sing praises (तस्मै) to that (इन्द्राय) electric force. (यस्य) His (संस्थे) chariot is yoked (हरी) with horse particles and anti particles. With His help (शत्रवः) forces of contraction (न) cannot (वृण्वते) emerge victorious (समत्सु) in the fight between forces of contraction and expansion.

Note: Here the seer visulises the cosmic phenomenon in his transcendental stage and witnesses a great struggle between the forces of expansion (electric force/Indra and radiation pressure /Ruder) and the forces of contraction of universe (surface tension/Vṛtra and gravitation force). He also witnesses the victory of forces of expansion over the forces of contraction. Indra, the electric force, has been described with horse yoked in his chariot. This horse is not an ordinary horse, but a charged particle. It is called horse (*aśva*), because of its fast speed like *aśva* (horse). *Ṛgevda* (1.163.3) calls *aśva* by the name '*Trit*' which means that aśva particle carries one third charge. Quark particles carry one third charge. As such *aśva* can be identified as one of the quark particles. Since, *aśva* particle is a charged particle, it exert electric force (Indra). Thus Indra's chariot yoked with horses means nothing but the exertion of Indra (electric force) from *aśva* particle.

Scientific 2: (गायत) Sing praises (तस्मै) to that (इन्द्राय) sun. (यस्य) His (संस्थे) chariot is yoked (हरी) with horses of light and attraction. With His help (शत्रवः) forces of darkness and destruction (न) cannot (वृण्वते) emerge victorious (समत्सु) in the fight between forces of darkness/destruction and the forces of light/construction.

Socio-political 1: (गायत) Sing praises (तस्मै) to that (इन्द्राय) ruler. (यस्य) His (संस्थे) state is yoked (हरी) with horses of justice and punishment. With His help (शत्रवः) anti-national elements (न) cannot (वृण्वते) flourish (समत्सु) in the fight between bad and good elements.

४५. सुतपाव्ने सुता इमे शुचयो यन्ति वीतये। सोमासो दध्याशिरः।।५।।

सुतपाव्ने। सुताः। इमे। शुचयः। यन्ति। वीतये। सोमासः। दधिऽआशिरः।।

Saṁhitāpāṭha

sutapāvne sutā ime śucayo yanti vītaye. somāso dadhyāśiraḥ.

Padapāṭha

sutapāvne. sutāḥ. ime. śucayaḥ.yanti. vītaye. somāsaḥ.dadhi-āśiraḥ.

Grammatical Notes:

सुतपाव्ने (sutapāvne)—Suta+Adādigaṇa root √pā 'to protect' or √pūñ 'to purify'+vanip[1].

सुताः (sutāḥ)—Nom. pl. of suta. Svādigaṇa root √ṣu 'to squeez' 'to press' or Bhvādigaṇa root √ṣu 'to deliver' 'to prosper'+kta (primary suffix)[2] or 'kta' (Uṇādi suffix). It gets acute accent on suffix.[3]

इमे (ime)—Nom. pl. of demonstrative pronoun 'idam'. Being a pronominal form, it bears an acute accent.

शुचयः (śucayaḥ)—Divādigaṇa root √śucir 'to purify'+in (Uṇādi suffix)[4]. Yāska derives it from √śuci 'to burn' and Sāyaṇa derives it from śuca 'to shine'. But these two roots are not registered in the Dhatupāṭha of Pāṇini. Therefore, Swami Dayananda derives it from Divādigaṇa root √śucir 'to purify'. Being fromed of 'nit' suffix, it is accented on the first syllable[5].

---

1. Cf. Pāṇ. आतो मनिन्क्वनिप० - 3.2.74
2. Cf. Pāṇ. क्तक्तवतु निष्ठा -1.1.26
3. Cf. Pāṇ. आद्युदात्तश्च - 3.1.3
4. Cf. *Uṇādi sūtra*—इगुपधात् कित् - 4.120.
5. Cf. Pāṇ. ञ्नित्यादिर्नित्यम् - 6.1.197

यन्ति (yanti)—Adādigaṇa root √iṇa 'to go'+laṭ lakāra third person pl. Being a verbal form preceded by a non—verbal form, it goes without accent [1].

वीतये (vītaye)—Bhvādigaṇa root √vī 'to move', 'to pervade', 'to generate', 'to shine', 'to eat'+ktin (Uṇādi suffix)[2]. It is also accented on the suffix.

सोमासः (somāsaḥ)—Nom. pl. of soma. Nom. pl. nominal suffix -jas is replaced by -asuk.[3] Bhvādigaṇa root √ṣu 'to deliver', 'to glorify' or Svādigaṇa root √ṣuñ 'to squeez' or √ṣu 'to inspire'+man (Uṇādi suffix)[4]. Due to 'nit' (having indicatory 'n') suffix, the word soma gets the accent on the first syllable[5].

दध्याशिरः (dadhi-āśiraḥ)—Bahuvrīhi compound. {Juhotyādigaṇa √dadhi 'to sustain', 'bring up'+kin[6]} + + {Krayādigaṇa root √śṛ 'to kill'+kvip suffix}. Being a Bahuvrīhi compound, it is accented on the first member[7]. The first member, being formed of 'nit' suffix, is accented on the first syllable[8].

Word meanings:

सुतपाव्ने (sutapāvne)—for use, exploitation, drinker of soma (electric charge)

सुताः[9] (sutāḥ)—resources created in nature, induced

---

1. Cf. Pāṇ. तिङ्ङतिङः - 8.1.28
2. Cf. Pāṇ. मन्त्रे वृषेषचमनविदभूवीरा उदात्तः - 3.3.93
3. Cf. Pāṇ. आज्जसेरसुक् - 7.1.50
4. *artti-stu-su-hu-sṛ-dhṛ-kṣi-kṣu-bhā-yā-vā-padi-uakṣi-nī-bhyo man- Uṇādi sūtra*—1.140.
5. Cf. Paṇini (6.1.197)—*ñnityādinityam.*
6. Cf. Pāṇ. आदृगमहनजनः किकिनौ लिट् च - 3.2.171
7. Cf. Pāṇ. बहुव्रीहौ प्रकृत्या पूर्वपदम् - 6.2.1
8. Cf. Pāṇ. ञ्नित्यादिर्नित्यम् - 6.1.197
9. सुतस्य अभिषुतस्य नि० 13.6. सुतेषु सोमेषु नि० 5.22. सुतः, सुतम् इत्यन्ननामनी निघं० 2.7.

इ॒मे (ime) —these

शुच॑यः[1] (śucayaḥ)—pure

य॒न्ति॒[2] (yanti)— to go, to beg

वी॒तये॑[3] (vītaye)—for consumption

सोमा॑सः[4] (somāsaḥ)—natural resources, electric charge

सुतस्य अभिषुतस्य नि० 13.6. सुतेषु सोमेषु नि० 5.22. सुतः, सुतम् इत्यन्ननामनी निघं० 2.7.

1. शुचिः शोचतेर्ज्वलतिकर्मणाः। अयमपीतरः शुचिरेतस्मादेव। निष्षिक्तमस्मात् पापकमिति नैरुक्ताः नि० 6.1. एतौ (शुक्रश्च शुचिश्च) एव ग्रैष्मौ (मासौ) स यदेतयोर्बलिष्ठं तपति तेन हैतौ शुक्रश्च शुचिश्च श० 4.3.1.15.
2. यन्ति याच्ञाकर्मा निघं० 3.19.
3. वीतये पानाय नि० 5.18. वीतिः (यजु० 11.46) अग्नऽआयाहि वीतयऽइत्यवितवऽइत्येतत् श० 6.4.4.9.
4. सोम-ओषधिः सोमः सुनोतेर्यदेनमभिषुण्वन्ति नि० 11.2. सोमः-स्वा वै मऽएषेति तस्मात्सोमो नाम श० 3.9.4.22. सत्यं (वै) श्रीर्ज्योतिः सोमः श० 5.1.2.10. श्रीर्वै सोमः श० 4.1.3.9. सोमो राजा राजपतिः तै० 2.5.7.3. असौ वै सोमो राजा विचक्षणश्चन्द्रमाः कौ० 4.4. सोमो राजाचन्द्रमाः श० 10.4.2.1. चन्द्रमा वै सोमः कौ० 16.5. वृत्रो वै सोम आसीत् श०3.4.3.13. संवत्सरो वै सोमो राजा कौ० 7.10. सोमो हि प्रजापतिः श० 5.1.5.26. सोमो वैष्णवो राजेत्याह तस्याप्सरसो विशः श० 13.4.3.8. जुष्टा विष्णव इति। जुष्टा सोमायेत्येवैतदाह (विष्णुः-सोमः) श० 3.2.4.12. तद् यदेवेदं क्रीतो विशतीव तदु हास्य (सोमस्य) वैष्णवं रूपम् कौ० 8.2. सोमोवै पवमानः श० 2.2.3.22. एष (वायुः) वै सोमस्योद्गीथो यत्पवते तां० .6.18. तस्मात् सोमं सर्वेभ्यो देवेभ्यो जुह्वति तस्मादाहुः सोमः सर्वा देवता इति श० 1.6.3.21. सोमो वाऽइन्द्रः श० 2.2.3.23. सोमो रात्रिः श० 3.4.4.15. सोम एव सकृत इति गो० उ० 2.24. सोमो वै चतुर्होता तै० 2.3.1.1. सोमो वै पर्णः श० 6.5.1.1. सोमो वै पलाशः कौ० 2.2. पशुर्वै प्रत्यक्षं सोमः श०5.1.3.7. सोम एवैव प्रत्यक्षं यत्पशुः कौ० 12.6. पशवः सोमोः राजा तै० 1.4.7.6. सोमो वै दधि तै० 1.4.7.6. एष वै यजमानो यत्सोमः तै० 1.3.3.5. द्यावापृथिव्योर्वा एष गर्भो यत्सोमो राजा ऐ० 2.26. क्षत्रं सोमः ऐ० 2.38. यशो वै सोमः श० 4.2.4.9. यशो (ऋ० 10.72.10.) वै सोमो राजा ऐ० 1.13. प्राणः सोमः श० 7.3.1.2. रसः सोमः श० 7.3. 1.3. तस्मात् सोमो राजा सर्वाणि नक्षत्राण्युपैति प० 3.12. तै० 1.1.3.10. अन्तरिक्षदेवत्यो हि सोमः गो० उ० 2.4. गिरिषु हि सोमः श० 3.3.4.7. घ्नन्ति खलु वाऽएतत्सोमं यदभिषुण्वन्ति तै० 2.2.8.1. सोमो राजा मृगशीर्षेण आगन् श० 3.1.2.2. सोमवीरुधां पते तै० 3.11.4.1. आपः सोमः सुतः श० 7.1.1.22. आपो ह्येतस्य (सोमस्य) लोकः श० 4.4.5.21. पुमान् वै

दध्याशिरः (dadhyāśiraḥ)—nourishing, curd or coagulated butter pervading the universe or inhomogeneous universe.

Anvaya (Sequencial placement of words)

ime somāsaḥ sutapāvne vītaye yanti. sutāḥ śucayaḥ dadhyāśiraḥ.

Meaning of Mantra in different contexts :

Spiritual: (सोमासः) All natural resources in the universe (सुताः) have been created by Brahman (सुतपाव्ने) for the use/exploitation and (वीतये) consumption of the individuated beings. (इमे) These resources created in nature are (शुचयः) pure (without any adultration), and (दध्याशिरः) nourishing.

Scientific: (सोमासः) The electric force (यन्ति) depends upon (सुतपाव्ने) the magnitude of induced electric charge (वीतये) for its drink. (इमे) These electric charges (शुचयः) shines like fire and (सुताः) induced (दध्याशिरः) while the universe was becoming inhomogeneous.

Note : The electric force depends upon the magnitude of electric charge, greater the charge, larger the force. Had there been no electric charge, there would have been no electric force. This process of electric charges exerting electric force is called as soma-pāna (drinking of soma) by Indra in the Veda. That is why, the seer calls the electric charge as the protector of electric force. Here *dadhi* (curd or coagulated butter) referes to universe becoming inhomogeneous. In earlier state universe was *salila*, completely homogeneous. By that time *sattva*, *rajas* and *tamas* were also in homogeneous state. This state was known as *prakṛti*. The evolutionary state was described as *vikṛti*, which was the inhomogeneous state of *sattva*, *rajas* and *tamas*. With the rise of inhomogeneity, particles began to from. Particles can be thought of as condensation of energy. With the origin of particles, electric charge was also induced. The word *suta* refers to the induced electric charge in the Vedas.

सोमः स्त्री सुरा तै० 1.3.3.4.

४६. त्वं सुतस्य पीतये सद्यो वृद्धो अजायथाः।
इन्द्र ज्यैष्ठ्याय सुक्रतो॥६॥

त्वम्। सुतस्य। पीतये। सद्यः। वृद्धः। अजायथाः। इन्द्र। ज्यैष्ठ्याय।
सुक्रतोइति सुक्रतो।

Saṁhitāpāṭha

tvaṁ sutasya pītaye sadyo vṛddho ajāyathāḥ. indra jyaiṣ ṭhyāya sukrato.

Padapāṭha

tvam. sutasya. pītaye. sadyaḥ. vṛddhaḥ. ajāyathāḥ. indra. jyaiṣṭhyāya. sukrato.

Grammatical Notes:

त्वम् (tvam)—Nom. sing. of second person pronoun 'Yusmad'. Being a pronominal form, it is accented.

सुतस्य (sutasya)—Gen. sing. of suta. Svādigaṇa root √ ṣu 'to squeez' 'to press' or Bhvādigaṇa root √ṣu 'to deliver' 'to prosper'+kta (primary suffix) [1] or kta (Uṇādi suffix). It gets acute accent on suffix. [2]

पीतये (pītaye) —Bhvādigaṇa root √ pā 'to drink'+ktin suffix[3]. Being formed of 'nit' suffix, it should have been accented on the first syllable. But it is exceptionally accented on the suffix.

सद्यः (sadyaḥ)—Samāna+dya[4]. It is accented on the suffix[5].

---

1. Cf. Pāṇ. क्तक्तवतु निष्ठा -1.1.26
2. Cf. Pāṇ. आद्युदात्तश्च - 3.1.3
3. Cf. Pāṇ. स्थागापापचो भावे - 3.3.95
4. Cf. Pāṇ. सद्यः परुत्० - 5.3.22
5. Cf. Pāṇ. आद्युदात्तश्च- 3.1.3

वृद्धः (vṛddhaḥ)—Bhvādigaṇa root √vṛdhu 'to increase'+kta suffix. It is also accented on the suffix[1].

अजायथाः (ajāyathāḥ)—Divādigaṇa root √ janī 'to appear'+loṭ lakāra second person sing. Being a verbal form preceded by a non—verbal form, it goes without accent[2].

इन्द्र (indra)—Voc. sing. of Indra. Bhvādigaṇa root √idi 'to prosper'+ran (Uṇādi suffix).[3] 'Nit' suffix (of which final 'n' is elided) makes it accented on the first syllable[4].

ज्यैष्ठ्याय (jyaiṣṭhyāya)—Vṛddha (jyā)+iṣṭhan suffix+ṣyañ in the sense of 'nature'. Jyeṣṭhasya bhāvaḥ jyaiṣṭham[5] i.e. the nature of Jyeṣṭha is jyaiṣṭham. Being formed of 'ñit' suffix, it is accented on the first syllable[6].

सुक्रतो (sukrato)—Voc. sing. of Sukratu. Su+Taṇādigaṇa root √kṛñ 'to do'+ktuḥ. (Uṇādi suffix) in the nom. or instrumental+sense[7]. Being a voc. case not located in the beginning of a hemistich, it loses its accent[8].

Word meanings:

त्वम् (tvam)—you

सुतस्य[9] (sutasya)—natural resources, induced electric charge

---

1. Cf. Pāṇ. आद्युदात्तश्च- 3.1.3
2. Cf. Pāṇ. तिङ्ङतिङः - 8.1.28
3. Cf. *Uṇādi.* ऋज्रेन्द्राग्रवज्र० - 2.28.
4. Cf. Pāṇ. ञ्नित्यादिर्नित्यम् - 6.1.197
5. Cf. Pāṇ. गुणवचनब्राह्मणादिभ्यः कर्मणि - 5.1.124
6. Cf. Pāṇ. ञ्नित्यादिर्नित्यम् - 6.1.197
7. Cf. *Uṇādi* कृञः कतुः - 1.76.
8. Cf. Pāṇ. आमन्त्रितस्य च - 8.1.19
9. सुतस्य अभिषुतस्य नि० 13.6. सुतेषु सोमेषु नि० 5.22. सुतः, सुतम् इत्यन्ननामनी निघं० 2.7.

पीतये (pītaye) —for use, exploitation, for drinking

सद्यः (sadyaḥ)—immediately

वृद्धः (vṛddhaḥ)—grow up in knowledge, augmented vigour

अजायथाः (ajāyathāḥ)—to grow

इन्द्र[1] (indra)—Address to Indra. Individuated being, electric force

ज्यैष्ठ्याय[2] (jyaiṣṭhyāya)—for the larger interest of humanity or creation

सुक्रतो[3] (sukrato)—Address to Sukratu. Possessed of best intellectual power and ability of action, performer of good works.

सुतस्य अभिषुतस्य नि० 13.6. सुतेषु सोमेषु नि० 5.22. सुतः, सुतम् इत्यन्ननामनी निघं० 2.7.

1. इन्द्रः पदनाम निघं० 5.4. इन्द्रः-इरां दृणातीति वा इरां ददातीति वा, इरां दधातीति वा। इरां दारयत इति वा। इरां धारयत इति वा। इन्दवे द्रवतीति वा। इन्दौ रमत इति वा। इन्धे भूतानीति वा। 'तद्यदेनं प्राणैः समैन्धंस्तदिन्द्रस्येन्द्रत्वमिति विज्ञायते।' इदं करणादित्याग्रायणः। इदं दर्शनादित्यौपमन्यवः। इन्दतेर्वैश्वर्यकर्मणः। इन्दञ्छत्रूणां दारयिता वा द्रावयिता वा। आदरयिता च यज्वनाम् नि० 10.8. एष वै शुक्रो य एष (सूर्यः) तपत्येष (सूर्यः) उ एवेन्द्रः श० 4.5.5.7, 4.5.9.4. अथ यः स इन्द्रोऽसौ स आदित्यः श० 8.5.3.2. यो वै वायुः स इन्द्रो य इन्द्रः स वायुः श० 4.1.3.19. स योऽयं मध्ये प्राणः। एष एवेन्द्रस्तानेष प्राणान्मध्यत इन्द्रियैणैन्द्ध तस्मादिन्ध इन्धो ह वै तमिन्द्र इत्याचक्षते परोऽक्षम् श० 6.1.1.2. हृदयमेवेन्द्रः श० 12.9.1.15. यन्मनः स इन्द्रः गो० उ० 4.11. मन एवेन्द्रः श० 12.9.1.13. इन्द्रो वै यजमानः श०2.1.2.11 क्षत्रियो यदुच यजमानः श० 5.3.5.27. एन्द्रो वै राजन्य तै० 3.8.23.2. इन्द्रः क्षत्रम् श० 10.4. 1.5. वीर्यं वा इन्द्रः तां० 9.7.5, 8. इन्द्रो यज्ञस्य नेता श० 4.1.2.15.
2. प्रजापतिर्वाव ज्येष्ठः तै० सं० 7.1.1.4. यद्वै ज्येष्ठं तन्महत् ऐ०आ० 1.3.7 ज्यैष्ठ्यं वा अग्निष्टोमः जै० 2.378.
3. क्रतुं कर्म वा प्रज्ञां वा नि० 2.28. क्रतुः-कर्मनाम निघं० 2.1. प्रज्ञानाम निघं० 3.9. क्रतुना कर्मणा नि० 10.10. कृत्वे अपत्याय नि० 11.27. सुक्रतवः-सुकर्माणः नि० 8.7. स यदेव मनसाऽकामयतऽइदं मे स्यादिदं कुर्वीयेति स एव क्रतुः श० 4.1.4.1. क्रतुर्मनोजवः श० 3.3.4. 7. हृत्सु ह्यसं क्रतुर्मनोजवः प्रविष्टः श० 3.3.4.7. क्रतुं दक्षं वरुणं सं शिशाधि ऋ० 8.42.3 इति वीर्यं प्रज्ञानं वरुण संशिशाधीति ऐ० 1.13. मित्र एव क्रतुः श० 4.1.4.1.

Anvaya (Sequencial placement of words)

tvam sukrato indra sadyaḥ vṛddhaḥ ajāyathāḥ sutasya pītaye jyaiṣṭhyāya.

Meaning of Mantra in different contexts :

Spiritual: (त्वम्) You, (इन्द्र) O individuated being! are (सुक्रतो) possessed of best intellectual power and ability of action. So (सद्यः) immediately (वृद्धः अजायथाः) grow up in knowledge (पीतये) for exploiting natural resources properly (ज्यैष्ठ्याय) for the larger interest of the humanity and not for selfish motives.

Note: Vedas want only the genious and knowledgeable persons to exploit the natural resources for larger interest of the humanity and not the laymen or fools who have commercial selfish motives behind.

Scientific: (त्वम्) You, O electric force! (सुक्रतो) performer of good work like expansion of the universe, (सद्यः) immediately (वृद्धः अजायथाः) grow up in power (पीतये) for somapĒna (process of electric charges exerting electric force) (ज्यैष्ठ्याय) for the larger interest of the creation.

४७. आ त्वा॑ विशन्त्वा॒शव॒: सोमा॑स इन्द्र गिर्वणः।
शं ते॑ सन्तु॒ प्रचे॑तसे।।७।।

आ। त्वा॒। वि॒श॒न्तु॒। आ॒शव॑:। सोमा॑सः। इ॒न्द्र॒। गि॒र्व॒ण॒:। शम्। ते॒।
स॒न्तु॒। प्रऽचे॑तसे।।

Saṁhitāpāṭha

ā tvā viśantvāśavaḥ somāsa indra girvaṇaḥ śaṁ te santu pracetase.

Padapāṭha

ā. tvā. viśantu. āśavaḥ. somāsaḥ. indra. girvaṇaḥ. śam. te. santu. pracetase.

Grammatical Notes:

आ (ā)—A prefix meaning proximity, conjunction and simli. Being a prefix, it is accented on the first syllabl[1].

त्वा॒ (tvā)—Acc.sing. enclitic form of second person pronoun 'Yusmad'[2]. Being an enclitic form, it is not accented[3].

वि॒श॒न्तु॒ (viśantu)—Tudādigaṇa root √viśa 'to enter'+loṭ lakāra third person pl. Being a verbal form preceded by a non—verbal form, it is not accented[4].

आ॒शव॑: (āśavaḥ)—Svādigaṇa root √aśūṅ 'to pervade'+uṇa (Uṇādi suffix)[5]. It receives suffixal accent. Attributive epithet of somāsaḥ.

---

1. Cf. *Phiṭ sūtra*—उपसर्गाश्चाभिवर्जम् -81.
2. Cf. Pāṇ. त्वामौ द्वितीयायाः - 8.1.23
3. Cf. Pāṇ. युस्मदस्मदोः षष्ठी-चतुर्थी.द्वितीयास्थयोर्वान्नावौ- 8.1.20
4. Cf. Pāṇ. तिङ्ङतिङः - 8.1.28
5. Cf. *Uṇādi sūtra*—कृवापाजि० 1.1

सोमा॑सः (somāsaḥ)—Nom. pl. of soma. Nom. pl. nominal suffix—jas is replaced by—asuk.[1] Bhvādigaṇa root √ṣu 'to deliver', 'to glorify' or Svādigaṇa root √ṣuñ 'to squeez' or √ṣu 'to inspire'+man (Uṇādi suffix)[2]. Due to 'nit' (having indicatory 'n') suffix, the word soma gets the accent on the first syllable [3].

इ॒न्द्र॒ (indra)—Voc. sing. of Indra. Bhvādigaṇa root √idi 'to prosper'+ran (Uṇādi suffix).[4] 'Being a voc. form not located in the beginning of a hemistich,it goes without accent[5].

गि॒र्व॒ण॒ः (girvaṇaḥ)—Voc. sing. of Girvaṇa. Gīḥ+Tanādigaṇa root √vana 'to beg' or Bhvādigaṇa root √'vana 'to divide'+asun (Uṇādi suffix). Being a voc. form not located in the beginning of a hemistich, it goes without accent[6]. Attributive epithet of Indra.

शम् (śam)—Divādigaṇa root √śamu 'to extinguish'+ghañ suffix.

ते॒ (te)—Dat. gen. sing. enclitic form of second person pronoun 'Yusmad'[7]. Being an enclitic form, it is not accented[8].

स॒न्तु॒ (santu)—Adādigaṇa root √as 'to be'+laṭ lakāra third person pl. Being a verbal form preceded by a

---

1. Cf. Pāṇ. आज्जसेरसुक् - 7.1.50
2. *artti-stu-su-hu-sṛ-dhṛ-kṣi-kṣu-bhā-yā-vā-padi-uakṣi-nī-bhyo man—Uṇādi sutra*,1.140.
3. Cf. Paṇini (6.1.197)—*ñnityādinityam.*
4. Cf. Uṇādi. ऋज्रेन्द्राग्रवज्र॰ - 2.28.
5. Cf. Pāṇ. आमन्त्रितस्य च - 8.1.19
6. Cf. Pāṇ. आमन्त्रितस्य च - 8.1.19
7. Cf. Pāṇ. तेमयावेकवचनस्य - 8.1.22.
8. Cf. Pāṇ. युस्मदस्मदोः षष्ठी चतुर्थी द्वितीया स्थयोर्वान्नावौ - 8.1.20.

non—verbal form, it is not accented[1].

प्रचैतसे (pracetase)—Bahuvrīhi (possessive) compound.

Pra+Bhvādigaṇa root √citī 'to be conscious'+asun (Uṇādi suffix)[2]. Being a Bahuvrīhi (possesive) compound, it will receive accent on the first member. The first member, being a prefix, carries acute accent[3]. As such, it is accented on the first syllable.

Word meanings:

आ[4] (ā)—

त्वा (tvā) —to you

विशन्तु (viśantu) —to reach, to enter

आशवः[5] (āśavaḥ)—Attributive of Somāsaḥ. extant, prevailing, quick moving

सोमासः[6] (somāsaḥ)—natural resources, electric froce

---

1. Cf. Pāṇ. तिङ्ङतिङः - 8.1.28
2. Cf. *Uṇādi sūtra*—सर्वधातुभ्योऽसुन् - 4.190
3. Cf. *Phiṭ sūtra*—उपसर्गश्चाभिवर्जम् - 81
4. अर्वागर्थे नि० 1.3. एतस्मिन्नेवार्थे (समुच्चयार्थे) देवेभ्यश्च पितृभ्य एत्याकारः नि० 1.4. उपमार्थे दृश्यते नि० 3.16. अध्यर्थे दृश्यते नि० 5.5.
5. आशुः क्षिप्रनाम, निघं० 2.15. अश्वनाम निघं० 1.14. आ इति शु इति च क्षिप्रनामनी भवतः।

नि० 6.1. आशु भार्गवं भवति तां० 14.9.9. अहर्वा एतदव्लीयत तद्देवा आशुनाभ्यधिन्वथ्ठंस्तदाशोराशुत्वम् तां० 14.9.10. आशवः क्षिप्रकारिणः नि० 9.5.

6. सोम-ओषधिः सोमः सुनोतेर्यदेनमभिषुण्वन्ति नि० 11.2. सोमः-स्वा वै मऽएषेति तस्मात्सोमो नाम श० 3.9.4.22. सत्यं (वै) श्रीर्ज्योतिः सोमः श० 5.1.2.10. श्रीर्वै सोमः श० 4.1.3.9. सोमो राजा राजपतिः तै० 2.5.7.3. असौ वै सोमो राजा विचक्षणश्चन्द्रमाः कौ० 4.4. सोमो राजाचन्द्रमाः श० 10.4.2.1. चन्द्रमा वै सोमः कौ० 16.5. वृत्रो वै सोम आसीत् श०3.4.3.13. संवत्सरो वै सोमो राजा कौ० 7.10. सोमो हि प्रजापतिः श० 5.1.5.26. सोमो वैष्णवो राजेत्याह तस्याप्सरसो विशः श० 13.4.3.8. जुष्टा विष्णव इति। जुष्टा सोमायेत्येवैतदाह (विष्णुः-सोमः) श० 3.2.4.12. तद् यदेवेदं क्रीतो विशतीव तदु हास्य (सोमस्य) वैष्णवं रूपम् कौ० 8.2.

इन्द्र[1] (indra)—Address to Indra. electric force, scholar

गिर्वणः [2] (girvaṇaḥ)—Address to Girvaṇa. Attributive of Indra. praise worthy

शम्[3] (śam)—peaceful, useful

ते (te)—yours

सोमोवै पवमानः श० 2.2.3.22. एष (वायुः) वै सोमस्योद्गीथो यत्पवते तां० .6.18. तस्मात् सोमं सर्वेभ्यो देवेभ्यो जुह्वति तस्मादाहुः सोमः सर्वा देवता इति श० 1.6.3.21. सोमो वाऽइन्द्रः श० 2.2.3.23. सोमो रात्रिः श० 3.4.4.15. सोम एव सक्त इति गो० उ० 2.24. सोमो वै चतुर्होता तै० 2.3.1.1. सोमो वै पर्णः श० 6.5.1.1. सोमो वै पलाशः कौ० 2.2. पशुर्वै प्रत्यक्षं सोमः श०5.1.3.7. सोम एवैव प्रत्यक्षं यत्पशुः कौ० 12.6. पशवः सोमोः राजा तै० 1.4.7.6. सोमो वै दधि तै० 1.4.7.6. एष वै यजमानो यत्सोमः तै० 1.3.3.5. द्यावापृथिव्योर्वा एष गर्भो यत्सोमो राजा ऐ० 2.26. क्षत्रं सोमः ऐ० 2.38. यशो वै सोमः श० 4.2.4.9. यशो (ऋ० 10. 72.10.) वै सोमो राजा ऐ० 1.13. प्राणः सोमः श० 7.3.1.2. रसः सोमः श० 7.3.1.3. तस्मात् सोमो राजा सर्वाणि नक्षत्राण्युपैति प० 3.12. तै० 1.1.3.10. अन्तरिक्षदेवत्यो हि सोमः गो० उ० 2.4. गिरिषु हि सोमः श० 3.3.4.7. घ्नन्ति खलु वाऽएतत्सोमं यदभिषुण्वन्ति तै०2.2. 8.1.सोमो राजा मृगशीर्षेण आगन् श० 3.1.2.2. सोमवीरुधां पते तै० 3.11.4.1. आपः सोमः सुतः श० 7.1.1.22. आपो ह्येतस्य (सोमस्य) लोकः श० 4.4.5.21. पुमान् वै सोमः स्त्री सुरा तै० 1.3.3.4.

1. इन्द्रः पदनाम निघं० 5.4. इन्द्रः-इरां दृणातीति वा इरां ददातीति वा, इरां दधातीति वा। इरां दारयत इति वा। इरां धारयत इति वा। इन्दवे द्रवतीति वा। इन्दौ रमत इति वा। इन्धे भूतानीति वा। 'तद्यदेनं प्राणैः समैन्धंस्तदिन्द्रस्येन्द्रत्वमिति विज्ञायते।' इदं करणादित्याग्रायणः। इदं दर्शनादित्यौपमन्यवः। इन्दतेर्वैश्वर्यकर्मणः। इन्दञ्छत्रूणां दारयिता वा द्रावयिता वा। आदरयिता च यज्वनाम् नि० 10.8. एष वै शुक्रो य एष (सूर्यः) तपत्येष (सूर्यः) उ एवेन्द्रः श० 4.5.5.7, 4.5.9.4. अथ यः स इन्द्रोऽसौ स आदित्यः श० 8.5.3.2. यो वै वायुः स इन्द्रो य इन्द्रः स वायुः श० 4.1.3.19. स योऽयं मध्ये प्राणः। एष एवेन्द्रस्तानेष प्राणान्मध्यत इन्द्रियैणैन्द्ध तस्मादिन्ध इन्धो ह वै तमिन्द्र इत्याचक्षते परोऽक्षम् श० 6.1.1.2. हृदयमेवेन्द्रः श० 12.9.1.15. यन्मनः स इन्द्रः गो० उ० 4.11. मन एवेन्द्रः श० 12.9.1.13. इन्द्रो वै यजमानः श०2.1.2.11 क्षत्रियो यदु च यजमानः श० 5.3.5.27. एन्द्रो वै राजन्य तै० 3.8.23.2. इन्द्रः क्षत्रम् श०10.4. 1.5. वीर्यं वा इन्द्रः तां० 9.7.5, 8. इन्द्रो यज्ञस्य नेता श० 4.1.2.15.
2. गिर्वणो देवो भवति, गीर्भिरेनं वनयन्ति नि० 6.15.
3. शम् सुखनाम निघं० 3.6. शम् सुखम् नि० 11.30.

स॒न्तु॒ (santu)—be

प्रचे॑तसे[1] (pracetase)—intelligent, wise

Anvaya (Sequencial placement of words)

indra girvaṇaḥ tvā āśavaḥ somāsaḥ ā viśantu. te pracetase śam santu.

Meaning of Mantra in different contexts :

आ। त्वा॒। वि॒श॒न्तु॒। आ॒शव॑ः। सोमा॑सः। इ॒न्द्र॒। गि॒र्व॒ण॒ः। शम्। ते॒।
स॒न्तु॒। प्रऽचे॑तसे॥

Spiritual: (गिर्वणः) O praise worthy (इन्द्र) scholar! let these (आशवः) all pervading (सोमासः) natural resources (आ विशन्तु) reach (त्वा) you. (ते) Let all these resources (सन्तु) be (शम्) be peaceful and useful for (प्रचेतसे) the wise person

Scientific: (गिर्वणः) O praise worthy (इन्द्र) electric force! let (आशवः) the quick moving (सोमासः) electric charge (आ विशन्तु) reach (त्वा) you. (ते) Let all these electric charges (सन्तु) be (प्रचेतसे) for your intelligent act (expansion of universe) and (शम्) peace.

---

1. चेतः प्रज्ञानाम निघं० 3.9. प्रचेताः-प्रवृद्धचेताः नि० 8.5. प्रचेतसः-प्रवृद्धचेतसः नि० 9.19.

४८. त्वां स्तोमा॑ अवीवृधन् त्वामु॒क्था श॑तक्रतो।
त्वां व॑र्धन्तु नो॒ गिर॑ः॥८॥

त्वाम्। स्तोमा॑ः। अ॒वी॒वृ॒ध॒न्। त्वाम्। उ॒क्था। श॒त॒क्र॒तो॒ इति॑ शतक्रतो।
त्वाम्। व॒र्ध॒न्तु॒। न॒ः। गिर॑ः॥

Saṁhitāpāṭha

tvāṁ stomā avīvṛdhana tvāmukthā śatakrato. tvāṁ vardhantu no girah.

Padapāṭha

tvām. stomāḥ. avīvṛdhana. tvām. ukthā. śatakrato iti śatakrato. tvām. vardhantu. naḥ. giraḥ.

Grammatical Notes:

त्वाम् (tvām)—Acc. sing. of second person pronoun 'Yusmad'. Being a pronominal form it bears acute accent.

स्तोमा॑ः (stomāḥ) —Adādigaṇa root √ sṭuñ 'to extol'+man (Uṇādi suffix)[1].

अ॒वी॒वृ॒ध॒न् (avīvṛdhana)—Bhvādigaṇa root √vṛdhu 'to increase'+luṅ lakāra (aorist) third person pl. Being a verbal form preceded by a non—verbal form, it remains unaccented [2].

त्वाम् (tvām)—Acc. sing. of second person pronoun 'Yusmad'. Being a pronominal form, it bears acute accent.

उ॒क्था (ukthā)—Adādigaṇa root √vaca 'to speak'+thak

1 Cf. *Uṇādi sūtra*—अर्त्तिस्तुसु० - 1.140

2. Cf. Pāṇ. तिङ्ङतिङः - 8.1.28

(Uṇādi suffix)[1]. It retains suffixal accent[2].

शतक्रतो (śatakrato)—Voc. sing. of śatakratu. Being a voc. case not located in the beginning of a hemistich, it does not carry accent[3].

त्वाम् (tvām)—Acc. sing. of second person pronoun 'Yusmad'. Being a pronominal form it bears an acute accent.

वर्धन्तु (vardhantu)—Bhvādigaṇa root √vṛdhu 'to increase'+loṭ lakāra third person pl. Being a verbal form preceded by a non—verbal form, it remains unaccented[4].

नः (naḥ)—Acc./dat./gen. pl. enclitic form of first person pronoun 'Asmad'[5]. Being an enclitic form it is not accented.[6]

गिरः (giraḥ)—Nom. pl. of gīḥ. Tudādigaṇa root √gṛ 'to gulp' or 'to swallow' or Krayādigaṇa root √gṛ 'to make sound'+kvip suffix. 'Sup' suffixes (nominal suffixes) are never accented, as such only the root accent will prevail making it to be accented on the first syllable.

Word meanings:

त्वाम् (tvām)—you

स्तोमाः[7] (stomāḥ) —chants of Sāmaveda

---

1. Cf. *Uṇādi sūtra*—पातृतुदिवनि० 2.7.
2. Cf. Pāṇ. आद्युदात्तश्च- 3.1.3
3. Cf. Pāṇ. आमन्त्रितस्य च - 8.1.19
4. Cf. Pāṇ. तिङ्ङतिङः - 8.1.28
5. Cf. *vahuvacanasyavasnasau*—Pāṇ. 8.1.21.
6. Cf. Pāṇ. युस्मदस्मदोः षष्ठी चतुर्थी द्वितीया स्थयोर्वान्नावौ 8.1.20.
7. स्तोमः स्तवनात् नि० 7.22. स्तोमः-सप्तस्तोमः श० 8.5.2.8. त्रिवृत्पञ्चदशः सप्दश एकविंश एते वै स्तोमानां वीर्यवत्तमाः तां० 6.3.15. यदु ह किं च देवा कुर्वते स्तोमेनैव तत् कुर्वते श० 8.4.3.2. स्तोमो वै देवेषु तरो नामासीत् तां० 8.3.3. स्तोम वै परमाः स्वर्गा लोकाः ऐ० 4.18.

अवीवृधन् (avīvṛdhana)—magnified

त्वाम् (tvām)—you

उक्था[1] (ukthā)—hymns of Ṛgveda.

शतक्रतो[2] (śatakrato)—Address to Śatakratu. performer of act for 100 Brāhma years or 100 human years in case of human beings

त्वाम् (tvām)—you

वर्धन्तु (vardhantu)—magnify, laud, speak highly of, glorify

नः (naḥ)—our

गिरः[3] (giraḥ)—praises

Anvaya (Sequencial placement of words)

śatakrato tvām stomāḥ avīvṛdhana, tvām ukthā, tvām vardhantu naḥ giraḥ

Meaning of Mantra in different contexts :

स्तोमा वै त्रयः स्वर्गा लोकाः ऐ० 4.18. स्तोमो हि पशुः तां० 5.10.8. अन्नं वै स्तोमाः श० 9.3.3.6. प्राणा वै स्तोमा० श० 8.4.1.3. वीर्यं वै स्तोमाः तां० 2.5.4. वीरजननं वै स्तोमः तां० 21.9.3. गायत्री मात्रो वै स्तोमः कौ 19.8.

1. उक्थम् प्राण उ ऽएवोक्तस्यान्नमेव थं तदुक्थम् श० 10.4.1.23. एष (अग्निः) उऽएवोक्स्यैतदन्नं थ्क्नं तदुक्थम् श० 10.4.1.4. अग्निर्वा ऽउक्तस्याहुतय एव थन् श०10.6.2.8. आदित्यो वा उक्। तस्य चन्द्रमा एव थम् श० 10.6.2.9. प्राणो वा ऽउक्थस्यान्नमेव थम् श० 10.6.2.10. वागुक्थम् ष० 1.5. अन्नमुक्थानि कौ० 11.8., 17.7. प्रजा वा उक्थानि तै० 1.8.7.2. पशव उक्थानि ऐ० 4.1, 12 गो० उ० 6.7. तै० 1.8.7.2. पशवो वा उक्थानि कौ० 28.10, 29.8. ष० 3.11. तै० 1.2.2.2. तां० 4.5.18. अन्तरिक्षमुक्थेन (अभ्यजयन्) तां० 9.2. 9.
2. शतं दशदशतः नि० 3.10. शतम् बहुनाम निघं० 3.1. क्रतुः कर्मनाम निघं० 2.1. प्रज्ञानाम निघं० 3.9. शतक्रतुः इन्द्र आसीत् सीरपतिः शतक्रतुः तै० 2.4.8.7
3. गी वाङ् नाम निघं० 1.11. वाग्वै गीः श० 7.2.2.4. विशो गिरः श० 3.6.1.24.।

Spiritual: (शतक्रतो) O *Śatakratu* (performer of act of creation for 100 Brāhma years) Brahman! (स्तोमाः) the chants of *Sāmaveda* (अवीवृधन् त्वाम्) tells your glory, (उक्था) the hymns of the *Ṛgveda* (अवीवृधन् त्वाम्) tells you glory. (नः गिरः) Our praises also (वर्धन्तु त्वाम्) glorify you.

Scientific: (शतक्रतो) O *Śatakratu* (performer of act of expansion of the universe for 100 Brāhma years) electric force! (स्तोमाः) the chants of *Sāmaveda* (अवीवृधन् त्वाम्) speak highly of you, (उक्था) the hymns of the *Ṛgveda* (अवीवृधन् त्वाम्) speak highly of you; (नः गिरः) Our praises also (वर्धन्तु त्वाम्) glorify you.

Socio-political 1: (शतक्रतो) O *Śatakratu*, ruler (having a rule of 100 years), (स्तोमाः) the chants of *Sāmaveda* (अवीवृधन् त्वाम्) lauds you, (उक्था) the hymns of the *Ṛgveda* (अवीवृधन् त्वाम्) lauds you; (नः गिरः) Our praises also (वर्धन्तु त्वाम्) glorify you.

Socio-political 2: (शतक्रतो) O *Śatakratu,* teacher (performing the act of teaching for 100 years), (स्तोमाः) the chants of *Sāmaveda* (अवीवृधन् त्वाम्) lauds you, (उक्था) the hymns of the *Ṛgveda* (अवीवृधन् त्वाम्) lauds you; (नः गिरः) Our praises also (वर्धन्तु त्वाम्) glorify you.

४९. अक्षितोतिः सनेदिमं वाजमिन्द्रः सहस्रिणम्।
यस्मिन् विश्वानि पौंस्या।।९।।

अक्षितऽऊतिः। सनेत्। इमम्। वाजम्। इन्द्रः। सहस्रिणम्। यस्मिन्। विश्वानि। पौंस्या।

Saṁhitāpāṭha

akṣitotiḥ sanedimaṁ vājamindraḥ sahasriṇam. yasmin viśvāni paunsyā.

Padapāṭha

akṣita-ūtiḥ sanet. imam. vājam. indraḥ. sahasriṇam. yasmin. viśvāni. paunsyā.

Grammatical Notes:

अक्षितोतिः (akṣitotiḥ)—Bahuvrīhi (possessive) compound.

{Nañ+Tanādigaṇa root √kṣiṇu 'to kill' +kta in the accusative sense}+{Bhvādigaṇa root √ava 'to protect', 'to move', 'to love'+ktin[1]}. Being a Bahuvrīhi compound, the first member receives the accent and here the first member is accented on 'nañ'.

सनेत् (sanet)—Bhvādigaṇa root √ṣaṇ 'to divide' or Tanādigaṇa root √ṣaṇu 'to donate'+liṅ lakāra (subjunctive) third person sing. Being a verbal form preceded by a non-verbal form, it remains unaccented[2].

इमम् (imam)—Acc. sing. masc. of demonstrative pronoun 'idam', Being a pronominal form, it is accented.

वाजम् (vājam)—Acc. sing. of vāja. Bhvādigaṇa root √vaja 'to go'+ghañ suffix. It is accented on the first syllable,

1. Cf. Pāṇ. ऊतियूतिजूतिसाति० -3.3.97

2. Cf. Pāṇ. तिङ्ङतिङः - 8.1.28

being read in the list of 'vṛṣa' group of words.[1]

इन्द्रः (indraḥ)—Nom. sing. of Indra. Bhvādigaṇa root √idi 'to prosper'+ran (Uṇādi suffix).[2] 'Nit' suffix (of which final 'n' is elided) makes it accented on the first syllable[3].

सहस्रिणम् (sahasriṇam)—Sahasra+iniḥ suffix[4]. Sāyaṇa tries to derive this form with the suffix 'iniḥ' prescribed in Pāṇini 'ata iniṭhanau'—5.2.115. This is quite wrong concept. Pāṇini has already prescribed 'iniḥ' suffix in his succinct aphorism 5.2.102. Swami Dayananda has quoted Pāṇini's prescriptive formula correctly. It receives suffixal accent [5].

यस्मिन् (yasmin)—Loc. sing. masc. of demonstrative Pronoun 'Yad'. Being a pronominal form it receives an accent.

विश्वानि (viśvāni)—Voc. pl. of viśva. Tudādigaṇa root √ viśa 'to enter'+kvan (Uṇādi suffix).[6] It is accented on the first syllable, being a voc. form located in the beginning of hemistich. [7] Accent on the initial syllable, is also due to its being formed of 'nit' suffix[8].

पौंस्या (paunsyā)—{Adādigaṇa root √pā 'to protect'+ḍumsun (Uṇādi suffix)[9]}+{ṣyañ suffix in abstract or accusative

---

1. Cf. Pāṇ. वृषादीनां च - 6.1.203.
2. Cf. Uṇādi. ऋज्रेन्द्राग्रवज्र० - 2.28.
3. Cf. Pāṇ. ञ्नित्यादिर्नित्यम् - 6.1.197
4. Cf. Pāṇ. तपःसहस्राभ्यां विनीनी 5.2.102.
5. Cf. Pāṇ. आद्युदात्तश्च - 3.1.3
6. Cf. *Uṇādi sūtra* अशुप्रुषिलिटि कणि० - 1.151.
7. Cf. Pāṇ. आमन्त्रितस्य च० 6.1.198.
8. Cf. Pāṇ. ञ्नित्यादिर्नित्यम् - 6.1.197
9. Cf. *Uṇādi sūtra*—पातेर्डुम्सुन् - 4.178

sense [1] or yañ suffix in the sense of 'welfare' or 'goodenss' or 'being the product of'}. Being formed of 'ñit' suffix, it is accented on the first syllable [2].

Word meanings:

अक्षितोतिः (akṣitotiḥ)—whose knowledge is imperishable, who never fails to protect, custodian, unobstructed protector

सनेत् (sanet) —to make receive,

इमम् (imam)—this

वाजम् (vājam)—food, natural resources

वाजः अन्ननाम निघं० 2.7. बलनाम निघं० 2.9. वाजेभिरन्नैः नि० 11.26. अन्नं वै वाजः तै० 1.3.6.2. श० 5.1.4.3. ता० 13.9.13. अन्नं वाजः श०5.1.1.16. अन्नं वै वाजः श० 1.4.1.9. वीर्यं वै वाजः श० 3.3.4.7. ओषधयः खलु वै वाजः तै० 1.3.7.1. वाजो वै पशवः ऐ० 5.8. वाजो वै स्वर्गो लोकः तां० 18.7.12. गो० उ० 5.8. वाग्वै वाजस्य प्रसवः तै० 1.3.2.5. सोमो वै वाजः मै० 4.5.4. सर्वं सोमं पिपासति वाजः ह गच्छति मै० 1.11.5. अमृतोऽन्नं वै वाज जै० 2.193.

इन्द्रः[3] (indraḥ)—God, electric force, ruler

---

1. Cf. Pāṇ. गुणवचनब्राह्मणादिभ्यः कर्मणि च - 5.1.124
2. Cf. Pāṇ. ञ्नित्यादिर्नित्यम् - 6.1.197
3. इन्द्रः पदनाम निघं० 5.4. इन्द्रः-इरां दृणातीति वा इरां ददातीति वा, इरां दधातीति वा। इरां दारयत इति वा। इरां धारयत इति वा। इन्दवे द्रवतीति वा। इन्दौ रमत इति वा। इन्धे भूतानीति वा। 'तद्यदेनं प्राणैः समैन्धंस्तदिन्द्रस्येन्द्रत्वमिति विज्ञायते।' इदं करणादित्याग्रायणः। इदं दर्शनादित्यौपमन्यवः। इन्दतेर्वैश्वर्यकर्मणः। इन्दञ्छत्रूणां दारयिता वा द्रावयिता वा। आदरयिता च यज्वनाम् नि०10.8. एष वै शुक्रो य एष (सूर्यः) तपत्येष (सूर्यः) उ एवेन्द्रः श० 4.5.5.7, 4. 5.9.4. अथ यः स इन्द्रोऽसौ स आदित्यः श० 8.5.3.2. यो वै वायुः स इन्द्रो य इन्द्रः स वायुः श०4.1.3.19. स योऽयं मध्ये प्राणः। एष एवेन्द्रस्तानेष प्राणान्मध्यत इन्द्रियैणैन्द्ध तस्मादिन्ध इन्धो ह वै तमिन्द्र इत्याचक्षते परोऽक्षम् श० 6.1.1.2. हृदयमेवेन्द्रः श० 12.9.1.15. यन्मनः स इन्द्रः गो० उ० 4.11. मन एवेन्द्रः श० 12.9.1.13. इन्द्रो वै यजमानः श० 2.1.2.11 क्षत्रियो

स॒ह॒स्रिणम्[1] (sahasriṇam)—hundreds of thousands

यस्मिन् (yasmin)—in which, in whom

विश्वानि[2] (viśvāni)—Address to Viśva. all

पौंस्या (paunsyā)—power, comfort

Anvaya (Sequencial placement of words)

akṣitotiḥ indraḥ imam sahasriṇam vājam sanet. yasmin viśvāni paunsyā.

Meaning of Mantra in different contexts :

Spiritual: (इन्द्रः) Brahman, (अक्षितोतिः) whose knowledge is imperishable, (सनेत्) make us receive (इमम्) these (सहस्रिणम्) thousands of (वाजम्) natural resources and food grains (यस्मिन्) which consists of (विश्वानि) all sorts of (पौंस्या) comforts and energy.

Scientific: (इन्द्रः) Electric force, (अक्षितोतिः) custodian of this universe, (सनेत्) enjoys (इमम्) these (सहस्रिणम्) thousands of (वाजम्) electric charges (यस्मिन्) which consists of (विश्वानि) all (पौंस्या) power for Indra to to fight out the forces of contraction.

Socio-political 1: (इन्द्रः) Ruler, (अक्षितोतिः) unobstructed protector of the public interest, (सनेत्) make us receive (इमम्) these (सहस्रिणम्) thousands of (वाजम्) facilities (यस्मिन्) which lead us to (विश्वानि) all sorts of (पौंस्या) comforts.

यदु चयजमानः श० 5.3.5.27. एन्द्रो वै राजन्य तै० 3.8.23.2. इन्द्रः क्षत्रम् श० 10.4.1.5. वीर्यं वा इन्द्रः तां० 9.7.5, 8. इन्द्रो यज्ञस्य नेता श० 4.1.2.15.

1. सहस्रमिति बहुनाम निघं० 3.1.
2. यद्वै विश्वं सर्वं तत् श० 3.1.2.11. तदन्नं वै विश्वम्प्राणो मित्रम् जै० उ० 3.3.6.

५०. मा नो मर्त्ता अभि द्रुहन् तनूनामिन्द्र गिर्वणः।
ईशानो यवया वधम्।।१०।।

मा। नः। मर्त्ताः। अभि। द्रुहन्। तनूनाम्। इन्द्र। गिर्वणः। ईशानः।
यवय। वधम्।।

Saṁhitāpāṭha

mā no martā abhi druhan tanūnām indra girvaṇaḥ.
īśāno yavayā vadham.

Padapāṭha

mā. naḥ. marttāḥ. abhi. druhan. tanūnām. indra. girvaṇaḥ.
īśānaḥ. yavaya. vadham.

Grammatical Notes:

मा (mā)—negation Being a particle, it is accented on the first syllable[1].

नः (naḥ) —Acc./dat./gen. pl. enclitic form of first person pronoun 'Asmad'[2]. Being an enclitic form it is not accented.[3]

मर्त्ताः (marttāḥ)—Tudādigaṇa root √mṛṅ 'to die'+tan (Uṇādi suffix)[4]. Being formed of 'nit' suffix, it is accented on the first syllable [5].

अभि (abhi)—A particle meaning 'in front of'. Being a particle, it should have been accented on the first syllable. But as an exception to the main rule, it is

1. Cf. *Phiṭ sūtra*—निपाताः आद्युदात्ताः - 80
2. Cf. *vahuvacanasyavasnasau*—Pāṇ. 8.1.21.
3. Cf. Pāṇ. युस्मदस्मदोः षष्ठी चतुर्थी द्वितीया स्थयोर्वान्नावौ 8.1.20.
4. Cf. *Uṇādi sūtra* हसिमृग्रिण० 3.86
5. Cf. Pāṇ. ञ्नित्यादिर्नित्यम् - 6.1.197

accented on the last syllable[1].

द्रुह॒न् (druhan)—Divādigaṇa root √druha 'desire to kill'+luṅ lakāra (aorist) in the sense of loṭ (imperative) third person pl. Sāyaṇa considers it to be the form of leṭ lakāra used in the sense of liṅ (subjunctive). Being a verbal form preceded by a non—verbal form, it goes without accent[2].

त॒नू॒नाम् (tanūnām)—Tanādigaṇa root √tanu 'to extend'+ūḥ[3] or uḥ[4] (Uṇādi fem.suffix). It receives accent on the suffix[5].

इ॒न्द्र॒ (indra)—Voc. sing. of Indra. Bhvādigaṇa root √idi 'to prosper'+ran (Uṇādi suffix).[6] 'Being a voc. form not located in the beginning of a hemistich, it goes without accent[7].

गि॒र्व॒णः॒ (girvaṇaḥ)—Voc. sing. of Girvaṇa. Gīḥ+Tanādigaṇa root √vana 'to beg' or Bhvādigaṇa root √'vana 'to divide'+asun (Uṇādi suffix). Being a voc. form not located in the beginning of a hemistich, it goes without accent[8]. Attributive epithet of Indra.

ईशा॑नः (īśānaḥ)—Nom. sing. of īśāna. Adādīgaṇa root √īśa 'to prosper'+śānac (present active participle). Śānac, being a sārvadhātuk suffix[9], remains unaccented, as such the root portion is accented.

---

1. Cf. *Phiṭ sūtra* एवमादीनामन्तः - 82
2. Cf. Pāṇ. तिङ्ङतिङः - 8.1.28
3. Cf. *Uṇādi sūtra* कृषिचमि० 1.80.
4. Cf. *Uṇādi sūtra* भृमृशीङ् 1.7.
5. Cf. Pāṇ. आद्युदात्तश्च - 3.1.3
6. Cf. *Uṇādi.* ऋज्रेन्द्राग्रवज्र० - 2.28.
7. Cf. Pāṇ. आमन्त्रितस्य च - 8.1.19
8. Cf. Pāṇ. आमन्त्रितस्य च - 8.1.19
9. Cf. Pāṇ. तिङ्शित्सार्वधातुकम् - 3.4.113

यवय (yavaya)—Adādigaṇa root √yu 'to mix and unmix'+ṇic suffix (for verbal use)+loṭ lakāra second person sing. Being used as a verbal form preceded by a non-verbal form, it looses its accent[1].

वधम् (vadham)—Adādigaṇa root √han 'to kill', 'to move'+ap. Here 'han' is substituted by 'vadha' which is accented on the last syllable[2].

Word meanings:

मा[3] (mā)—negation

नः (naḥ) —us

मर्त्ताः[4] (marttāḥ)—mortal beings

अभि[5] (abhi)—in front of

द्रुहन् (druhan)—keep enmity

तनूनाम्[6] (tanūnām)—us

इन्द्र[7] (indra)—Address to Indra. God, electric force, ruler

---

1. Cf. Pāṇ. तिङ्ङतिङः - 8.1.28
2. Cf. Pāṇ. हनश्च वधः - 3.3.76
3. मेति प्रतिषेधे नि० 1.5
4. मर्त्त इति मनुष्यनाम निघं० 2.6.
5. अभीत्याभिमुख्यम् निघं० 1.3.
6. आत्मा वै तनुः श० 6.7.2.6. सा मे ते (सुपर्णस्य गरुत्मतः) तनूर्वामदेव्यम् मै० 2.7.8.
7. इन्द्रः पदनाम निघं० 5.4. इन्द्रः-इरां दृणातीति वा इरां ददातीति वा, इरां दधातीति वा। इरां दारयत इति वा। इरां धारयत इति वा। इन्दवे द्रवतीति वा। इन्दौ रमत इति वा। इन्धे भूतानीति वा। 'तद्यदेनं प्राणैः समैन्धंस्तदिन्द्रस्येन्द्रत्वमिति विज्ञायते।' इदं करणादित्याग्रायणः। इदं दर्शनादित्यौपमन्यवः। इन्दतेर्वैश्वर्यकर्मणः। इन्दञ्छत्रूणां दारयिता वा द्रावयिता वा। आदरयिता च यज्वनाम् नि० 10.8. एष वै शुक्रो य एष (सूर्यः) तपत्येष (सूर्यः) उ एवेन्द्रः श० 4.5.5.7, 4.5.9.4. अथ यः स इन्द्रोऽसौ स आदित्यः श० 8.5.3.2. यो वै वायुः स इन्द्रो य इन्द्रः स वायुः श० 4.1.3.19. स योऽयं मध्ये प्राणः। एषे एवेन्द्रस्तानेश्ज्ञ प्राणान्मध्यत इन्द्रियैणैन्द्ध तस्मादिन्ध इन्धो ह वै तमिन्द्रइत्याचक्षते परोऽक्षम् श० 6.1.1.2. हृदयमेवेन्द्रः श० 12.9.1.15.

गिर्वणः[1] (girvaṇaḥ)—Address to girvaṇa. Praise-worthy

ईशानः[2] (īśānaḥ)—powerful

यवय (yavaya)—keep off

वधम्[3] (vadham)—violence

Anvaya (Sequencial placement of words)

girvaṇaḥ indra marttāḥ naḥ tanūnām mā abhi druhan.
īśānaḥ vadham yavaya.

Meaning of Mantra in different contexts :

Spiritual: (इन्द्र) Brahman, (गिर्वणः) who is praise-worthy, (मर्त्ताः) let the mortal beings (मा) never (अभिद्रुहन्) keep enmity (नः) with us. (ईशानः) You are powerful, (यवय) keep (तनूनाम्) us (वधम्) off violence.

Scientific: (इन्द्र) Electric force, (गिर्वणः) worthy of praise, (मर्त्ताः) let the forces of destruction/contraction (मा) never do (अभिद्रुहन्) any injury (नः) to us. (ईशानः) You are powerful, (यवय) keep (तनूनाम्) us (वधम्) off violence being perpetrated by the forces of contraction.

Socio-political 1: (इन्द्र) Ruler, (गिर्वणः) worthy of praise, (मर्त्ताः) let the ultras/terrorists in your state (मा) never do (अभिद्रुहन्) any harm (नः) to us. (ईशानः) You are powerful, (यवय) keep (तनूनाम्) us (वधम्) off violence perpetrated by the anti-nationals and terrorists.

यन्मनः स इन्द्रः गो० उ०4.11.मन एवेन्द्रः श० 12.9.1.13. इन्द्रो वै यजमानः श० 2.1.2.11 क्षत्रियो यदु च यजमानः श०5.3.5.27. एन्द्रो वै राजन्य तै० 3.8.23.2. इन्द्रः क्षत्रम् श० 10.4. 1.5. वीर्यं वाइन्द्रः तां०9.7.5, 8. इन्द्रो यज्ञस्य नेता श० 4.1.2.15.

1. गिर्वणो देवो भवति, गीर्भिरेनं वनयन्ति नि० 6.15.
2. आदित्यो वा ऽ ईशान आदित्यो ह्यस्य सर्वस्येष्टे श० 6.1.3.17. एतान्यष्टौ (रुद्रः, सर्वशर्वः, पशुपतिः उग्रः, अशनिः, भवः, महान्देवः, ईशानः) अग्निरूपाणि। कुमारो नवमः श०6.1.3.18. यदीशानोऽन्नं तेन कौ० 6.8.
3. वधः बलनाम निघं० 2.9. वज्रनाम निघं० 2.20.

www.ingramcontent.com/pod-product-compliance
Lightning Source LLC
Chambersburg PA
CBHW051723040426
42447CB00008B/943
9788187710264